Rogers Cadenhead

Sams **Teach Yourself**

Java™

in **24**
Hours

Eighth Edition

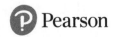 **Pearson**

Sams Teach Yourself Java in 24 Hours, Eighth Edition

ISBN-13: 978-0-672-33794-9

ISBN-10: 0-672-33794-0

Library of Congress Control Number: 2017946911

Printed in the United States of America

1   17

Trademarks

All terms mentioned in this book that are known to be trademarks or service marks have been appropriately capitalized. Pearson cannot attest to the accuracy of this information. Use of a term in this book should not be regarded as affecting the validity of any trademark or service mark.

Warning and Disclaimer

Special Sales

For information about buying this title in bulk quantities, or for special sales opportunities (which may include electronic versions; custom cover designs; and content particular to your business, training goals, marketing focus, or branding interests), please contact our corporate sales department at corpsales@pearsoned.com or (800) 382-3419.

For government sales inquiries, please contact governmentsales@pearsoned.com.

For questions about sales outside the U.S., please contact intlcs@pearsoned.com.

Editor
Mark Taber

Senior Project Editor
Lori Lyons

Project Manager
Dhayanidhi Karunanidhi

Copy Editor
Abigail Manheim Bass

Technical Editor
Boris Minkin

Table of Contents

Dedication

For Roger Cadenhead, Sr. (1946–2017)

My dad, pictured with me in 1970, loaned me the Timex Sinclair 1000 on which I first attempted to program a computer at age 12. He never got it back:

I learned several things as his first-born son:

1. When a train crossing starts clanging and the arms come down, that means "hurry up and see if you can beat the train." .

2. If your dad leaves you on an elevator, stay on the elevator. He'll eventually figure out you're gone and find you.

3. When your dad says, "hold my beer while I try this," step back at least 10 feet for safety reasons.

Dad was a microelectronic engineer, rock-ribbed Republican, ham radio operator K5PCS and one half of the June 1980 father-son championship at the Hulen Mall Putt-Putt. You could start a conversation with him on the weather and find yourself an hour later in a discourse on the root causes of World War I. He was buried in Honey Grove, Texas, which he loved, beside the mother and grandmother who raised him. His death means that someone else is now the No. 1 critic of Texas Rangers general manager Jon Daniels.

About the Author

Rogers Cadenhead is a writer, computer programmer, and web developer who has written more than 25 books on programming- and Internet-related topics, including *Sams Teach Yourself Java in 21 Days*. He maintains the Drudge Retort and other websites that receive more than 20 million visits a year. This book's official website is at www.java24hours.com and he can be reached on Twitter at @rcade.

Acknowledgments

To the folks at Pearson—especially Mark Taber, Lori Lyons, Abigail Manheim Bass, Boris Minkin, and Dhayanidhi Karunanidhi. No author can produce a book like this on his own. Their excellent work will give me plenty to take credit for later.

To my wife, Mary, and my sons, Max, Eli, and Sam.

Accessing the Free Web Edition

Your purchase of this book in any format, print or electronic, includes access to the corresponding Web Edition, which provides several special features to help you learn:

▶ The complete text of the book online

▶ Updates and corrections as they become available

The Web Edition can be viewed on all types of computers and mobile devices with any modern web browser that supports HTML5.

To get access to the Web Edition of *Sams Teach Yourself Java in 24 Hours, Eighth Edition,* all you need to do is register this book:

1. Go to www.informit.com/register

2. Sign in or create a new account

3. Enter ISBN: 9780672337949

4. Answer the questions as proof of purchase

The Web Edition will appear under the Digital Purchases tab on your Account page.

Click the Launch link to access the product.

Introduction

As the author of computer books, I spend a lot of time lurking in the computer section of bookstores, observing the behavior of readers while I'm pretending to read the latest issue of *Soap Opera Digest* magazine.

Because of my research, I've learned that if you have picked up this book and turned to this introduction, I only have 13 more seconds before you put it down and head to the coffee bar for a double-tall-decaf-skim-with-two-shots-of-vanilla-hold-the-whip latte.

So I'll keep this brief: Computer programming with Java is easier than it looks.

I'm not supposed to tell you that because thousands of programmers have used their Java skills to get high-paying jobs in software development, server programming, and Android app creation. The last thing any programmer wants is for the boss to know that anyone with persistence and a little free time can learn this language, the most popular programming language on the planet. By working your way through each of the one-hour tutorials in *Sams Teach Yourself Java in 24 Hours*, you'll be able to learn Java programming quickly.

Anyone can learn how to write computer programs, even if you can't program a DVR. Java is one of the best programming languages to learn because it's a useful, powerful, modern technology that's embraced by companies around the world.

This book is aimed at non-programmers, new programmers who think they hate this stuff, and experienced programmers who want to get up to speed swiftly with Java. It uses Java 9, the latest and greatest version of the language.

Java is an enormously popular programming language because of the things it makes possible. You can create programs that feature a graphical user interface, connect to web services, run on an Android phone or tablet, and more.

This language turns up in some amazing places. One of them is Minecraft, the gaming phenomenon written entirely in Java. (In this book you learn how to create Java programs that run in that game alongside creepers and zombie pigmen!)

This book teaches Java programming from the ground up. It introduces the concepts in English instead of jargon with step-by-step examples of working programs you will create. Spend 24 hours with this book and you'll be writing your own Java programs, confident in your ability to use the language and learn more about it. You also will have skills that are becoming increasingly important—such as Internet computing, graphical user interface design, app creation, and object-oriented programming.

These terms might not mean much to you now. In fact, they're probably the kind of thing that makes programming seem intimidating and difficult. However, if you can use a computer to create a photo album on Facebook, pay your taxes, or work an Excel spreadsheet, you can learn to write computer programs by reading *Sams Teach Yourself Java in 24 Hours*.

NOTE

At this point, if you would rather have coffee than Java, please reshelve this book with the front cover facing outward on an endcap near a lot of the store's foot traffic.

HOUR 1
Becoming a Programmer

This Hour's To-Do List:

▶ Find out the reasons to learn Java.
▶ Discover how programs work.
▶ Select a Java development tool.
▶ Get ready to write your first program.

You've probably heard that computer programming is insanely difficult. It requires a degree in computer science, thousands of dollars in computer hardware and software, a keen analytical mind, the patience of Job, and a strong liking for caffeinated drinks.

Aside from the part about caffeine, you heard wrong. Programming is easier than you might think, despite what programmers have been telling people for years to make it easier for us to land high-paying jobs.

This is a great time to learn programming. Countless programming tools are being made available as free downloads on the Web, and thousands of programmers distribute their work as open source so other people can examine how the software was written, fix errors, and contribute improvements. In a recovering economy, many companies are hiring programmers.

It's a great time to learn Java, because the language is everywhere. Billions of mobile devices use Android, an operating system whose apps are all written in Java. If you have an Android phone, you've been enjoying the work of Java programmers every time you look up a movie, rock out on streaming radio, or sling an antagonistic avian at a poorly built fortress of swine.

This book aims to teach Java programming to three kinds of people:

1. Nervous novices who never tried to program before

2. Bitter beginners who tried programming but hated it like Lord Voldemort hates orphaned British schoolchildren

3. Impatient intellectuals who know another programming language and want to get up to speed quickly on Java

To achieve this goal, this book uses the English language as much as possible instead of technical jargon or obscure acronyms. All new programming terms are thoroughly explained as they are introduced.

If I've succeeded, you will finish this book with enough programming skills to be a danger to yourself and others. You'll be able to write programs, plunge into programming classes and books with more confidence, and learn new languages more easily. (Programming languages, to be clear. This book won't help you master Spanish, Esperanto, or Klingon.)

You also will have skills with Java, the most widely used programming language on the planet.

The first hour of this book provides an introduction to programming and guidance on setting up your computer so you can use it to write and run Java programs.

Choosing a Language

If you're comfortable enough with a computer to prepare a nice-looking résumé, balance a checkbook, or share your vacation photos on Instagram, you can create computer software.

The key to learning how to program is to start with the right language. The programming language you choose often depends on the tasks you want to accomplish. Each language has strengths and weaknesses. Back in my day, young whippersnappers, people learned to program with the BASIC language because it was created with beginners in mind.

NOTE

The BASIC language was invented to be easy for students to learn (the B in BASIC stands for Beginner's). The downside to using some form of BASIC is that it's easy to fall into sloppy programming habits with the language.

The most popular language that employs BASIC today is Visual Basic, a programming language from Microsoft that has moved far beyond its roots. VB, as it also is called, is designed for creating programs to run on computers and mobile devices that use the Windows operating system. Another popular language is PHP, a scripting language for creating websites. Other widely used languages you may have heard about include C++, Ruby, Javascript, and Python.

Each of these languages has its adherents, but the most widely taught in computer science classes at the high school and collegiate level is Java.

The Java programming language, which is offered by Oracle, is more difficult to learn than some other languages such as VB and PHP, but it's a great starting place for several reasons. One advantage of learning Java is that you can use it across a variety of operating systems and computing environments. Java programs can be desktop software, web applications, web servers,

Android apps, and more, running on Windows, Mac, Linux, and other operating systems. This versatility is referenced by the ambitious early Java slogan "Write once, run anywhere."

NOTE

Early Java programmers had a less flattering slogan: "Write once, debug everywhere." The language has come a long way, baby, since the first version was released in 1996.

Another important advantage is that Java requires a highly organized approach for getting programs to work. You must be particular about how you write programs and how they store and alter data.

When you start writing Java programs, you might not see the language's persnickety behavior as an advantage. You could tire of writing a program and having several errors to fix before the program even can be run. The benefit of this extra effort is that the software you create is more reliable, useful, and error-free.

In the coming hours, you learn all of Java's rules and the pitfalls to avoid.

Java was invented by the Canadian computer scientist James Gosling as a better way to create computer programs. While working at Sun Microsystems in 1991, Gosling was unhappy with the way the C++ programming language was performing on a project, so he created a new language that did the job better. It's a matter of contentious debate whether Java is superior to other programming languages, of course, but the success of the language demonstrates the strength of his initial design. Fifteen billion devices across the world are running Java, a number so amazing I'm going to repeat it. Fifteen billion! More than 1,000 books have been published about the language since its introduction. (This is my twentieth.)

Regardless of whether Java is the best language, it definitely is a great language to learn. You get your first chance to try out Java during Hour 2, "Writing Your First Program."

Learning one programming language makes it much easier to learn subsequent languages. Many are similar to each other, so you aren't starting from scratch when you plunge into a new one. For instance, many C++ and Smalltalk programmers find it fairly easy to learn Java because Java borrows ideas from those earlier languages. Similarly, C# adopts many ideas from Java, so it's easier to pick up for Java programmers.

NOTE

C++ is mentioned several times this hour, so you might be tripping over the term, wondering what it means—and how it's pronounced. C++ is pronounced "C-Plus-Plus," and it's a programming language developed by Danish computer scientist Bjarne Stroustrop at Bell Laboratories. C++ is an enhancement of the C programming language, hence the Plus-Plus part of the name. Why not just call it C+? The Plus-Plus part is a computer programming joke you'll understand later in this book.

Telling the Computer What to Do

A computer program, also called software, is a way to tell a computer to perform a task. Everything that the computer does, from booting up to shutting down, is done by a program. Mac OS X is a program; Minecraft is a program; the driver software that controls your printer is a program; even the dreaded blue screen of death on a crashed Windows PC is a program.

Computer programs are made up of a list of commands the computer handles in a specific order when the program is run. Each command is called a statement.

If your house had its own butler and you were a control freak with a Type-A personality, you could give your servant a detailed set of instructions to follow every day, like this:

> Dear Mr. Jeeves,
>
> Please take care of these errands for me while I'm out asking Congress for a bailout:
>
> Item 1: Vacuum the living room.
>
> Item 2: Go to the store.
>
> Item 3: Pick up soy sauce, wasabi, and as many California sushi rolls as you can carry.
>
> Item 4: Return home.
>
> Sincerely, your lord and master,
>
> Bertie Wooster

If you tell a human butler what to do, there's a certain amount of leeway in how your requests are fulfilled. If California rolls aren't available, Jeeves could bring Boston rolls home instead.

Computers don't do leeway. They follow instructions literally. The programs that you write are followed precisely, one instruction at a time.

The following example is a three-line computer program, written in BASIC. Take a look at it, but don't worry too much about what each line is supposed to mean.

```
1 PRINT "Hey Tom, it's Bob from the office down the hall."
2 PRINT "It's good to see you buddy, how've you been?"
3 INPUT A$
```

Translated into English, this program is equivalent to giving a computer the following to-do list:

> Dear personal computer,
>
> Item 1: Display the message, "Hey Tom, it's Bob from the office down the hall."
>
> Item 2: Ask the question, "It's good to see you buddy, how've you been?"

Item 3: Give the user a chance to answer the question.

Sincerely, your lord and master,

Ima Coder

Each line in a computer program is called a *statement*. A computer handles each statement in a program in a specific order, in the same way that a cook follows a recipe or Mr. Jeeves the butler follows the orders of Bertie Wooster. In BASIC, the line numbers are used to put the statements in the correct order. Other languages such as Java do not use line numbers, favoring different ways to tell the computer how to run a program.

Because of the way programs function, you can't blame the computer when something goes wrong as your program runs. The computer is doing exactly what you told it to do, so the blame for any errors usually lies with the programmer.

That's the bad news. The good news is you can't do any permanent harm. No computers will be injured as you learn to program in Java.

How Programs Work

The collection of statements that make up a computer program is called its *source code*.

Most computer programs are written in the same way that you write an email—by typing each statement into a text window. Some programming tools come with their own source code editor and others can be used with any text-editing software.

When you have finished writing a computer program, you save the file to disk. Computer programs often have their own filename extension to indicate what type of file they are. Java programs must have the extension `.java`, as in `Calculator.java`.

NOTE

Computer programs should be prepared as text files with no special formatting. Notepad, a text editor that comes with Windows, saves all files as unformatted text. You also can use TextEdit on Macs or the vi editor or emacs on Linux systems to create text files without formatting. An easier solution is coming up later this hour.

To run a program you have saved as a file, you need some help. The kind of help required depends on the programming language you're using. Some languages require an interpreter to run their programs. The interpreter examines each line of a computer program and executes that line, then proceeds to the next line. Many versions of BASIC are interpreted languages.

The biggest advantage of interpreted languages is that they are faster to test. When you are writing a BASIC program, you can try it out immediately, fix errors, and try again. The primary disadvantage is that interpreted languages run slower than other programs. Each line has to be translated into instructions the computer can run, one line at a time.

Other programming languages require a compiler. The compiler takes a program and translates it into a form that the computer can understand. It also makes the program run as efficiently as possible. The compiled program can be run directly without the need for an interpreter.

Compiled programs run more quickly than interpreted programs but take more time to test. You have to write your program and compile the whole thing before trying it out. If you find an error and fix it, you must compile the program again.

Java is unusual because it requires both a compiler and an interpreter. The compiler converts the statements that make up the program into bytecode. Once this bytecode has been created successfully, it can be run by an interpreter called the Java Virtual Machine.

The Java Virtual Machine, also called a JVM, is the thing that makes it possible for the same Java program to run without modification on different operating systems and different kinds of computing devices. The virtual machine turns bytecode into instructions that a particular device's operating system can execute.

NOTE

Java 9 introduces a new tool called JShell that acts like an interpreter, running a Java statement right when it is typed in. JShell works by putting the statement into a Java program, compiling that program into bytecode, and running it. This is a useful tool for learning and testing.

When Programs Don't Work

Many new programmers become discouraged when they start to test their programs. Errors appear everywhere. Some of these are syntax errors, which are identified by the computer as it looks at the program and becomes confused by the way a statement has been written. Other errors are logic errors, which only are noticed by the programmer as the program is being tested (or might be overlooked entirely). Logic errors often cause it to do something unintended.

As you begin writing your own programs, you become well acquainted with errors. They're a natural part of the process. Programming errors are called *bugs*, a term that dates back a century or more to describe errors in technical devices.

The process of fixing errors also has its own term: *debugging*.

It's no coincidence that there are so many ways to describe errors. You get a lot of debugging experience as you learn programming—whether you want it or not.

One of the first computer bugs was discovered in 1947 by a team that included the American computer scientist Grace Hopper. Hopper was testing a computer at Harvard when a relay malfunctioned. The cause wasn't a software problem—it was an actual bug! A team member debugged the computer by removing a dead moth and taped it into a logbook with the note, "First actual case of bug being found." The bug and logbook page can be viewed at www.doncio.navy.mil/CHIPS/ArticleDetails. aspx?id=3489.

Choosing a Java Programming Tool

To start writing Java programs, you must have a Java programming tool. Several such programs are available for Java, including the simple Java Development Kit and the more sophisticated Eclipse, IntelliJ IDEA, and NetBeans. The latter three tools are each an integrated development environment (IDE), a powerful tool used by professional programmers to get work done.

Whenever Oracle releases a new version of Java, the first tool that supports it is the Java Development Kit (JDK).

To create the programs in this book, you must use JDK version 9 or a programming tool that works on top of it. The JDK is a set of free command-line tools for creating Java software. It lacks a graphical user interface, so if you have never worked in a non-graphical environment such as the Windows command prompt or Linux command-line interface, you will find it challenging to use the JDK.

The NetBeans IDE, also offered for free by Oracle, is a much easier way to write and test Java code than the JDK. NetBeans includes a graphical user interface, source code editor, user interface designer, and project manager. It works in complement to the JDK, running it behind the scenes, so you must have both tools on your system when you begin developing Java programs.

Most of the programs in this book were created with NetBeans, which you can download and install separately from the JDK. You can use other Java tools as long as they support JDK 9.

NOTE

You don't have to use NetBeans in this book. If you can use the JDK or another tool to create, compile, and run a program, those tasks are all that most projects require. NetBeans is covered because for readers of past editions it has proven easier than the JDK. I use NetBeans for most of my Java programming.

In Hour 24, "Writing Android Apps," you will use the Android Studio IDE. Google, which created Android, recommends that free tool to Java programmers who are creating programs for Android.

Installing a Java Development Tool

Every hour of this book includes Java programming projects you can undertake to enhance your knowledge of the subject matter while it percolates in your brain.

You can't do any of that percolating if you lack a Java programming tool on your computer.

If you already have installed a tool that supports Java, you can use it to develop the tutorial programs in the next 23 hours. However, you already should have some familiarity with how to use the tool. Learning Java and a complex IDE at the same time can be daunting.

The recommended choice for programming as you read this book is NetBeans, which is free from Oracle's website at http://netbeans.org. Though NetBeans has advanced features that take time to learn, it makes it easy to create and run simple Java applications.

To find out how to download and install NetBeans, read Appendix A, "Using the NetBeans Integrated Development Environment."

Summary

During this hour, you were introduced to the concept of programming a computer—giving it a set of instructions called statements that tell it what to do. You also learned why you made a good call choosing to teach yourself Java instead of another programming language.

You also might have downloaded and installed a Java development tool to use on the programs you create in the hours to come.

Ask 10 programmers for the best programming language and you may get 10 answers, complete with "my language can beat up your language" taunts and "your source code is so bloated" jokes. Java scores highly in such arguments because it is widely adopted, extremely versatile, and smartly designed. You can accomplish a lot with this language, and it makes learning others a little easier.

If you are still confused about programs, programming languages, or Java in general, don't panic. Everything will begin to make sense in the next hour, "Writing Your First Program," which gently steps through the process of creating a Java program.

Workshop

Q&A

Q. BASIC? C++? Smalltalk? Java? What are the names of these languages supposed to mean?

A. BASIC gets its name from an acronym: Beginner's All-purpose Symbolic Instruction Code. C++ is a programming language that was created to be an improvement on the C language, which itself was an improvement of the B programming language. Smalltalk is an innovative object-oriented language developed in the 1970s that had numerous ideas adopted by Java.

Java goes against the tradition of naming a language with an acronym or other meaningful term. It's just the name that Java's developers liked the best, beating out WebRunner, Silk, Ruby, and others. (The Ruby programming language didn't exist back then.)

When I create my own programming language, it will be named Salsa. Everybody loves salsa.

Q. Why are interpreted languages slower than compiled ones?

A. They're slower for the same reason that a person interpreting a live speech in a foreign language is slower than a translator interpreting a printed speech. The live interpreter has to think about each statement that's being made as it happens, while the other interpreter can work on the speech as a whole and take shortcuts to speed up the process. Compiled languages can be much faster than interpreted languages because they do things to make the program run more efficiently.

Q. Do you only answer questions about Java?

A. Not at all. Ask me anything.

Q. Okay, what is the lowest score ever given on *Dancing with the Stars*?

A. The worst dance by a celebrity contestant on the hit ABC TV show in the United States was performed by the rapper Master P during the second season in 2006. His paso doble with professional dancer Ashly DelGrosso scored a lowest-ever 8. Judges Len Goodman and Bruno Tonioli scored it a 2 and judge Carrie Ann Inaba a 4.

Tonioli's take: "It was a nightmare. You looked like a child on the mall looking for his mother."

Goodman: "I know viewers think they're being kind by bringing you back. They're not. They're being cruel—to Ashly, to the judges."

Inaba: "I actually thought that that was your best dancing."

Master P only trained 20 hours for the show, compared to 130 for the other contestants at that point in the season. He also refused to wear dancing shoes and performed in basketball sneakers. The dance was his last before being voted off.

The dance can be seen on YouTube, where one commenter writes, "Thumbs up if you're watching this just to see the 2 paddle."

On *Dancing with the Stars* internationally, reality TV star Farmer Dave Graham got the lowest possible score—a 1 from all four judges for a total of 4—in Australia in 2007. He shared the performance on his YouTube account, writing, "Perhaps not the best claim to fame, but you take your world records where you can."

Quiz

Test your knowledge of the material covered in this hour by answering the following questions.

1. Which of the following is NOT a reason that people think computer programming is painfully difficult?

    A. Programmers spread that rumor to improve our employment prospects.

    B. Jargon and acronyms are all over the place.

    C. People who find programming too difficult are eligible for a government bailout.

2. What kind of tool runs a computer program by figuring out one line at a time?

    A. A slow tool

    B. An interpreter

    C. A compiler

3. Why did James Gosling hole up in his office and create Java?

    A. He was unhappy with the language he was using on a project.

    B. His rock band wasn't getting any gigs.

    C. When you can't visit YouTube at work, the Internet is pretty dull.

Answers

1. **C.** Computer book authors didn't get a bailout either.

2. **B.** Interpreters interpret one line at a time. Compilers figure out the instructions beforehand so the program can run faster.

3. **A.** He was frustrated with C++. Back in 1991 when he created Java, YouTube was the place that held YouToothpaste.

Activities

If you'd like to better introduce yourself to the subjects of Java and computer programming, do the following activities:

▶ To learn more about why to learn Java, read this Oracle University blog post: https://blogs.oracle.com/oracleuniversity/10-reasons-why-you-should-consider-learning-java.

▶ Using English sentences, write a set of instructions to convert a temperature from Celsius to Fahrenheit. Break the instructions into as many short one-sentence lines as you can.

To see solutions to the activities at the end of each hour, visit the book's website at www.java24hours.com.

HOUR 2
Writing Your First Program

This Hour's To-Do List:

- ▶ Type a Java program into a text editor.
- ▶ Organize a program with bracket marks.
- ▶ Store information in a variable.
- ▶ Display the information stored in a variable.
- ▶ Save, compile, and run a program.

As you learned during Hour 1, "Becoming a Programmer," a computer program is a set of instructions that tells a computer what to do. These instructions are given to a computer using a programming language.

During this hour, you create your first Java program by entering it into a text editor. When that's done, you save the program, compile it, and test it out. Then you break it on purpose and fix it again, just to show off.

What You Need to Write Programs

As explained in Hour 1, to create Java programs, you must have a programming tool that supports the Java Development Kit (JDK) such as the NetBeans integrated development environment (IDE). You need a tool that can compile and run Java programs and a text editor to write those programs.

With most programming languages, computer programs are written by entering text into a text editor (also called a source code editor). Some programming languages come with their own editor. NetBeans includes its own editor for writing Java programs.

Java programs are plain text files without any special formatting, such as centered text or boldface text. The NetBeans source code editor functions like a simple text editor with some useful enhancements for programmers. Text turns different colors as you type to identify different elements of the language. NetBeans also indents lines properly and provides helpful programming documentation inside the editor.

Because Java programs are text files, you can open and edit them with any text editor. You could write a Java program with NetBeans, open it in Windows Notepad and make changes, and open it again later in NetBeans without any problems.

Creating the Saluton Program

The first Java program that you create will display a traditional greeting from the world of computer science: "Saluton mondo!"

To prepare for the first programming project in NetBeans, if you haven't already done so, create a new project called Java24 by following these steps:

1. Choose the menu command File, New Project. The New Project dialog opens.

2. Choose the project category Java and the project type Java Application and then click Next.

3. Enter Java24 as the project's name. (If you created a project with this name previously, you see the error message "Project folder already exists and is not empty.")

4. Deselect the Create Main Class check box.

5. Click Finish.

The Java24 project is created in its own folder. You can use this project for the Java programs you write as you progress through this book.

Beginning the Program

NetBeans groups relate programs together into a project. If you don't have the Java24 project open, here's how to load it:

1. Choose File, Open Project. A file dialog appears.

2. Find and select the NetBeansProjects folder (if necessary).

3. Choose Java24 and click Open Project.

The Java24 project appears in the Projects pane next to a coffee cup icon and a + sign that can be expanded to see the files and folders that the project contains.

To add a new Java program to the currently open project, choose File, New File. The New File Wizard opens, as shown in Figure 2.1.

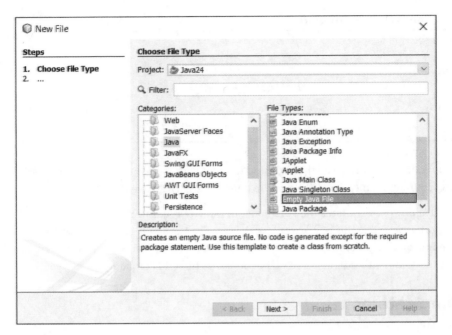

FIGURE 2.1
The New File Wizard.

The Categories pane lists the different kinds of Java programs you can create. Click the Java folder in this pane to see the file types that belong to this category. For this first project, choose the Empty Java File type (near the end in the File Types pane) and click Next.

A New Empty Java File dialog opens. Follow these steps to begin writing the program:

1. In the Class Name field, enter `Saluton`.

2. In the Package field, enter `com.java24hours`.

3. Click Finish.

So you can begin working right away on your program, an empty file named `Saluton.java` opens in the source code editor. Using the editor, begin your Java programming career by entering each line from Listing 2.1. These statements are called the program's source code.

CAUTION

Don't enter the line number and colon at the beginning of each line—these are used in this book to reference specific line numbers.

LISTING 2.1 **The** Saluton **Program**

```
1: package com.java24hours;
2:
3: class Saluton {
4:     public static void main(String[] arguments) {
5:         // My first Java program goes here
6:     }
7: }
```

Make sure to capitalize everything exactly as shown, and use your spacebar or Tab key to insert the blank spaces in front of Lines 4–6. When you're done, choose File, Save to save the file.

At this point, Saluton.java contains the bare bones of a Java program. You will create many programs that start exactly like this one, except for the word Saluton on Line 3. This word represents the name of your program and changes with each program you write. Line 5 should make sense to you, because it's a sentence in actual English. The rest is probably new to you.

The class Statement

The first line of the program is the following:

```
package com.java24hours;
```

A package is a way to group Java programs together. This line tells the computer to make com.java24hours the package name of the program.

After a blank line, the third line is this:

```
class Saluton {
```

Translated into English, it means, "Computer, give my Java program the name Saluton."

As you might recall from Hour 1, each instruction you give a computer is called a statement. The class statement is the way you give your computer program a name. It's also used to determine other things about the program, as you will see later. The significance of the term class is that Java programs also are called classes.

In this example, the program name Saluton matches the document's filename, Saluton. java. A Java program must have a name that matches the first part of its filename—the portion before the "." period character—and should be capitalized the same way.

If the program name doesn't match the filename, you get an error when you try to compile some Java programs, depending on how the class statement is being used to configure the program.

What the `main` Statement Does

The next line of the program is the following:

```
public static void main(String[] arguments) {
```

This line tells the computer, "The main part of the program begins here." Java programs are organized into different sections, so there needs to be a way to identify the part of a program that is executed first when the program is run.

The `main` statement is the entry point to most Java programs. The exceptions are applets, programs that are run on a web page by a web browser; servlets, programs run by a web server; and apps, programs run by a mobile device.

Most programs you write during upcoming hours of this book use `main` as their starting point. That's because you run them directly on your computer. Applets, apps, and servlets are run indirectly by another program or device.

To differentiate them from these other types, the programs that you run directly are called applications.

Those Squiggly Bracket Marks

In the `Saluton` program, Lines 3, 4, 6, and 7 contain a squiggly bracket mark of some kind—either a { or a }. These brackets are a way to group lines of your program (in the same way that parentheses are used in a sentence to group words). Everything between the opening bracket { and the closing bracket } is part of the same group.

These groupings are called blocks. In Listing 2.1, the opening bracket on Line 3 is associated with the closing bracket on Line 7, which makes your entire program a block. You use brackets in this way to show the beginning and end of a program.

Blocks can be located inside other blocks (just as parentheses are used in this sentence (and a second set is used here)). The `Saluton` program has brackets on Line 4 and Line 6 that establish another block. This block begins with the `main` statement. The lines inside the `main` statement's block will be run when the program begins.

TIP

NetBeans can help you figure out where a block begins and ends. Click one of the brackets in the source code of the `Saluton` program. The bracket you clicked turns yellow along with its corresponding bracket. The Java statements enclosed within the two yellow brackets are a block. This tip is not that useful on a short program like `Saluton`, but as you write much longer programs, it helps you avoid looking like a blockhead.

The following statement is the only thing located inside the block:

```
// My first Java program goes here
```

This line is a placeholder. The `//` at the beginning of the line tells the computer to ignore this line because it was put in the program solely for the benefit of humans who are looking at the source code. Lines that serve this purpose are called *comments*.

Right now, you have written a complete Java program. It can be compiled, but if you run it, nothing happens. The reason is that you haven't told the computer to do anything yet. The `main` statement block contains only a single comment, which is ignored by the computer. You must add some statements inside the opening and closing brackets of the `main` block.

Storing Information in a Variable

In the programs you write, you need a place to store information for a brief period of time. You can do this by using a variable, a storage place that can hold information such as integers, floating-point numbers, true-false values, characters, and lines of text. The information stored in a variable can change, which is how it gets the name variable.

In `Saluton.java` file, replace Line 5 with the following:

```
String greeting = "Saluton mondo!";
```

This statement tells the computer to store the text "Saluton mondo!" in a variable called `greeting`.

In a Java program, you must tell the computer what type of information a variable will hold. In this program, `greeting` is a string—a line of text that can include letters, numbers, punctuation, and other characters. Putting `String` in the statement sets up the variable to hold string values.

When you enter this statement into the program, a semicolon must be included at the end of the line. Semicolons end each statement in a Java program. They're like the period at the end of a sentence. The computer uses them to determine when one statement ends and the next one begins.

Putting only one statement on each line makes a program more understandable (for us humans).

Displaying the Contents of a Variable

If you run the program at this point, it still seems like nothing happens. The command to store text in the `greeting` variable occurs behind the scenes. To make the computer show that it is doing something, you can display the contents of that variable.

Insert another blank line in the `Saluton` program after the `String greeting = "Saluton mondo!"` statement. Use that empty space to enter the following statement:

```
System.out.println(greeting);
```

This statement tells the computer to display the value stored in the `greeting` variable. The `System.out.println` statement makes the computer display information on the system output device—your monitor.

Now you're getting somewhere.

Saving the Finished Product

Your program should now resemble Listing 2.2, although you might have used slightly different spacing in Lines 5–6. Make any corrections that are needed and save the file (by choosing File, Save).

LISTING 2.2   The Finished Version of the `Saluton` Program

```
1: package com.java24hours;
2:
3: class Saluton {
4:     public static void main(String[] arguments) {
5:         String greeting = "Saluton mondo!";
6:         System.out.println(greeting);
7:     }
8: }
```

When the computer runs this program, it executes each of the statements in the `main` statement block on Lines 5 and 6. Listing 2.3 shows what the program would look like if it was written in the English language instead of Java.

LISTING 2.3   A Line-by-Line Breakdown of the `Saluton` Program

```
1: Put this program in the com.java24hours package.
2:
3: The Saluton program begins here:
4:     The main part of the program begins here:
5:         Store the text "Saluton mondo!" in a String variable named greeting.
6:         Display the contents of the variable greeting.
7:     The main part of the program ends here.
8: The Saluton program ends here.
```

Listing 2.4 shows what the program would look like if written in Klingon, the language of the warrior race from *Star Trek*.

LISTING 2.4   The Saluton **Program in Klingon**

```
1: This program belongs to the house of com.java2hours!
2:
3: Begin the Saluton program here if you know what's good for you!
4:     The main part of the program begins here with honor!
5:         Store the gibberish "Saluton mondo!" in a String variable called
greeting!
6:         Display this gibberish from a tongue inferior to Klingon!
7:     End the main part of the program here to avoid my wrath!
8: End the Saluton program now and be grateful you were spared!
```

Compiling the Program into a Class File

Before you can run a Java program, you must compile it. When you compile a program, the instructions given to the computer in the program are converted into a form the computer can better understand.

NetBeans compiles programs automatically as they are saved. If you typed everything as shown in Listing 2.2, the program compiles successfully.

A compiled version of the program, a new file called Saluton.class, is created. All Java programs are compiled into class files, which are given the file extension .class. A Java program can be made up of several classes that work together, but in a simple program such as Saluton only one class is needed.

The compiler turns Java source code into bytecode, a form that can be run by the Java Virtual Machine (JVM).

NOTE

The Java compiler speaks up only when there's an error to complain about. If you compile a program successfully without any errors, nothing happens in response.

This is admittedly a bit anticlimactic. When I was starting out as a Java programmer, I was hoping successful compilation would be met with a grand flourish of celebratory horns.

Fixing Errors

As you compose a program in the NetBeans source editor, errors are flagged with a red alert icon to the left of the editor pane, as shown in Figure 2.2.

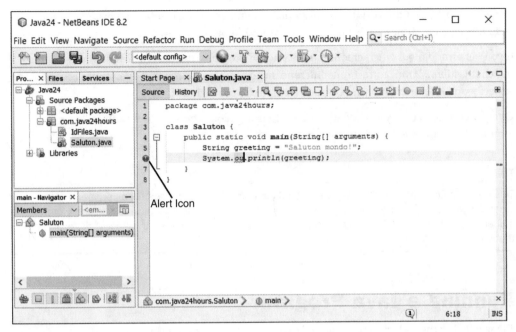

FIGURE 2.2
Spotting errors in the source editor.

The icon appears on the line that triggered the error. You can click this icon to display an error dialog that explains the compiler error with these details:

▶ The name of the Java program

▶ The type of error

▶ The line where the error was found

Here's an example of an error dialog you might see when compiling the `Saluton` program:

```
cannot find symbol.
symbol   : variable greeting
location: class Saluton
```

The error message is the first line of the dialog: "cannot find symbol." These messages often can be confusing to new programmers. When the error message doesn't make sense to you, don't spend much time trying to figure it out. Instead, look at the line where the error occurred and check for the most obvious causes.

For instance, can you determine what's wrong with the following statement?

```
System.out.println(greeting);
```

The error is a typo in the variable name, which should be `greeting` instead of `greting`. (Add this typo on purpose in NetBeans to see what happens.)

If you get error dialogs when creating the `Saluton` program, double-check that your program matches Listing 2.2 and correct any differences you find. Make sure that everything is capitalized correctly and all punctuation marks such as {,}, and ; are included.

Often, a close look at the line identified by the error dialog is enough to reveal the error (or errors) that need to be fixed.

TIP
_____

This book's official website at www.java24hours.com includes source files for all programs you create. If you can't find any typos or other reasons for errors in the `Saluton` program but there are still errors, go to the book's website and download `Saluton.java` from the Hour 2 page. Try to run that file instead.

_____

Running a Java Program

To see whether the `Saluton` program does what you want, run the class with the Java interpreter. In NetBeans, choose the menu command Run, Run File. An Output pane opens below the source code editor. In this pane, if there are no errors, the program displays the output, as shown in Figure 2.3.

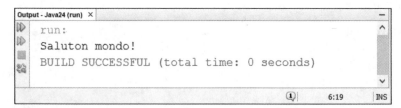

FIGURE 2.3
Running your first Java program.

If you see the text "Saluton Mondo!" you have just written your first working Java program! Your computer has just greeted the world—a tradition in the computer programming field that's as important to many of us as energy drinks, short-sleeved dress shirts, and League of Legends.

You might be asking yourself why "Saluton mondo!" is a traditional greeting. The phrase means "Hello world!" in Esperanto, an artificial language created by Ludwig Zamenhof in 1887 to facilitate international communication.

It's only a traditional greeting in the sense that I'm trying to start that tradition.

TIP

Oracle offers comprehensive documentation for the Java language on the Web. You don't need it to read this book, because each topic is discussed fully as it is introduced, but this reference comes in handy when you want to expand your knowledge and write your own programs.

The documentation can be downloaded, but it's more convenient to browse as needed on Oracle's website. The most up-to-date Java documentation is available at http://download.java.net/jdk9/docs/api.

Summary

During this hour, you got your first chance to create a Java program. You learned that in order to develop a Java program, you need to complete these four basic steps:

1. Write the program with a text editor or a tool such as NetBeans.

2. Compile the program into a class file.

3. Tell the Java Virtual Machine to run the class.

4. Call your mother.

Along the way, you were introduced to some basic computer programming concepts such as compilers, interpreters, blocks, statements, and variables. These will become clearer to you in successive hours. As long as you got the `Saluton` program to work during this hour, you're ready to proceed.

(The fourth step has nothing to do with Java programming. It's just something my mother suggested I put in the book.)

Workshop

Q&A

Q. How important is it to put the right number of blank spaces on a line in a Java program?

A. It's completely unimportant as far as the computer is concerned. Spacing is strictly for the benefit of people looking at a computer program—the Java compiler couldn't care less. You could have written the `Saluton` program without including blank spaces or using the Tab key to indent lines, and it would compile successfully.

Although the number of spaces in front of lines isn't important to the computer, you should use consistent spacing and indentation in your Java programs anyway. Why? Because spacing makes it easier for you to see how a program is organized and to which programming block a statement belongs.

The programs you write must be understandable to other programmers, including yourself when you look at the code weeks or months later to fix a bug or make an enhancement. Consistency in spacing and indentation are part of what's called a programming style. Good programmers adopt a style and practice it in all their work.

Q. A Java program has been described as a class and as a group of classes. Which is it?

A. Both. The simple Java programs you create during the next few hours are compiled into a single file with the extension `.class`. You can run these with the Java Virtual Machine. Java programs also can be made up of a set of classes that work together. This topic is fully explored during Hour 10, "Creating Your First Object."

Q. If semicolons are needed at the end of each statement, why does the comment line `// My first Java program goes here` not end with a semicolon?

A. Comments are completely ignored by the compiler. If you put `//` on a line in your program, this tells the Java compiler to ignore everything to the right of the `//` on that line. The following example shows a comment on the same line as a statement:

```
System.out.println(greeting); // hello, world!
```

Q. I couldn't find any errors in the line where the compiler noted an error. What can I do?

A. The line number displayed with the error message isn't always the place where an error needs to be fixed. Examine the statements that are directly above the error message to see whether you can spot any typos or other bugs. The error usually is within the same programming block.

Q. How can I visit Antarctica?

A. If you're not willing to become a scientific researcher or a support staffer such as a cook, electrician, or doctor, you can become one of the 10,000 people who visit the frozen continent annually as tourists.

Flyovers are available from Australia, New Zealand, and South America and cost around $1,000 per person.

Several cruise ships visit for a trip lasting from 10 days to three weeks, the most expensive of which is around $25,000. Some cruises offer a chance to kayak or hike among penguins, visit icebergs, and even camp overnight.

The Polar Cruises website at www.polarcruises.com provides more information for prospective Antarctica visitors.

The British Antarctic Survey offers a piece of advice for visitors: "Do not walk onto glaciers or large snowfields unless properly trained."

Quiz

Test your knowledge of the material covered in this hour by answering the following questions.

1. When you compile a Java program, what are you doing?

    A. Saving it to a disk

    B. Converting it into a form the computer can better understand

    C. Adding it to your program collection

2. What is a variable?

    A. Something that wobbles but doesn't fall down

    B. Text in a program that the compiler ignores

    C. A place to store information in a program

3. What is the process of fixing errors called?

    A. Defrosting

    B. Debugging

    C. Decomposing

Answers

1. **B.** Compiling a program converts a `.java` file into a `.class` file or a set of `.class` files.

2. **C.** Variables are one place to store information; later you learn about others such as arrays and constants. Weebles wobble but they don't fall down, and comments are text in a program that the compiler ignores.

3. **B.** Because errors in a computer program are called bugs, fixing those errors is called debugging. Some programming tools come with a tool called a debugger that helps you fix errors. NetBeans has one of debest debuggers.

Activities

If you'd like to explore the topics covered in this hour a little more fully, try the following activities:

▶ You can translate the English phrase "Hello world!" into other languages using the Google Translator at http://translate.google.com. Write a program that enables your computer to greet the world in a language such as French, Italian, or Portuguese.

▶ Go back to the `Saluton` program and add one or two errors. For example, take a semicolon off the end of a line or change the text `println` on one line to `print1n` (with a number 1 instead of the letter L). Save the program and try to compile it; then compare the error messages you see to the errors you caused.

To see solutions to these activities, visit the book's website at www.java24hours.com.

HOUR 3
Vacationing in Java

This Hour's To-Do List:

▶ Discover the history of Java.

▶ Learn the benefits of using the language.

▶ See examples of Java at work.

Before you venture further into Java programming, it's worthwhile to learn more about the language and see what programmers are doing with it today. Though Java has long outgrown its origins as a language focused on web browser programs, you can find millions of examples of how Java is used in mobile apps.

During this hour, we look at sites that feature Java programs, apps written in the language, and the history and development of the language.

To go on this vacation, you need a phone or tablet that runs Java programs.

Power up your device of choice, put on your best batik shirt, and get ready to take a vacation. You won't be leaving your house, and you won't experience the simpler pleasures of tourism, such as exotic locales, exotic locals, exotic food, exotic locals with food, and so on.

Look on the bright side though: no traveler's check hassles, no passports, and no worries about the water.

First Stop: Oracle

The Java vacation begins at www.java.com, a site published by Oracle, the company that develops the Java language.

A Java program that runs on a mobile device is called an *app*. Apps in Java appear primarily on Android devices. Java also appears on the Web: Desktop programs written in Java can be launched from a web browser, Java servlets are run by web servers to deliver web applications, and Java applets appear on web pages in browsers.

Figure 3.1 shows Celtic Heroes, a massively multiplayer online game powered by Java on Android. You can play the game for free by installing the app on Google Play or your device's app store.

FIGURE 3.1
The Java-powered app game Celtic Heroes.

When you run it, the game loads within seconds and you can create a character and explore a fantasy world.

Oracle's Java division leads the development of the Java language. *Java Magazine*, an online magazine available for free from Oracle at Java.com, showcases how Java is being used on Android phones, websites, and other platforms. Billions of devices run programs written with Java.

Oracle also offers a more technically oriented website for Java programmers at www.oracle.com/technetwork/java. This site is the place to find the latest released versions of NetBeans and the Java Development Kit along with other programming resources.

This trip around Java begins in Android because that has become the most thriving place for the language to be used. After you learn Java, you can apply your skills developing your own apps using the Android Software Development Kit (SDK), a free programming toolkit that runs on Windows, Mac OS, and Linux.

More than 300,000 apps have been created for Android phones and other devices that run the mobile operating system. You learn more about how to create them in Hour 24, "Writing Android Apps."

A Brief History of Java

Bill Joy, one of the executives at Sun Microsystems when the company created Java, called the language "the end result of 15 years of work to produce a better, more reliable way to write computer programs." Java's creation was a little more complicated than that.

Java was developed in 1990 by James Gosling as a language that would serve as the brains for smart appliances (interactive TVs, omniscient ovens, time-traveling Terminators, SkyNet military satellites that enslave mankind, and so on). Gosling was unhappy with the results he was getting by writing programs with a programming language called C++. In a burst of inspiration, he holed up in his office and wrote a new language to better suit his needs.

Gosling named his new language Oak after a tree he could see from his office window. The language was part of his company's strategy to make a fortune when interactive TV became a multimillion-dollar industry. That still hasn't happened today (though Amazon, Apple, Roku, and others are making a game attempt), but something completely different took place for Gosling's new language. Just as Oak was about to be scrapped, the Web became popular.

In a fortuitous circumstance, many qualities that made Gosling's language good on its appliance project made it suitable for adaptation to the Web. His team devised a way for programs to be run safely from web pages, and a catchy new name was chosen to accompany the language's new purpose: Java.

NOTE

You might have heard that Java is an acronym that stands for Just Another Vague Acronym. You also might have heard that it was named for Gosling's love of coffee.

The story behind Java's naming contains no secret messages or declarations of liquid love. Java was chosen as the name for the same reason that the comedian Jerry Seinfeld likes to say the word *salsa*: It just sounds cool.

Although Java can be used for many other things, the Web provided the original showcase it needed to seize the attention of the world's software developers. When the language rose to prominence, you had to be in solitary confinement or a long-term orbital mission to avoid hearing about it.

There have been 10 major releases of the Java language, each with some essential new features. Here are the first nine:

- **Java 1.0**—The original release (1995)

- **Java 1.1**—Java Database Connectivity (JDBC), improved graphical user interfaces (1997)

- **Java 2 version 1.2**—Inner classes, the Java Plug-in for web browsers, and data structures (1998)

- **Java 2 version 1.3**—Enhanced multimedia (2000)

- **Java 2 version 1.4**—Improved Internet support, XML processing, and assertions (2002)

- **Java 5**—Generics, new for loops, annotations, and automatic data conversion (2005)

- **Java 6**—The built-in Derby database and web services (2006)

- **Java 7**—Memory and resource management improvements and the Nimbus graphical user interface (2011)

- **Java 8**—Closures (2014)

The current release, Java 9, came out in 2017. Three years in the making, this new version introduces improvements to interfaces and closures, an advanced feature you learn about during Hour 16, "Using Inner Classes and Closures." There's also an HTTP client for receiving and sending data over the Web, as covered in Hour 21, "Using Java 9's New HTTP Client."

If you don't know what all these things are—such as inner classes, generics, or HTTP—don't freak out. You'll learn about them over the next 21 hours.

NOTE

Are you wondering why Java's versions are numbered so strangely, skipping from 2 to 6, calling the seventh version Java 6, and including an integer and decimal number in some versions? Me, too!

Java's major domos made some odd decisions along the way as new versions were released.

Fortunately, the numbering scheme has made more sense since 2006, with each new release an integer one higher than the last.

Going to School with Java

The Web includes numerous resources for educators and schoolchildren. Because Java apps can offer a more interactive experience than web pages, the language is a natural choice for programs that enhance learning.

For one such example, install the FreeBalls app to access a free particle motion simulator created by Ivan Maklyakov, a computer programmer in Russia. The program uses Java to demonstrate physics-based animation of thousands of particles made out of a solid or liquid. The motion is controlled by tilting the screen. Figure 3.2 shows the colorful result.

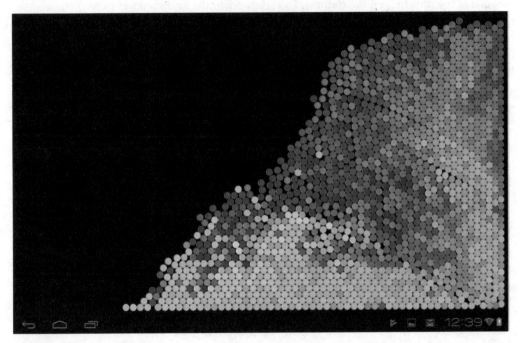

FIGURE 3.2
A physics simulator can be experienced interactively using a Java app.

Numerous educational programs are available for many operating systems, but one thing that makes this program stand out is its availability. The simulator can run on any Android device. You can run Java programs on any computer that has a Java Virtual Machine (JVM).

The JVM loaded by a mobile device or web browser is the same you used to run the `Saluton` application during Hour 2, "Writing Your First Program."

A Java program, such as the physics simulator, does not have to be written for a specific operating system. Because operating systems like Windows also are called platforms, this advantage is called platform independence. Java was created to work on multiple systems. Java's developers believed it needed to be multiplatform because it would be used on a variety of appliances and other electronic devices.

Users can run the programs you write with Java on a variety of systems without requiring any extra work from you. Under the right circumstances, Java can remove the need to create specific versions of a program for different operating systems and devices.

Lunch at Food Network

After working up an appetite on our first two stops, take a lunch break with Food Network in the Kitchen, a free Java app created by the gustatory television channel.

For each of the star chefs on the channel, Food Network in the Kitchen offers recipes, cooking notes, user comments, and videos. One of the advantages of the app format is that it can include interactive features in conjunction with articles. Figure 3.3 shows Giada de Laurentiis's recipe for pan-seared branzino that accompanies a video tutorial explaining how it was prepared. Remember to use your fish spatula!

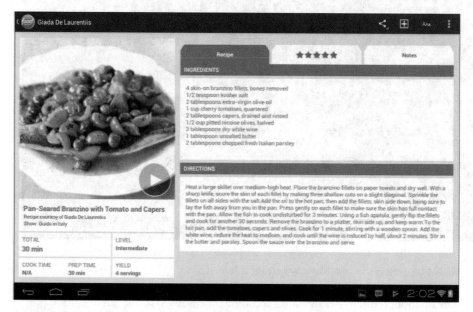

FIGURE 3.3
A recipe in the Food Network in the Kitchen app.

An app store like the one where Food Network in the Kitchen was found contains thousands of programs for users to try. Because these programs come from many developers, safeguards must be in place to protect users and their devices. One issue that has been hotly debated since Java's introduction is whether the language is secure.

Security is important because of the way Java programs work when they are delivered as apps. The apps you try during this hour are downloaded to your phone or tablet. When the program is finished downloading, it can be run.

Unless you know a whole lot of people, most apps you use are published by strangers. In terms of security, running their programs isn't a lot different than letting the general public come over and borrow your computer. If the Java language did not have safeguards to prevent abuse, its programs could introduce viruses onto your system, delete files, play the spoken-word song performances of William Shatner, and do other unspeakable things.

Java includes several kinds of security to make sure that its programs are safe when run from apps or web pages.

The language generally has been considered safe enough to be usable over the Web, but security holes exploited in recent years have led some security experts to recommend that users turn off Java entirely in their browsers. Most of the leading browsers today discourage users from running Java applets on websites.

Java is more commonly encountered by users on mobile apps, server programs, and desktop software. That's why this hour is being spent running apps instead of applets.

Watching the Skies at NASA

The first afternoon stop on the Java tour is a trip to space. NASA is a U.S. government agency that makes extensive use of Java. One example is ISS Detector, a free app from the developer RunaR that helps stargazers keep an eye out for the International Space Station and several orbiting satellites.

ISS Detector superimposes the current location and path of the ISS and satellites—over the night sky. In Figure 3.4, the app shows the Iridium 96 satellite (GALEX) making a path through the Eastern sky past Venus and Uranus beginning at 1:43 a.m.

FIGURE 3.4
The ISS Detector app monitors the location and path of orbiting satellites, a boon to metal birdwatchers.

The app redraws the position of each tracked satellite as it runs and changes the orientation of the sky map based on the direction the user is facing. This kind of real-time update is possible because the Java language is multithreaded. Multithreading is a way for the computer to do more than one thing at the same time. One part of a program takes care of one task, another part takes care of a different task, and the two parts can pay no attention to each other. Each part of a program in this example is called a thread.

In a program such as ISS Detector, each satellite could run in its own thread. If you use an operating system such as Windows 10, you're using a type of this behavior when you run more than one program at the same time. If you're at work playing Minecraft in one window while running a company sales report in another window and making a long-distance call to a friend, congratulate yourself—you're multithreading!

Getting Down to Business

At this point in your travels, you might have the impression that Java is primarily of use to space buffs, amateur chefs, and elven warriors. The next stop on our trip shows an example of Java getting down to business.

Install the Realtime Stock Quotes Java app from uInvest Studio which displays updated stock prices for a user's holdings. Figure 3.5 shows the current data for ticker symbol GOOG (Google's parent company Alphabet Inc.).

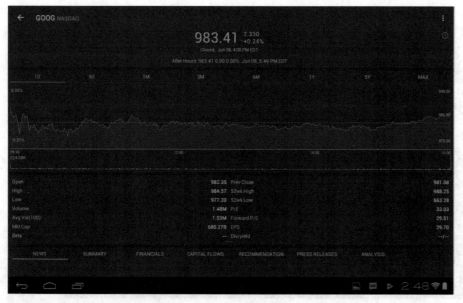

FIGURE 3.5
Stock market data presented in a uInvest Studio Java app.

You can think of a program like this stock ticker app in several ways. One is to think of a program as an object—something that exists in the world, takes up space, and has certain things it can do. Object-oriented programming (OOP), which Java uses, as you discover in Hour 10, "Creating Your First Object," is a way of creating computer programs as a group of objects. Each object handles a specific job and knows how to speak to other objects. For example, a stock ticker program could be set up as the following group of objects:

▶ A quote object, which represents an individual stock quote

▶ A portfolio object, which holds a set of quotes for specific stocks

▶ A ticker object, which displays a portfolio

▶ An Internet object, a user object, and many others

Under that model, the stock ticker software is a collection of all the objects necessary to get work done.

OOP is a powerful way to create programs, and it makes the programs you write more useful. Consider the stock software. If the programmer wants to use the quote capabilities of that program with some other software, the quote object can be used with the new program. No changes need to be made.

Programs created with objects are easier to maintain because they are better organized. An object contains the data necessary to do its job and the code required to do that work. Objects also make a program more extensible. A new object can be patterned after an existing one and enhanced with new capabilities.

Stopping by SourceForge for Directions

This world tour of Java programs is being led by a professional who is well versed in the hazards and highlights of app-based travel. You'll be venturing out on your own trips soon, so it's worthwhile to learn the lay of the land at an incredibly useful site for programmers: SourceForge, one of the best places to find complete examples of working programs written with Java (or any other language). Find it at www.sourceforge.net.

SourceForge is an enormous website devoted to collaborative programming projects. If you have an interest in working with others on a program you are developing, you can start a project on SourceForge, share all its files, recruit others, and communicate with them. The 430,000-plus projects on the site all are open source, which means that the programmers have shared all the source code. In case you're unfamiliar with the term, source code is another name for the text files that are used to create computer programs. The `Saluton.java` file you developed during Hour 2 is an example of source code.

If you use the search box atop the SourceForge home page to search for Java, you'll find more than 61,000 listings in the site's directory of projects.

One of the programs on SourceForge is JSoko, a Java version of the Japanese warehouse keeper game Sokoban (see Figure 3.6). The puzzle game features animation, graphics, keyboard control, and sound. To download the application and view its Java source code, visit https://sourceforge.net/projects/jsokoapplet to download the source code.

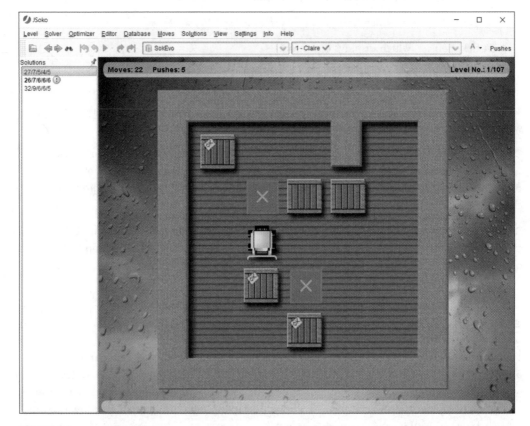

FIGURE 3.6
Source code for Java programs such as the open source Sokoban game JSoko can be found on SourceForge.

Java includes an enormous library of classes you can use in your own programs. JSoko employs the library's `Image` class (in `java.awt`) to display graphics such as boxes and its `AudioInputStream` class (in `javax.sound.sampled`) to play sounds as the truck moves and boxes are placed.

One reason so many programs are created with Java—on SourceForge and elsewhere—is because the language was designed to be easier to learn despite its powerful functionality.

An original design goal for the language was to make it quicker to master than C++, the language Gosling was having fits with on his smart-appliance project back in the 1990s. Much of Java is based on C++, so programmers who have learned to use that language find it easier to learn Java. However, some of the elements of C++ that are the hardest to learn and use correctly are not present in Java.

For people learning programming for the first time, Java is easier to learn than C++. Some languages are created to make it easier for experienced programmers to harness the capabilities of the computer in their programs. These languages include shortcuts and other features that programming veterans easily understand.

Java does not use some of these features, preferring to make the language as simple as an object-oriented programming language can be. Java was created to be easy to learn, easy to debug, and easy to use. Java includes numerous enhancements that make it a worthy competitor to other languages.

Summary

Now that the hour-long vacation is over, it's time to put away your luggage and get ready for a return to actual Java programming.

During the next 21 hours, you will master the basic building blocks of the Java language, learn how to create your own objects to accomplish tasks in object-oriented programming, design graphical user interfaces, and much more.

Unless you stopped reading this book to play Celtic Heroes.

Workshop

Q&A

Q. Why are Java applets no longer popular?

A. When the Java language was introduced in the mid-1990s, most people were learning the language to write applets. Java was the only way to create interactive programs that ran in a web browser. Over the years, alternatives emerged. Macromedia Flash, Microsoft Silverlight, and the new web publishing HTML5 standard all offer ways to put programs on web pages.

Applets were hampered by poor loading times, slow support for new versions of Java by browser developers, and security holes exploited by hackers. Though applets are disappearing from the web, Java has outgrown its origins as a web browser enhancement and is now a sophisticated general-purpose programming language.

Q. **What's the difference between Java SE (Java Standard Edition) and Java EE (Java Enterprise Edition)? Does Java EE cost money?**

A. Java Enterprise Edition is an expansion of the Java Standard Edition that includes packages to support advanced technology such as Enterprise JavaBeans, XML processing, and the development of servlets—Java programs that run on a web server. Java EE also includes an application server, a sophisticated environment for executing Java software that's tailored for corporations and other large organizations with heavy computing needs. The Java EE development kit can be downloaded at no cost from Oracle at www.oracle.com/technetwork/java/javaee.

Q. **What's a Chris Steak House, and why does Ruth have one?**

A. Ruth's Chris Steak House, the chain of more than 130 upscale steak restaurants across the United States and a handful of other countries, has an odd two-first-name name that reveals its humble origins and the stubborn streak of its founder.

The chain was founded in 1965 as a solitary New Orleans restaurant owned by Ruth Fertel, a single mother of two sons. Fertel saw a classified ad offering a restaurant for sale and took out a $22,000 home mortgage to buy it (equivalent to around $150,000 in present dollars).

She reached a deal to keep the name Chris Steak House with original owner Chris Matulich, but later had to relocate after a kitchen fire.

Fertel's contract did not permit her to use the Chris Steak House name anywhere but the original location, so she renamed it Ruth's Chris Steak House. Though she had no restaurant or culinary expertise, the business was so successful that she began offering it as a franchise within 12 years. She disregarded several suggestions over the years to change the name to broaden its appeal.

"I've always hated the name," she once told a reporter for *Fortune* magazine, "but we've always managed to work around it."

Fertel, who died in 2002, was born on February 5, 1927—the same day that Matulich opened the original steakhouse.

Quiz

If your mind hasn't taken a vacation by this point, test your knowledge of this hour with the following questions.

1. How did object-oriented programming get its name?

    A. Programs are considered to be a group of objects working together.

    B. People often object because it's hard to master.

    C. Its parents named it.

2. Where were Java apps designed to run?

   A. A web browser.

   B. An Android phone or tablet.

   C. A desktop computer.

3. What does a computer or device need to run Java programs?

   A. A Java compiler

   B. A Java Virtual Machine

   C. Both

Answers

1. A. It's also abbreviated as OOP.

2. B. All Android apps are written in Java. They can run on browsers and desktops, but were developed with mobile devices and tablets in mind.

3. B. The Java Virtual Machine (JVM) is an interpreter that converts Java bytecode into instructions the computer or device can run. A compiler is required to create Java programs, but not to run them.

Activities

Before unpacking your luggage, you can explore the topics of this hour more fully with the following activities:

▶ Use SourceForge at www.sourceforge.net to find out what card games have been developed using the Java language.

▶ Use Google Play on your Android device to search for physics simulations. Pick one that sounds interesting and install it.

Solutions for the activities in this book are presented on the book's website at www.java24hours.com.

Understanding How Java Programs Work

This Hour's To-Do List:

- ▶ Learn how applications work.
- ▶ Send arguments to an application.
- ▶ Learn how Java programs are organized.
- ▶ Use the Java Class Library.
- ▶ Try Java 9's new JShell tool.
- ▶ Create an object in an application.

An important distinction to make in Java programming is where your program is supposed to be running. Some programs are intended to work on your computer. Other programs are intended to run on a phone or tablet.

Java programs that run locally on your own computer are called applications, programs that are run by web servers are called servlets, and programs that run on mobile devices are called apps.

During this hour, you will create an application and run it on your computer.

Creating an Application

The `Saluton` program you wrote during Hour 2, "Writing Your First Program," is an example of a Java application. The next application you create calculates the square root of a number and displays the value.

With the Java24 project open in NetBeans, begin a new application:

1. Choose File, New File. The New File Wizard opens.

2. Choose the category `Java` and the file type `Empty Java File` and then click Next.

3. Enter the class name `Root`.

4. Enter the package name `com.java24hours`.

5. Click Finish.

NetBeans creates `Root.java` and opens the empty file in the source editor so you can begin working on it. Enter everything from Listing 4.1, remembering not to enter the line numbers and colons along the left side of the listing. The numbers are used to make parts of programs easier to describe in the book. When you're done, save the file by clicking the Save All button on the toolbar.

LISTING 4.1   **The Full Text of** `Root.java`

```
 1: package com.java24hours;
 2:
 3: class Root {
 4:     public static void main(String[] arguments) {
 5:         int number = 225;
 6:         System.out.println("The square root of "
 7:             + number
 8:             + " is "
 9:             + Math.sqrt(number)
10:         );
11:     }
12: }
```

The `Root` application accomplishes the following tasks:

▶ Line 1—The application is placed in the `com.java24hours` package.

▶ Line 5—An integer value of 225 is stored in a variable named `number`.

▶ Lines 6–10—This integer and its square root are displayed. The `Math.sqrt(number)` statement in Line 9 displays the square root.

If you have entered Listing 4.1 without any typos, including all punctuation and every word capitalized as shown, you can run the file in NetBeans by choosing Run, Run File. The output of the program appears in the Output pane, as shown in Figure 4.1.

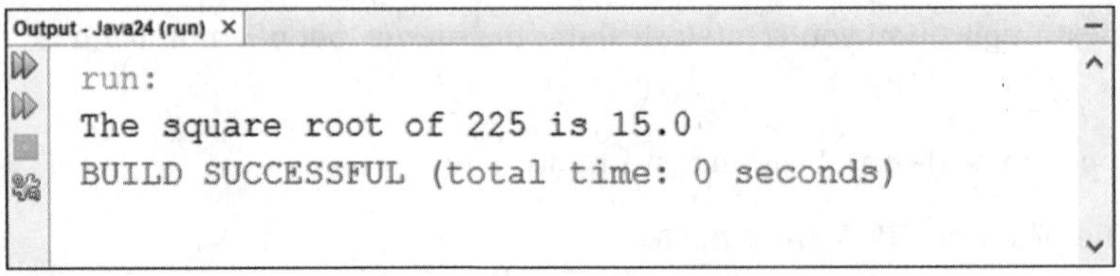

```
Output - Java24 (run)  ×
run:
The square root of 225 is 15.0
BUILD SUCCESSFUL (total time: 0 seconds)
```

FIGURE 4.1
The output of the `Root` application.

When you run a Java application, the Java Virtual Machine (JVM) looks for a `main()` block and starts handling Java statements within that block. If your program does not have a `main()` block, the JVM responds with an error.

The statement `Math.sqrt(number)` in line 9 demonstrates a built-in capability of the Java language—the ability to determine the square root of a number. There is a Java program named `Math` that has a method called `sqrt()` to find a specified number's square root.

The `Math` program is part of the Java Class Library, which you explore later this hour.

Sending Arguments to Applications

You can run Java applications from a command line using `java`, a program that invokes the JVM. NetBeans uses this program behind the scenes when you run programs. When a Java program is run as a command, the JVM loads the application. The command can include extra items of information, as in this example:

```
java TextDisplayer readme.txt /p
```

Any extra information sent to a program is called an argument. The first argument, if there is one, is provided one space after the name of the application. Each additional argument also is separated by a space. In the preceding example, the arguments are `readme.txt` and `/p`.

If you want to include a space inside an argument, you must put quotation marks around it, as in the following:

```
java TextDisplayer readme.txt /p "Page Title"
```

This example runs the TextDisplayer program with three arguments: `readme.txt`, `/p`, and `"Page Title"`. The quotation marks prevent `Page` and `Title` from being treated as separate arguments.

You can send as many arguments as you want to a Java application (within reason). To do something with them, you must write statements in the application to handle them.

To see how arguments work in an application, create a new class in the Java24 project:

1. Choose File, New File.

2. In the New File Wizard, choose the category `Java` and file type `Empty Java File`.

3. Give the class the name `BlankFiller`, the package `com.java24hours`, and click Finish.

Enter the text of Listing 4.2 in the source code editor and save it when you're done. Compile the program, correcting any errors that are flagged by the editor as you type.

LISTING 4.2   The Full Text of BlankFiller.java

```
 1: package com.java24hours;
 2:
 3: class BlankFiller {
 4:     public static void main(String[] arguments) {
 5:         System.out.println("The " + arguments[0]
 6:             + " " + arguments[1] + " fox "
 7:             + "jumped over the "
 8:             + arguments[2] + " dog."
 9:         );
10:     }
11: }
```

This application compiles successfully and can be run, but if you try it with the menu command Run, Run File, you get a complicated-looking error:

Output ▼

```
Exception in thread "main" java.lang.ArrayIndexOutOfBoundsException: 0
    at BlankFiller.main(BlankFiller.java:5)
```

This error occurs because the program expects to receive three arguments when it is run. You can specify arguments by customizing the project in NetBeans:

1. Choose the menu command Run, Set Project Configuration, Customize. The Project Properties dialog opens.

2. Enter com.java24hours.BlankFiller in the Main Class text field.

3. In the Arguments field, enter retromingent purple lactose-intolerant and click OK.

Because you've customized the project, you must run it a little differently. Choose the menu command Run, Run Main Project. The application uses the arguments you specified as adjectives to fill out a sentence, as shown in Figure 4.2.

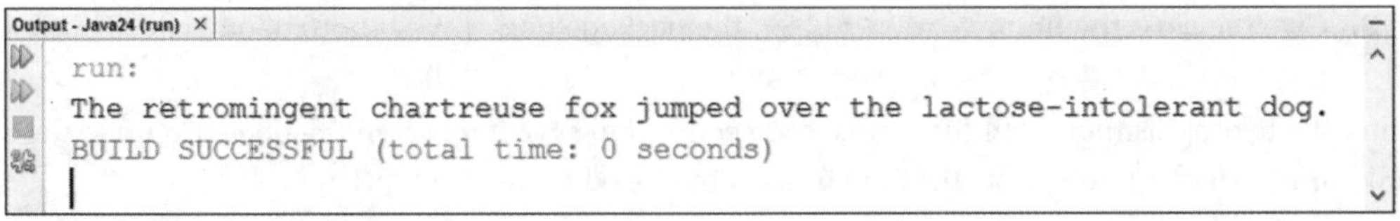

```
Output - Java24 (run)  ×
run:
The retromingent chartreuse fox jumped over the lactose-intolerant dog.
BUILD SUCCESSFUL (total time: 0 seconds)
```

FIGURE 4.2
The output of the BlankFiller application.

Return to the Project Properties dialog and designate three adjectives of your own choosing as arguments, making sure to always include at least three.

Arguments are a simple way to customize the behavior of a program. The arguments are stored in a type of variable called an array. You learn about arrays during Hour 9, "Storing Information with Arrays."

The Java Class Library

This book covers how to use the Java language to create your own programs from scratch. You learn all the keywords and operators that form the language and then put them to work writing statements that make a computer do interesting and useful things.

Although this approach is the best way to learn Java, it's a bit like showing someone how to build a car by making her build every part of the car from scratch first.

A lot of work already is done for you as a Java programmer, provided you know where to look for it.

Java comes with an enormous collection of code you can utilize in your own programs called the Java Class Library. This library is a collection of thousands of classes, many of which can be used in the programs that you write.

NOTE
There also are many class libraries provided by other companies and organizations. The Apache Project, the creators of the Apache web server, has more than a dozen Java open source projects. One is Tomcat, a set of classes for creating a web server that can run web applications implemented as Java servlets.

For more information on the project, visit http://tomcat.apache.org. To see all of Apache's Java projects, visit https://projects.apache.org.

The classes can be put to work in your programs in a manner somewhat similar to using a variable.

A class is used to create an object, which is like a variable but far more sophisticated. An object can hold data, like a variable does, and also perform tasks, like a program.

Oracle offers comprehensive documentation for the Java Class Library on the Web at http://download.java.net/jdk9/docs/api. This page is shown in Figure 4.3.

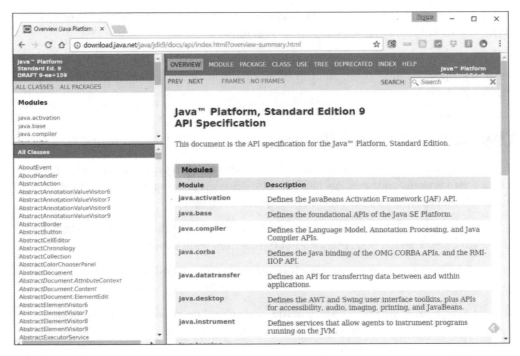

FIGURE 4.3
The Java Class Library documentation.

Java classes are organized into packages, which serve a similar function to a file folder on a computer. The programs you have created thus far belong to the com.java24hours package.

The home page for the documentation is divided into frames. The largest frame lists all of the packages that compose the Java Class Library, along with a description of each one.

The names of the packages help describe their purpose. For instance, java.io is a set of classes for input and output from disk drives, Internet servers, and other data sources; java.time contains classes related to times and dates; and java.util collects helpful utility classes.

On the documentation home page, in the largest frame is a list of packages with a short description of each one. Click the name of a package to learn more about it. A page loads listing the classes in the package.

Each class in the Java Class Library has its own page of documentation on this reference site, which consists of more than 22,000 pages. (You don't have to read all of them now, or ever.)

For this hour's final project, you will poke around the library and use an existing Java class to do some work for you.

The Dice program uses the Random class in the java.util package, which can be used to create random numbers.

The first thing you do in the program to use this class is import its package with this statement:

```
import java.util.*;
```

This makes it possible to refer to the Random class without using its full name, which is `java.util.Random`. Instead, you can simply refer to it as Random. The asterisk makes it possible to refer to all classes in a package by their shorter names.

If you only wanted to import the Random class, this statement would be used:

```
import java.util.Random;
```

A Java program can be thought of as an object that performs a task (or tasks). The Random class is a template that can be used to create a Random object. To create an object, use the new keyword followed by the name of the class and parentheses:

```
Random generator = new Random();
```

This creates a variable named generator that holds a new Random object. The object is a random-number generator that can produce random numbers. The tasks an object can do are called *methods*.

For this program, the object's nextInt() method will be employed to produce a random integer value:

```
int value = generator.nextInt();
```

Integers in Java range from –2,147,483,648 to 2,147,483,647. The generator chooses one of these numbers at random and it is assigned to the value variable.

Without the Random class from the Java Class Library, you'd have to create your own program to produce random numbers, which is a highly complex task. Random numbers are useful in games, educational programs, and other programs that must do something randomly.

In NetBeans, create a new empty Java file, name it Dice, and put it in the package com.java24hours. When the source code editor opens, enter the text of Listing 4.3 into that window and then click the Save button (or choose the menu command File, Save).

LISTING 4.3   **The Full Text of** Dice.java

```
1: package com.java24hours;
2:
3: import java.util.*;
4:
5: class Dice {
6:     public static void main(String[] arguments) {
7:         Random generator = new Random();
8:         int value = generator.nextInt();
```

```
 9:          System.out.println("The random number is "
10:              + value);
11:     }
12: }
```

Run the program by choosing Run, Run File. The output is shown in Figure 4.4, although your number will be different. (Actually, there's a one in four billion chance it will be the same number, which is even worse odds than a lottery.)

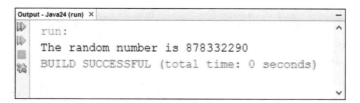

FIGURE 4.4
The output of the Dice program.

You now have a randomly selected integer to call your own. Take good care of it.

The Random class, like all classes in the Java Class Library, has extensive documentation you can read on Oracle's site. It describes the purpose of the class, the package it belongs to, how to create an object of this class, and what methods it has that can be called to make it do something.

Follow these steps to see this documentation:

1. In your web browser, load the page http://download.java.net/jdk9/docs/api.

2. In a navigation bar atop the page at upper left, click the Frames link. The documentation opens in several frames.

3. In the Modules frame at upper left, click java.base.

4. In the main frame, scroll down until you see the link to the package java.util. Click this link. Documentation for the package is displayed.

5. In the main frame, scroll down and click the Random link.

As a Java programmer with slightly under four hours' experience, you likely will find the documentation to be mind-bendingly tough to understand. This is no cause for alarm. It's written for experienced programmers.

But as you read this book and become curious about how Java's built-in classes are being used, you can get some value from looking at the official documentation for a class. One way to use it is to look up the methods in that class, each of which performs a job.

On the `Random` documentation, you can scroll down to the explanation for the `nextInt()` method, which was used on line 8 of Listing 4.3. Figure 4.5 shows this section of the page.

FIGURE 4.5
Oracle's documentation for the `Random` class.

NOTE

All the Java classes this book covers are described within its pages, so the online documentation is not required to progress through these 24 hours and become a Java programmer. Because the classes used in this book have many additional features beyond what an introductory book can cover, the Java Class Library documentation can supplement your learning.

Trying Java Statements in JShell

Java 9 debuts a fun-filled, new tool to make the language easier for beginners to learn. JShell, a command-line program included in the Java Development Kit (JDK), can be used to type in a single Java statement and see what it does.

JShell is a *language shell*, an interactive environment that makes it possible to play with Java by entering commands. Each command is a Java statement. Once you hit Enter, the statement is executed by the JVM as if it was part of a complete Java program.

To run JShell, in your file system find the folder where you installed the JDK. This folder has a subfolder called `bin`. Open that folder and double-click `jshell`.

A window opens where you can enter Java code and see what it does.

A JShell window is shown in Figure 4.6.

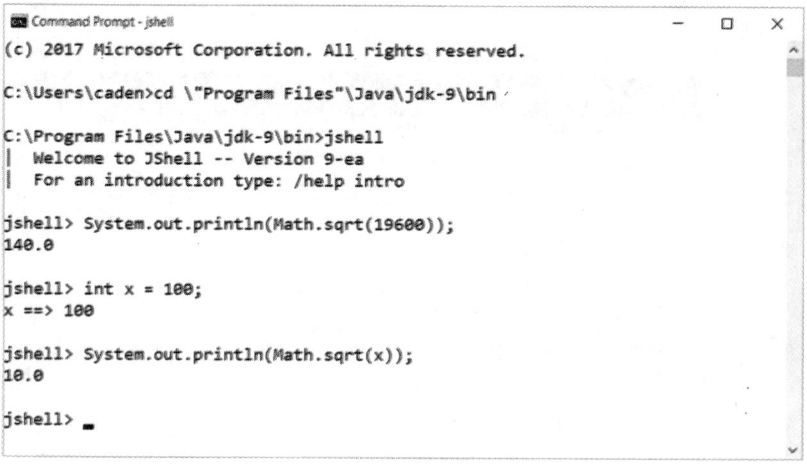

```
Command Prompt - jshell                                    —   □   ×
(c) 2017 Microsoft Corporation. All rights reserved.

C:\Users\caden>cd \"Program Files"\Java\jdk-9\bin

C:\Program Files\Java\jdk-9\bin>jshell
|  Welcome to JShell -- Version 9-ea
|  For an introduction type: /help intro

jshell> System.out.println(Math.sqrt(19600));
140.0

jshell> int x = 100;
x ==> 100

jshell> System.out.println(Math.sqrt(x));
10.0

jshell>
```

FIGURE 4.6
Playing in the Java sandbox using JShell.

JShell commands are typed at the `jshell>` prompt. In Figure 4.6, a series of three statements are entered:

1. `System.out.println(Math.sqrt(19600));`, which displays the square root of an integer.

2. `int x = 100;`, which sets the x variable's value.

3. `System.out.println(x);`, which displays the square root of x.

After each command, JShell shows the value produced by that statement. When a variable is created, it stays in memory and can appear in subsequent statements, like how the x integer was used in Figure 4.6.

The statements in JShell don't have to end with a semi-colon ";" character, unlike the ones in a full Java program.

When you're ready to exit JShell, use the command `/exit`.

A language shell such as JShell also is called a *REPL*, an acronym that stands for Read-Eval-Print Loop. The term comes from the Lisp language, which featured an interactive shell beloved by programmers.

A REPL is a great hands-on way to experiment with the programming techniques you learn in this book. Take a statement you read about and try creating a similar one to see what it does.

Summary

During this hour, you had a chance to create a Java program, send arguments to a program, and make use of existing programs in the Java Class Library.

The next several hours continue to focus on applications as you become more experienced as a Java programmer. Applications are quicker to test because they don't require you to do any extra work to run them, as you do for the other kinds of programs.

This hour is the first of several that discuss how to make use of objects and their methods in a Java program. You will return to this subject in Hour 10, "Creating Your First Object."

Workshop

Q&A

Q. Do all arguments sent to a Java application have to be strings?

A. Java stores all arguments as strings when an application runs. When you want to use one of these arguments as an integer or some other nonstring type, you have to convert the value. You learn how to do this during Hour 11, "Describing What Your Object Is Like."

Q. Does the line of succession to the British throne run out at some point?

A. Under Parliamentary law that has been in place since 1701, the British monarch must be a Protestant descendant of Sophia of Hanover, a German princess who was the heiress to the crown when the law was passed.

There are a finite number of people who are descendants of Sophia, so there's always somebody last in the regal line. The British government lists only the first 38, so genealogists have attempted to fill out the rest of the list themselves.

The last person in the line of succession is Karin Vogel, a German pain therapist in her thirties. She was 4,973rd in line as of 2011, genealogists determined after an exhaustive search that took years. So if all the people ahead of her drop out of the running (to, say, spend more time learning Java programming), Vogel takes over the mortgage on Buckingham Palace and becomes Her Majesty Karin the First.

Vogel is Sophia's great-great-great-great-great-great-great-great-granddaughter. She told the *Wall Street Journal* that becoming monarch would be "too stressful."

With the birth of Prince William and Princess Kate's son, George, more officially known as His Royal Highness Prince George Alexander Louis of Cambridge, Vogel dropped to 4,974.

Quiz

Test your knowledge of the material covered in this hour by answering the following questions.

1. Which type of Java program can be run by a mobile device?

   A. Apps

   B. Applications

   C. None

2. What does JVM stand for?

   A. Journal of Vacation Marketing

   B. Jacksonville Veterans Memorial

   C. Java Virtual Machine

3. If you get into a fight with someone over the way to send information to a Java application, what are you doing?

   A. Struggling over strings

   B. Arguing about arguments

   C. Feudin' for functionality

Answers

1. **A.** Apps run as part of a mobile device such as a phone or tablet, whereas applications are run almost everywhere else.

2. **A.**, **B.**, or **C.** Trick question! The initials stand for all three things, though Java Virtual Machine is the one you need to remember for the next 20 hours.

3. **B.** Applications receive information in the form of arguments. Can't we all just get along?

Activities

If you'd like to apply your acumen to applications, the following activities are suggested:

▶ Using the Root application as a guide, create a NewRoot application that can display the square root of 625.

▶ Using the Root application as a guide, create a NewRoot application that can display the square root of a number submitted as an argument.

Solutions for the activities in this book are presented on the book's website at www.java24hours.com.

HOUR 5
Storing and Changing Information in a Program

This Hour's To-Do List:

- ▶ Create a variable.
- ▶ Use different types of variables.
- ▶ Store values in variables.
- ▶ Use variables in mathematical expressions.
- ▶ Store one variable's value in another variable.
- ▶ Increase and decrease a variable's value.

In Hour 2, "Writing Your First Program," you used a variable, a special storage place designed to hold information. The information stored in variables can be changed as a program runs. Your first program stored a string of text in a variable. Strings are only one type of information that can be stored in variables. They also can hold characters, integers, floating-point numbers, and objects.

During this hour, you learn more about using variables in your Java programs.

Statements and Expressions

Computer programs are a set of instructions that tell the computer what to do. Each instruction is called a statement. The following example from a Java program is a statement:

```
int highScore = 450000;
```

You can use brackets to group a set of statements together in a Java program. These groupings are called *block statements*. Consider the following portion of a program:

```
1: public static void main(String[] arguments) {
2:     int a = 3;
3:     int b = 4;
4:     int c = 8 * 5;
5: }
```

Lines 2–4 of this example are in a block statement. The opening bracket on Line 1 denotes the beginning of the block, and the closing bracket on Line 5 denotes the end of the block.

Some statements are called *expressions* because they involve a mathematical expression and produce a result. Line 4 in the preceding example is an expression because it sets the value of the c variable equal to 8 multiplied by 5. You work with expressions during this hour.

Assigning Variable Types

Variables are the main way that a computer remembers something while it runs a program. The Saluton program in Hour 2 used the greeting variable to hold "Saluton mondo!" The computer needed to remember that text so that the message could be displayed later.

In a Java program, variables are created with a statement that must include two things:

▶ The name of the variable

▶ The type of information the variable will store

Variables also can include the value of the information being stored.

To see the different types of variables and how they are created, fire up NetBeans and create a new empty Java file with the class name Variable.

Start writing the program by entering the following lines:

```
package com.java24hours;

class Variable {
    public static void main(String[] arguments) {
        // Coming soon: variables
    }
}
```

Go ahead and save this before proceeding.

Integers and Floating-Point Numbers

So far, the Variable program has a main() block with only one statement in it—the comment // Coming soon: variables. Delete the comment and enter the following statement in its place:

```
int tops;
```

This statement creates a variable named tops. It does not specify a value for tops, so for the moment this variable is an empty storage space. The int text at the beginning of the statement designates `tops` as a variable that is used to store integer numbers. You can use the `int` type to store most of the non-decimal numbers you need in your computer programs. It can hold any integer ranging from around –2.14 billion to 2.14 billion.

Add a blank line after the `int tops` statement and enter the following statement:

```
float gradePointAverage;
```

This statement creates a variable with the name `gradePointAverage`. The `float` text stands for floating-point numbers. Floating-point variables are used to store numbers that might contain a decimal point.

The `float` variable type holds decimal numbers of up to 38 figures. The larger `double` type holds decimal numbers up to 300 figures.

Characters and Strings

Because the variables you have dealt with thus far are numeric, you might have the impression that all variables are used to store numbers. Think again. You also can use variables to store text. Two types of text can be stored as variables: characters and strings. A character is a single letter, number, punctuation mark, or symbol. A string is a group of characters.

Your next step in creating the `Variable` program is to create a `char` variable and a `String` variable. Add these two statements after the `float gradePointAverage` line:

```
char key = 'C';
String productName = "Larvets";
```

As you might have noticed, these two statements use different characters around the text values. When you are using character values in your program, you must put single quotation marks on both sides of the character value being assigned to a variable. For string values, you must surround them with double quotation marks.

Quotation marks prevent the character or string from being confused with a variable name or another part of a statement. Take a look at the following statement:

```
String productName = Larvets;
```

This statement might look like one telling the computer to create a string variable called `productName` with the text value of `Larvets`. However, because there are no quotation marks around the word `Larvets`, the computer is being told to set the `productName` value to the same value as a variable named `Larvets`. (If there is no variable named `Larvets`, the program fails to compile with an error.)

After you add the `char` and `String` statements, your program should resemble Listing 5.1. Make any necessary changes and save the file.

LISTING 5.1   **The** `Variable` **Program**

```
 1: package com.java24hours;
 2:
 3: class Variable {
 4:     public static void main(String[] arguments) {
 5:         int tops;
 6:         float gradePointAverage;
 7:         char key = 'C';
 8:         String productName = "Larvets";
 9:     }
10: }
```

The last two variables in the `Variable` program use the = sign to assign a starting value when the variables are created. You can use this option for any variables you create in a Java program, as you discover later in this hour.

NOTE

Although the other variable types are all lowercase letters (`int`, `float`, and `char`), the capital letter is required in the word `String` when creating string variables. A string in a Java program is different from the other types of information you use in variable statements. You learn about this distinction in Hour 6, "Using Strings to Communicate."

This program can be run but produces no output.

Other Numeric Variable Types

The types of variables you have been introduced to so far are the main ones you will use for most of your Java programming. You can employ a few other types of variables in less common circumstances.

One is `byte`, which holds integer numbers that range from –128 to 127. The following statement creates a variable called `escapeKey` with an initial value of 27:

```
byte escapeKey = 27;
```

The second, `short`, can be used for integers that are smaller in size than the `int` type. A short integer can range from –32,768 to 32,767, as in the following statement:

```
short roomNumber = 222;
```

The last of the numeric variable types, `long`, is used for integers that are too big for the `int` type to hold. A `long` integer can be from –9.22 quintillion to 9.22 quintillion, which is a large enough number to cover everything but government spending.

When you are working with enormous numbers in Java, it can be difficult to see at a glance the value of the number, as in this statement:

```
long salary = 264400000000L;
```

Unless you count the zeros, you probably can't tell that it's $264.4 billion. Java makes it possible to organize large numbers with underscore ('_') characters. Here's an example:

```
long salary = 264_400_000_000L;
```

The underscores are ignored, so the variable still equals the same value. They just make numbers more human-readable.

The capital "L" at the end of the number specifies it as a `long` value. If the "L" was omitted, the Java compiler would have assumed the number was an `int` and flagged an "integer number too large" error.

CAUTION

If the use of underscores in a number is flagged as an error in the NetBeans source code editor, the IDE has been set up to use an older version of Java. To correct this problem, in the Projects pane, right-click the name of the current project (likely `Java24`) and choose Properties. The Project Properties dialog opens with Sources chosen in the Categories pane. Check the Source/Binary Format drop-down to make sure it is the current version of Java.

The `boolean` **Variable Type**

Java has a type of variable called `boolean` that can be used only to store the value `true` or the value `false`. At first glance, a `boolean` variable might not seem particularly useful unless you plan to write a lot of true-or-false quizzes. However, `boolean` variables are used in a variety of situations in your programs. The following are some examples of questions that `boolean` variables can be used to answer:

▶ Has the user pressed a key?

▶ Is the game over?

▶ Is my bank account overdrawn?

▶ Do these pants make my butt look fat?

▶ Are these the droids I'm looking for?

Booleans are the place to hold the answer to yes/no and true/false questions.

The following statement creates a `boolean` variable called gameOver:

```
boolean gameOver = false;
```

This variable has the starting value of `false`, so a statement like this could indicate in a game program that the game isn't over yet. Later, when something happens to end the game, the `gameOver` variable can be set to `true`.

Although the two possible boolean values look like strings in a program, you should not surround them with quotation marks. Hour 7, "Using Conditional Tests to Make Decisions," further explores `boolean` variables.

NOTE

Boolean numbers are named for George Boole (1815–1864). Boole, a mathematician who was mostly self-taught until adulthood, invented Boolean algebra, which has become a fundamental part of computer programming, digital electronics, and logic. One imagines that he did pretty well on true-false tests as a child.

Naming Your Variables

Variable names in Java can begin with a letter, underscore character "_", or a dollar sign $. The rest of the name can be any letters or numbers. You can give your variables almost any name you like but should be consistent in how you name them. This section outlines the generally recommended naming method for variables.

Java is case sensitive when it comes to variable names, so you must always capitalize variable names the same way. For example, if the `gameOver` variable is referred to as `GameOver` somewhere in the program, an error prevents the program from being compiled.

A variable's name should describe its purpose in some way. The first letter should be lowercase, and if the variable name has more than one word, make the first letter of each subsequent word a capital letter. For instance, if you want to create an integer variable to store the all-time high score in a game program, you can use the following statement:

```
int allTimeHighScore;
```

You can't use punctuation marks or spaces in a variable name, so neither of the following works:

```
int all-TimeHigh Score;
int all Time High Score;
```

If you try these variable names in a program, NetBeans responds by flagging the error with the red alert icon alongside the line in the source editor.

NOTE

Variable names aren't the only aspect of Java that's case sensitive. Everything else you can give a name to in a program, including classes, packages, and methods, must be referred to using consistent capitalization.

Keywords that are used by the language, such as `public`, `class`, `true`, and `false`, cannot be used as the names of variables.

Java 9 adds another restriction: a variable name cannot be a single underscore _ character. This statement used to be permitted in Java:

```
int _ = 747;
```

Try it now, and an error results with the message that '_' is a keyword.

Storing Information in Variables

You can store a value in a variable at the same time that you create the variable in a Java program. You also can put a value in the variable at any time later in the program.

To set a starting value for a variable upon its creation, use the equal sign (=). Here's an example of creating a double floating-point variable called `pi` with the starting value of 3.14:

```
double pi = 3.14;
```

All variables that store numbers can be set up in a similar fashion. If you're setting up a character or a string variable, quotation marks must be placed around the value as described earlier in this hour.

You also can set one variable equal to the value of another variable if they both are of the same type. Consider the following example:

```
int mileage = 300;
int totalMileage = mileage;
```

First, an integer variable called `mileage` is created with a starting value of 300. Next, an integer variable called `totalMileage` is created with the same value as `mileage`. Both variables have the starting value of 300. In future hours, you learn how to convert one variable's value to the type of another variable.

CAUTION

If you do not give a variable a starting value, you should give it a value before you use it in another statement. If you don't, when your program is compiled, you might get an error stating that the variable "may not have been initialized."

As you've learned, Java has similar numeric variables that hold values of different sizes. Both `int` and `long` hold integers, but `long` holds a larger range of possible values. Both `float` and `double` carry floating-point numbers, but `double` is bigger.

You can append a letter to a numeric value to indicate the value's type, as in this statement:

```
float pi = 3.14F;
```

The "F" after the value 3.14 indicates that it's a `float` value. If the letter was omitted, Java assumes that 3.14 is a `double` value.

The letter "L" is used for `long` integers and "D" for `double` floating-point values.

Another naming convention in Java is to capitalize every letter in the names of variables that do not change in value. These variables are called *constants*. The following creates four constants:

```
final int TOUCHDOWN = 6;
final int FIELDGOAL = 3;
final int CONVERSION = 2;
final int PAT = 1;
```

Because constants never change in value, you might wonder why one ever should be used—you can just use the value assigned to the constant instead. One advantage of using constants is that they make a program easier to understand.

In the preceding four statements, the name of the constant was capitalized. This is not required in Java, but it has become a standard convention among programmers to distinguish constants from other variables.

All About Operators

Statements can use mathematical expressions by employing the operators +, -, *, /, and %. You use these operators to crunch numbers throughout your Java programs.

An addition expression in Java uses the + operator, as in these statements:

```
double weight = 205;
weight = weight + 10;
```

The second statement uses the + operator to set the `weight` variable equal to its current value plus 10.

A subtraction expression uses the - operator:

```
weight = weight - 15;
```

This expression sets the `weight` variable equal to its current value minus 15.

A division expression uses the / sign:

```
weight = weight / 3;
```

This sets the `weight` variable to its current value divided by 3.

To find a remainder from a division expression, use the % operator (also called the modulo operator). The following statement finds the remainder of 245 divided by 3:

```
int remainder = 245 % 3;
```

A multiplication expression uses the * operator. Here's a statement that employs a multiplication expression as part of a more complicated statement:

```
int total = 500 + (score * 12);
```

The `score * 12` part of the expression multiplies `score` by 12. The full statement multiplies `score` by 12 and then adds 500 to the result. If `score` equals 20, the result of the expression is that `total` equals 740: 500 + (20 * 12).

Incrementing and Decrementing a Variable

A common task in programs is changing the value of a variable by one. You can increase the value by one, which is called incrementing the variable, or decrease the value by one, which is decrementing the variable. There are operators to accomplish both tasks.

To increment the value of a variable by one, use the ++ operator, as in the following statement:

```
power++;
```

This statement adds one to the value stored in the `power` variable.

To decrement the value of a variable by one, use the -- operator:

```
rating--;
```

This statement reduces `rating` by one.

You also can put the increment and decrement operators in front of the variable name, as in the following statements:

```
++power;
--rating;
```

Putting the operator in front of the variable name is called prefixing, and putting it after the name is called postfixing.

NOTE

Confused yet? This is easier than it sounds, if you think back to elementary school when you learned about prefixes. Just as a prefix such as "sub-" or "un-" goes at the start of a word like sub-urban or unexpected, a prefix operator goes at the start of a variable name. A postfix operator goes at the end.

The difference between prefixed and postfixed operators becomes important when you use the increment and decrement operators inside an expression.

Consider the following statements:

```
int x = 3;
int answer = x++ * 10;
```

What does the answer variable equal after these statements are handled? You might expect it to equal 40—which would be true if 3 was incremented by 1, which equals 4, and then 4 was multiplied by 10.

However, answer ends up with the value 30 because the postfixed operator was used instead of the prefixed operator.

When a postfixed operator is used on a variable inside an expression, the variable's value doesn't change until after the expression has been completely evaluated. The statement int answer = x++ * 10 does the same thing in the same order as the following two statements:

```
int answer = x * 10;
x++;
```

The opposite is true of prefixed operators. If they are used on a variable inside an expression, the variable's value changes before the expression is evaluated.

Consider the following statements:

```
int x = 3;
int answer = ++x * 10;
```

This does result in the answer variable being equal to 40. The prefixed operator causes the value of the x variable to be changed before the expression is evaluated. The statement int answer = ++x * 10 does the same thing, in order, as these statements:

```
x++;
int answer = x * 10;
```

It's easy to become exasperated with the ++ and -- operators because they're not as straightforward as many of the concepts you encounter in this book.

I hope I'm not breaking some unwritten law of programmers by telling you this, but you don't need to use the increment and decrement operators in your own programs. You can achieve the same results by using the + and – operators like this:

```
x = x + 1;
y = y - 1;
```

Incrementing and decrementing are useful shortcuts, but taking the longer route in an expression is fine, too.

NOTE

Back in Hour 1, "Becoming a Programmer," the name of the C++ programming language was described as a joke you'd understand later. Now that you've been introduced to the increment operator ++, you have all the information you need to figure out why C++ has two plus signs in its name instead of just one. Because C++ adds new features and functionality to the C programming language, it can be considered an incremental increase to C—hence the name C++.

After you complete all 24 hours of this book, you too will be able to tell jokes like this that are incomprehensible to more than 99 percent of the world's population.

Operator Precedence

When you are using an expression with more than one operator, you need to know what order the computer uses as it works out the expression. Consider the following statements:

```
int y = 10;
x = y * 3 + 5;
```

Unless you know what order the computer uses when working out the math in these statements, you cannot be sure what the x variable will equal. It could be set to either 35 or 80, depending on whether y * 3 is evaluated first or 3 + 5 is evaluated first.

The following evaluation order is used when working out an expression:

1. Incrementing and decrementing take place first.

2. Multiplication, division, and modulus division occur next.

3. Addition and subtraction follow.

4. Comparisons take place next.

5. The equal sign = is used to set a variable's value.

Because multiplication takes place before addition, you can revisit the previous example and come up with the answer: y is multiplied by 3 first, which equals 30, and then 5 is added. The x variable is set to 35.

Comparisons are discussed during Hour 7. The rest has been described during this hour, so you should be able to figure out the result of the following statements:

```
int x = 5;
int number = x++ * 6 + 4 * 10 / 2;
```

These statements set the number variable equal to 50.

How does the computer come up with this total? First, the increment operator is handled, and x++ sets the value of the x variable to 6. However, make note that the ++ operator is postfixed after x in the expression. This means that the expression is evaluated with the original value of x.

Because the original value of x is used before the variable is incremented, the expression becomes the following:

```
int number = 5 * 6 + 4 * 10 / 2;
```

Now, multiplication and division are handled from left to right. First, 5 is multiplied by 6, 4 is multiplied by 10, and that result is divided by 2 (4 * 10 / 2). The expression becomes the following:

```
int number = 30 + 20;
```

This expression results in the number variable being set to 50.

If you want an expression to be evaluated in a different order, you can use parentheses to group parts of an expression that should be handled first. For example, the expression x = 5 * 3 + 2; would normally cause x to equal 17 because multiplication is handled before addition. However, look at a modified form of that expression:

```
x = 5 * (3 + 2);
```

In this case, the expression within the parentheses is handled first, so the result equals 25. You can use parentheses as often as needed in a statement.

Using Expressions

When you were in school, as you worked on a particularly unpleasant math problem, did you ever complain to a higher power, protesting that you would never use this knowledge in your life? Sorry to break this to you, but your teachers were right—your math skills come in handy in your computer programming. That's the bad news.

The good news is that the computer does any math you ask it to do. Expressions are used frequently in your computer programs to accomplish tasks such as the following:

▶ Changing the value of a variable

▶ Counting the number of times something has happened in a program

▶ Using a mathematical formula in a program

As you write computer programs, you find yourself drawing on your old math lessons as you use expressions. Expressions can use addition, subtraction, multiplication, division, and modulus division.

To see expressions in action, return to NetBeans and create a new Java file with the class name `PlanetWeight`. This program tracks a person's weight loss and gain as she travels to other bodies in the solar system. Enter the full text of Listing 5.2 in the source editor. Each part of the program is discussed in turn.

LISTING 5.2   **The `PlanetWeight` Program**

```
 1: package com.java24hours;
 2:
 3: class PlanetWeight {
 4:     public static void main(String[] arguments) {
 5:         System.out.print("Your weight on Earth is ");
 6:         double weight = 178;
 7:         System.out.println(weight);
 8:
 9:         System.out.print("Your weight on Mercury is ");
10:         double mercury = weight * .378;
11:         System.out.println(mercury);
12:
13:         System.out.print("Your weight on the Moon is ");
14:         double moon = weight * .166;
15:         System.out.println(moon);
16:
17:         System.out.print("Your weight on Jupiter is ");
18:         double jupiter = weight * 2.364;
19:         System.out.println(jupiter);
20:     }
21: }
```

When you're done, save the file and it should compile automatically. Run the program with the menu command Run, Run File. The output is shown in the Output pane in Figure 5.1.

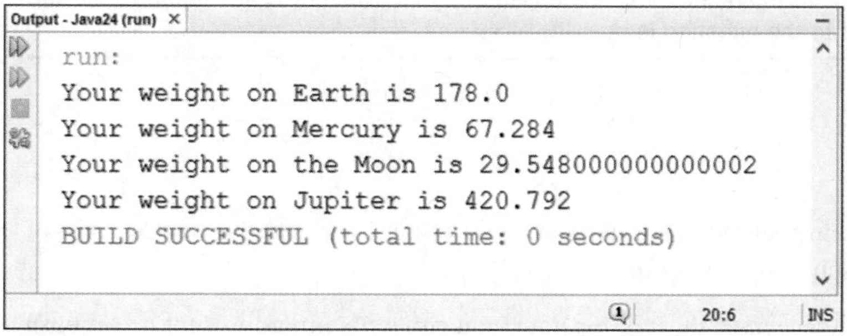

```
Output - Java24 (run)  ×
run:
Your weight on Earth is 178.0
Your weight on Mercury is 67.284
Your weight on the Moon is 29.548000000000002
Your weight on Jupiter is 420.792
BUILD SUCCESSFUL (total time: 0 seconds)
                                    20:6    INS
```

FIGURE 5.1
The output of the `PlanetWeight` program.

As in other programs you have created, the `PlanetWeight` program uses a `main()` block statement for all its work. This statement can be broken into the following four sections:

1. Lines 5–7: The person's weight is set initially to 178.

2. Lines 9–11: Mercury weight loss is calculated.

3. Lines 13–15: Moon weight loss is calculated.

4. Lines 17–19: Jupiter weight gain is calculated.

Line 6 creates the `weight` variable and designates it as a large floating-point variable with `double`. The variable is given the initial value 178 and used throughout the program to monitor the person's weight.

The next line is similar to several statements in the program:

```
System.out.println(weight);
```

The `System.out.println()` command displays a string that is contained within its parentheses. On Line 5, the `System.out.print()` command displays the text "Your weight on Earth is ". There are several `System.out.print()` and `System.out.println()` statements in the program.

The difference between them is that `print()` does not start a new line after displaying the text, whereas `println()` does.

NOTE

For the sample value, the `PlanetWeight` application used a weight of 178 pounds, which just happens to be the average weight of a person in North America according to a BMC Health Study. That compares to the average 164-pound Oceanian, 156-pound European, 150-pound Latin American, 134-pound African, and 127-pound Asian.

So if you're reading this in North America and someone asks you, "Would you like an apple pie with that?" the correct answer to the question is no.

Summary

Now that you have been introduced to variables and expressions, you can give a wide range of instructions to your computer in a program.

With the skills you have developed during this hour, you can write programs that accomplish many of the same tasks as a calculator, handling sophisticated mathematical equations with ease.

You've also learned that a trip to the Moon is an effective weight-loss plan.

Numbers are only one kind of thing that can be stored in a variable. You also can store characters, strings of characters, and special `true` or `false` values called Boolean variables. The next hour expands your knowledge of `String` variables and how they are stored and used.

Workshop

Q&A

Q. Is a line in a Java program the same thing as a statement?

A. No. The programs you create in this book put one statement on each line to make the programs easier to understand; it's not required.

The Java compiler does not consider lines, spacing, or other formatting issues when compiling a program. The compiler just wants to see semicolons at the end of each statement. This line would work just fine in Java:

```
int x = 12; x = x + 1;
```

Putting more than one statement on a line makes a program more difficult for humans to understand when they read its source code. For this reason, it is not recommended.

Q. Why should the first letter of a variable name be lowercase, as in `gameOver`?

A. It's a naming convention that helps your programming in two ways. First, it makes variables easier to spot among the other elements of a Java program. Second, by following a consistent style in the naming of variables, you eliminate errors that can occur when you use a variable in several places in a program. The style of capitalization used in this book is the one that's been adopted by most Java programmers over the years.

Q. Can I specify integers as binary values in Java?

A. You can. Put the characters "0b" in front of the number and follow it with the bits in the value. Since 1101 is the binary form for the number 13, the following statement sets an integer to 13:

```
int z = 0b0000_1101;
```

The underscore is just there to make the number more readable, just like with large numbers. The underscore is ignored by the Java compiler.

Hexadecimal values can be represented with numbers preceded by "0x", as in Super Bowl 0x33, in which the New England Patriots defeated the Atlanta Falcons by a score of 0x22 to 0x1C.

Q. What the heck are Larvets?

A. Larvets, the product mentioned in this hour, is a snack made from edible worms that have been killed, dried, and mixed with the same kinds of scrumptious food-like flavoring as Doritos chips. You can order Larvets in three flavors—BBQ, cheddar cheese, and Mexican spice—from the mail-order retailer HotLix at the website www.hotlix.com or by calling 1-800-EAT-WORM.

Quiz

Test your knowledge of variables, expressions, and the rest of the information in this hour by answering the following questions.

1. What do you call a group of statements contained with an opening bracket and a closing bracket?

    A. A block statement

    B. Groupware

    C. Bracketed statements

2. A `boolean` variable is used to store `true` or `false` values.

    A. True

    B. False

    C. No, thanks. I already ate.

3. What characters cannot be used to start a variable name?

    A. A dollar sign

    B. Two forward slash marks (//)

    C. A letter

Answers

1. A. The grouped statements are called a block statement or a block.

2. A. `true` and `false` are the only answers a `boolean` variable can store.

3. B. Variables can start with a letter, a dollar sign ($), or an underscore character (_). If you started a variable name with two slash marks, the rest of the line would be ignored because the slash marks are used to start a comment line.

Activities

You can review the topics of this hour more fully with the following activities:

▶ Expand the `PlanetWeight` program to track a person's weight on Venus (90.7% of Earth weight) and his weight on Uranus (88.9% Earth)—and stop snickering because I mentioned Uranus.

▶ Create a short Java program that uses an x integer and a y integer and displays the result of x squared plus y squared.

To see Java programs that implement these activities, visit the book's website at www.java24hours.com.

Using Strings to Communicate

This Hour's To-Do List:

- ▶ Use strings to store text.
- ▶ Display strings in a program.
- ▶ Include special characters in a string.
- ▶ Paste two strings together.
- ▶ Include variables in a string.
- ▶ Compare two strings.
- ▶ Determine the length of a string.

Your computer programs are capable of quietly doing their work and never stopping for a chat.

But when a program needs to tell the world something, the simplest way to do so is through the use of strings.

Java programs use strings as the primary means to communicate with users. *Strings* are collections of text—letters, numbers, punctuation, and other characters. During this hour, you learn all about working with strings.

Storing Text in Strings

Strings store text and present it to users. The most basic element of a string is a character. A character is a single letter, number, punctuation mark, or other symbol.

In Java programs, a character is one of the types of information that can be stored in a variable. Character variables are created with the `char` type in a statement such as the following:

```
char keyPressed;
```

This statement creates a variable named `keyPressed` that can hold a character. When you create character variables, you can set them up with an initial value, as in the following:

```
char quitKey = '@';
```

The value of the character must be surrounded by single quotation marks.

A string is a collection of characters. You can set up a variable to hold a string value by following `String` with the name of the variable, as in this statement:

```
String fullName = "Fin Shepard";
```

This statement creates a string variable called `fullName` containing the text "Fin Shepard," the hero in the cinematic masterpiece *Sharknado*. A string is denoted with double quotation marks around the text in a Java statement. These quotation marks are not included in the string itself.

Unlike the other types of variables you have used—int, `float`, `char`, `boolean`, and so on—the name of the `String` type is capitalized.

In Java, strings are a special kind of information called objects, and the types of all objects are capitalized in the language. You learn about objects during Hour 10, "Creating Your First Object." The important thing to note during this hour is that strings are different from the other variable types, and because of this difference, `String` is capitalized.

Displaying Strings in Programs

The most basic way to display a string in a Java program is with the `System.out.println()` statement. This statement takes strings and other variables inside the parentheses and displays their values on the system output device, which is the computer's monitor. Here's an example:

```
System.out.println("We can't just wait here for sharks to rain down on us.");
```

This statement causes the following text to be displayed:

```
We can't just wait here for sharks to rain down on us.
```

Displaying text on the screen often is called printing, which is what `println()` stands for—print line. You can use the `System.out.println()` statement to display text within double quotation marks and also variables, as you see later. Put all the material you want to be displayed within the parentheses.

Another way to display text is to call `System.out.print()`. This statement displays strings and other variables inside the parentheses, but unlike `System.out.println()`, it enables subsequent statements to display text on the same line.

You can use `System.out.print()` several times in a row to display several things on the same line, as in this example:

```
System.out.print("There's ");
System.out.print("a ");
System.out.print("shark ");
System.out.print("in ");
System.out.print("your ");
```

```
System.out.print("pool.");
System.out.println();
```

These statements cause the following text to be displayed:

```
There's a shark in your pool.
```

The call to `println()` with no argument ends the line.

Using Special Characters in Strings

When a string is being created or displayed, its text must be enclosed within double quotation marks. These quotation marks are not displayed, which raises a question: What if you want to display a double quotation mark?

To display that character, Java has a special code that can be put into a string: `\"`. Whenever this code is encountered in a string, it is replaced with a double quotation mark. For example, examine the following:

```
System.out.println("Anthony Ferrante directed \"Sharknado\".");
```

This code is displayed as the following:

```
Anthony Ferrante directed "Sharknado".
```

You can insert other special characters into a string in this manner. The following list shows these special characters; note that each is preceded by a backslash (\).

Special Characters	Display
\'	Single quotation mark
\"	Double quotation mark
\\	Backslash
\t	Tab
\b	Backspace
\r	Carriage return
\f	Formfeed
\n	Newline

The newline character causes the text following that character to be displayed at the beginning of the next line. Look at this example:

```
System.out.println("Script by\nThunder Levin");
```

This statement would be displayed like this:

```
Script by
Thunder Levin
```

Pasting Strings Together

When you use `System.out.println()` and work with strings in other ways, you can paste two strings together by using +, the same operator that is used to add numbers.

The + operator has a different meaning in relation to strings. Instead of performing some math, it pastes two strings together. This action can cause strings to be displayed together or make one big string out of two smaller ones.

Linking two things together in a string is called *concatenation*.

NOTE

You'll probably see the term "concatenation" in other books as you build your programming skills, so it's worth knowing. However, pasting is the term used here when one string and another string are joined together. Pasting sounds like fun. Concatenating sounds like something that should never be done in the presence of an open flame.

The following statement uses the + operator to display a long string:

```
System.out.println("\"\'Sharknado\' is an hour and a half of your "
    + "life that you'll never get back.\nAnd you won't want to.\"\n"
    + "\t-- David Hinckley, New York Daily News");
```

Instead of putting this entire string on a single line, which would make it harder to understand when you look at the program later, you can use the + operator to break the text over two lines of the program's Java source code. When this statement is displayed, it appears as the following:

```
"'Sharknado' is an hour and a half of your life that you'll never get back.
And you won't want to."
    -- David Hinckley, New York Daily News
```

Several special characters are used in the string: \", \', \n, and \t. To better familiarize yourself with these characters, compare the output with the `System.out.println()` statement that produced it.

Using Other Variables with Strings

Although you can use the + operator to paste two strings together, you use it more often to link strings and variables. Take a look at the following:

```
int length = 86;
char rating = 'R';
System.out.println("Running time: " + length + " minutes");
System.out.println("Rated " + rating);
```

This code will be displayed as the following:

```
Running time: 86 minutes
Rated R
```

This example displays a unique facet about how the + operator works with strings. It can cause variables that are not strings to be treated just like strings when they are displayed. The variable length is an integer set to the value 86. It is displayed between the strings "Running time: " and "minutes". The System.out.println() statement is being asked to display a string plus an integer, plus another string. This statement works because at least one part of the group is a string. The Java language offers this functionality to make displaying information easier.

One thing you might want to do with a string is paste something to it several times, as in the following example:

```
String searchKeywords = "";
searchKeywords = searchKeywords + "shark ";
searchKeywords = searchKeywords + "hurricane ";
searchKeywords = searchKeywords + "danger";
```

This code would result in the searchKeywords variable being set to "shark hurricane danger". The first line creates the searchKeywords variable and sets it to be an empty string because there's nothing between the double quotation marks. The second line sets the searchKeywords variable equal to its current string plus the string "shark" added to the end. The next two lines add "hurricane" and "danger" in the same way.

As you can see, when you are pasting more text at the end of a variable, the name of the variable is listed twice. Java offers a shortcut to simplify this process: the += operator. The += operator combines the functions of the = and + operators. With strings, it is used to add something to the end of an existing string. The searchKeywords example can be shortened by using +=, as shown in the following statements:

```
String searchKeywords = "";
searchKeywords += "shark ";
searchKeywords += "hurricane ";
searchKeywords += "danger";
```

This code produces the same result: searchKeywords is set to "shark hurricane danger".

Advanced String Handling

There are several other ways you can examine a string variable and change its value. These advanced features are possible because strings are objects in the Java language. Working with strings develops skills you'll use on other objects later.

Comparing Two Strings

One thing you test often in your programs is whether one string is equal to another. You do this by using equals() in a statement with both of the strings, as in this example:

```
String favorite = "chainsaw";
String guess = "pool cue";
System.out.println("Is Fin's favorite weapon a " + guess + "?");
System.out.println("Answer: " + favorite.equals(guess));
```

This example uses two different string variables. One, favorite, stores the name of Fin's favorite shark-hunting instrument: a chainsaw. The other, guess, stores a guess as to what his favorite might be. The guess is that Fin prefers a pool cue.

The third line displays the text "Is Fin's favorite weapon a" followed by the value of the guess variable, and then a question mark. The fourth line displays the text "Answer:" and then contains something new:

```
favorite.equals(guess)
```

This part of the statement is a method, a way to accomplish a task in a Java program. This method's task is to determine if one string has the same value as another. If the two string variables have the same value, calling the method displays the text "true". If not, the text "false" is displayed. The following is the output of this example:

```
Is Fin's favorite weapon a pool cue?
Answer: false
```

The call to equals() produces a Boolean value that can be stored in a variable. Consider this revised statement:

```
boolean checker = favorite.equals(guess);
```

If the favorite and guess strings have the same value, checker equals true. Otherwise, it equals false.

One thing that's often required when working with strings is to test whether a string is empty. An empty string, also called a null string, has nothing inside the double quotation marks. This statement looks for one:

```
if (favorite.equals("")) {
    System.out.println("No favorite has been defined");
}
```

There's also an `equalsIgnoreCase()` method that will make the comparison without regard to how the strings are capitalized. When `favorite` equals "chainsaw", another strong would be equal if it was "chainsaw", "Chainsaw", or "CHAINSAW".

Determining the Length of a String

It also can be useful to determine the length of a string in characters. You do this with the `length()` method. This method works in the same fashion as the `equals()` method, except that only one string variable is involved. Look at the following example:

```
String cinematographer = "Ben Demaree";
int nameLength = cinematographer.length();
```

This example sets `nameLength`, an integer variable, equal to 11. The `cinematographer.length()` method counts the number of characters in the string variable called `cinematographer` and stores this count in the `nameLength` integer variable.

Copying a String with a New Case

Because computers take everything literally, it's easy to confuse them. Although a human would recognize that the text Ian Ziering and the text IAN ZIERING refer to the same thing, most computers would disagree. The `equals()` method discussed previously in this hour would state authoritatively that "Ian Ziering" is not equal to "IAN ZIERING".

To get around some of these obstacles, Java has methods that take a string variable and create another that's all uppercase letters or all lowercase letters, `toUpperCase()` and `toLowerCase()`, respectively. The following example shows the `toUpperCase()` method in action:

```
String fin = "Ian Ziering";
String change = fin.toUpperCase();
```

This code sets the string variable `change` equal to the `fin` string variable converted to all uppercase letters—"IAN ZIERING". The `toLowerCase()` method works in the same fashion but returns an all-lowercase string value.

Note that the `toUpperCase()` method does not change the case of the string variable it is called on. In the preceding example, the `fin` variable is still equal to "Ian Ziering".

Looking for a String

Another common task when handling strings is to see whether one string can be found inside another. To look inside a string, use its `indexOf()` method. Put the string you are looking for inside the parentheses. If the string is not found, `indexOf()` produces the value –1. If the string is found, `indexOf()` produces an integer that represents the position where the string begins.

Positions in a string are numbered upwards from 0, beginning with the first character in the string. In the string "Sharknado", the text "nado" begins at position 5.

One possible use of the indexOf() method would be to search the entire script of *Sharknado* for the place where the heroes are flying a helicopter into a tornado to drop a bomb into it and Nova says, "We're gonna need a bigger chopper."

If the entire script of *Sharknado* was stored in a string called script, you could search it for that quote with the following statement.

```
int position = script.indexOf("We're gonna need a bigger chopper");
```

If that text can be found in the script string, position equals the position at which the text begins. Otherwise, it equals –1.

If you're looking for one string inside another but don't care about the position, a string's contains() method returns a boolean value. It is true if the looked-for string is found and false otherwise. Here's an example:

```
if (script.contains("There's a shark in your pool")) {
    int stars = 4;
}
```

CAUTION

The indexOf() and contains() methods are case sensitive, which means that they look only for text capitalized exactly like the search string. If the string contains the same text capitalized differently, indexOf() produces the value –1 and contains() returns false.

The indexOf() method also can be used to find a character in a string.

Presenting Credits

To reinforce the string-handling features that have been covered up to this time in the hour, you write a Java program to display credits for a feature film. You can probably guess the film.

Return to the Java24 project in NetBeans and create a new empty Java file called Credits in the com.java24hours package. Enter the text of Listing 6.1 into the source editor and save the file when you're done.

LISTING 6.1 The Credits Program

```
1: package com.java24hours;
2:
3: class Credits {
4:     public static void main(String[] arguments) {
```

```
 5:          // set up film information
 6:          String title = "Sharknado";
 7:          int year = 2013;
 8:          String director = "Anthony Ferrante";
 9:          String role1 = "Fin";
10:          String actor1 = "Ian Ziering";
11:          String role2 = "April";
12:          String actor2 = "Tara Reid";
13:          String role3 = "George";
14:          String actor3 = "John Heard";
15:          String role4 = "Nova";
16:          String actor4 = "Cassie Scerbo";
17:          // display information
18:          System.out.println(title + " (" + year + ")\n" +
19:              "A " + director + " film.\n\n" +
20:              role1 + "\t" + actor1 + "\n" +
21:              role2 + "\t" + actor2 + "\n" +
22:              role3 + "\t" + actor3 + "\n" +
23:              role4 + "\t" + actor4);
24:      }
25: }
```

Look over the program and see whether you can figure out what it's doing at each stage. Here's a breakdown of what's taking place:

▶ Line 3 gives the Java program the name Credits.

▶ Line 4 begins the main() block statement in which all the program's work gets done.

▶ Lines 6–16 set up variables to hold information about the film, its director, and stars. One of the variables, year, is an integer. The rest are string variables.

▶ Lines 18–23 are one long System.out.println() statement. Everything between the first parenthesis on Line 18 and the last parenthesis on Line 23 is displayed onscreen. The newline character (\n) causes the text after it to be displayed at the beginning of a new line. The tab character (\t) inserts tab spacing in the output. The rest are either text or string variables that should be shown.

▶ Line 24 ends the main() block statement.

▶ Line 25 ends the program.

If you do encounter error messages, correct any typos you find in the Credits program and save it again. NetBeans compiles the program automatically. When you run the program, you see an output window like the one in Figure 6.1.

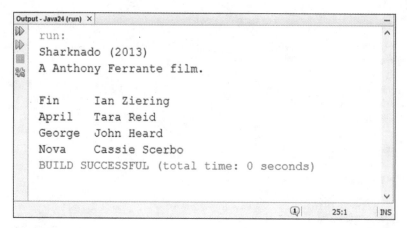

FIGURE 6.1
The output of the `Credits` program.

Summary

When your version of Credits looks like Figure 6.1, give yourself some credit. Six hours into this book, you're writing longer Java programs and dealing with more sophisticated issues. Strings are something you use every time you sit down to write a program. You'll be using strings in many ways to communicate with users.

Workshop

Q&A

Q. How can I set the value of a string variable to be blank?

A. Use an empty string, a pair of double quotation marks without any text between them. The following code creates a new string variable called georgeSays and sets it to nothing:

```
String georgeSays = "";
```

Q. I can't seem to get the `toUpperCase()` method to change a string so that it's all capital letters. What am I doing wrong?

A. When you call a `String` object's `toUpperCase()` method, it doesn't actually change the `String` object it is called on. Instead, it creates a new string that is set in all uppercase letters. Consider the following statements:

```
String firstName = "Baz";
String changeName = firstName.toUpperCase();
System.out.println("First Name: " + firstName);
```

This code displays the text "First Name: Baz" because `firstName` contains the original string. If you switched the last statement to display the `changeName` variable instead, it would output "First Name: BAZ".

Strings do not change in value in Java after they are created.

Q. Do all methods in Java display `true` or `false` in the same way that the `equals()` method does in relation to strings?

A. Methods have different ways of producing a response after they are used. When a method sends back a value, as the `equals()` method does, it's called returning a value. The `equals()` method is set to return a boolean value. Other methods might return a string, an integer, another type of variable, or nothing at all—which is represented by `void`.

Q. Why do schools assign grades the letters A, B, C, D, and F but not E?

A. The letter grade E already was being used in an alternative grading system. Until the mid-20th century, in the United States the most popular grading system was to assign E for excellent, S for satisfactory, N for needs improvement, or U for the dreaded unsatisfactory. So when the ABCD system came along, giving a failing student an E was considered a not-so-excellent idea.

ESNU grading remains in wide use in elementary schools.

Quiz

The following questions build character by testing your knowledge of the care and feeding of strings.

1. My friend concatenates. Should I report him to the authorities?

A. No. It's only illegal during the winter months.

B. Yes, but not until I sell the story to TMZ first.

C. No. All he's doing is pasting two strings together in a program.

2. Why is the word `String` capitalized, whereas `int` and others are not?

A. `String` is a full word, but `int` ain't.

B. Like all objects that are a standard part of Java, `String` has a capitalized name.

C. Poor quality control at Oracle.

3. Which of the following characters puts a single quotation mark in a string?

A. `<quote>`

B. `\'`

C. `'`

Answers

1. **C.** Concatenation is just another word for pasting, joining, melding, or otherwise connecting two strings together. It happens when you use the + and += operators on strings.

2. **B.** The types of objects available in Java are all capitalized, which is the main reason variable names have a lowercase first letter. It makes it harder to mistake them for objects.

3. **B.** The single backslash is what begins one of the special characters that can be inserted into strings.

Activities

You can review the topics of this hour more fully with the following activities:

▶ Write a short Java program called `Favorite` that puts the code from this hour's "Comparing Two Strings" section into the `main()` block statement. Test it out to make sure it works as described and says that Fin's favorite shark-killing weapon is not the pool cue. When you're done, change the initial value of the `guess` variable from "pool cue" to "chainsaw". See what happens.

▶ Modify the `Credits` program so the names of the director and all performers are displayed entirely in uppercase letters.

To see Java programs that implement these activities, visit the book's website at www.java-24hours.com.

HOUR 7
Using Conditional Tests to Make Decisions

This Hour's To-Do List:

- ▶ Use the `if` statement for basic conditional tests.
- ▶ Test whether one value is greater than or less than another.
- ▶ Test whether two values are equal or unequal.
- ▶ Use `else` statements as the opposite of `if` statements.
- ▶ Chain several conditional tests together.
- ▶ Use the `switch` statement for complicated conditional tests.
- ▶ Create tests with the ternary operator.

When you write a computer program, you provide the computer with a list of instructions called statements, and these instructions are followed to the letter. You can tell the computer to work out some unpleasant mathematical formulas, and it works them out. Tell it to display some information, and it dutifully responds.

There are times when you need the computer to be more selective about what it does. For example, if you have written a program to balance your checkbook, you might want the computer to display a warning message if your account is overdrawn. The computer should display this message only if your account is overdrawn. If it isn't, the message would be inaccurate and emotionally upsetting.

The way to accomplish this task in a Java program is to use a *conditional*, a statement that causes something to happen in a program only if a specific condition is met. During this hour, you learn how to use the conditionals `if`, `else`, and `switch`.

When a Java program makes a decision, it does so by employing a conditional statement. During this hour, you check the condition of things in your Java programs using the conditional keywords `if`, `else`, `switch`, `case`, and `break`. You also use the conditional operators `==`, `!=`, `<`, `>`, `<=`, `>=`, and `?`, along with `boolean` variables.

`if` **Statements**

The most basic way to test a condition in Java is by using an `if` statement. The `if` statement tests whether a condition is true or false and takes action only if the condition is true.

You use `if` along with the condition to test, as in the following statement:

```
long account = -17_000_000_000_000L;
if (account < 0) {
    System.out.println("Account overdrawn; you need a bailout");
}
```

The `if` statement checks whether the `account` variable is below 0 by using the less-than operator `<`. If it is, the block within the `if` statement is run, displaying a message.

The block runs only if the condition is true. In the preceding example, if the `account` variable has a value of 0 or higher, the `println()` statement is ignored. Note that the condition you test must be surrounded by parentheses, as in `(account < 0)`.

The less-than operator `<` is one of several operators you can use with conditional statements.

Less-Than and Greater-Than Comparisons

In the preceding section, the `<` operator is used the same way as in math class: as a less-than sign. There also is a greater-than conditional operator `>`, which is used in the following statements:

```
int elephantWeight = 900;
int elephantTotal = 13;
int cleaningExpense = 200;

if (elephantWeight > 780) {
    System.out.println("Elephant too big for tightrope act");
}

if (elephantTotal > 12) {
    cleaningExpense = cleaningExpense + 150;
}
```

The first `if` statement tests whether the value of the `elephantWeight` variable is greater than 780. The second `if` statement tests whether the `elephantTotal` variable is greater than 12.

If the two preceding statements are used in a program where `elephantWeight` is equal to 600 and `elephantTotal` is equal to 10, the statements within each `if` block are ignored.

You can determine whether something is less than or equal to something else with the `<=` operator. Here's an example:

```
if (account <= 0) {
    System.out.println("You are flat broke");
}
```

There's also a >= operator for greater-than-or-equal-to tests.

Equal and Not Equal Comparisons

Another condition to check in a program is equality. Is a variable equal to a specific value? Is one variable equal to the value of another? These questions can be answered with the == operator, as in the following statements:

```
char answer = 'b';
char rightAnswer = 'c';
int studentGrade = 85;
if (answer == rightAnswer) {
    studentGrade = studentGrade + 10;
}

if (studentGrade == 100) {
    System.out.println("Show off!");
}
```

CAUTION

The operator used to conduct equality tests has two equal signs: ==. It's easy to confuse this opera-tor with the = operator, which is used to assign a value to a variable. Always use two equal signs in a conditional statement.

You also can test inequality, whether something is not equal to something else, with the != operator, as follows:

```
if (answer != rightAnswer) {
    score = score - 5;
}
```

You can use the == and != operators with every type of variable except for strings, because strings are objects.

Organizing a Program with Block Statements

Up to this point, the if statements in this hour have been accompanied by a block contained within { and } brackets. (I believe the technical term for these characters is "squiggly bracket marks.")

Previously, you have seen how block statements are used to mark the beginning and end of the main() block of a Java program. Each statement within main() is handled when the program is run.

An if statement does not require a block statement. It can occupy a single line, as in this example:

```
if (account <= 0) System.out.println("No more money");
```

When there's no block, the statement that follows the if conditional is executed only if the condition is true.

The following statements use if statements to keep score in a football game, adding 7 to the total after a touchdown or 3 after a field goal. (If your football doesn't have touchdowns or field goals, that's another football entirely.)

Here's the code:

```
int total = 0;
int score = 7;
if (score == 7) {
    System.out.println("You score a touchdown!");
}
if (score == 3) {
    System.out.println("You kick a field goal!");
}
total = total + score;
```

You can use block statements in if statements to make the computer do more than one thing if a condition is true. The following is an example of an if statement that includes a block statement:

```
int playerScore = 12000;
int playerLives = 3;
int difficultyLevel = 10;

if (playerScore > 9999) {
    playerLives++;
    System.out.println("Extra life!");
    difficultyLevel = difficultyLevel + 5;
}
```

The brackets are used to group all statements that are part of the if statement. If the variable playerScore is greater than 9,999, three things happen:

▶ The value of the playerLives variable increases by 1 (because the increment operator ++ is used).

▶ The text "Extra life!" is displayed.

▶ The value of the difficultyLevel variable increases by 5.

If the variable `playerScore` is not greater than 9,999, nothing happens. All three statements inside the `if` statement block are ignored.

if-else **Statements**

There are times when you want to do something if a condition is true and something else if the condition is false. You can do this by using the `else` statement in conjunction with the `if` statement, as in the following code:

```
int answer = 17;
int correctAnswer = 13;

if (answer == correctAnswer) {
    score += 10;
    System.out.println("That's right. You get 10 points");
} else {
    score -= 5;
    System.out.println("Sorry, that's wrong. You lose 5 points");
}
```

The `else` statement does not have a condition listed alongside it, unlike the `if` statement. That's because the `else` statement is matched with the `if` statement that immediately precedes it. You also can use `else` to chain several `if` statements together, as in the following example:

```
char grade = 'A';

if (grade == 'A') {
    System.out.println("You got an A. Awesome!");
} else if (grade == 'B') {
    System.out.println("You got a B. Beautiful!");
} else if (grade == 'C') {
    System.out.println("You got a C. Concerning!");
} else {
    System.out.println("You got an F. You'll do well in Congress!");
}
```

By putting together several `if` and `else` statements in this way, you can handle a variety of conditions. The preceding example sends a different message to A students, B students, C students, and future legislators.

switch **Statements**

The `if` and `else` statements are good for situations with two possible conditions, but there are times when you have more than two.

With the preceding grade example, you saw that if and else statements can be chained to handle several different conditions.

Another way to do this is with the switch statement, which can test for a variety of different conditions and respond accordingly. In the following code, the grading example has been rewritten with a switch statement:

```
char grade = 'B';

switch (grade) {
    case 'A':
        System.out.println("You got an A. Awesome!");
        break;
    case 'B':
        System.out.println("You got a B. Beautiful!");
        break;
    case 'C':
        System.out.println("You got a C. Concerning!");
        break;
    default:
        System.out.println("You got an F. You'll do well in Congress!");
}
```

The first line of the switch statement specifies the variable that is tested—in this example, grade. Then, the switch statement uses the { and } brackets to form a block statement.

Each case statement checks the test variable in the switch statement against a specific value. The value used in a case statement can be a character, integer, or string. In the preceding example, there are case statements for the characters 'A', 'B', and 'C'. Each has one or two statements that follow it. When one of these case statements matches the variable in switch, the computer executes all statements after the case statement until it encounters a break statement.

For example, if the grade variable has the value of 'B', the text "You got a B. Good work!" is displayed. The next statement is break, so nothing else in the switch statement is executed. The break statement tells the computer to break out of the switch statement.

Forgetting to use break statements in the case sections of a switch statement can lead to undesired results. If there were no break statements in this grading example, the first three "You got a" messages would be displayed whether the grade variable equals 'A', 'B', or 'C'.

The default statement is used as a catch-all if none of the preceding case statements is true. In this example, it occurs if the grade variable does not equal 'A', 'B', or 'C'. You do not have to use a default statement with every switch block statement in your programs. When it is omitted, nothing happens if none of the case statements has the correct value.

The hour's first project, the Commodity class in Listing 7.1, uses switch to either buy or sell an unspecified commodity. The commodity costs $20 when purchased and earns $15 profit when sold.

A switch-case statement tests the value of a string named command, running one block if it equals "BUY" and another if it equals "SELL".

In NetBeans, create an empty Java file with the class name Commodity in the package com.java24hours, then fill it with Listing 7.1.

LISTING 7.1 The full text of Commodity.java

```
1: package com.java24hours;
2:
3: class Commodity {
4:     public static void main(String[] arguments) {
5:         String command = "BUY";
6:         int balance = 550;
7:         int quantity = 42;
8:
9:         switch (command) {
10:             case "BUY":
11:                 quantity += 5;
12:                 balance -= 20;
13:                 break;
14:             case "SELL":
15:                 quantity -= 5;
16:                 balance += 15;
17:         }
18:         System.out.println("Balance: $" + balance + "\n"
19:             + "Quantity: " + quantity);
20:     }
21: }
```

This application sets the command string to "BUY" in line 5. When the switch in line 9 is tested, the case block in lines 11–13 is run. The quantity of the commodity increases by 5 and the balance is lowered by $20.

When the Commodity program is run, it produces the output shown in Figure 7.1.

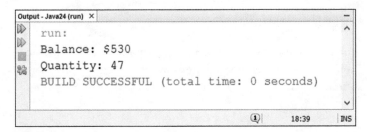

FIGURE 7.1
The output of the Commodity program.

The Ternary Operator

The most complicated conditional statement in Java is the ternary operator ?.

The ternary operator assigns a value or displays a value based on a condition. For example, consider a video game that sets the `numberOfEnemies` variable to one of two values based on whether the `skillLevel` variable is greater than 5. One way you can accomplish this is with an `if-else` statement:

```
if (skillLevel > 5) {
    numberOfEnemies = 20;
} else {
    numberOfEnemies = 10;
}
```

A shorter but more complicated way to do this is with the ternary operator. A ternary expression has five parts:

▶ The condition to test, surrounded by parentheses, as in `(skillLevel > 5)`

▶ A question mark (?)

▶ The value to use if the condition is true

▶ A colon (:)

▶ The value to use if the condition is false

To use the ternary operator to set `numberOfEnemies` based on `skillLevel`, you could use the following statement:

```
int numberOfEnemies = (skillLevel > 5) ? 20 : 10;
```

You also can use the ternary operator to determine what information to display. Consider the example of a program that displays the text "Ms." or "Mr." depending on the value of the `gender` variable. Here's a statement that accomplishes this:

```
String gender = "female";
System.out.print( (gender.equals("female")) ? "Ms." : "Mr." );
```

The ternary operator can be useful, but it's also the hardest conditional in Java for beginners to understand. As you learn Java, you don't encounter any situations where the ternary operator must be used instead of `if-else` statements.

Watching the Clock

This hour's final project provides another look at each of the conditional tests you can use in your programs. For this project, you use Java's built-in timekeeping feature, which keeps track of the current date and time, and present this information in sentence form.

Load NetBeans or another development tool you're using to create Java programs, and give a new document the name Clock.java and package com.java24hours. This program is long, but most of it consists of multi-line conditional statements. Type the full text of Listing 7.2 into the source code editor and save the file as Clock.java when you're done.

LISTING 7.2   The full text of Clock.java

```
 1: package com.java24hours;
 2:
 3: import java.time.*;
 4: import java.time.temporal.*;
 5:
 6: class Clock {
 7:     public static void main(String[] arguments) {
 8:         // get current time and date
 9:         LocalDateTime now = LocalDateTime.now();
10:         int hour = now.get(ChronoField.HOUR_OF_DAY);
11:         int minute = now.get(ChronoField.MINUTE_OF_HOUR);
12:         int month = now.get(ChronoField.MONTH_OF_YEAR);
13:         int day = now.get(ChronoField.DAY_OF_MONTH);
14:         int year = now.get(ChronoField.YEAR);
15:
16:         // display greeting
17:         if (hour < 12) {
18:             System.out.println("Good morning.\n");
19:         } else if (hour < 17) {
20:             System.out.println("Good afternoon.\n");
21:         } else {
22:             System.out.println("Good evening.\n");
23:         }
24:
25:         // begin time message by showing the minutes
26:         System.out.print("It's");
27:         if (minute != 0) {
28:             System.out.print(" " + minute + " ");
29:             System.out.print( (minute != 1) ? "minutes" :
30:                 "minute");
31:             System.out.print(" past");
32:         }
33:
```

```
34:        // display the hour
35:        System.out.print(" ");
36:        System.out.print( (hour > 12) ? (hour - 12) : hour );
37:        System.out.print(" o'clock on ");
38:
39:        // display the name of the month
40:        switch (month) {
41:            case 1:
42:                System.out.print("January");
43:                break;
44:            case 2:
45:                System.out.print("February");
46:                break;
47:            case 3:
48:                System.out.print("March");
49:                break;
50:            case 4:
51:                System.out.print("April");
52:                break;
53:            case 5:
54:                System.out.print("May");
55:                break;
56:            case 6:
57:                System.out.print("June");
58:                break;
59:            case 7:
60:                System.out.print("July");
61:                break;
62:            case 8:
63:                System.out.print("August");
64:                break;
65:            case 9:
66:                System.out.print("September");
67:                break;
68:            case 10:
69:                System.out.print("October");
70:                break;
71:            case 11:
72:                System.out.print("November");
73:                break;
74:            case 12:
75:                System.out.print("December");
76:        }
77:
78:        // display the date and year
79:        System.out.println(" " + day + ", " + year + ".");
80:    }
81: }
```

After the program is saved, before you run it, look the code over to get an idea about how the conditional tests are being used.

CAUTION

Because this program uses newer features of Java, it won't compile if the current NetBeans project is set to use an earlier version of the language. To make sure the correct setting has been chosen, choose File, Project Properties. In the Project Properties dialog, look for the Source/Binary Format value. It should be JDK 9.

With the exception of Lines 3–4 and Lines 8–14, the `Clock` program contains material that has been covered up to this point. After a series of variables are set up to hold the current date and time, a series of `if` or `switch` conditionals are used to determine what information should be displayed.

This program contains several uses of `System.out.println()` and `System.out.print()` to display strings.

Lines 8–14 refer to a `LocalDateTime` variable called now. The `LocalDateTime` variable type is capitalized because `LocalDateTime` is an object.

You learn how to create and work with objects during Hour 10, "Creating Your First Object." For this hour, focus on what's taking place in those lines rather than how it's happening.

The `Clock` program is made up of the following sections:

▶ Line 3 enables your program to use a class that is needed to track the current date and time: `java.time.LocalDateTime`.

▶ Line 4 enables the program to use the class `java.time.temporalfield.ChronoField`, which sounds like something from a time travel movie.

▶ Lines 6–7 begin the `Clock` program and its `main()` statement block.

▶ Line 9 creates a `LocalDateTime` object called now that contains the current date and time of your system. The now object changes each time you run this program. (Unless the physical laws of the universe are altered and time stands still.)

▶ Lines 10–14 create variables to hold the `hour`, `minute`, `month`, `day`, and `year`. The values for these variables are pulled from the `LocalDateTime` object, which is the storehouse for all this information. The information within the parentheses, such as `ChronoField.DAY_OF_MONTH`, indicates which part of the date and time to pull.

▶ Lines 17–23 display one of three possible greetings: "Good morning.", "Good afternoon.", or "Good evening." The greeting to display is selected based on the value of the `hour` variable.

▶ Lines 26–32 display the current minute along with some accompanying text. If the value of minute is equal to 0, Lines 28–31 are ignored because of the if statement in Line 27. This statement is necessary because it would not make sense for the program to tell someone that it's 0 minutes past an hour. Line 28 displays the current value of the minute variable. A ternary operator is used in Lines 29–30 to display either the text "minutes" or "minute," depending on whether minute is equal to 1.

▶ Lines 35–37 display the current hour by using another ternary operator. This ternary conditional statement in Line 36 causes the hour to be displayed differently if it is larger than 12, which prevents the computer from stating times like "15 o'clock."

▶ Lines 40–76, almost half of the program, are a long switch statement that displays a different name of the month based on the integer value stored in the month variable.

▶ Line 79 finishes off the display by showing the current date and the year.

▶ Lines 80–81 close out the main() statement block and then the entire Clock program.

When you run this program, the output should display a sentence based on the current date and time. The output of the application in the Output pane is shown in Figure 7.2.

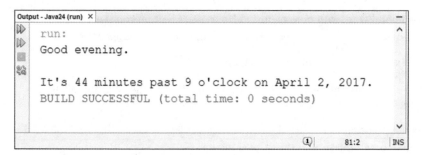

FIGURE 7.2
The output of the Clock program.

Run the program several times to see how it keeps up with the clock.

NOTE

The Clock application uses the Date/Time API introduced recently in Java. Earlier versions of Java used a different set of classes to work with dates and times. As you may recall from Hour 4, "Understanding How Java Programs Work," the Java Class Library includes thousands of classes that perform useful tasks. The java.time and java.time.temporal packages used in this program are part of the Date/Time API.

Summary

Now that you can use conditional statements, the intelligence of your Java programs has improved greatly. Your programs can evaluate information and use it to react differently in different situations, even if information changes as the program is running. They can decide between two or more alternatives based on specific conditions.

Programming a computer forces you to break a task down into a logical set of steps to undertake and decisions that must be made. Using the `if` statement and other conditionals in programming also promotes a type of logical thinking that can reap benefits in other aspects of your life:

- *"If* that candidate is elected president in November, I will move to Canada."

- *"If* my OK Cupid date likes me, I'll pay for dinner at an expensive restaurant, *else* we will go to Taco Bell."

- *"If* I violate my probation, the only team that will draft me is the Dallas Cowboys."

Workshop

Q&A

Q. The `if` statement seems like the one that's most useful. Is it possible to use only `if` statements in programs and never use the others?

A. It's possible to do without `else` or `switch`, and many programmers never use the ternary operator `?`. However, `else` and `switch` often are beneficial to use in your programs because they make the programs easier to understand. A set of `if` statements chained together can become unwieldy.

Q. During this hour, opening and closing brackets { and } sometimes are not used with an `if` statement if it is used with only one statement. Isn't it mandatory to use brackets?

A. No. Brackets can be used as part of any `if` statement to surround the part of the program that's dependent on the conditional test. Using brackets is a good practice to get into because it prevents a common error that might take place when you revise the program. If you don't add brackets in an `if` conditional with a single statement, what happens when you later add a second statement but neglect to add brackets? I'll answer my own question: Unexpected things, and the word "unexpected" is almost never good in programming.

Q. Must `break` be used in each section of statements that follows a `case`?

A. You don't have to use `break`. If you do not use it at the end of a group of statements, all the remaining statements inside the `switch` block statement are handled, regardless of the `case` value they are being tested with.

However, in most cases you're likely to want a `break` statement at the end of each group.

Q. Why did the Thompson Twins get that name when they were a trio, were not related, and none of them was named Thompson?

A. Band members Tom Bailey, Alannah Currie, and Joe Leeway called themselves the Thompson Twins in honor of Thomson and Thompson, a pair of bumbling detectives featured in the Belgian comic books *The Adventures of Tintin*.

The bowler-wearing detectives were physically indistinguishable except for a minor difference in the shape of their mustaches. Despite being terrible at their jobs, they were inexplicably assigned to important and sensitive missions. They often pursued Tintin for crimes that he did not commit.

As their names would indicate, the detectives were not related either.

Quiz

The following questions see what condition your condition is in after you've studied conditional statements in Java.

1. Conditional tests result in either a `true` or `false` value. Which variable type does this remind you of?

    A. None. Stop pestering me with all these questions.

    B. The `long` variable type.

    C. The `boolean` type.

2. Which statement is used as a catch-all category in a `switch` block statement?

    A. `default`

    B. `otherwise`

    C. `onTheOtherHand`

3. What's a conditional?

    A. The thing that repairs messy split ends and tangles after you shampoo.

    B. Something in a program that tests whether a condition is true or false.

    C. The place where you confess your sins to a religious authority figure.

Answers

1. **C.** The `boolean` variable type only can equal `true` or `false`, making it similar to conditional tests. If you answered A., I'm sorry, but there are only 17 hours left and we've got a lot left to cover. Java doesn't teach itself.

2. **A.** `default` statements are handled if none of the other `case` statements matches the `switch` variable.

3. **B.** The other answers describe conditioner and a confessional.

Activities

To improve your conditioning in terms of Java conditionals, review the topics of this hour with the following activities:

▶ Add "//" in front of a `break` statement on one of the lines in the `Clock` program to make it a comment; then compile it and see what happens when you run it. Try it again with a few more `break` statements removed.

▶ Create a short program that stores a value of your choosing from 1 to 100 in an integer variable called `grade`. Use this `grade` variable with a conditional statement to display a different message for all 'A', 'B', 'C', 'D', and 'F' students. Try it first with an `if` statement, and then try it with a `switch` statement.

To see Java programs that implement these activities, visit the book's website at www.java24hours.com.

Repeating an Action with Loops

This Hour's To-Do List:

- ▶ Use the `for` loop.
- ▶ Use the `while` loop.
- ▶ Use the `do-while` loop.
- ▶ Exit a loop prematurely.
- ▶ Name a loop.

One of the more annoying punishments for schoolchildren is to make them write something over and over again on a chalkboard. On *The Simpsons*, in one of his frequent trips to the board, Bart Simpson had to write, "I will stop asking when Santa goes to the bathroom," dozens of times. This punishment might work on children but would be completely useless on a computer. A computer program can repeat a task with ease.

Programs are ideally suited to do the same thing over and over because of loops. A loop is a statement or block that is repeated in a program. Some loops run a fixed number of times. Others run indefinitely.

There are three loop statements in Java: `for`, `do`, and `while`. Each can work like the others, but it's beneficial to learn how all three operate. You often can simplify a loop section of a program by choosing the right statement.

`for` **Loops**

In your programming, you find many circumstances in which a loop is useful. You can use them to keep doing something several times, such as when an antivirus program opens each new email as it comes in to look for viruses. You also can use loops to cause the computer to do nothing for a brief period, such as an animated clock that moves a minute hand once per minute.

A loop statement causes a computer program to return to the same place more than once, like a stunt plane completing an acrobatic loop.

Java's most complex loop statement is `for`. A `for` loop repeats a section of a program a fixed number of times. Take a look at one here:

```
for (int dex = 0; dex < 1000; dex++) {
    if (dex % 12 == 0) {
        System.out.println("#: " + dex);
    }
}
```

This loop displays every number from 0 to 999 that is evenly divisible by 12.

A `for` loop has a variable that determines when the loop should begin and end. This variable is called the *counter* (or index). The counter in the preceding loop is the variable `dex`.

A `for` loop has three parts within the parentheses that follow the `for` keyword: the initialization, conditional, and change sections. These sections are divided by semi-colons (;). The example illustrates these three sections:

▶ The initialization section—In the first part, the `dex` variable is given an initial value of 0.

▶ The conditional section—In the second part, there is a conditional test like one you might use in an `if` statement: `dex < 1000`.

▶ The change section—The third part is a statement that changes the value of the `dex` variable, in this example by using the increment operator.

In the initialization section, you set up the counter variable. You can create the variable in the `for` statement, as the preceding example does with the integer variable `dex`. You also can create the variable elsewhere in the program. The variable should be given a starting value in this section. The variable has this value when the loop starts.

The conditional section contains a test that must remain `true` for the loop to keep looping. When the test is `false`, the loop ends. In this example, the loop ends when the `dex` variable is equal to or greater than 1,000.

The last section of the `for` statement contains a statement that changes the value of the counter variable. This statement is handled each time the loop goes around. The counter has to change in some way or the loop never ends. In the example, `dex` is incremented by one in the change section. If `dex` was not changed, it would stay at its original value of 0 and the conditional `dex < 1000` always would be true.

The `for` statement's block is executed during each trip through the loop.

The preceding example had the following statements inside the `for` block:

```
if (dex % 12 == 0) {
    System.out.println("#: " + dex);
}
```

These statements are executed 1,000 times. The loop starts by setting the dex variable equal to 0. During each pass through the loop, it adds 1 to dex. When dex is no longer less than 1,000, the loop stops looping.

NOTE

An unusual term you might hear in connection with loops is iteration. An iteration is a single trip through a loop. The counter variable that is used to control the loop is called an iterator.

As you have seen with `if` statements, a `for` loop does not require brackets if it contains only a single statement. This is shown in the following example:

```
for (int p = 0; p < 500; p++)
    System.out.println("I will not sell miracle cures");
```

This loop displays the text "I will not sell miracle cures" 500 times. Although brackets are not required around a single statement inside a loop, you can use them to make the block easier to spot, like so:

```
for (int p = 0; p < 500; p++) {
    System.out.println("I will not sell miracle cures");
}
```

The first program you create during this hour displays the first 200 multiples of 9: 9, 18, 27, and so on, up to 1,800 (9 × 200). In NetBeans, create a new empty Java file named Nines in the com.java24hours package and enter the text of Listing 8.1. When you save the file, it is stored as Nines.java.

LISTING 8.1   The Full Text of Nines.java

```
 1: package com.java24hours;
 2:
 3: class Nines {
 4:     public static void main(String[] arguments) {
 5:         for (int dex = 1; dex <= 200; dex++) {
 6:             int multiple = 9 * dex;
 7:             System.out.print(multiple + " ");
 8:         }
 9:     System.out.println();
10:     }
11: }
```

The `Nines` program contains a `for` statement in Line 5. This statement has three sections:

▶ Initialization—`int dex = 1`, which creates an integer variable called `dex` and gives it an initial value of 1.

▶ Conditional—`dex <= 200`, which must be true during each trip through the loop. When it is not true, the loop ends.

▶ Change—`dex++`, which increments the `dex` variable by 1 during each trip through the loop.

Run the program by choosing Run, Run File in NetBeans. The program produces the output shown in Figure 8.1.

```
Output - Java24 (run)  ×
   run:
    9 18 27 36 45 54 63 72 81 90 99 108 117 126 135 144 153 162 171 180 189 198 207
   216 225 234 243 252 261 270 279 288 297 306 315 324 333 342 351 360 369 378 387
   396 405 414 423 432 441 450 459 468 477 486 495 504 513 522 531 540 549 558 567
   576 585 594 603 612 621 630 639 648 657 666 675 684 693 702 711 720 729 738 747
   756 765 774 783 792 801 810 819 828 837 846 855 864 873 882 891 900 909 918 927
   936 945 954 963 972 981 990 999 1008 1017 1026 1035 1044 1053 1062 1071 1080 108
   9 1098 1107 1116 1125 1134 1143 1152 1161 1170 1179 1188 1197 1206 1215 1224 123
   3 1242 1251 1260 1269 1278 1287 1296 1305 1314 1323 1332 1341 1350 1359 1368 137
   7 1386 1395 1404 1413 1422 1431 1440 1449 1458 1467 1476 1485 1494 1503 1512 152
   1 1530 1539 1548 1557 1566 1575 1584 1593 1602 1611 1620 1629 1638 1647 1656 166
   5 1674 1683 1692 1701 1710 1719 1728 1737 1746 1755 1764 1773 1782 1791 1800
   BUILD SUCCESSFUL (total time: 0 seconds)
                                                                      12:1      INS
```

FIGURE 8.1
The output of the `Nines` program.

The output window in NetBeans does not wrap text, so all the numbers appear on a single line. To make the text wrap, right-click anywhere in the Output pane and choose Wrap Text from the pop-up menu.

`while` **Loops**

The `while` loop is simpler than a `for` loop. The only thing it needs is a conditional test that accompanies the `while` statement, as in this code:

```
int gameLives = 3;
while (gameLives > 0) {
    // the statements inside the loop go here
}
```

This loop continues repeating until the gameLives variable is no longer greater than 0.

The while statement tests the condition at the beginning of the loop before any statements in the loop have been handled. If the tested condition is false when a program reaches the while statement for the first time, the statements inside the loop are ignored.

If the while condition is true, the loop goes around once and tests the while condition again. If the tested condition never changes inside the loop, the loop keeps looping forever.

The following statements use a while loop to display the same line of text several times:

```
int limit = 5;
int count = 1;
while (count < limit) {
    System.out.println("Pork is not a verb");
    count++;
}
```

A while loop uses one or more variables set up before the loop statement. In this example, two integer variables are put to work: limit, which has a value of 5, and count, which has a value of 1.

The while loop displays the text "Pork is not a verb" four times. If you gave the count variable an initial value of 6 instead of 1, the text never would be displayed.

do-while **Loops**

The do-while loop is similar to the while loop, but the conditional test goes in a different place. The following is an example of a do-while loop:

```
int gameLives = 0;
do {
    // the statements inside the loop go here
} while (gameLives > 0);
```

Like the while loop, this loop continues looping until the gameLives variable is no longer greater than 0. The do-while loop is different because the conditional test is conducted after the statements inside the loop, instead of before them.

When the do loop is reached for the first time as a program runs, the statements between the do and while are handled automatically, then the while condition is tested to determine whether the loop should be repeated. If the while condition is true, the loop goes around one more time. If the condition is false, the loop ends. Something must happen inside the do and while statements that changes the condition tested with while, or the loop continues indefinitely. The statements inside a do-while loop always are handled at least once.

The following statements cause a do-while loop to display the same line of text several times:

```
int limit = 5;
int count = 1;
do {
    System.out.println("I am not allergic to long division");
    count++;
} while (count < limit);
```

Like a while loop, a do-while loop uses one or more variables that are set up before the loop statement.

The loop displays the text "I am not allergic to long division" four times. If you gave the count variable an initial value of 6 instead of 1, the text would be displayed once, even though count is never less than limit.

In a do-while loop, the statements inside the loop are executed at least once even if the loop condition is false the first time around. This difference is why there's a do-while loop as a companion to the while loop.

Exiting a Loop

The normal way to exit a loop is for the tested condition to become false. This is true of all three types of loops in Java. There might be times when you want a loop to end immediately, even if the condition being tested is still true. You can accomplish this with a break statement, as shown:

```
int index = 0;
while (index <= 1000) {
    index = index + 5;
    if (index == 400) {
        break;
    }
}
```

A break statement ends the loop that contains the statement.

In this example, the while loop is designed to loop until the index variable is greater than 1,000. However, a special case causes the loop to end earlier than that: If index equals 400, the break statement is executed, ending the loop immediately.

Another special-circumstance statement you can use inside a loop is continue. The continue statement causes the loop to exit its current trip through the loop and start over at the first statement of the loop. Consider the following code:

```
int index = 0;
while (index <= 1000) {
    index = index + 5;
    if (index == 400) {
        continue;
    }
    System.out.println("The index is " + index);
}
```

Inside this loop, the statements are handled normally unless the value of index equals 400. In that case, the continue statement causes the loop to go back to the while statement instead of proceeding normally to the System.out.println() statement. Because of the continue statement, the loop never displays the following text:

```
The index is 400
```

You can use the break and continue statements with all three kinds of loops.

The break statement makes it possible to create a loop in your program that's designed to run forever, as in this example:

```
while (true) {
    if (quitKeyPressed == true) {
        break;
    }
}
```

This example assumes that something in another part of the program will cause the quitKeyPressed variable to equal true. Until that occurs, the while loop will keep on looping forever—because its condition always equals true and that can never change.

Naming a Loop

Like other statements in Java programs, loops can be placed inside other loops. The following shows a for loop inside a while loop:

```
int points = 0;
int target = 100;
while (target <= 100) {
    for (int i = 0; i < target; i++) {
        if (points > 50) {
            break;
        }
        points = points + i;
    }
}
```

In this example, the `break` statement causes the `for` loop to end if the `points` variable is greater than 50. However, the `while` loop never ends because `target` is never greater than 100.

In some cases, you might want to break out of more than one loop at the same time. To make this possible, you have to give the outer loop—in this example, the `while` statement—a name. To name a loop, put the name on the line before the beginning of the loop and follow it with a colon (`:`).

When the loop has a name, use the name after the `break` or `continue` statement to indicate the loop to which the `break` or `continue` statement applies. The following example repeats the previous one with the exception of one thing: If the `points` variable is greater than 50, both loops end.

```
int points = 0;
int target = 100;
targetLoop:
while (target <= 100) {
    for (int i = 0; i < target; i++) {
        if (points > 50) {
            break targetLoop;
        }
        points = points + i;
    }
}
```

When a loop's name is used in a `break` or `continue` statement, the name does not include a colon.

Complex `for` **Loops**

A `for` loop can be more complex than shown up to this point in the hour. The loop can include more than one variable in its initialization, conditional, and change sections. A `for` loop can have more than one variable set up during the initialization section and more than one statement in the change section, as in the following code:

```
int i, j;
for (i = 0, j = 0; i * j < 1000; i++, j += 2) {
    System.out.println(i + " * " + j + " = " + (i * j));
}
```

In each section of the `for` loop separated by semicolons (`;`), commas are used to separate the variables, as in `i = 0, j = 0`. The example loop displays a list of equations where the `i` and `j` variables are multiplied together. The `i` variable increases by 1, and the `j` variable increases by 2 during each trip through the loop. When `i` multiplied by `j` is equal or greater than 1,000, the loop ends.

Sections of a `for` loop also can be empty. An example of this is when a loop's counter variable already has been created with an initial value in another part of the program, as in the following:

```
int displayCount = 1;
int endValue = 13;
for ( ; displayCount < endValue; displayCount++) {
    // loop statements would be here
}
```

Testing Your Computer Speed

This hour's next project is a Java program that performs a benchmark, a test that measures how fast computer hardware or software is running. The `Benchmark` program uses a loop statement to repeatedly perform the following mathematical expression:

```
double x = Math.sqrt(index);
```

This statement calls the `Math.sqrt()` method to find the square root of a number. You learn more about methods during Hour 11, "Describing What Your Object Is Like."

The benchmark you're creating counts how many times a Java program can calculate a square root in one minute.

Use NetBeans to create a new empty Java file called `Benchmark` in the package `com. java24hours`. Enter the text of Listing 8.2 and save the program when you're done.

LISTING 8.2   The Full Source Code of `Benchmark.java`

```
 1: package com.java24hours;
 2:
 3: class Benchmark {
 4:     public static void main(String[] arguments) {
 5:         long startTime = System.currentTimeMillis();
 6:         long endTime = startTime + 60000;
 7:         long index = 0;
 8:         while (true) {
 9:             double x = Math.sqrt(index);
10:             long now = System.currentTimeMillis();
11:             if (now > endTime) {
12:                 break;
13:             }
14:             index++;
15:         }
16:         System.out.println(index + " loops in one minute.");
17:     }
18: }
```

The following things take place in the program:

▶ Line 5—The `startTime` variable is created with the current time in milliseconds as its value, measured by calling the `currentTimeMillis()` method of Java's `System` class.

▶ Line 6—The `endTime` variable is created with a value 60,000 higher than `startTime`. Since one minute equals 60,000 milliseconds, this sets the variable one minute past `startTime`.

▶ Line 7—A `long` named `index` is set up with an initial value of 0.

▶ Line 8—The `while` statement begins a loop using `true` as the conditional, which causes the loop to continue forever (in other words, until something else stops it).

▶ Line 9—The square root of `index` is calculated and stored in the x variable.

▶ Line 10—Using `currentTimeMillis()`, the now variable is created with the current time.

▶ Lines 11–13—If now is greater than `endTime`, this signifies that the loop has been running for one minute and `break` ends the `while` loop. Otherwise, it keeps looping.

▶ Line 14—The `index` variable is incremented by 1 with each trip through the loop.

▶ Line 16—Outside the loop, the program displays the number of times it performed the square root calculation.

The output of the application is shown in the Output pane in Figure 8.2.

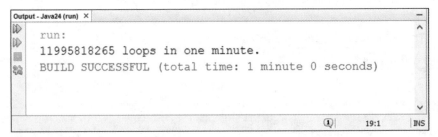

FIGURE 8.2
The output of the `Benchmark` program.

The `Benchmark` program is an excellent way to see whether your computer is faster than mine. During the testing of this program, my laptop performed around 11.99 billion calculations. If your computer has better results, don't just send me your condolences. Buy more of my books so I can upgrade my PC.

Summary

Loops are a fundamental part of most programming languages. Animation created by displaying several graphics in sequence is one of many tasks you could not accomplish in Java or any other programming language without loops.

Every one of Bart Simpson's chalkboard punishments has been documented on the Web. Visit http://simpsons.wikia.com/wiki/List_of_chalkboard_gags to see the list.

Workshop

Q&A

Q. The term "initialization" has been used in several places. What does it mean?

A. It means to give something an initial value and set it up. When you create a variable and assign a starting value to it, you are initializing the variable.

Q. If a loop never ends, how does the program stop running?

A. Usually in a program where a loop does not end, something else in the program is set up to stop execution in some way. For example, a loop in a game program could continue indefinitely while the player still has lives left.

One bug that crops up often as you work on programs is an infinite loop, a loop that never stops because of a programming mistake. If one of the Java programs you run is stuck in an infinite loop, press the red alert icon to the left of the Output pane.

Q. How can I buy stock in the Green Bay Packers?

A. Unless the publicly owned NFL team decides to hold another stock sale, the only way to become a stockholder is to inherit shares in a will.

The Packers have sold stock in 1923, 1935, 1950, 1997, and 2011. Approximately 360,000 people own five million shares in the team, despite the fact that they have very limited rights associated with the stock.

Holders don't earn a dividend and can't profit from their shares. They only can sell them back to the team and lose money in the deal. No individual can own more than 200,000 shares.

They do receive exclusive team merchandise offers and can attend an annual meeting to elect the seven-member board that manages the team.

In the 1923 stock sale that formed the franchise, 1,000 fans bought shares for $5 each. The 2011 sale raised $67 million for an upgrade to Lambeau Field, the team's stadium.

More information on the stock can be found on the Web at www.packers.com/community/shareholders.html.

Quiz

The following questions test your knowledge of loops. In the spirit of the subject matter, repeat each of these until you get them right.

1. What must be used to separate each section of a `for` statement?

   A. Commas

   B. Semicolons

   C. Off-duty police officers

2. Which statement causes a program to go back to the statement that began a loop and then keep going from there?

   A. `continue`

   B. `next`

   C. `skip`

3. Which loop statement in Java always runs at least once?

   A. `for`

   B. `while`

   C. `do-while`

Answers

1. **B.** Commas are used to separate things within a section, but semicolons separate sections.

2. **A.** The `break` statement ends a loop entirely, and `continue` skips to the next go-round of the loop.

3. **C.** The `do-while` conditional isn't evaluated until after the first pass through the loop.

Activities

If your head isn't going in circles from all this looping, review the topics of this hour with the following activities:

▶ Modify the `Benchmark` program to test the execution of simple mathematical calculation, such as multiplication or division.

▶ Write a short program using loops that finds the first 400 numbers that are multiples of 13.

To see Java programs that implement these activities, visit the book's website at www.java24hours.com.

HOUR 9
Storing Information with Arrays

This Hour's To-Do List:

- ▶ Create an array.
- ▶ Set the size of an array.
- ▶ Store a value in an array element.
- ▶ Change the information in an array.
- ▶ Make multidimensional arrays.
- ▶ Sort an array.

No one benefited more from the development of the computer than Santa Claus. For centuries, humankind has put an immense burden on him to gather and process information. Old St. Nick has to keep track of the following things:

- ▶ Naughty children

- ▶ Nice children

- ▶ Gift requests

- ▶ Homes with impassable chimneys

- ▶ Women who want more from Santa than Mrs. Claus will let him give

- ▶ Countries that shoot unidentified aircraft first and ask questions later

Computers were a great boon to the North Pole. They are ideal for the storage, categorization, and study of information.

The most basic way that information is stored in a computer program is by putting it into a variable. So far, all variables you've worked with have been a single item of information, such as a floating-point number or a string.

Santa's list of nice children is an example of a larger collection of similar information. To keep track of a list of this kind, you can use arrays.

An array is a group of related variables that share the same type. Any type of information that can be stored as a variable can become the items stored in an array. Arrays can be used to keep track of more sophisticated types of information than a single variable, but they are almost as easy to create and manipulate.

Creating Arrays

Arrays are variables grouped together under a common name. The term array should be familiar to you—think of a saleswoman showing off her array of products or a game show with a dazzling array of prizes. Like variables, arrays are created by stating the type of variable being organized into the array and the name of the array. A pair of square brackets ([]) follow the type to distinguish arrays from variables.

You can create arrays for any type of information that can be stored as a variable. The following statement creates an array of string variables:

```
String[] naughtyChild;
```

Here are two statements that create arrays of integers and Boolean values, respectively:

```
int[] reindeerWeight;
boolean[] hostileAirTravelNations;
```

NOTE

Java is flexible about where the square brackets are placed when an array is created. You can put them after the variable name instead of the variable type, as in the following:

```
String niceChild[];
```

To make arrays easier to spot in your programs (for humans), you should stick to one style rather than switching back and forth. Programs that use arrays in this book always place the brackets after the variable or object type.

The previous examples create variables to hold arrays, but do not store any values in them. To do this, you can use the new keyword along with the variable type, or store values in the array within { and } marks. When using new, you must specify how many different items are stored in the array. Each item in an array is called an element. The following statement creates an array and sets aside space for the values that it holds:

```
int[] elfSeniority = new int[250];
```

This example creates an array of integers called elfSeniority. The array has 250 elements that can store the months that each of Santa's elves has been employed at the Pole. (If Santa runs a union shop, this information is extremely important to track.)

When you create an array with the `new` statement, you must specify the number of elements. Each element of the array is given an initial value that depends on the type of the array. All numeric arrays have the initial value 0, `char` arrays equal `'\0'`, and `boolean` arrays have the value `false`. A `String` array and all other objects are created with the initial value of `null`.

For arrays that are not extremely large, you can set up their initial values at the same time that you create them. The following example creates an array of strings and gives them initial values:

```
String[] reindeerNames = { "Dasher", "Dancer", "Prancer", "Vixen",
    "Comet", "Cupid", "Donner", "Blitzen" };
```

The information that should be stored in elements of the array is placed between { and } brackets with commas separating each element. The number of elements in the array is set to the number of elements in the comma-separated list.

Array elements are numbered, beginning with 0 for the first element. A specific element can be accessed by referring to this number within [and] brackets. The preceding statement accomplishes the same thing as the following code:

```
String[] reindeerNames = new String[8];
reindeerNames[0]  = "Dasher";
reindeerNames[1]  = "Dancer";
reindeerNames[2]  = "Prancer";
reindeerNames[3]  = "Vixen";
reindeerNames[4]  = "Comet";
reindeerNames[5]  = "Cupid";
reindeerNames[6]  = "Donner";
reindeerNames[7]  = "Blitzen";
```

Each element of the array must be of the same type. Here, a string is used to hold each of the reindeer names.

After the array is created, you cannot make room for more elements. Even if you recall the most famous reindeer of all, you can't add "Rudolph" as the ninth element of the `reindeerNames` array. The Java compiler won't let poor Rudolph join in any `reindeerNames`.

Using Arrays

You use arrays in a program as you would in any variable, with one difference: The element number of the array item must be provided between the square brackets next to the array's name. You can use an array element anywhere a variable could be used, as in these statements:

```
elfSeniority[193] += 1;
niceChild[9428] = "Eli";
currentNation = 413;
if (hostileAirTravelNations[currentNation] == true) {
    sendGiftByMail();
}
```

Because the first element of an array is numbered 0 instead of 1, this means that the highest number is one less than you might expect. Consider the following statement:

```
String[] topGifts = new String[10];
```

This statement creates an array of string variables numbered from 0 to 9. If you referred to `topGifts[10]` somewhere in the program, you would get an error message referring to an `ArrayIndexOutOfBoundsException`.

Exception is another word for error in Java programs. This exception is an "array index out of bounds" error, which means that a program tried to use an array element that doesn't exist within its defined boundaries. You learn more about exceptions during Hour 14, "Handling Errors in a Program."

If you want to check the upper limit of an array so you can avoid going beyond that limit, a variable called `length` is associated with every array. The `length` variable is an integer that contains the number of elements an array holds. The following example creates an array and then reports its length:

```
String[] reindeerNames = { "Dasher", "Dancer", "Prancer", "Vixen",
    "Comet", "Cupid", "Donder", "Blitzen", "Rudolph" };
System.out.println("There are " + reindeerNames.length + " reindeer.");
```

In this example, the value of `reindeerNames.length` is 9, which means that the highest element number you can specify is 8.

You can work with text in Java as a string or an array of characters. When you're working with strings, one useful technique is to put each character in a string into its own element of a character array. To do this, call the string's `toCharArray()` method, which produces a char array with the same number of elements as the length of the string.

This hour's first project uses both techniques introduced in this section. The `SpaceRemover` program displays a string with all space characters replaced by periods (`.`).

To get started, open the Java24 project in NetBeans, choose File, New File and create a new Empty Java File called `SpaceRemover` in the `com.java24hours` package. Enter Listing 9.1 in the source editor and save it when you're done.

LISTING 9.1   The Full Text of `SpaceRemover.java`

```
1: package com.java24hours;
2:
3: class SpaceRemover {
4:     public static void main(String[] arguments) {
5:         String mostFamous = "Rudolph the Red-Nosed Reindeer";
6:         char[] mfl = mostFamous.toCharArray();
```

```
 7:              for (int dex = 0; dex < mfl.length; dex++) {
 8:                  char current = mfl[dex];
 9:                  if (current != ' ') {
10:                      System.out.print(current);
11:                  } else {
12:                      System.out.print('.');
13:                  }
14:              }
15:              System.out.println();
16:          }
17: }
```

Run the program with the command Run, Run File to see the output shown in Figure 9.1.

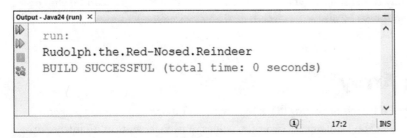

FIGURE 9.1
The output of the SpaceRemover program.

The SpaceRemover application stores the text "Rudolph the Red-Nosed Reindeer" in two places: a string called mostFamous and a char array called mfl. The array is created in Line 6 by calling the toCharArray() method of mostFamous, which fills an array with one element for each character in the text. The character 'R' goes into element 0, 'u' into element 1, and so on, up to the final 'r' in element 29.

The for loop in Lines 7–14 looks at each character in the mfl array. If the character is not a space, it is displayed. If it is a space, a '.' character is displayed instead.

Multidimensional Arrays

The arrays thus far in the hour all have one dimension, so you can retrieve an element using a single number. Some types of information require more dimensions to store as arrays, such as points in an (x,y) coordinate system. One dimension of the array could store the x coordinate and the other dimension could store the y coordinate.

To create an array that has two dimensions, you must use an additional set of square brackets when creating and using the array, as in these statements:

```
boolean[][] selectedPoint = new boolean[50][50];
selectedPoint[4][13] = true;
selectedPoint[7][6] = true;
selectedPoint[11][22] = true;
```

This example creates an array of Boolean values called `selectedPoint`. The array has 50 elements in its first dimension and 50 elements in its second dimension, so there are 2,500 individual array elements (50 × 50). When the array is created, each element is given the default value of `false`. Three elements are given the value `true`: a point at the (x,y) position of 4,13, one at 7,6, and one at 11,22.

Arrays can have as many dimensions as you need, but keep in mind that they can take up a lot of memory. Creating the 50 by 50 `selectedPoint` array was equivalent to creating 2,500 individual variables.

Sorting an Array

When you have grouped a bunch of similar items together into an array, one thing you can do is rearrange items. The following statements swap the values of two elements in an integer array called `numbers`:

```
int[] numbers = { 3, 7, 9, 12, 5, 0, 8, 19 };
int temporary = numbers[5];
numbers[5] = numbers[6];
numbers[6] = temporary;
```

These statements result in `numbers[5]` and `numbers[6]` trading values with each other. The integer variable called `temporary` is used as a temporary storage place for one of the values being swapped. Sorting is the process of arranging a list of related items into a set order, such as when a list of numbers is sorted from lowest to highest.

Santa Claus could use sorting to arrange the order of gift recipients by last name with Willie Aames and Hank Aaron raking in their Yuletide plunder much earlier than alphabetical unfortunates Steve Zahn and Mark Zuckerberg.

Sorting an array is easy in Java because the `Arrays` class does all the work. `Arrays`, which is part of the `java.util` group of classes, can rearrange arrays of all variable types.

To use the Arrays class in a program, undertake the following steps:

1. Use the import java.util.* statement to make it easier to use java.util classes in the program.

2. Create the array.

3. Use the sort() method of the Arrays class to rearrange an array.

An array of variables that is sorted by the Arrays class is rearranged into ascending numerical order. Characters and strings are arranged in alphabetical order.

To see this in action, create a new Empty Java File named NameSorter in the com.java24hours package and enter the text of Listing 9.2 in the source editor.

LISTING 9.2   The Full Source Code of NameSorter.java

```
 1: package com.java24hours;
 2:
 3: import java.util.*;
 4:
 5: class NameSorter {
 6:     public static void main(String[] arguments) {
 7:         String names[] = { "Glimmer", "Marvel", "Rue", "Clove",
 8:             "Thresh", "Foxface", "Cato", "Peeta", "Katniss" };
 9:         System.out.println("The original order:");
10:         for (int i = 0; i < names.length; i++) {
11:             System.out.println(i + ": " + names[i]);
12:         }
13:         System.out.println();
14:         Arrays.sort(names);
15:         System.out.println("The new order:");
16:         for (int i = 0; i < names.length; i++) {
17:             System.out.println(i + ": " + names[i]);
18:         }
19:         System.out.println();
20:     }
21: }
```

When you run this program, it displays a list of nine names in their original order, sorts the names, and then redisplays the list. Figure 9.2 shows the output.

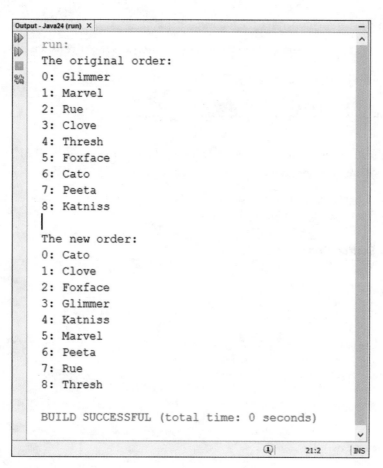

FIGURE 9.2
The output of the NameSorter program.

When you're working with strings and the basic types of variables such as integers and floating-point numbers, you only can sort them by ascending order using the Arrays class. You can write code to do your own sorts by hand if you desire a different arrangement of elements during a sort or you want better efficiency than the Arrays class provides.

Counting Characters in Strings

The letters that appear most often in English are E, R, S, T, L, N, C, D, M, and O, in that order. This is a fact worth knowing if you ever find yourself on the syndicated game show *Wheel of Fortune*.

NOTE

If you're unfamiliar with the show, *Wheel of Fortune* is a game in which three contestants guess the letters of a phrase, name, or quote. If they get a letter right and it's a consonant, they win the amount of money spun on a big wheel. To re-create the experience, play hangman with your friends in front of a studio audience, hand out random amounts of money when someone guesses a letter correctly, and give the winner a new Shark Rotator vacuum.

Your next Java program counts letter frequency in as many different phrases and expressions as you care to type. An array is used to count the number of times that each letter appears. When you're done, the program presents the number of times each letter appeared in the phrases.

Create a new Empty Java File in NetBeans called `Wheel.java`, put it in the `com.java24hours` package, fill it with the contents of Listing 9.3, and save the file when you're finished. Feel free to add additional phrases between Lines 17 and 18, formatting them exactly like Line 17.

LISTING 9.3   **The Full Source Code of** `Wheel.java`

```
 1: package com.java24hours;
 2:
 3: class Wheel {
 4:     public static void main(String[] arguments) {
 5:         String phrase[] = {
 6:             "A STITCH IN TIME SAVES NINE",
 7:             "DON'T EAT YELLOW SNOW",
 8:             "TASTE THE RAINBOW",
 9:             "EVERY GOOD BOY DOES FINE",
10:             "I WANT MY MTV",
11:             "I LIKE IKE",
12:             "PLAY IT AGAIN, SAM",
13:             "FROSTY THE SNOWMAN",
14:             "ONE MORE FOR THE ROAD",
15:             "HOME FIELD ADVANTAGE",
16:             "SHEFFIELD WEDNESDAY",
17:             "GROVER CLEVELAND OHIO",
18:             "SPAGHETTI WESTERN",
19:             "TEEN TITANS GO",
20:             "IT'S A WONDERFUL LIFE"
21:         };
22:         int[] letterCount = new int[26];
23:         for (int count = 0; count < phrase.length; count++) {
24:             String current = phrase[count];
25:             char[] letters = current.toCharArray();
26:             for (int count2 = 0;  count2 < letters.length; count2++) {
27:                 char lett = letters[count2];
28:                 if ( (lett >= 'A') & (lett <= 'Z') ) {
29:                     letterCount[lett - 'A']++;
```

```
30:                        }
31:                    }
32:                }
33:            for (char count = 'A'; count <= 'Z'; count++) {
34:                System.out.print(count + ": " +
35:                    letterCount[count - 'A'] +
36:                    " ");
37:                if (count == 'M') {
38:                    System.out.println();
39:                }
40:            }
41:            System.out.println();
42:        }
43: }
```

If you run the program without adding your own phrases, the output should be Figure 9.3.

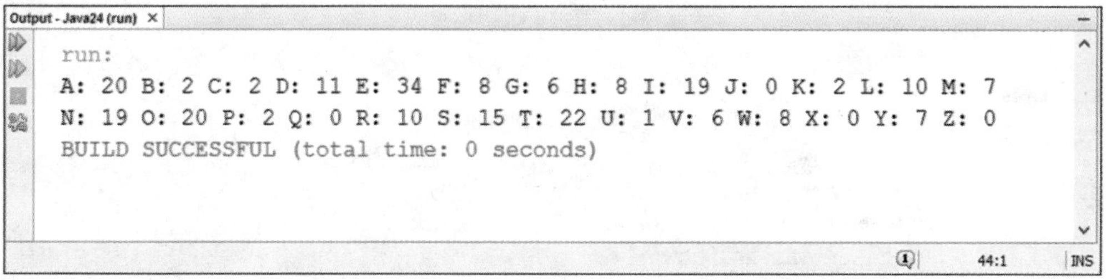

FIGURE 9.3
The output of the Wheel program.

The following things are taking place in the Wheel program:

▶ Lines 5–21—Phrases are stored in a string array called phrase.

▶ Line 22—An integer array called letterCount is created with 26 elements. This array is used to store the number of times each letter appears. The order of the elements is from 'A' to 'Z'. letterCount[0] stores the count for letter 'A', letterCount[1] stores the count for 'B', and so on, up to letterCount[25] for 'Z'.

▶ Line 23—A for loop cycles through the phrases stored in the phrase array. The phrase. length variable is used to end the loop after the last phrase is reached.

▶ Line 24—A string variable named current is set with the value of the current element of the phrase array.

▶ Line 25—A character array is created and stores all the characters in the current phrase.

▶ Line 26—A for loop cycles through the letters of the current phrase. The letters. length variable is used to end the loop after the last letter is reached.

▶ Line 27—A character variable called `lett` is created with the value of the current letter. In addition to their text value, characters have a numeric value. Because elements of an array are numbered, the numeric value of each character is used to determine its element number.

▶ Lines 28–30—An `if` statement weeds out all characters that are not part of the alphabet, such as punctuation and spaces. An element of the `letterCount` array is increased by 1 depending on the numeric value of the current character, which is stored in `lett`. The numeric values of the alphabet range from 65 for 'A' to 90 for 'Z'. Because the `letterCount` array begins at 0 and ends at 25, 'A' (65) is subtracted from `lett` to determine which array element to increase.

▶ Line 33—A `for` loop cycles through the alphabet from 'A' to 'Z'.

▶ Lines 34–40—The current letter is displayed followed by a semicolon and the number of times the letter appeared in the phrases stored in the `phrase` array. When the current letter is 'M', a newline is displayed so the output is spread out over two lines.

This project shows how two nested `for` loops can be used to cycle through a group of phrases one letter at a time. Java attaches a numeric value to each character; this value is easier to use than the character inside arrays.

NOTE

The numeric values associated with each of the characters from 'A' to 'Z' are those used by the ASCII character set. The ASCII character set is part of Unicode, the full character set supported by the Java language. Unicode includes support for more than 60,000 different characters used in the world's written languages. ASCII is limited to just 256.

Summary

Arrays make it possible to store complicated types of information in a program and manipulate that information. They're ideal for anything that can be arranged in a list and can be accessed easily using the loop statements that you learned about during Hour 8, "Repeating an Action with Loops."

To be honest, the information-processing needs of Santa Claus probably have outgrown arrays. More children are manufactured each year, and the gifts they want are constantly increasing in complexity and expense.

Your programs are likely to use arrays to store information that is unwieldy to work with using variables, even if you're not making any lists or checking them twice.

Workshop

Q&A

Q. Is the numeric range of the alphabet, from 65 for 'A' to 90 for 'Z', part of the basic Java language? If so, what are 1 through 64 reserved for?

A. The numbers 1 through 64 include numerals, punctuation marks, and some unprintable characters, such as linefeed, newline, and backspace. A number is associated with each printable character that can be used in a Java program, as well as some unprintable ones. Java uses the Unicode numbering system. The first 127 characters are from the ASCII character set, which you might have used in another programming language.

Q. In a multidimensional array, is it possible to use the `length` variable to measure different dimensions other than the first?

A. You can test any dimension of the array. For the first dimension, use `length` with the name of the array, as in `x.length`. Subsequent dimensions can be measured by using `length` with the `[0]` element of that dimension. Consider an array called `data` that was created with the following statement:

```
int[][][] data = new int[12][13][14];
```

The dimensions of this array can be measured by using the `data.length` variable for the first dimension, `data[0].length` for the second, and `data[0][0].length` for the third.

Q. Why does New England Patriots head coach Bill Belichick wear that scruffy hoodie on the sidelines?

A. When you have the highest number of wins over a decade than any coach in NFL history—140 from 2003 to 2012—your boss lets you set your own dress code. Sportswriters believe that Belichick began wearing the cut-off hoodie in response to an NFL deal with Reebok that required all coaches to wear licensed team apparel.

"He decided that if they were going to make him wear team apparel then he'd sift through the options and put on the absolute ugliest thing he could find," Dan Wetzel of Yahoo! Sports explained. "He chose a grey sweatshirt, often with a hood."

Belichick's passive-aggressive fashion statement has turned the hoodie into one of the team's best-selling items.

Quiz

If your brain were an array, you could test its `length` by answering each of the following questions about arrays.

1. What types of information are arrays best suited for?

    A. Lists

    B. Pairs of related information

    C. Trivia

2. What variable can you use to check the upper boundary of an array?

    A. `top`

    B. `length`

    C. `limit`

3. How many reindeer does Santa have, including Rudolph?

    A. 8

    B. 9

    C. 10

Answers

1. **A.** Lists that contain nothing but the same type of information—strings, numbers, and so on—are well-suited for storage in arrays.

2. **B.** The `length` variable contains a count of the number of elements in an array.

3. **B.** Santa had "eight tiny reindeer," according to Clement Clarke Moore's "A Visit from St. Nicholas," so Rudolph makes nine.

Activities

To give yourself an array of experiences to draw from later, you can expand your knowledge of this hour's topics with the following activities:

▶ Create a program that uses a multidimensional array to store student grades. The first dimension should be a number for each student, and the second dimension should be for each student's grades. Display the average of all the grades earned by each student and an overall average for every student.

▶ Write a program that stores the first 400 numbers that are multiples of 13 in an array.

To see Java programs that implement these activities, visit the book's website at www.java24hours.com.

HOUR 10
Creating Your First Object

This Hour's To-Do List:

▶ Create an object.
▶ Describe an object with attributes.
▶ Determine how objects behave.
▶ Combine objects.
▶ Inherit from other objects.
▶ Convert objects and other types of information.

One of the more fearsome examples of jargon that you encounter during these 24 hours is *object-oriented programming* (OOP). This complicated term describes, in an elegant way, what a computer program is and how it works.

Before OOP, a computer program was usually described under the simplest definition you've learned in this book: a set of instructions listed in a file and handled in some kind of reliable order.

By thinking of a program as a collection of objects, you figure out the tasks a program must accomplish and assign the tasks to the objects where they best belong.

How Object-Oriented Programming Works

You can think of the Java programs you create as objects, just like physical objects that exist in the real world. Objects exist independently of other objects, interact in specific ways, and can be combined with other objects to form something bigger. If you think of a computer program as a group of objects that interact with each other, you can design a program that's more reliable, easier to understand, and reusable in other projects.

In Hour 22, "Creating Java2D Graphics," you create a Java program that displays pie graphs—circles with different-colored pie slices to represent data. The chart created by that program is shown in Figure 10.1.

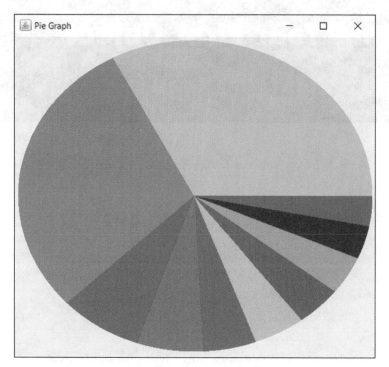

FIGURE 10.1
A pie chart produced by a Java program.

Each object has things that make it different from other objects. Pie charts are circular, whereas bar graphs represent data as a series of rectangles. A pie chart is an object that is made up of smaller objects—individual slices of different colors, a legend identifying what each slice represents, and a title. If you break down computer programs in the same way a pie chart is broken down, you're engaging in OOP.

In OOP, an object contains two things: attributes and behavior. *Attributes* are things that describe the object and show how it is different from other objects. *Behavior* is what an object does.

You create objects in Java by using a class as a template. A *class* is a master copy of the object that determines the attributes and behavior an object should have. The term class should be familiar to you because Java programs are called classes. Every program you create with Java is a class that you can use as a template for the creation of new objects. As an example, any Java program that uses strings is using objects created from the String class. This class contains attributes that determine what a String object is and behavior that determines what String objects can do.

With OOP, a computer program is a group of objects that work together to get something done. Some simple programs might seem as though they consist of only one object: the class file. Even those programs are using other objects to get work done.

Objects in Action

Consider the program that displays a pie chart. A `PieChart` object could consist of the following:

▶ Behavior to calculate the size of each pie slice

▶ Behavior to draw the chart

▶ An attribute to store the title of the chart

It might seem odd to ask the `PieChart` object to draw itself because graphs don't draw themselves in the real world. Objects in OOP work for themselves whenever possible. This capability makes it easier to incorporate them in other programs. If a `PieChart` object did not know how to draw itself, for instance, every time you used that `PieChart` object in another program, you would have to create behavior to draw it.

For another example of OOP, consider the autodialer program that Matthew Broderick's character used in the classic hacker movie *WarGames* to find computers he could break into.

NOTE

An autodialer is software that uses a device called a modem to dial a series of phone numbers in sequence. The purpose of such a program is to find other computers that answer the phone, so you can call them later to see what they are.

Readers younger than 30 might find it hard to believe that computers used to make connections to each other with phone calls. You had to know a computer's phone number to connect to it, and if it already was talking to another computer, you got a busy signal.

Now I probably need to explain what a busy signal is.

To quote the poet T.S. Eliot, "I grow old … I grow old."

Using an autodialer today would attract the attention of your local phone company and law enforcement. Back in the 1980s, it was a good way to be rebellious without leaving the house. David Lightman (the character portrayed by Broderick) used his autodialer to look for a video game company's private computer system so he could play the company's new game before it was released. Instead, Lightman found a secret government computer that could play everything from chess to Global Thermonuclear War.

An autodialer, like any computer program, can be thought of as a group of objects that work together. It could be broken down into the following:

▶ A Modem object, which knows its attributes such as connection speed and has behavior to make the modem dial a number and detect when another computer has answered the call

▶ A Monitor object, which keeps track of what numbers are called and which ones are computers

Each object exists independently of the other.

One advantage of designing a completely independent Modem object is that it could be used in other programs that need modem functionality.

Another reason to use self-contained objects is that they are easier to debug. Computer programs quickly grow unwieldy in size. If you're debugging something like a Modem object and you know it's not dependent on anything else, you can focus on making sure the Modem object does the job it's supposed to do and holds the information that it needs to do its job.

Learning an object-oriented language such as Java as your first programming language can be advantageous because you're not unlearning the habits of other styles of programming.

What Objects Are

Objects are created by using a class of objects as a template. The following statements create a class:

```
public class Modem {
}
```

An object created from this class can't do anything because it doesn't have any attributes or behavior. You need to add those to make the class useful, as in the following statements:

```
public class Modem {
    int speed;

    public void displaySpeed() {
        System.out.println("Speed: " + speed);
    }
}
```

The Modem class now should be starting to look like programs you've written during Hours 1 through 9. The Modem class begins with a class statement, except that it has the word public in it. This means that the class is available for use by the public—in other words, by any program that wants to use Modem objects.

The first part of the `Modem` class creates an integer variable called `speed`. This variable is an attribute of the object.

The second part of the `Modem` class is a method called `displaySpeed()`. This method is part of the object's behavior. It contains one statement, `System.out.println()`, which reveals the modem's `speed` value.

An object's variables are called instance variables or member variables.

If you want to use a `Modem` object in a program, you create the object with the following statement:

```
Modem device = new Modem();
```

This statement creates a `Modem` object called `device`. After you have created an object, you can set its variables and call its methods. Here's how to set the value of the `speed` variable of the `device` object:

```
device.speed = 28800;
```

To make this modem display its speed by calling the `displaySpeed()` method, you call the method:

```
device.displaySpeed();
```

The `Modem` object named `device` could respond to this statement by displaying the text "Speed: 28800."

Understanding Inheritance

A big advantage to OOP is *inheritance*, which enables one object to inherit behavior and attributes from another object.

When you start creating objects, you sometimes find that a new object you want is a lot like an object you already have.

What if David Lightman wanted an object that could handle error correction and other advanced modem features that weren't around in 1983 when *WarGames* was released? Lightman could create a new `ErrorCorrectionModem` object by copying the statements of the `Modem` object and revising them. However, if most of the behavior and attributes of `ErrorCorrectionModem` are the same as those of `Modem`, this is a lot of unnecessary work. It also means that Lightman would have two separate programs to update if something needed to be changed later.

Through inheritance, a programmer can create a new class of objects by defining how they are different from an existing class. Lightman could make `ErrorCorrectionModem` inherit from `Modem`, and all he would need to write are things that make error-correction modems different than modems.

A class of objects inherits from another class by using the `extends` statement. The following is a skeleton of an `ErrorCorrectionModem` class that inherits from the `Modem` class:

```
public class ErrorCorrectionModem extends Modem {
    // program goes here
}
```

Building an Inheritance Hierarchy

Inheritance, which enables a variety of related classes to be developed without redundant work, makes it possible for code to be passed down from one class to another class to another class. This parent-to-child grouping of classes is called a *class hierarchy*, and all the standard classes you can use in your Java programs are part of a hierarchy.

Understanding a hierarchy is easier if you understand subclasses and superclasses. A class that inherits from another class is called a *subclass*. The class that is inherited from is called a *superclass*.

In the preceding *WarGames* example, the `Modem` class is the superclass of the `ErrorCorrectionModem` class. `ErrorCorrectionModem` is the subclass of `Modem`.

A class can have more than one class that inherits from it in the hierarchy—another subclass of `Modem` could be `ISDNModem` because ISDN modems have behavior and attributes that make them different from error-correction modems. If there was a subclass of `ErrorCorrectionModem` such as `InternalErrorCorrectionModem`, it would inherit from all classes above it in the hierarchy—both `ErrorCorrectionModem` and `Modem`. These inheritance relationships are shown in Figure 10.2.

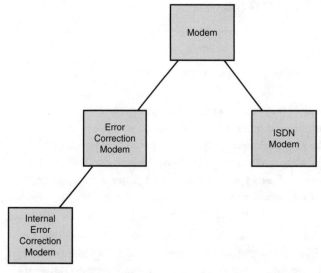

FIGURE 10.2
An example of a class hierarchy.

The classes that make up the Java language extensively use inheritance, so understanding it is essential. You learn more about the subject during Hour 12, "Making the Most of Existing Objects."

Converting Objects and Simple Variables

One of the most common tasks you need to accomplish in Java is to convert information from one form into another. Several types of conversions you can do include the following:

▶ Converting an object into another object

▶ Converting a simple variable into another type of variable

▶ Using an object to create a simple variable

▶ Using a simple variable to create an object

Simple variables are the basic data types you learned about during Hour 5, "Storing and Changing Information in a Program." Some of these types are `int`, `float`, `char`, `long`, `double`, `byte`, and `short`.

When using a method or an expression in a program, you must use the right type of information that's expected by these methods and expressions. A method that expects a `Calendar` object must receive a `Calendar` object, for instance. If you used a method that takes a single integer argument and you sent it a floating-point number instead, an error would occur when you attempted to compile the program.

NOTE
_____

When a method requires a string argument, you can use the + operator to combine several different types of information in that argument. As long as one of the things being combined is a string, the combined argument is converted into a string.

_____

Converting information to a new form is called *casting*. Casting produces a new value that is a different type of variable or object than its source. You don't actually change the value when casting. Instead, a new variable or object is created in the format you need.

The terms source and destination are useful when discussing the concept of casting. The *source* is some kind of information in its original form—whether it's a variable or an object. The *destination* is the converted version of the source in a new form.

Casting Simple Variables

With simple variables, casting occurs most commonly between numeric variables such as integers and floating-point numbers. One type of variable that cannot be used in any casting is Boolean values.

To cast information into a new format, you precede it with the new format surrounded by parentheses. For example, if you want to cast something into a `long` variable, you precede it with `(long)`. The following statements cast a `float` value into an `int`:

```
float source = 7.00F;
int destination = (int) source;
```

In variable casting where the destination holds larger values than the source, the value is converted easily, such as when a `byte` is cast into an `int`. A `byte` holds values from –128 to 127, whereas an `int` holds values from –2.1 billion to 2.1 billion. No matter what value the `byte` variable holds, the new `int` variable has plenty of room for it.

You sometimes can use a variable in a different format without casting it at all. For example, you can use `char` variables as if they were `int` variables. Also, you can use `int` variables as if they were `long` variables, and any numeric type can be used as a `double`.

In most cases, because the destination provides more room than the source, the information is converted without changing its value. The main exceptions occur when an `int` or `long` variable is cast to a `float`, or a `long` is cast into a `double`.

When you are converting information from a larger variable type into a smaller type, you must explicitly cast it, as in the following statements:

```
int xNum = 103;
byte val = (byte) xNum;
```

Here, casting converts an integer value called `xNum` into a `byte` variable called `val`. This is an example where the destination variable holds a smaller range of values than the source variable. A `byte` holds integer values ranging from –128 to 127, and an `int` holds a much larger range of integer values.

When the source variable in a casting operation has a value that doesn't fit in the destination variable type, Java changes the value to make the cast fit successfully. This can produce unexpected results and should be avoided.

Casting Objects

You can cast objects into other objects when the source and destination are related by inheritance. One class must be a subclass of the other.

Some objects do not require casting at all. You can use an object where any of its superclasses are expected. All objects in Java are subclasses of the `Object` class, so you can use any object as an argument when an `Object` is expected.

You also can use an object where one of its subclasses is expected. However, because subclasses usually contain more information than their superclasses, you might lose some of this information. For instance, if the object doesn't have a method that the subclass would contain, an error results if that missing method is used in the program.

To use an object in place of one of its subclasses, you must cast it explicitly with statements such as the following:

```
public void paintComponent(Graphics comp) {
    Graphics2D comp2D = (Graphics2D) comp;
}
```

This casts a `Graphics` object called `comp` into a `Graphics2D` object called `comp2D`. You don't lose any information in the cast, but you gain all the methods and variables the subclass defines.

Converting Simple Variables to Objects and Back

There are classes in Java for each of the simple variable types including `Boolean`, `Byte`, `Character`, `Double`, `Float`, `Integer`, `Long`, and `Short`. All these classes are capitalized because they are objects, not simple variable types.

Working with these objects is as easy as using their corresponding types. The following statement creates an `Integer` object with the value 5309:

```
Integer suffix = 5309;
```

This statement creates an `Integer` object called `suffix` that represents the `int` value 5309.

After you have created an object like this, you can use it like any other object. To get an `int` value from the preceding `suffix` object, you could use the following statement:

```
int newSuffix = suffix;
```

This statement causes the `newSuffix` variable to have the value 5309, expressed as an `int` value.

Java's capability to use the basic data type and object forms of a value interchangeably is made possible through autoboxing and unboxing.

Autoboxing casts a simple variable value to the corresponding class.

Unboxing casts an object to the corresponding simple value.

These features work behind the scenes, assuring that when you are expecting a simple data type like `float`, an object is converted to the matching data type with the same value. When you're expecting an object like `Float`, a data type is converted to an object as necessary.

One common conversion from an object to a variable is to use a string in a numeric expression. When the string's value could become an integer, this can be done using the `parseInt()` method of the `Integer` class, as in this example:

```
String count = "25";
int myCount = Integer.parseInt(count);
```

This converts a string with the text "25" into an integer with the value 25. If the string value was not a valid integer, the conversion would not work.

The next project you create is `NewRoot`, an application that converts a string value in a command-line argument to a numeric value, a common technique when you're taking input from a user at the command line.

Return to your `Java24` project in NetBeans, choose File, New File, and then create a new Empty Java File named `NewRoot` in the `com.java24hours` package. Enter Listing 10.1 in the source editor and remember to save the file.

LISTING 10.1   The Full Text of `NewRoot.java`

```
 1: package com.java24hours;
 2:
 3: class NewRoot {
 4:     public static void main(String[] arguments) {
 5:         int number = 100;
 6:         if (arguments.length > 0) {
 7:             number = Integer.parseInt(arguments[0]);
 8:         }
 9:         System.out.println("The square root of "
10:             + number
11:             + " is "
12:             + Math.sqrt(number)
13:         );
14:     }
15: }
```

Before you run the program, you must configure NetBeans to run it with a command-line argument:

1. Choose the menu command Run, Set Project Configuration, Customize. The Project Properties window opens.

2. Enter `com.java24hours.NewRoot` as the Main Class.

3. Enter `9025` in the Arguments field.

4. Click OK to close the dialog.

To run the program, choose Run, Run Main Project (instead of Run, Run File). The program displays the number and its square root, as shown in Figure 10.3.

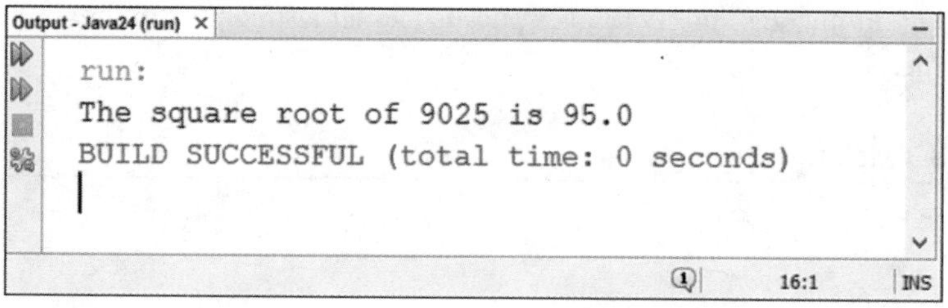

```
Output - Java24 (run)  ×
run:
The square root of 9025 is 95.0
BUILD SUCCESSFUL (total time: 0 seconds)

                                        16:1    INS
```

FIGURE 10.3
The output of the NewRoot program.

The NewRoot application is an expansion of an earlier tutorial from Hour 4, "Understanding How Java Programs Work," that displayed the square root of the integer 225.

That program would have been more useful if it took a number submitted by a user and displayed its square root. This requires conversion from a string to an integer. All command-line arguments are stored as elements of a String array, so you must cast them to numbers before using them in mathematical expressions.

To create an integer value based on the contents of a string, you call the Integer.parseInt() method with the string as the only argument, as in Line 7:

```
number = Integer.parseInt(arguments[0]);
```

The arguments[0] array element holds the first command-line argument submitted when the application is run. When the program was run with "9025" as an argument, the string "9025" was converted to the int 9025.

Change the command-line argument from 9025 to other numbers, and run the program several more times.

Creating an Object

To see a working example of classes and inheritance in this hour's next project, you create classes that represent two types of objects: cable modems, which are implemented as the CableModem class, and DSL modems, which are implemented as the DslModem class. The workshop focuses on simple attributes and behavior for these objects:

▶ Each object should have a speed that it can display.

▶ Each object should be able to connect to the Internet.

One thing that cable modems and DSL modems have in common is that they both have a speed. Because this is something they share, it can be put into a class that is the superclass of both the `CableModem` and `DslModem` classes. Call this class `Modem`. In NetBeans, create a new empty Java class called `Modem` in the `com.java24hours` package. Enter Listing 10.2 in the source editor and save the file.

LISTING 10.2   The Full Text of `Modem.java`

```
1: package com.java24hours;
2:
3: public class Modem {
4:     int speed;
5:
6:     public void displaySpeed() {
7:         System.out.println("Speed: " + speed);
8:     }
9: }
```

This file is compiled automatically as `Modem.class`. You cannot run this program directly, but you can use it in other classes. The `Modem` class can handle one of the things that the `CableModem` and `DslModem` classes have in common. By using the `extends` statement when you are creating the `CableModem` and `DslModem` classes, you can make each of them a subclass of `Modem`.

Start a new Empty Java File in NetBeans with the class name `CableModem` in the `com.java24hours` package. Enter Listing 10.3 and save the file.

LISTING 10.3   The Full Text of `CableModem.java`

```
 1: package com.java24hours;
 2:
 3: public class CableModem extends Modem {
 4:     String method = "cable connection";
 5:
 6:     public void connect() {
 7:         System.out.println("Connecting to the Internet ...");
 8:         System.out.println("Using a " + method);
 9:     }
10: }ok
```

Create a third file in NetBeans named `DslModem` in the `com.java24hours` package. Enter Listing 10.4 and save the file.

LISTING 10.4   **The Full Text of** DslModem.java

```
 1: package com.java24hours;
 2:
 3: public class DslModem extends Modem {
 4:     String method = "DSL phone connection";
 5:
 6:     public void connect() {
 7:         System.out.println("Connecting to the Internet ...");
 8:         System.out.println("Using a " + method);
 9:     }
10: }
```

If there were no errors, you now have three class files: Modem.class, CableModem.class, and DslModem.class. However, you cannot run any of these class files because they do not have main() blocks like the ones in other programs you've created. You need to create a short application to test out the class hierarchy you have just built.

Return to NetBeans and create a new Empty Java File with the class name ModemTester in com.java24hours. Enter Listing 10.5 in the source editor and save the file.

LISTING 10.5   **The Full Text of** ModemTester.java

```
 1: package com.java24hours;
 2:
 3: public class ModemTester {
 4:     public static void main(String[] arguments) {
 5:         CableModem surfBoard = new CableModem();
 6:         DslModem gateway = new DslModem();
 7:         surfBoard.speed = 500000;
 8:         gateway.speed = 400000;
 9:         System.out.println("Trying the cable modem:");
10:         surfBoard.displaySpeed();
11:         surfBoard.connect();
12:         System.out.println("Trying the DSL modem:");
13:         gateway.displaySpeed();
14:         gateway.connect();
15:     }
16: }
```

When you run the program, you should see output matching Figure 10.4.

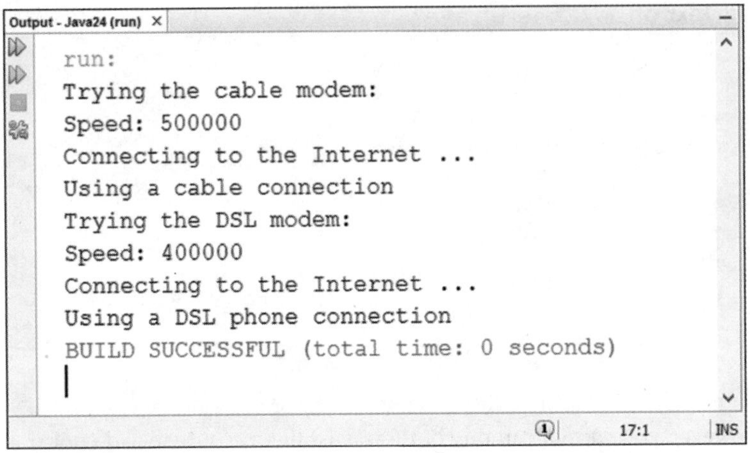

```
Output - Java24 (run)  ×                                           —
  ⏵  run:                                                          ⌃
  ⏵  Trying the cable modem:
  ◼  Speed: 500000
  ⚙  Connecting to the Internet ...
     Using a cable connection
     Trying the DSL modem:
     Speed: 400000
     Connecting to the Internet ...
     Using a DSL phone connection
     BUILD SUCCESSFUL (total time: 0 seconds)
     |
                                                                  ⌄
                                        ⓘ        17:1       INS
```

FIGURE 10.4
The output of the `ModemTester` program.

The following things are taking place in the program:

▶ Lines 5–6—Two new objects are created: a `CableModem` object called `surfBoard` and a `DslModem` object called `gateway`.

▶ Line 7—The `speed` variable of the `CableModem` object named `surfBoard` is set to 500000.

▶ Line 8—The `speed` variable of the `DslModem` object named `gateway` is set to 400000.

▶ Line 10—The `displaySpeed()` method of the `surfBoard` object is called. This method is inherited from `Modem`—even though it isn't present in the `CableModem` class, you can call it.

▶ Line 11—The `connect()` method of the `surfBoard` object is called.

▶ Line 12—The `displaySpeed()` method of the `gateway` object is called.

▶ Line 13—The `connect()` method of the `gateway` object is called.

Summary

After creating your first class of objects and arranging several classes into a hierarchy, you ought to be more comfortable with the term object-oriented programming and the fun acronym OOP. You learn more about object behavior and attributes in the next two hours as you start creating more sophisticated objects.

Terms such as program, class, and object make more sense as you become more experienced with this style of development. OOP is a concept that takes some time to get used to. When you have mastered it, you'll find that it's an effective way to design, develop, and debug computer programs.

Workshop

Q&A

Q. Can classes inherit from more than one class?

A. It's possible with classes in some programming languages (such as C++), but not Java. Multiple inheritance is a powerful feature, but it also makes OOP harder to learn and use. Java's developers decided to limit inheritance to one superclass for any class, although a class can have numerous subclasses. One way to compensate for this limitation is to inherit methods from a special type of class called an interface. You learn more about interfaces during Hour 15, "Creating a Threaded Program."

Q. When would you want to create a method that isn't `public`?

A. The main time to do that is when the method is strictly for the use of the program you're writing. If you're creating a game program and your `shootRayGun()` method is highly specific to the game you're writing, it could be a private method. To keep a method from being `public`, leave off the `public` statement in front of the method's name.

Q. Why is it possible to use `char` values as if they were `int` values?

A. A character can be used as an `int` variable because each character has a corresponding numeric code that represents its position in the character set. If you have a variable named k with the value 67, the cast `(char) k` produces the character value 'C' because the numeric code associated with a capital C is 67, according to the ASCII character set. The ASCII character set is part of the Unicode character standard adopted by the Java language.

Q. Does Tabasco hot sauce spoil?

A. No, it doesn't, though if you keep an opened bottle around for several years it will change color. The ingredients of vinegar, red pepper, and salt are an extremely inhospitable environment for bacterial growth.

McIlhenny Company, the makers of Tabasco, say the original brand has a shelf life of five years. Other versions have a shelf life from 18 months to three years.

As a huge fan of the product, I find it hard to believe anyone is keeping a bottle of Tabasco around long enough for this to be an issue.

Quiz

The following questions test your knowledge of objects and the programs that use them.

1. What statement is used to enable one class to inherit from another class?

   A. `inherits`

   B. `extends`

   C. `handItOverAndNobodyGetsHurt`

2. Why are compiled Java programs saved with the `.class` file extension?

   A. Java's developers think it's a classy language.

   B. It's a subtle tribute to the world's teachers.

   C. Every Java program is a class.

3. What are the two things that make up an object?

   A. Attributes and behavior

   B. Commands and data files

   C. Spit and vinegar

Answers

1. **B.** The `extends` statement is used because the subclass is an extension of the attributes and behavior of the superclass and of any superclasses above that in the class hierarchy.

2. **C.** Your programs are always made up of at least one main class and any other classes that are needed.

3. **A.** In a way, **B** also is true because commands are comparable to behavior, and data files are analogous to attributes.

Activities

If you don't object, you can `extends` your knowledge of this hour's topics with the following activities:

▶ Create a `Commodore64Modem` class with a speed of 300 and its own `connect()` method.

▶ Add a `disconnect()` method to one of the classes in the `Modem` project, deciding where it should go to support modem disconnection in cable, DSL, and Commodore 64 modems.

To see Java programs that implement these activities, visit the book's website at www. java24hours.com.

HOUR 11

Describing What Your Object Is Like

This Hour's To-Do List:

- ▶ Create variables for an object or class.
- ▶ Use methods with objects and classes.
- ▶ Call a method and return a value.
- ▶ Create a constructor.
- ▶ Send arguments to a method.
- ▶ Use `this` to refer to an object.
- ▶ Create new objects.

As you learned during the past hour's introduction to object-oriented programming (OOP), an object is a way of organizing a program so it has everything it needs to accomplish a task. Objects consist of attributes and behavior.

Attributes are the information stored within an object. They can be variables such as integers, characters, and Boolean values, or objects such as `String` and `Calendar` objects. Behavior is the groups of statements used to handle specific jobs within the object. Each of these groups is called a method.

Up to this point, you have been working with methods and variables of objects without knowing it. Anytime your statement had a period in it that wasn't a decimal point or part of a string, an object was involved.

Creating Variables

In this hour, you are looking at a sample class of objects called `Gremlin` whose sole purpose in life is to replicate themselves. A `Gremlin` has several different things it needs to do its work, and these are implemented as the behavior of the class. The information that's needed for the methods are stored as attributes.

The attributes of an object represent variables needed for the object to function. These variables could be simple data types such as integers, characters, and floating-point numbers, or they could be arrays or objects of classes such as String or Calendar. You can use an object's variables throughout its class, in any of the methods the object contains. By convention, you create variables immediately after the class statement that creates the class and before any methods.

One of the things that a Gremlin object needs is a unique identifier to set it apart from others of its kind (class).

The Gremlin object holds this identifier in an integer variable called guid. The following statements begin a class called Gremlin with an attribute called guid and two other attributes:

```
public class Gremlin {
    public int guid;
    public String creator = "Chris Columbus";
    int maximumAge = 240;
}
```

All three variables are attributes for the class: guid, maximumAge, and creator.

Putting a statement such as public in a variable declaration statement is called access control because it determines how other objects made from other classes can use that variable—or if they can use it at all.

Making a variable public makes it possible to modify the variable from another program that is using the Gremlin object.

If the other program wants to assign another creator, for instance, it can change creator to that value. The following statements create a Gremlin object called gizmo and set its creator variable:

```
Gremlin gizmo = new Gremlin();
gizmo.creator = "Joe Dante";
```

In the Gremlin class, the creator variable also is public, so it can be changed freely from other programs. The other variable, maximumAge, only can be used within the class itself.

When you make a variable in a class public, the class loses control over how that variable is used by other programs. In many cases, this might not be a problem. For example, the creator variable can be changed to any name that identifies the creator of the gremlin.

Restricting access to a variable keeps errors from occurring if the variable is set incorrectly by another program. The maximumAge variable contains the number of hours the gremlin will exist in its current form. It wouldn't make sense for maximumAge to be set to a negative value. If the Gremlin class of objects needs to guard against this problem, you need to do these two things:

▶ Switch the variable from public to protected or private, two other statements that provide more restrictive access.

▶ Add behavior to change the value of the variable and report the value of the variable to other programs.

You can use a `protected` variable only in the same class as the variable, any subclasses of that class, or by classes in the same package. A package is a group of related classes that serve a common purpose. An example is the `java.util` package, which contains classes that offer useful utilities such as date and time programming and file archiving. When you use the `import` statement in a Java program with an asterisk, as in `import java.util.*`, you are making it easier to refer to the classes of that package in a program.

A `private` variable is restricted even further than a `protected` variable—you can use it only in the same class. Unless you know that a variable can be changed to anything without affecting how its class functions, you should make the variable `private` or `protected`.

The following statement makes `guid` a `private` variable:

```
private int guid;
```

If you want other programs to use the `guid` variable in some way, you have to create behavior that makes it possible. This task is covered later in the hour.

There also is another type of access control: the lack of any `public`, `private`, or `protected` statement when the variable is created.

In most of the programs you have developed prior to this hour, you didn't specify any access control. When no access control is set, the variable is available only to classes in the same package. This is called default or package access.

Creating Class Variables

When you create an object, it has its own version of all variables that are part of the object's class. Each object created from the `Gremlin` class of objects has its own version of the `guid`, `maximumAge`, and `creator` variables. If you modified one of these variables in an object, it would not affect the same variable in another `Gremlin` object.

There are times when an attribute should describe an entire class of objects instead of a specific object itself. These are called class variables. If you want to keep track of how many `Gremlin` objects are being used in a program, you could use a class variable to store this information. Only one copy of the variable exists for the whole class. The variables you have been creating for objects thus far can be called object variables because they are associated with a specific object.

Both types of variables are created and used in the same way, but `static` is part of the statement that creates class variables. The following statement creates a class variable for the `Gremlin` example:

```
static int gremlinCount = 0;
```

Changing the value of a class variable is no different than changing an object's variables. If you have a `Gremlin` object called `stripe`, you could change the class variable `gremlinCount` with the following statement:

```
stripe.gremlinCount++;
```

Because class variables apply to an entire class, you also can use the name of the class instead:

```
Gremlin.gremlinCount++;
```

Both statements accomplish the same thing, but an advantage to using the name of the class when working with class variables is that it shows immediately that `gremlinCount` is a class variable instead of an object variable. If you always use object names when working with class variables, you can't tell whether they are class or object variables without looking carefully at the source code.

Class variables also are called static variables.

CAUTION
___
Although class variables are useful, you must take care not to overuse them. These variables exist for as long as the class is running. If a large array of objects is stored in class variables, it will take up a sizeable chunk of memory and never release it.
___

Creating Behavior with Methods

Attributes are the way to keep track of information about a class of objects, but for a class to do the things it was created to do, you must create behavior. Behavior describes the parts of a class that accomplish specific tasks. Each of these sections is called a method.

You have been using methods throughout your programs up to this point without knowing it, including one in particular: `println()`. This method displays text onscreen. Like variables, methods are used in connection with an object or a class. The name of the object or class is followed by a period and the name of the method, as in `object2.move()` or `Integer.parseInt()`.

NOTE
___
The `System.out.println()` method might seem confusing because it has two periods instead of one. This is because two classes are involved in the statement: the `System` class and the `PrintStream` class. The `System` class has a static variable called `out` that is a `PrintStream` object. `println()` is a method of the `PrintStream` class. The `System.out.println()` statement means, in effect, "Use the `println()` method of the `out` instance variable of the `System` class." You can chain together references in this way.
___

Declaring a Method

You create methods with a statement that looks similar to the statement that begins a class. Both can take arguments between parentheses after their names, and both use { and } marks at the beginning and end. The difference is that methods can send back a value after they are handled. The value can be one of the simple types such as integers or boolean values, or it can be a class of objects.

The following is an example of a method the `Gremlin` class can use to create a new gremlin:

```
public Gremlin replicate(String creator) {
    Gremlin noob = new Gremlin();
    noob.creator = "Steven Spielberg";
    return noob;
}
```

This method takes a single argument: a string variable called `creator`, which is a variable that represents the name of the creator.

In the statement that begins the method, `Gremlin` precedes the name of the method, `replicate`. This statement signifies that a `Gremlin` object is sent back after the method is handled. The `return` statement is what actually sends the object back. In this method, the value of `noob` is returned.

If a method should not return a value, use the keyword `void` in the statement that declares the method.

When a method returns a value, you can use the method as part of an expression. For example, if you created a `Gremlin` object called `haskins`, you could use statements such as these:

```
if (haskins.active() == true) {
    System.out.println(haskins.guid + " is active.");
}
```

You can use a method that returns a value at any place in the program where you could have used a variable.

Earlier in the hour, you switched the `guid` variable to `private` to prevent it from being read or modified by other programs.

When an instance variable is private, there's still a way to make it possible for `guid` to be used elsewhere: Create `public` methods in the `Gremlin` class that get the value of `guid` and set `guid` to a new value. These new methods should be `public`, unlike the `guid` variable itself, so they can be called in other programs.

Consider the following two methods:

```
public int getGuid() {
    return guid;
}
```

```
public void setGuid(int newValue) {
    if (newValue > 0) {
        guid = newValue;
    }
}
```

These methods are called *accessor methods* because they enable the guid variable to be accessed from other objects.

The getGuid() method is used to retrieve the current value of guid. The getGuid() method does not have any arguments, but it still must have parentheses after the method name. The setGuid() method takes one argument, an integer called newValue. This argument is the new value of guid. If newValue is greater than 0, the change will be made.

In this example, the Gremlin class controls how the guid variable can be used by other classes. This process is called *encapsulation*, and it's a fundamental concept of OOP. The better your objects are able to protect themselves against misuse, the more useful they are when you put them to work in other programs.

Although guid is private, the new methods getGuid() and setGuid() are able to work with guid because they are in the same class.

TIP
_____

An integrated development environment (IDE) often can create accessor methods automatically. NetBeans offers this capability. To see it in action, open the Modem class from Hour 10, "Creating Your First Object." Right-click anywhere in the source code editor and choose the menu command Refactor, Encapsulate Fields. A dialog opens. Click Select All, then click Refactor. NetBeans turns the speed variable private and creates new getSpeed() and setSpeed() methods.

_____

Similar Methods with Different Arguments

As you have seen with the setGuid() method, you can send arguments to a method to affect what it does. Different methods in a class can have different names, but methods also can have the same name if they have different arguments.

Two methods can have the same name if they have a different number of arguments or the arguments are of different variable types. For example, it might be useful for the Gremlin class of objects to have two tauntHuman() methods. One could have no arguments and would deliver a generic taunt. The other could specify the taunt as a string argument. The following statements implement these methods:

```
void tauntHuman() {
    System.out.println("That has gotta hurt!");
}
```

```
void tauntHuman(String taunt) {
    System.out.println(taunt);
}
```

The methods have the same name, but the arguments differ: one has no argument, the other has a single `String` argument. The arguments to a method are called the method's signature. A class can have different methods with the same name as long as each method has a different signature.

Constructors

When you want to create an object in a program, the `new` statement is used, as in the following example:

```
Gremlin clorr = new Gremlin();
```

This statement creates a new `Gremlin` object called `clorr`. When you use the `new` statement, a special method of that object's class is called. This method is called a constructor because it handles the work required to create the object. The purpose of a constructor is to set up any variables and call the methods that must take place for the object to function properly.

Constructors are defined like other methods, except they cannot return a value. The following are two constructors for the `Gremlin` class of objects:

```
public Gremlin() {
    creator = "Michael Finnell"; // creator is a string
    maximumAge = 240; // maximumAge is an int
}

public Gremlin(String name, int size) {
    creator = name;
    maximumAge = size;
}
```

Like other methods, constructors can use the arguments they are sent to define more than one constructor in a class. In this example, the first constructor would be called when a `new` statement such as the following is used:

```
Gremlin blender = new Gremlin();
```

The other constructor could be called only if a string and an integer are sent as arguments with the `new` statement, as in this example:

```
Gremlin plate = new Gremlin("Zach Galligan", 960);
```

If you don't include any constructors in a class, it inherits a single constructor with no arguments from its superclass. There also might be other constructors that it inherits, depending on the superclass used.

In any class, there must be a constructor that has the same number and type of arguments as the new statement that's used to create objects of that class. In the example of the Gremlin class, which has Gremlin() and Gremlin(String name, int size) constructors, you only could create Gremlin objects with two different types of new statements: one without arguments and one with a string and an integer as the only two arguments.

CAUTION

If your subclass defines a constructor with one or more arguments, the class will no longer inherit a constructor with no arguments from its superclass. For this reason, you must always define a no-argument constructor when your class has other constructors.

Class Methods

Like class variables, class methods are a way to provide functionality associated with an entire class instead of a specific object. Use a class method when the method does nothing that affects an individual object of the class. In Hour 10, you used the parseInt() method of the Integer class to convert a string to a variable of the type int:

```
int fontSize = Integer.parseInt(fontText);
```

This is a class method. To make a method into a class method, use static in front of the method name, as in the following code:

```
static void showGremlinCount() {
    System.out.println("There are " + gremlinCount + " gremlins");
}
```

The gremlinCount class variable was used earlier to keep track of how many Gremlin objects have been created by a program. The showGremlinCount() method is a class method that displays this total, and you can call it with a statement such as the following:

```
Gremlin.showGremlinCount();
```

Variable Scope within Methods

When you create a variable or an object inside a method in one of your classes, it is usable only inside that method. The reason for this is the concept of variable scope. Scope is the block in which a variable exists in a program. If you go outside of the part of the program defined by the scope, you can no longer use the variable.

The { and } brackets in a program define the boundaries for a variable's scope. Any variable created within these marks cannot be used outside of them. For example, consider the following statements:

```
if (numFiles < 1) {
    String warning = "No files remaining.";
}
System.out.println(warning);
```

This code does not work—and does not compile in NetBeans—because the warning variable was created inside the brackets of the if block. Those brackets define the scope of the variable. The warning variable does not exist outside of the brackets, so the System.out.println() method cannot use it as an argument.

When you use a set of brackets inside another set of brackets, you need to pay attention to the scope of the enclosed variables. Take a look at the following example:

```
if (humanCount < 5) {
    int status = 1;
    if (humanCount < 1) {
        boolean firstGremlin = true;
        status = 0;
    } else {
        firstGremlin = false;
    }
}
```

See any problems? In this example the status variable can be used anywhere within the block, but the statement that assigns a value of false to the firstGremlin variable causes a compiler error. Because firstGremlin is created within the scope of the if (humanCount < 1) statement, it doesn't exist inside the scope of the else statement that follows.

To fix the problem, firstGremlin must be created outside both of these blocks so that its scope includes both of them. One solution is to create firstGremlin one line after status is created.

Rules that enforce scope make programs easier to debug because scope limits the area in which you can use a variable. This reduces one of the most common errors that can crop up in programming: using the same variable two different ways in different parts of a program.

The concept of scope also applies to methods because they are defined by an opening bracket and closing bracket. A variable created inside a method cannot be used in other methods. You only can use a variable in more than one method if it was created as an object variable or class variable.

Putting One Class Inside Another

Although a Java program is called a class, there are many occasions when a program requires more than one class to get its work done. These programs consist of a main class and any helper classes that are needed.

When you divide a program into multiple classes, there are two ways to define the helper classes. One way is to define each class separately, as in the following example:

```
public class Wrecker {
    String creator = "Phoebe Cates";

    public void destroy() {
        GremlinCode gc = new GremlinCode(1024);
    }
}

class GremlinCode {
    int vSize;

    GremlinCode(int size) {
        vSize = size;
    }
}
```

In this example, the GremlinCode class is a helper class for the Wrecker class. Helper classes sometimes are defined in the same source code file as the class they're assisting. When the source file is compiled, multiple class files are produced. The preceding example produces the files Wrecker.class and GremlinCode.class when compiled.

CAUTION

If more than one class is defined in the same source file, only one of the classes can be `public`. The other classes should not have `public` in their class statements. The name of the source code file must match the `public` class that it defines.

When creating a main class and a helper class, you also can put the helper inside the main class. When this is done, the helper class is called an inner class.

You place an inner class within the opening bracket and closing bracket of another class:

```
public class Wrecker {
    String creator = "Hoyt Axton";

    public void destroy() {
        GremlinCode vic = new GremlinCode(1024);
    }

    class GremlinCode {
        int vSize;

        GremlinCode(int size) {
```

```
                vSize = size;
        }
    }
}
```

You can use an inner class in the same manner as any other kind of helper class. The main difference—other than its location—is what happens after the compiler gets through with these classes. Inner classes do not get the name indicated by their class statement. Instead, the compiler gives them a name that includes the name of the main class.

In the preceding example, the compiler produces Wrecker.class and Wrecker$GremlinCode.class.

NOTE

Inner classes enable some complex programming techniques in Java that will make more sense after you have more experience with the language. Five more hours, to be precise. This book gets back to the subject in Hour 16, "Using Inner Classes and Closures."

Using the this Keyword

Because you can refer to variables and methods in other classes along with variables and methods in your own classes, the variable you're referring to can become confusing in some circumstances. One way to make things clearer is with the this statement—a way to refer within a program to the program's own object.

When you are using an object's methods or variables, you put the name of the object in front of the method or variable name, separated by a period. Consider these examples:

```
Gremlin mogwai = new Gremlin();
mogwai.creator = "LoveHandles";
mogwai.setGuid(75);
```

These statements create a new Gremlin object called mogwai, set the name variable of mogwai, and then call the setGuid() method of mogwai.

There are times in a program when you need to refer to the current object—in other words, the object represented by the program itself. For example, inside the Gremlin class, you might have a method that has its own variable called creator:

```
public void checkCreator() {
    String creator = null;
}
```

In this example, a variable called `creator` exists within the scope of the `checkCreator()` method, but it isn't the same variable as an object variable called `creator`. If you want to refer to the current object's `creator` variable, you have to use the `this` statement, as in the following:

```
System.out.println(this.creator);
```

By using `this`, you make it clear to which variable or method you are referring. You can use `this` anywhere in a class where you would refer to an object by name. If you want to send the current object as an argument to a method, for example, you could use a statement such as the following:

```
verifyData(this);
```

In many cases, the `this` keyword is not needed to make it clear that you're referring to an object's variables and methods. However, there's no detriment to using `this` any time you want to be sure you're referring to the right thing.

The `this` keyword comes in handy in a constructor when setting the value of an object's instance variables. Consider a `Gremlin` object that has `creator` and `maximumAge` variables. This constructor sets them:

```
public Gremlin(String creator, int maximumAge) {
    this.creator = creator;
    this.maximumAge = maximumAge;
}
```

Using Class Methods and Variables

For this hour's first project, you create a simple `Gremlin` object that can count the number of `Gremlin` objects that a program has created and report the total.

You know the drill: Choose File, New File in NetBeans and create a new Empty Java File called `Gremlin` in the `com.java24hours` package. Enter Listing 11.1 in the source editor. Click Save.

LISTING 11.1   The Full Text of `Gremlin.java`

```
1: package com.java24hours;
2:
3: public class Gremlin {
4:     static int gremlinCount = 0;
5:
6:     public Gremlin() {
7:         gremlinCount++;
8:     }
9:
```

```
10:      static int getGremlinCount() {
11:          return gremlinCount;
12:      }
13: }
```

Save the file, which NetBeans compiles automatically. This class lacks a main() method and thus cannot be run directly. To test out this new Gremlin class, you need to create a second class that can create Gremlin objects.

The GremlinLab class is a simple application that creates Gremlin objects and then counts the number of objects that have been created with the getGremlinCount() class method of the Gremlin class.

Open a new file with NetBeans and enter Listing 11.2. Save the file as GremlinLab.java when you're done.

LISTING 11.2   The Full Text of GremlinLab.java

```
 1: package com.java24hours;
 2:
 3: public class GremlinLab {
 4:      public static void main(String[] arguments) {
 5:          int numGremlins = Integer.parseInt(arguments[0]);
 6:          if (numGremlins > 0) {
 7:              Gremlin[] gremlins = new Gremlin[numGremlins];
 8:              for (int i = 0; i < numGremlins; i++) {
 9:                  gremlins[i] = new Gremlin();
10:              }
11:              System.out.println("There are " + Gremlin.getGremlinCount()
12:                  + " gremlins.");
13:          }
14:      }
15: }
```

The GremlinLab class is an application that takes one argument when you run it at the command line: the number of Gremlin objects to create. To specify the command-line argument in NetBeans, do the following:

1. Choose Run, Set Project Configuration, Customize. The Project Properties dialog opens.

2. Enter GremlinLab in the Main Class field and in the Arguments field, enter the number of Gremlin objects you'd like the program to create.

3. Click OK to close the dialog.

To run a program you've configured with arguments, choose Run, Run Main Project in NetBeans.

Arguments are read into an application using a string array that's sent to the main() method. In the GremlinLab class, this occurs in Line 4.

To work with an argument as an integer, the argument must be converted from a String object to an integer. This requires the use of the parseInt() class method of the Integer class. In Line 5, an int variable named numGremlins is created from the first argument sent to the program on the command line.

If the numGremlins variable is greater than 0, the following things take place in the GremlinLab application:

▶ Line 7—An array of Gremlin objects is created with the numGremlins variable determining the number of objects in the array.

▶ Lines 8–10—A for loop is used to call the constructor method for each Gremlin object in the array.

▶ Lines 11–12—After all the Gremlin objects have been constructed, the getGremlinCount() class method of the Gremlin class is used to count the number of its objects that have been created. This should match the argument that was set when you ran the GremlinLab application.

If the numGremlins variable is not greater than 0, nothing happens in the GremlinLab application.

After the GremlinLab.java file has been compiled, test it with any command-line argument you'd like to try. The number of Gremlin objects that can be created depends on the memory that's available on your system when you run the GremlinLab application. On my laptop, anything greater than 80 million gremlins causes the program to crash after displaying an OutOfMemoryError message.

If you don't specify more Gremlin objects than your system can handle, the output should be something like Figure 11.1.

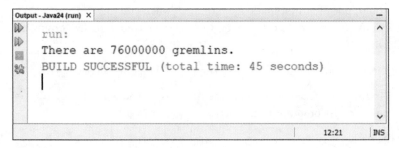

FIGURE 11.1
The output of the GremlinLab program.

Summary

You now have completed two of the three hours devoted to object-oriented concepts in this book. You've learned how to create an object, give behavior and attributes to the object and its class of objects, and convert objects and variables into other forms by using casting.

Thinking in terms of objects is one of the tougher challenges of the Java programming language. After you start to understand it, however, you realize that the entire language makes use of objects and classes.

During the next hour, you learn how to give your objects parents and children.

Workshop

Q&A

Q. Do you have to create an object to use class variables or methods?

A. No. Because class variables and methods aren't associated with a specific object, you don't need to create an object solely for the purpose of using them. The use of the `Integer.parseInt()` method is an example of this because you don't have to create a new `Integer` object just to convert a string to an `int` value.

Q. Is there a list of all the built-in methods that Java supports?

A. Oracle offers full documentation for all classes in the Java language, including all public methods you can use, on the Web at http://download.java.net/java/jdk9/docs/api/index.html.

Q. Is there a way to control how much memory a Java program uses?

A. The memory available to the Java Virtual Machine when it runs an application is controlled by two things: the total physical memory available on the computer and the amount the JVM is configured to use. The default memory allocation is 256MB. A different amount can be set with the `-Xmx` command-line argument.

To set this in NetBeans, choose Run, Set Project Configuration, Customize. The Project Properties dialog opens with the Run settings at the front. In the VM Options field, enter `-Xmx1024M` to allocate 1024MB of memory to the JVM. Alter that number for more or less memory. Also fill out the Main Class and Arguments fields and run the program by choosing Run, Run Project.

Q. What do I have to do to be ranked in men's tennis?

A. There are currently 2,104 male tennis players ranked in the ATP World Tour tennis rankings. If your goal is to do at least as well as the lowest ranked player, you must reach the round of 16 in an ITF Futures tournament.

At the time of this writing, Aziz Ouakaa is ranked in 2,104th place among men's singles players. Ouakaa achieved this distinction by earning only one point in the 12 tournaments he's entered the past 52 weeks. Several hundred other players also have earned one point, but they did it in fewer tournaments.

Ouakaa, a 17-year-old from Tunisia, played the Vietnam F1 futures tournament in March 2013. There was a 32-player qualifier and a 32-player field. Oaukaa beat Rafael Moreno-Higueras of Spain in three sets. He advanced to play Baptiste Crepatte of France in the second round and lost in two sets. His year-to-date prize winnings are $1,194.

There's probably a Futures tournament near you. More than 500 take place around the world each year. Visit www.itftennis.com for the calendar and entry information.

Good luck! If you reach the finals at Wimbledon, I want a seat in the players' box.

Quiz

The following questions see if you have the attributes and behavior to understand OOP techniques.

1. In a Java class, a method is an example of what?

    A. Attributes

    B. Statements

    C. Behavior

2. If you want to make a variable a class variable, what statement must you use when it is created?

    A. `new`

    B. `public`

    C. `static`

3. What is the name for the part of a program in which a variable lives?

    A. Its nest

    B. The scope

    C. Variable valley

Answers

1. **C.** A method is made up of statements, but it's an example of behavior.

2. **C.** If the `static` statement is left off, the variable is an object variable instead of a class variable.

3. **B.** The compiler fails with an error when a variable is used outside of its scope.

Activities

If all this talk of gremlins didn't scare you off, you can increase your knowledge of this hour's topics with the following activity:

▶ Add a `private` variable to the `Gremlin` class that stores an integer called `guid`. Create methods to return the value of `guid` and change the value of `guid` only if the new value is between `1,000,000` and `9,999,999`.

▶ Write a Java application that takes an argument as a string, converts it to a float variable, converts that to a `Float` object, and finally turns that into an `int` variable. Run it a few times with different arguments to see how the results change.

To see Java programs that implement these activities, visit the book's website at www.java24hours.com.

Making the Most of Existing Objects

Java objects are ideally suited for childbearing. When you create an object—a set of attributes and behavior—you have designed something that's ready to pass these qualities on to offspring. These child objects take on a lot of the same attributes and behavior of the parent. They also can do some things differently than the parent.

This system is called inheritance, and it's something every superclass (parent) gives to its subclasses (children). Inheritance is one of the most useful aspects of object-oriented programming (OOP), and you learn about it during this hour.

Another useful aspect of OOP is the capability to create an object that you can use with different programs. Reusability makes it easier to develop error-free, reliable programs.

The Power of Inheritance

You have used inheritance every time you worked with one of the standard Java classes such as `String` or `Integer`. Java classes are organized into a pyramid-shaped hierarchy of classes in which all classes descend from the `Object` class.

A class of objects inherits from all superclasses that are above it. To get a working idea of how this operates, consider the `InputStreamReader` class. This class is a superclass of `FileReader`, a class that reads lines of text from a file. The `FileReader` class is a subclass of `InputStreamReader`.

A partial family tree of `InputStreamReader` is shown in Figure 12.1. Each of the boxes is a class, and the lines connect a superclass to any subclasses below it.

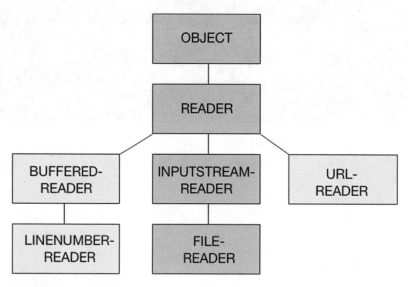

FIGURE 12.1
The family tree of the `InputStreamReader` class.

At the top is the `Object` class. `InputStreamReader` has two superclasses above it in the hierarchy: `Reader`, and `Object`. It has one subclass below it in the hierarchy: `FileReader`.

The `InputStreamReader` class inherits attributes and behavior from the `Reader` and `Object` classes because each is directly above it in the hierarchy of superclasses. `InputStreamReader` does not inherit anything from the orange classes in Figure 12.1, `BufferedReader`, `UrlReader`, and `LineNumberReader`, because they are not above it in the hierarchy.

If this seems confusing, think of the hierarchy as a family tree. `InputStreamReader` inherits from its parent and on upward. The `InputStreamReader` class doesn't inherit from its siblings or its cousins, however.

Creating a new class boils down to the following task: You only must define the ways in which it is different from an existing class. The rest of the work is done for you.

Inheriting Behavior and Attributes

The behavior and attributes of a class are a combination of two things: its own behavior and attributes and all the behavior and attributes it inherits from its superclasses.

The following are some of the behavior and attributes of `InputStreamReader`:

▶ The `equals()` method determines whether an `InputStreamReader` object has the same value as another object.

▶ The `getEncoding()` method returns the name of the character encoding used by the stream.

▶ The `reset()` method moves the stream's current position back to the starting point.

▶ The `mark()` method notes the current position.

The `InputStreamReader` class can use all these methods, even though `getEncoding()` is the only one it didn't inherit from another class. The `equals()` method is defined in `Object`, and both `reset()` and `mark()` come from `Reader`.

Overriding Methods

Some methods defined in the `InputStreamReader` class of objects also are defined in one of its superclasses. As an example, the `close()` method is part of both the `InputStreamReader` class and the `Reader` class. When a method is defined in a subclass and its superclass, the subclass method is used. This enables a subclass to change, replace, or completely wipe out some of the behavior or attributes of its superclasses.

Creating a new method in a subclass to change behavior inherited from a superclass is called *overriding* the method. You need to override a method any time the inherited behavior produces an undesired result or you want to do something different.

Establishing Inheritance

A class is defined as the subclass of another class using the `extends` statement, as in the following:

```
class FileReader extends InputStreamReader {
    // behavior and attributes go here
}
```

The `extends` statement establishes the `FileReader` class of objects as a subclass of `JInputStreamReader`. All file readers must be subclasses of input stream readers. They need the functionality this class provides to read a file over an input stream.

One method that `FileReader` could override is the `close()` method, which does what is necessary to close the file after the text has been read. The `close()` method, implemented by the `Reader` class, is passed all the way down to `FileReader`.

To override a method, you must declare the method in the same way it was declared in the superclass from which it was inherited. A `public` method must remain public, the value sent back by the method must be the same, and the number and type of arguments to the method must not change.

The `read()` method of the `Reader` class begins as follows:

```
public int read(char[] buffer) {
```

When `FileReader` overrides this method, it must begin with a statement like this:

```
public int read(char[] cbuf) {
```

The only difference lies in the name of the char array, which does not matter when determining if the methods are created in the same way. These two statements match because the following things match:

▶ Both methods are `public`.

▶ Both methods return an integer.

▶ Both have a `char` array as their only argument.

When you override a method in a subclass, you should preface the method declaration with @ Override, as in this example:

```
@Override
public void setPosition(int x, int y) {
    if ( (x > 0) & (y > 0) ) {
        super.setPosition(x, y);
    }
}
```

The `@Override` text is a special comment called an *annotation* that tells the Java compiler more than it could figure out on its own. By preceding a method with the `@Override` annotation, you give the compiler an opportunity to check whether the method really overrides a superclass method. If it doesn't—for example, you might have left off the second integer argument—the program won't compile.

Without the annotation, the compiler can't look for this potential problem. The method without the second integer would just appear like any other method.

Using `this` and `super` in a Subclass

Two keywords that are extremely useful in a subclass are `this` and `super`.

As you learned during the previous hour, the `this` keyword is used to refer to the current object. When you're creating a class and you need to refer to the specific object created from that class, you can use `this`, as in the following statement:

```
this.title = "Cagney";
```

This statement sets the object's `title` instance variable to the text "Cagney."

The `super` keyword serves a similar purpose: It refers to the immediate superclass of the object. You can use `super` in several different ways:

▶ To refer to a constructor of the superclass, as in `super("Adam", 12);`

▶ To refer to a variable of the superclass, as in `super.hawaii = 50`

▶ To refer to a method of the superclass, as in `super.dragnet();`

One way you use the `super` keyword is in the constructor of a subclass. Because a subclass inherits the behavior and attributes of its superclass, you must associate each constructor of that subclass with a constructor of its superclass. Otherwise, some of the behavior and attributes might not be set up correctly, and the subclass isn't able to function properly.

A variable accessed through `super` can't be `private` because those are not available in a subclass.

To associate the constructors, the first statement of a subclass constructor must be a call to a constructor of the superclass. This requires the `super` keyword, as in the following statements:

```
public DataReader(String name, int length) {
    super(name, length);
}
```

This example is the constructor of a subclass, which is using the statement `super(name, length)` to call a comparable constructor in its superclass.

If you don't use `super()` to call a constructor in the superclass, Java automatically calls `super()` with no arguments when the subclass constructor begins. If this superclass constructor doesn't exist or provides unexpected behavior, errors will result, so it's better to call a superclass constructor yourself.

Working with Existing Objects

OOP encourages reuse. If you develop an object for use with one Java programming project, it should be possible to incorporate that object into another project without modification.

If a Java class is well designed, it's possible to make that class available for use in other programs. The more objects available for use in your programs, the less work you have to do when creating your own software. If there's an excellent spell-checking object that suits your needs, you can use it instead of writing your own. Ideally, you can even give your boss a false impression about how long it took to add spell-checking functionality to your project and use this extra time to make personal long-distance calls from the office.

NOTE
The author of this book, like many in his profession, is self-employed and works out of his home. Please keep this in mind when evaluating his advice on how to conduct yourself in the workplace.

When Java was first introduced, the system of sharing objects was largely an informal one. Programmers developed their objects to be as independent as possible and protected them against misuse through the use of private variables and public methods to read and write those variables.

Sharing objects becomes more powerful when there's a standard approach to developing reusable objects such as JavaBeans.

The benefits of a standard include the following:

▶ There's less need to document how an object works because anyone who knows the standard already knows a lot about how it functions.

▶ You can design development tools that follow the standard, making it possible to work more easily with these objects.

▶ Two objects that follow the standard can interact with each other without special programming to make them compatible.

JavaBeans are objects that follow a strict set of rules for how they are created and their instance variables are used. A Java class that follows the rules is called a *bean*. The NetBeans IDE can be used to make beans. An introductory tutorial on using JavaBeans in NetBeans is at http://wiki. netbeans.org/NetBeansJavaBeansTutorial.

Storing Objects of the Same Class in Array Lists

An important decision to make when writing a computer program is where to store data. In the first half of this book, you've discovered three useful places to keep information:

▶ Basic data types such as `int` and `char` (or their corresponding classes)

▶ Arrays

▶ `String` objects

There are far more places to store information, because any Java class can hold data. One of the most useful is `ArrayList`, a data structure that holds objects of the same class or a common superclass.

As the class name suggests, array lists are like arrays, which also hold elements of related data, but they can grow or shrink in size at any time.

The `ArrayList` class belongs to the `java.util` package of classes, one of the most useful in the Java Class Library. An `import` statement makes it available in your program:

```
import java.util.ArrayList;
```

An array list holds objects that either belong to the same class or share the same superclass. They are created by referencing two classes: the `ArrayList` class and the class the list holds.

The name of the class held by the list is placed within < and > characters, as in this statement:

```
ArrayList<String> structure = new ArrayList<String>();
```

The preceding statement creates a list that holds strings. Identifying a list's class in this manner utilizes generics, a way to indicate the kinds of objects a data structure such as an array list holds. If you were using lists with an older version of Java, you would have written a constructor like this:

```
ArrayList structure = new ArrayList();
```

Although you can still do this, generics make your code more reliable because they give the compiler a way to prevent more errors. Here, they stop you from misusing an array list by putting the wrong class of objects in it. If you attempt to put an Integer object in a list that's supposed to hold String objects, the compiler fails with an error.

Unlike arrays, array lists aren't created with a fixed number of elements they hold. The list is created with 10 elements. If you know you're storing a lot more objects than that, you can specify a size as an argument to the constructor. Here's a statement that creates a 300-element list:

```
ArrayList<String> structure = new ArrayList<String>(300);
```

You can add an object to a list by calling its add() method, using the object as the only argument:

```
structure.add("Vance");
structure.add("Vernon");
structure.add("Velma");
```

You add objects in order, so if these are the first three objects added to structure, element 0 is "Vance", element 1 is "Vernon", and element 2 is "Velma".

You retrieve an element from a list by calling its get() method with the element's index number as the argument:

```
String name = structure.get(1);
```

This statement stores "Vernon" in the name string.

To see if a list contains an object in one of its elements, call its contains() method with that object as an argument:

```
if (structure.contains("Velma")) {
    System.out.println("Velma found");
}
```

You can remove an object from a list using itself or its index number:

```
structure.remove(0);
structure.remove("Vernon");
```

These two statements leave "Velma" as the only string in the list.

Looping Through an Array List

Java includes a special `for` loop that makes it easy to load an array list and examine each of its elements in turn.

This loop has just two parts, which is one less than the `for` loops you learned about in Hour 8, "Repeating an Action with Loops."

The first part is the initialization section: the class and name of a variable that holds each object retrieved from the list. This object should belong to the same class that holds the list.

The second part identifies the list.

Here's code that loops through the `structure` list, displaying each name to the screen:

```
for (String name : structure) {
    System.out.println(name);
}
```

The hour's first project is `StringLister`, an application that takes array lists and the special `for` loop for a spin, presenting a list of strings in alphabetical order. The list comes from an array and command-line arguments.

With your Java24 project open within NetBeans, choose File, New File, and then create a new Empty Java File named `StringLister` in the `com.java24hours` package. Enter Listing 12.1 in the source editor and save the file.

LISTING 12.1   The Full Text of `StringLister.java`

```
 1: package com.java24hours;
 2:
 3: import java.util.*;
 4:
 5: public class StringLister {
 6:     String[] names = { "Carly", "Sam", "Kiki", "Lulu",
 7:         "Hayden", "Elizabeth", "Kristina", "Molly", "Laura" };
 8:
 9:     public StringLister(String[] moreNames) {
10:         ArrayList<String> list = new ArrayList<String>();
11:         for (int i = 0; i < names.length; i++) {
12:             list.add(names[i]);
13:         }
14:         for (int i = 0; i < moreNames.length; i++) {
15:             list.add(moreNames[i]);
16:         }
17:         Collections.sort(list);
18:         for (String name : list) {
19:             System.out.println(name);
20:         }
21:     }
22:
```

```
23:     public static void main(String[] arguments) {
24:         StringLister lister = new StringLister(arguments);
25:     }
26: }
```

Before you run the application, you should use the Run, Set Project Configuration, Customize command to set the main class to com.java24hours.StringLister and the argument to one or more names separated by spaces, such as Scotty Sonny Jason Dillon. Then choose Run, Run Project to see the result.

The names specified at the command line are added to the names stored in an array in Lines 6–7. Because the total number of names is not known until the program runs, an array list serves as a better storage place for these strings than an array.

The list's strings are sorted in alphabetical order using a method of the Collections class:

Collections.sort(list);

This class, like ArrayList, belongs to the java.util package. Array lists and other useful data structures are called collections in Java.

When you run the program, the output should be a list of names in alphabetical order (see Figure 12.2). The flexible size of array lists enables your additional names to be added to the data structure and sorted along with the others.

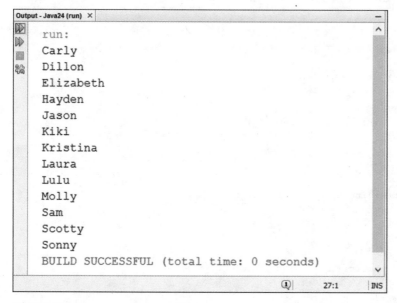

FIGURE 12.2
The output of the StringLister program.

Creating a Subclass

To see an example of inheritance at work, in the next project you create a class called `Point3D` that represents a point in three-dimensional space. You can express a two-dimensional point with an (x,y) coordinate. Three-dimensional space adds a third coordinate, which can be called z.

The `Point3D` class of objects can do three things:

▶ Keep track of an object's (x,y,z) coordinate

▶ Move an object to a new (x,y,z) coordinate

▶ Move an object by a specified amount of x, y, and z values

Java already has a standard class that represents two-dimensional points called `Point`. This class can be found in the `java.awt` package.

It has two integer variables called `x` and `y` that store a `Point` object's (x,y) location. It also has a `move()` method to place a point at the specified location and a `translate()` method to move an object by an amount of x and y values.

In the Java24 project in NetBeans, create a new Empty Java File called `Point3D` in the `com.java24hours` package and enter the text of Listing 12.2 into the file. Save it when you're done.

LISTING 12.2   The Full Text of `Point3D.java`

```
 1: package com.java24hours;
 2:
 3: import java.awt.*;
 4:
 5: public class Point3D extends Point {
 6:     public int z;
 7:
 8:     public Point3D(int x, int y, int z) {
 9:         super(x,y);
10:         this.z = z;
11:     }
12:
13:     public void move(int x, int y, int z) {
14:         this.z = z;
15:         super.move(x, y);
16:     }
17:
18:     public void translate(int x, int y, int z) {
19:         this.z += z;
20:         super.translate(x, y);
21:     }
22: }
```

The Point3D class does not have a main() method, so you cannot run it as an application, but you can use it in Java programs anywhere a three-dimensional point is needed.

The Point3D class only must do work that isn't being done by its superclass, Point. This primarily involves keeping track of the integer variable z and receiving it as an argument to the move() method, translate() method, and Point3D() constructor.

All the methods use the keywords super and this. The this statement is used to refer to the current Point3D object, so this.z = z in Line 10 sets the object variable z equal to the z value that is sent as an argument to the method in Line 8.

The super statement refers to the current object's superclass, Point. It is used to set variables and call methods that are inherited by Point3D. The statement super(x,y) in Line 9 calls the Point(x,y) constructor in the superclass, which then sets the (x,y) coordinates of the Point3D object. Because Point already is equipped to handle the x and y axes, it would be redundant for the Point3D class of objects to do the same thing.

To test out the new Point3D class, create a program that uses Point and Point3D objects and moves them around. Create a new file in NetBeans called PointTester in the com.java24hours package and enter Listing 12.3 into it. The file compiles automatically when it is saved.

LISTING 12.3   The Full Text of PointTester.java

```
 1: package com.java24hours;
 2:
 3: import java.awt.*;
 4:
 5: class PointTester {
 6:     public static void main(String[] arguments) {
 7:         Point location1 = new Point(11,22);
 8:         Point3D location2 = new Point3D(7,6,64);
 9:
10:         System.out.println("The 2D point is at (" + location1.x
11:             + ", " + location1.y + ")");
12:         System.out.println("It's being moved to (4, 13)");
13:         location1.move(4,13);
14:         System.out.println("The 2D point is now at (" + location1.x
15:             + ", " + location1.y + ")");
16:         System.out.println("It's being moved -10 units on both the x "
17:             + "and y axes");
18:         location1.translate(-10,-10);
19:         System.out.println("The 2D point ends up at (" + location1.x
20:             + ", " + location1.y + ")\n");
21:
22:         System.out.println("The 3D point is at (" + location2.x
23:             + ", " + location2.y + ", " + location2.z + ")");
24:         System.out.println("It's being moved to (10, 22, 71)");
```

```
25:            location2.move(10,22,71);
26:            System.out.println("The 3D point is now at (" + location2.x
27:                + ", " + location2.y + ", " + location2.z + ")");
28:            System.out.println("It's being moved -20 units on the x, y "
29:                + "and z axes");
30:            location2.translate(-20,-20,-20);
31:            System.out.println("The 3D point ends up at (" + location2.x
32:                + ", " + location2.y + ", " + location2.z + ")");
33:        }
34: }
```

When you run the file by choosing Run, Run File, you see the output shown in Figure 12.3. If the program cannot be run, look for the red alert icon alongside the source editor that indicates the line that triggered an error.

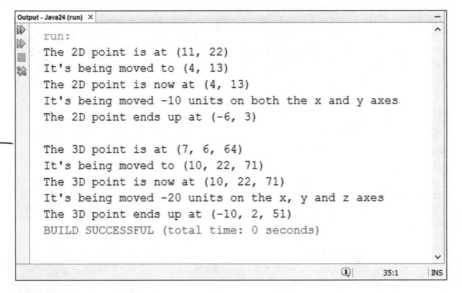

FIGURE 12.3
The output of the `PointTester` program.

Summary

When people talk about the miracle of birth, they're probably not speaking of the way a superclass in Java can give birth to subclasses or the way behavior and attributes are inherited in a hierarchy of classes.

If the real world worked the same way that OOP does, every descendant of Mozart could choose to be a brilliant composer. All descendants of Mark Twain could be poetic about Mississippi riverboat life. Every skill your ancestors worked to achieve would be handed to you without an ounce of toil.

On the scale of miracles, inheritance isn't quite up to par with continuing the existence of a species or throwing consecutive no-hitters in baseball. However, it's an effective way to design software with a minimum of redundant work.

Workshop

Q&A

Q. Most Java programs created up to this point have not used extends to inherit from a superclass. Does this mean they exist outside of the class hierarchy?

A. All classes you create in Java are part of the hierarchy because the default superclass for the programs you write is `Object` when you aren't using the `extends` keyword. The `equals()` and `toString()` methods of all classes are part of the behavior that automatically is inherited from `Object`.

Q. Why do people yell "eureka!" when they've discovered something?

A. Eureka is borrowed from ancient Greek, where it meant "I have found it!" The phrase was supposedly exclaimed by the Greek scholar Archimedes when he stepped into a bath.

What did the Greek discover in the bathtub? The rising water level, which led him to understand that the volume of displaced water must equal the volume of his body parts.

The story about Archimedes was spread two centuries later by Vitruvius in his multivolume *De Architectura*, a book about architecture.

"Eureka" has been in the California state seal since 1849, referring to the exclamation that accompanied the discovery of gold near Sutter's Mill a year earlier.

Quiz

To determine what kind of knowledge you inherited from the past hour's work, answer the following questions.

1. If a superclass handles a method in a way you don't want to use in the subclass, what can you do?

   A. Delete the method in the superclass.

   B. Override the method in the subclass.

   C. Write a nasty letter to the editor of the *San Jose Mercury News* hoping that Java's developers read it.

   2. What methods can you use to retrieve an element stored in an array list?

       A. `get()`

       B. `read()`

       C. `elementAt()`

   3. What statement can you use to refer to the methods and variables of the current object?

       A. `this`

       B. `that`

       C. `theOther`

Answers

   1. **B.** Because you can override the method, you don't have to change any aspect of the super-class or the way it works.

   2. **A.** The `get()` method has one argument—the index number of the element.

   3. **A.** The `this` keyword refers to the object in which it appears.

Activities

If a fertile imagination has birthed in you a desire to learn more, you can spawn more knowledge of inheritance with the following activities:

▶ Create a `Point4D` class that adds a `t` coordinate to the (x,y,z) coordinate system created by the `Point3D` class. The `t` coordinate stands for time, so you need to ensure that it is never set to a negative value.

▶ Take the members of a football team's offense: lineman, wide receiver, tight end, running back, and quarterback. Design a hierarchy of classes that represent the skills of these players, putting common skills higher up in the hierarchy. For example, blocking is behavior that probably should be inherited by the linemen and tight end classes, and speed is something that should be inherited by wide receivers and running backs.

To see Java programs that implement these activities, visit the book's website at www.java24hours.com.

Storing Objects in Data Structures

This Hour's To-Do List:

▶ Create an array list.

▶ Add and remove items from the list.

▶ Use generics to improve list reliability.

▶ Search a list for an object.

▶ Loop through the contents of a list.

▶ Create a hash map of keys and values.

▶ Add and remove items from the map.

▶ Retrieve a map entry's key and value.

▶ Loop through the keys and values of a map.

Programmers are hoarders.

In computer programming, you spend a lot of time collecting information and looking for a place to store it. The information can come in the form of a primitive data type such as a `float`, or as an object of a particular class. It can be read from a drive, retrieved from a server, typed in by a user, or gathered through other means.

After you have the information, you must decide where to put it while a program is running in the Java Virtual Machine. Items that are related to each other by data type or class can be stored in an array.

This is sufficient for many purposes, but as your programs grow in sophistication, your needs as a hoarder will increase.

During this hour you learn about two classes in Java that are designed for information hoarders: array lists and hash maps.

Array Lists

In Hour 9, "Storing Information with Arrays," you were introduced to arrays, an extremely handy way to work with groups of variables and objects in programs. Arrays are so essential to Java that they are a built-in data type like integers and characters. An array packages together elements of the same type or class.

As useful as arrays can be, they are limited by the fact that the size of an array does not change. After an array is created to hold 90 elements, it can't be altered to hold a larger or smaller amount. The size is fixed. (The fancy way of saying this is to call the array's size "immutable.")

There's a class in the `java.util` package that does everything an array can do without that limitation: `ArrayList`.

An *array list* is a data structure that holds objects of the same class or a common superclass. The list can grow or shrink as needed while a program is running.

The simplest way to create an array list is by calling its constructor with no arguments:

```
ArrayList servants = new ArrayList();
```

Array lists can be created by specifying an initial capacity, which provides some guidance on how many elements the list might hold. The capacity is set as an integer argument to the constructor, as in this statement that sets an array list's capacity to 30:

```
ArrayList servants = new ArrayList(30);
```

Although this looks a lot like creating an array and determining its exact size, the capacity is just a hint. If the capacity is exceeded, the array list will be adjusted accordingly and continue to function properly. The better you estimate the capacity, the more efficient the list will be as the program runs.

The list holds objects that belong to the same class or share a superclass.

When you create an array list, you know the class or superclass the list is intended to hold. This can be specified in the constructor within < and > signs, a feature of Java called generics. Here's an improvement of the constructor for a list that holds `String` objects:

```
ArrayList<String> servants = new ArrayList<String>();
```

This statement creates an array list of `String` objects. Only that class or a subclass can be stored in the list. Otherwise, the compiler detects an error.

To add an object, call the array list's `add(Object)` method with that object as the argument. Here are statements that add five strings:

```
servants.add("Bates");
servants.add("Anna");
```

```
servants.add("Thomas");
servants.add("Mrs. O'Brien");
servants.add("Daisy");
```

Each element is added to the end of the list, so the first string in `servants` is "Bates" and the last is "Daisy".

There's a corresponding `remove(Object)` method that takes the object out of the list:

```
servants.remove("Mrs. O'Brien");
```

The size of an array list is the number of elements it currently holds. Retrieve this information by calling the list's `size()` method, which returns an integer:

```
int servantCount = servants.size();
```

When you have used generics to specify the class the list contains, it's simple to use a `for` loop to iterate through each element of the list:

```
for (String servant : servants) {
    System.out.println(servant);
}
```

The first argument to `for` is a variable where an element should be stored. The second is the array list. Other data structures can employ the same loop.

The `add(Object)` method stores the object at the end of the list. Objects also can be added to a list by specifying the position within the list where the object should be stored. This requires the `add(int, Object)` method, which takes the position as the first argument:

```
ArrayList<String> aristocrats = new ArrayList<String>();
aristocrats.add(0, "Lord Robert");
aristocrats.add(1, "Lady Mary");
aristocrats.add(2, "Lady Edith");
aristocrats.add(3, "Lady Sybil");
aristocrats.add(0, "Lady Grantham");
```

The last statement in the preceding example adds "Lady Grantham" at the top of the list instead of the bottom, putting her above "Lord Robert" and the others.

The position specified as the first argument must be no greater than the `size()` of the list. If "Lord Robert" had been added with 1 as the position instead of 0, the program would fail with an `IndexOutOfBoundsException`.

An element can be removed from a list by specifying its position as the argument to `remove(int)`:

```
aristocrats.remove(4);
```

The element at a specified position in a list can be retrieved by calling get(int) with that position. Here's a for loop that pulls each string out of a list and displays it:

```
for (int i = 0; i < aristocrats.size(); i++) {
    String aristocrat = aristocrats.get(i);
    System.out.println(aristocrat);
}
```

Often it is necessary to find out whether an array list contains a specific object. This can be determined by calling the list's indexOf(Object) method with that object as the argument. The method returns the position of the object, or –1 if it cannot be found in the list:

```
int hasCarson = servants.indexOf("Carson");
```

There's also a contains() method that returns true or false based on whether the specified object can be found. Here's a revision of the previous example to use it:

```
boolean hasCarson = servants.contains("Carson");
```

The hour's first project employs these techniques on a simple game in which shots are fired at (x,y) points on a 10-by-10 grid. Some points contain a target and others do not.

The targets are represented by the Point class in the java.awt package. A point is created by calling the Point(int, int) constructor with the x and y coordinates as the two arguments.

This statement creates a point at (5,9):

```
Point p1 = new Point(5,9);
```

Here's a 10-by-10 grid with that point marked by an X and empty spaces m——arked by a "." period character:

Output ▼

```
   1  2  3  4  5  6  7  8  9
1  .  .  .  .  .  .  .  .  .
2  .  .  .  .  .  .  .  .  .
3  .  .  .  .  .  .  .  .  .
4  .  .  .  .  .  .  .  .  .
5  .  .  .  .  .  .  .  .  .
6  .  .  .  .  .  .  .  .  .
7  .  .  .  .  .  .  .  .  .
8  .  .  .  .  .  .  .  .  .
9  .  .  .  .  X  .  .  .  .
```

Columns go from left to right and represent the x coordinate. Rows extend from top to bottom and represent the y coordinate.

Before this project, you saw how array lists could hold strings. They can hold `Point` or any other class of objects. This statement creates a list of points:

```
ArrayList<Point> targets = new ArrayList<Point>();
```

The Java compiler won't allow any class other than `Point` or its subclasses to be added to the array list.

In NetBeans or another programming tool, create a Java file named `Battlepoint` and designate `com.java24hours` as its package. Enter the text of Listing 13.1 into the file.

LISTING 13.1   The Full Text of `Battlepoint.java`

```
 1: package com.java24hours;
 2:
 3: import java.awt.*;
 4: import java.util.*;
 5:
 6: public class Battlepoint {
 7:     ArrayList<Point> targets = new ArrayList<Point>();
 8:
 9:     public Battlepoint() {
10:         // create targets to shoot at
11:         createTargets();
12:         // display the game map
13:         showMap();
14:         // shoot at three points
15:         shoot(7,4);
16:         shoot(3,3);
17:         shoot(9,2);
18:         // display the map again
19:         showMap();
20:     }
21:
22:     private void showMap() {
23:         System.out.println("\n   1  2  3  4  5  6  7  8  9");
24:         for (int column = 1; column < 10; column++) {
25:             for (int row = 1; row < 10; row++) {
26:                 if (row == 1) {
27:                     System.out.print(column + " ");
28:                 }
29:                 System.out.print(" ");
30:                 Point cell = new Point(row, column);
31:                 if (targets.indexOf(cell) > -1) {
32:                     // a target is at this position
33:                     System.out.print("X");
34:                 } else {
35:                     // no target is here
```

```
36:                          System.out.print(".");
37:                      }
38:                      System.out.print(" ");
39:                  }
40:                  System.out.println();
41:              }
42:              System.out.println();
43:          }
44:
45:          private void createTargets() {
46:              Point p1 = new Point(5,9);
47:              targets.add(p1);
48:              Point p2 = new Point(4,5);
49:              targets.add(p2);
50:              Point p3 = new Point(9,2);
51:              targets.add(p3);
52:          }
53:
54:          private void shoot(int x, int y) {
55:              Point shot = new Point(x,y);
56:              System.out.print("Firing at (" + x + "," + y + ") ... ");
57:              if (targets.indexOf(shot) > -1) {
58:                  System.out.println("you sank my battlepoint!");
59:                  // delete the destroyed target
60:                  targets.remove(shot);
61:              } else {
62:                  System.out.println("miss.");
63:              }
64:          }
65:
66:          public static void main(String[] arguments) {
67:              new Battlepoint();
68:          }
69: }
```

Comments in the Battlepoint application describe each part of the constructor and important parts of the conditional logic in the program.

The application creates targets as three Point objects and adds them to an array (Lines 45–52). A map is displayed showing these targets (Lines 22–43).

Next, shots are taken at three points by calling the shoot(int, int) method (Lines 54–64). Each time, the application reports back whether the shot hit one of the targets. If it does, the target is removed from the array list.

Finally, the map is displayed again and the application terminates.

The output is shown in Figure 13.1.

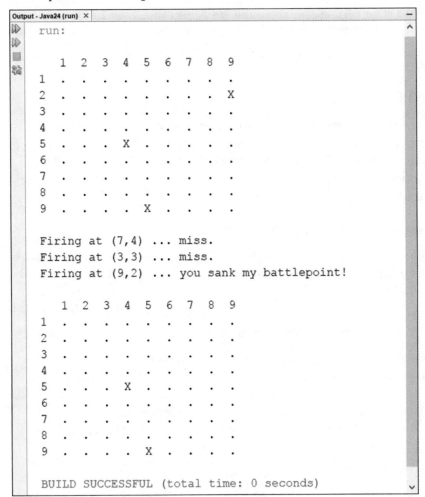

```
Output - Java24 (run)  ×                                              —
▷   run:
▷
■       1  2  3  4  5  6  7  8  9
⚇    1  .  .  .  .  .  .  .  .  .
     2  .  .  .  .  .  .  .  .  X
     3  .  .  .  .  .  .  .  .  .
     4  .  .  .  .  .  .  .  .  .
     5  .  .  .  X  .  .  .  .  .
     6  .  .  .  .  .  .  .  .  .
     7  .  .  .  .  .  .  .  .  .
     8  .  .  .  .  .  .  .  .  .
     9  .  .  .  .  X  .  .  .  .

     Firing at (7,4) ... miss.
     Firing at (3,3) ... miss.
     Firing at (9,2) ... you sank my battlepoint!

        1  2  3  4  5  6  7  8  9
     1  .  .  .  .  .  .  .  .  .
     2  .  .  .  .  .  .  .  .  .
     3  .  .  .  .  .  .  .  .  .
     4  .  .  .  .  .  .  .  .  .
     5  .  .  .  X  .  .  .  .  .
     6  .  .  .  .  .  .  .  .  .
     7  .  .  .  .  .  .  .  .  .
     8  .  .  .  .  .  .  .  .  .
     9  .  .  .  .  X  .  .  .  .

     BUILD SUCCESSFUL (total time: 0 seconds)
```

FIGURE 13.1
Putting Point objects in an array list and shooting at them.

The three targets are shown in the top map of Figure 13.1. One target is removed after it is hit. The bottom map in the output reflects this change.

When a target is hit by a shot, it is removed from the targets array list by calling the remove(Object) method with the shot's point as the argument.

NOTE

In the `shoot()` method of the `Battlepoint` application, the `Point` object that will be removed from the array list is the one that represents the shot. This has the same (x,y) coordinates as the target that was hit.

Hash Maps

The ability to use one piece of information to access another is common in programming. An array list is the simplest example of this among the data structures, where an index number is used to retrieve one object from the list. Here's an example that pulls the first string from the `aristocrats` array list:

```
String first = aristocrats.get(0);
```

Arrays also use index numbers to retrieve each item in the array.

Hash maps are a data structure in Java that use an object to retrieve another object. The first object is the *key* and the second is the *value*. This structure is implemented as the `HashMap` class in the `java.util` package.

The name refers to how keys are mapped to values. An example of this kind of structured data is a phone contact list. A person's name (a string) can be used to retrieve the person's phone number.

A hash map can be created by calling its constructor with no arguments:

```
HashMap phonebook = new HashMap();
```

Two things can be specified in a new hash map that control how efficient it is: the initial capacity and the load factor. These are set with two arguments, with the capacity first and load factor second:

```
HashMap phonebook = new HashMap(30, 0.7F);
```

The capacity is the number of buckets in which hash map values can be stored. The load factor is the number of buckets that can be used before the capacity automatically is increased. The value is a floating-point number ranging from 0 (empty) to 1.0 (full), so a 0.7 means that when the buckets are 70 percent full, the capacity increases. The defaults are a capacity of 16 and load factor of .75, which often are sufficient.

Generics should be used to indicate the classes of the keys and values. They are placed within < and > characters and the class names separated by a comma, as in this example:

```
HashMap<String, Long> phonebook = new HashMap<>();
```

This creates a hash map called `phonebook` with keys that are strings and values that are `Long` objects. The second set of < and > characters is empty, which assumes the same classes as those in the previous < and > in the statement.

Objects are stored in a hash map by calling its put(`Object, Object`) method with two arguments: the key and value:

```
phonebook.put("Butterball Turkey Line", 8002888372L);
```

This stores an item in the map with the key "Butterball Turkey Line" and a Long object for the value 8002888372, the phone number of that service.

NOTE

These statements are putting Long objects in the hash map using long values. This would have been an error in early versions of Java, because a primitive data type such as long couldn't be used where an object was required.

But it's no longer an error because of autoboxing and unboxing, a feature of Java that automatically converts between primitive types and their equivalent object classes. When the Java compiler sees a long like 8002888372, it converts it to a Long object representing that value.

An object can be retrieved from the map with its key by calling get(`Object`) with the key as the only argument:

```
long number = phonebook.get("Butterball Turkey Line");
```

The get() method returns null if there's no value matching that key. This would cause a problem with the preceding example, because null is not a suitable long value.

Another way to handle that potential problem is to call getOrDefault(`Object, Object`). If the key specified as the first argument is not found, the second argument is returned by default, as in this statement:

```
long number = phonebook.getOrDefault("Betty Crocker", -1L);
```

A third way to avoid the problem is for number to be declared as a Long object instead of a long primitive type. The number object could accept null as a value.

If a number matching the key "Betty Crocker" is found in the map, that number is returned. Otherwise, −1 is returned.

There are two methods that indicate whether a key or value is present in the map: containsKey(`Object`) and containsValue(`Object`). These return a Boolean of either true or false.

Hash maps, like array lists, have a size() method that reveals the number of items in the data structure.

Looping through a map can be performed by using an entry set, a collection of all the entries in the map. The entrySet() method returns these entries as a Set object (using the Set interface in java.util).

Each item in the set is represented by `Map.Entry`, an inner class in the `Map` class of `java.util`. When you have an `Entry` object, you can call its `getKey()` method to retrieve the key and `getValue()` to retrieve the value.

The following `for` loop uses entry sets and entries to access all keys and values in a phonebook hash map:

```
for (Map.Entry<String, Long> entry : map.entrySet()) {
    String key = entry.getKey();
    Long value = entry.getValue();
    // ...
}
```

The `FontMapper` project puts all of this together, using a hash map to manage a collection of fonts.

The `Font` class in the `java.awt` package is used to create fonts and use them to display text in a graphical user interface. A font includes the name of the font, the point size, and whether its style is plain, bold, or italic.

Hash maps can contain any class of objects. In NetBeans, create a Java file in the `com.java24hours` package and give it the name `FontMapper`. Enter Listing 13.2 into the file and save it.

LISTING 13.2   The Full Text of `FontMapper.java`

```
 1: package com.java24hours;
 2:
 3: import java.awt.*;
 4: import java.util.*;
 5:
 6: public class FontMapper {
 7:     public FontMapper() {
 8:         Font courier = new Font("Courier New", Font.PLAIN, 6);
 9:         Font times = new Font("Times New Roman", Font.BOLD, 12);
10:         Font verdana = new Font("Verdana", Font.ITALIC, 25);
11:         HashMap<String, Font> fonts = new HashMap<>();
12:         fonts.put("smallprint", courier);
13:         fonts.put("body", times);
14:         fonts.put("headline", verdana);
15:         for (Map.Entry<String, Font> entry : fonts.entrySet()) {
16:             String key = entry.getKey();
17:             Font value = entry.getValue();
18:             System.out.println(key + ": " + value.getSize() + "-pt "
19:                 + value.getFontName());
20:         }
21:     }
```

```
22:
23:     public static void main(String[] arguments) {
24:         new FontMapper();
25:     }
26: }
```

The FontMapper application creates three Font objects in Lines 8–10 and then adds them to a hash map called fonts in Lines 12–14. They're stored in the map with a string key that describes the font's purpose: "smallprint", "body", and "headline".

A for loop in Lines 15–20 loops through the hash map using an entry set and each individual entry in the set.

The output of the application is displayed in Figure 13.2.

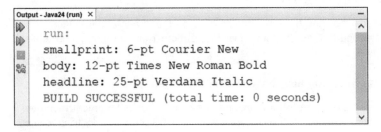

FIGURE 13.2
Storing Font objects in a hash map.

Summary

Array lists and hash maps are two of the more useful data structures in the java.util package. The array list class expands on the functionality of arrays, making it possible to overcome the fixed-size limitation of that data type. Hash maps enable any kind of object to be used as the key to retrieve a value.

There also are bit sets (the BitSet class), which hold the bit values of 0 and 1; stacks (Stack), which are a last-in, first-out collection of data similar to array lists; the sorted structures TreeMap and TreeSet; and properties (Properties), a specialized hash map that holds configuration properties for a program in a file or another permanent storage place.

Workshop

Q&A

Q. What does it mean when a class is synchronized?

A. Synchronization is how the Java Virtual Machine ensures that an object's instance variables and methods are accessed in a consistent and accurate manner by other users of the object.

This concept will make more sense when you learn about threads in Hour 15, "Creating a Threaded Program." Java programs can be designed to do more than one task simultaneously. Each task is put in its own thread.

When multiple threads are accessing the same object, it's vital that the object acts the same in each thread. So when the method of a class requires synchronization, as vectors and hash tables do, the Java Virtual Machine has to work harder and might encounter errors that may cause a thread to stop running.

Array lists and hash maps replicate the functionality of vectors and hash tables because data structures were needed that don't require synchronization. They run much more efficiently as a consequence.

Q. Have the Washington Generals ever beaten the Harlem Globetrotters?

A. The Generals have beaten the Globetrotters seven times over the decades, most recently in 1971. Playing in Martin, Tennessee, the Generals won 100–99 on a shot by team owner Louis "Red" Klotz.

Although the Generals are known today for being patsies, they began in 1921 as the Philadelphia Sphas, a legitimate team that played in the Eastern and American basketball leagues. The Sphas—an acronym for South Philadelphia Hebrew Association—won 10 championships. Klotz was a former Sphas player who bought the team and changed the name to the Generals in 1952 when they became the permanent touring partner of Harlem's famous team.

The 1971 victory ended a 2,495-game winning streak for the Globetrotters.

Quiz

The following questions test how much knowledge you've hoarded about data structures.

1. Which of the following cannot grow or shrink in size after it is created?

    A. Array lists

    B. Arrays

    C. Hash maps

2. What's the name of the method to find out how many items are in an array
   list or hash map?

   A. `length()`

   B. `size()`

   C. `count()`

3. What data type or class can be used as the keys in a hash map?

   A. `int` or `Integer`

   B. `String`

   C. Any class of object

Answers

1. **B.** The size of an array is determined when it is created and cannot be altered. Array lists
   and hash maps change size as needed.

2. **B.** The `size()` method indicates the current number of items in that data structure.

3. **A**, **B**, or **C.** Hash maps can use any class as the keys and any class as the values. Using
   an `int` would cause the `Integer` class to be used.

Activities

You can apply your well-structured programming knowledge with the following activities:

▶ Write a program that uses one of this hour's data structures for a company email address
   list, with each email associated with that person's name.

▶ Extend the `FontMapper` program to take a new font's name, size, and style as command-
   line arguments and add it to the hash map before its keys and values are displayed.

To see Java programs that implement these activities, visit the book's website at
www.java24hours.com.

Handling Errors in a Program

This Hour's To-Do List:

- ▶ Learn why errors are called exceptions.
- ▶ Respond to exceptions in your Java programs.
- ▶ Create methods that ignore an exception.
- ▶ Use methods that cause exceptions.
- ▶ Create your own exceptions.

Errors—the bugs, blunders, and typos that prevent a program from running correctly—are a natural part of the software development process. "Natural" is probably the kindest word that's ever been used to describe them. In my own programming, when I can't find the cause of an elusive error, I use words that would make an insult comic blush.

Some errors are flagged by the compiler and prevent you from creating a class. Others are noted by the interpreter in response to a problem that keeps it from running successfully. Java divides errors into two categories:

- ▶ Exceptions—Events that signal an unusual circumstance has taken place as a program runs
- ▶ Errors—Events that signal the interpreter is having problems that might be unrelated to your program

Errors normally aren't something a Java program can recover from, so they're not the focus of this hour. You might have encountered an `OutOfMemoryError` as you worked on Java programs, which means the program got so big it ran out of memory on the computer. There's nothing that can be done in a Java program to handle that kind of error after it occurs. The program exits with the error.

Exceptions often can be dealt with in a way that keeps a program running properly.

Exceptions

Although you are just learning about them now, you have probably become well acquainted with exceptions during the previous 13 hours. These errors turn up when you write a Java program that compiles successfully but encounters a problem as it runs.

For example, a common programming mistake is to refer to an element of an array that doesn't exist, as in the following statements:

```
String[] greek = { "Alpha", "Beta", "Gamma" };
System.out.println(greek[3]);
```

The `String` array `greek` has three elements. Because the first element of an array is numbered 0 rather than 1, the first element is `greek[0]`, the second `greek[1]`, and the third `greek[2]`. This makes the statement attempting to display `greek[3]` erroneous. The preceding statements compile successfully, but when you run the program, the Java Virtual Machine halts with a message such as the following:

Output ▼

```
Exception in thread "main" java.lang.ArrayIndexOutBoundsException: 3
    at SampleProgram.main(SampleProgram.java:4)
```

This message indicates that the application has generated an exception, which the JVM noted by displaying an error message and stopping the program.

The error message refers to a class called `ArrayIndexOutOfBoundsException` in the `java.lang` package. This class is an exception, an object that represents an exceptional circumstance that has taken place in a program.

Exception handling is a way that classes can communicate with each other in the event of an error or other unusual circumstance.

When a Java class encounters an exception, it alerts users of the class to the error. In this example, the user of the class is the JVM.

NOTE

Two terms are used to describe this process: *throw* and *catch*. Objects throw exceptions to alert other objects that they have occurred. These exceptions are caught by other objects or the Java Virtual Machine.

All exceptions are subclasses of `Exception` in the `java.lang` package. The `ArrayIndexOutOfBoundsException` does what you would expect—it reports that an array element has been accessed outside the array's boundaries.

There are hundreds of exceptions in Java. Many such as the array exception indicate a problem that can be fixed with a programming change. These are comparable to compiler errors. After you correct the situation, you don't have to concern yourself with the exception any longer.

Other exceptions must be dealt with every time a program runs by using five new keywords: try, catch, finally, throw, and throws.

Catching Exceptions in a try-catch Block

Up to this point, you have dealt with exceptions by fixing the problem that caused them. There are times you can't deal with an exception in that manner and must handle the issue within a Java class.

As an introduction to why this is useful, enter the short Java application in Listing 14.1 in a new Java file called Calculator in the com.java24hours package and save the file.

LISTING 14.1   The Full Text of Calculator.java

```
 1: package com.java24hours;
 2:
 3: public class Calculator {
 4:     public static void main(String[] arguments) {
 5:         float sum = 0;
 6:         for (String argument : arguments) {
 7:             sum = sum + Float.parseFloat(argument);
 8:         }
 9:         System.out.println("Those numbers add up to " + sum);
10:     }
11: }
```

The Calculator application takes one or more numbers as command-line arguments, adds them up, and displays the total.

Because all command-line arguments are represented by strings in a Java application, the program must convert them into floating-point numbers before adding them together. The Float.parseFloat() class method in Line 7 takes care of this, adding the converted number to a variable named sum.

Before running the application, set the following command-line arguments in NetBeans with the command Run, Set Project Configuration, Customize: 7 4 8 1 4 1 4. Choose Run, Run Main Project to run the application and you should see the output in Figure 14.1.

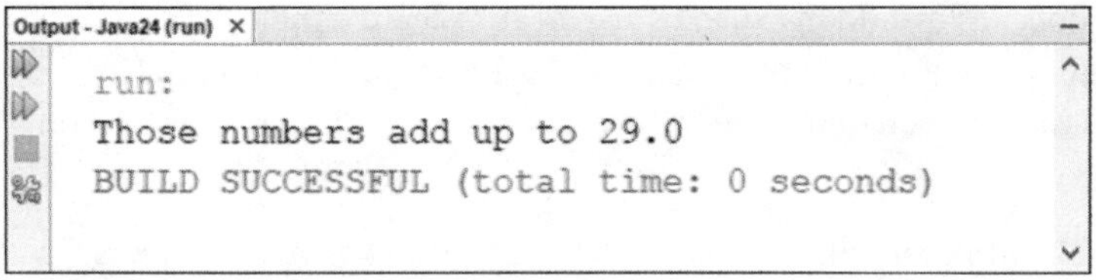

```
Output - Java24 (run)  ×
 ⫸
 ⫸    run:
 ■    Those numbers add up to 29.0
 ⅗    BUILD SUCCESSFUL (total time: 0 seconds)
```

FIGURE 14.1
The output of the `Calculator` application.

Run the program several times with different numbers as arguments. It should handle them successfully, which might make you wonder what this project has to do with exceptions.

To see the relevance, change the `Calculator` application's command-line arguments to 1 3 5x.

The third argument contains a typo—there shouldn't be an x after the number 5. The `Calculator` application has no way to know this is a mistake, so it tries to add 5x to the other numbers, causing the following exception to be displayed:

Output ▼

```
Exception in thread "main" java.lang.NumberFormatException: For input
string: "5x" at sun.misc.FloatingDecimal.readJavaFormatString
(FloatingDecimal.java:1241)
    at java.lang.Float.parseFloat(Float.java:452)
    at Calculator.main(Calculator.java:7)
Java Result: 1
```

This message can be informative to a programmer, but it's not something you'd want a user to see. It would be better to hide the error message and deal with the problem in the program.

Java programs can take care of their own exceptions by using a `try-catch` block statement, which takes the following form:

```
try {
    // statements that might cause the exception
} catch (Exception e) {
    // what to do when the exception occurs
}
```

A `try-catch` block must be used on any exception that you want a method of a class to handle. The `Exception` object that appears in the `catch` statement should be one of three things:

▶ The class of the exception that might occur

▶ More than one class of exception, separated by pipe "|" characters

▶ A superclass of several different exceptions that might occur

The `try` section of the `try-catch` block contains the statement (or statements) that might throw an exception. In the `Calculator` application, the call to the `Float.parseFloat(String)` method in Line 7 of Listing 14.1 throws a `NumberFormatException` whenever it is used with a string argument that can't be converted to a floating-point value.

To improve the `Calculator` application so that it never stops running with this kind of error, you can use a `try-catch` block.

Create a new Java file called `NewCalculator` in the `com.java24hours` package and enter the text of Listing 14.2.

LISTING 14.2   The Full Text of `NewCalculator.java`

```
 1: package com.java24hours;
 2:
 3: public class NewCalculator {
 4:     public static void main(String[] arguments) {
 5:         float sum = 0;
 6:         for (String argument : arguments) {
 7:             try {
 8:                 sum = sum + Float.parseFloat(argument);
 9:             } catch (NumberFormatException e) {
10:                 System.out.println(argument + " is not a number.");
11:             }
12:         }
13:         System.out.println("Those numbers add up to " + sum);
14:     }
15: }
```

After you save the application, customize the project configuration and run `com.java24hours.NewCalculator` with the command-line argument `1 3 5x`. You should see the output shown in Figure 14.2.

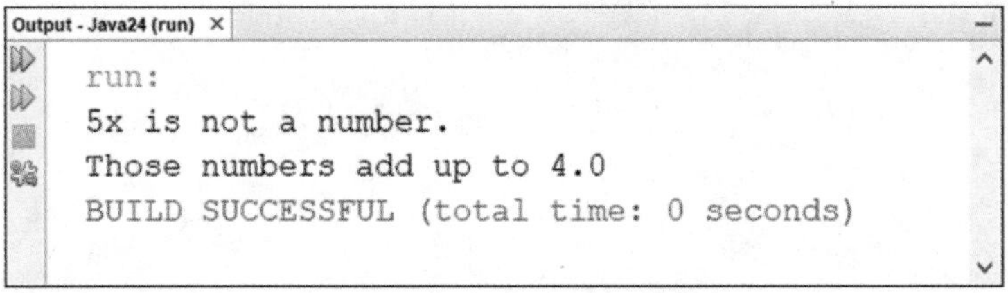

FIGURE 14.2
The output of the `NewCalculator` application.

The `try-catch` block in Lines 7–11 deals with `NumberFormatException` errors thrown by `Float.parseFloat()`. These exceptions are caught within the `NewCalculator` class: for any argument that is not a number, an error message is displayed. Because the exception is handled within the class, the JVM does not display an error. You often can deal with problems related to user input and other unexpected data by using `try-catch` blocks.

Catching Several Different Exceptions

A `try-catch` block can be used to handle several different kinds of exceptions, even if they are thrown by different statements.

One way to handle multiple classes of exceptions is to devote a `catch` block to each one, as in this code:

```
String textValue = "35";
int value;
try {
    value = Integer.parseInt(textValue);
} catch (NumberFormatException exc) {
    // code to handle exception
} catch (ArithmeticException exc) {
    // code to handle exception
}
```

You also can handle multiple exceptions in the same `catch` block by separating them with pipe "|" characters and ending the list with a name for the exception variable. Here's an example:

```
try {
    value = Integer.parseInt(textValue);
} catch (NumberFormatException | ArithmeticException exc) {
    // code to handle exceptions
}
```

If a `NumberFormatException` or `ArithmeticException` is caught, it will be assigned to the `exc` variable.

Listing 14.3 contains an application called `NumberDivider` that takes two integer command-line arguments and uses them in an integer division expression.

This application must be able to deal with two potential problems in user input:

▶ Non-integer arguments

▶ Division by zero

Create a new Java file for `NumberDivider` in the `com.java24hours` package and enter the text of Listing 14.3 into the source editor.

LISTING 14.3   **The Full Text of** `NumberDivider.java`

```
 1: package com.java24hours;
 2:
 3: public class NumberDivider {
 4:     public static void main(String[] arguments) {
 5:         if (arguments.length == 2) {
 6:             int result = 0;
 7:             try {
 8:                 result = Integer.parseInt(arguments[0]) /
 9:                     Integer.parseInt(arguments[1]);
10:                 System.out.println(arguments[0] + " divided by " +
11:                     arguments[1] + " equals " + result);
12:             } catch (NumberFormatException e) {
13:                 System.out.println("Both arguments must be integers.");
14:             } catch (ArithmeticException e) {
15:                 System.out.println("You cannot divide by zero.");
16:             }
17:         }
18:     }
19: }
```

Using command-line arguments to specify two arguments, you can run it with integers, floating-point numbers, and non-numeric arguments.

The `if` statement in Line 5 of Listing 14.3 checks to make sure that two arguments are sent to the application. If not, the program exits without displaying anything.

The `NumberDivider` application performs integer division, so the result is an integer. In integer division, 5 divided by 2 equals 2, not 2.5.

If you use a floating-point or non-numeric argument, a `NumberFormatException` is thrown by Lines 8–9 and caught by Line 14.

If you use an integer as the first argument and a zero as the second argument, an `ArithmeticException` is thrown in Lines 8–9 and caught by Line 14.

Some sample output from a successful run of the program is shown in Figure 14.3.

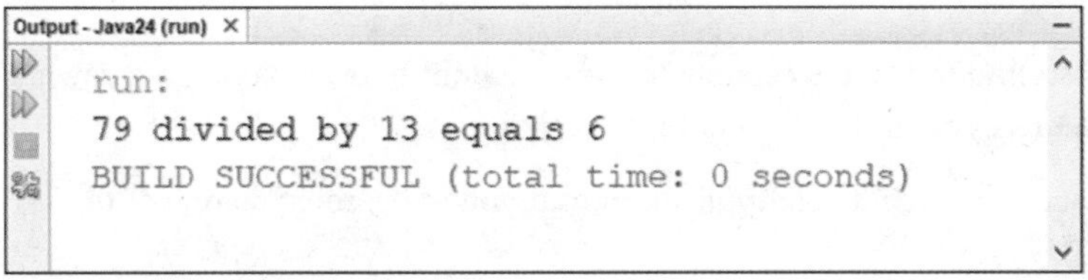

```
Output - Java24 (run) ✕                                    —
 run:
 79 divided by 13 equals 6
 BUILD SUCCESSFUL (total time: 0 seconds)
```

FIGURE 14.3
The output of the `NumberDivider` application.

Handling Something After an Exception

When you are dealing with multiple exceptions by using `try` and `catch`, there are times when you want the program to do something at the end of the block whether an exception occurred or not.

You can handle this by using a `try-catch-finally` block, which takes the following form:

```
try {
    // statements that might cause the exception
} catch (Exception e) {
    // what to do when the exception occurs
} finally {
    // statements to execute no matter what
}
```

The statement or statements within the `finally` section of the block are executed after everything else in the block, even if an exception occurs.

One place this is useful is in a program that reads data from a file on disk, which you do in Hour 20, "Reading and Writing Files." There are several ways an exception can occur when you are accessing data: the file might not exist, a disk error could occur, and so on. If the statements to read the disk are in a `try` section and errors are handled in a `catch` section, you can close the file in the `finally` section. This makes sure that the file is closed whether or not an exception is thrown as it is read.

Throwing Exceptions

When you call a method of another class, that class can control how the method is used by throwing exceptions.

As you make use of the classes in the Java class library, the compiler often displays a message about an exception being handled incorrectly. Here's one example:

Output ▼

```
NetReader.java:14: unreported exception java.net.MalformedURLException; must be
caught or declared to be thrown
```

Whenever you see an error stating that an exception "must be caught or declared to be thrown," it indicates the method you are trying to use throws that exception.

Any class that calls these methods, such as an application that you write, must do one of the following things:

▶ Handle the exception with a `try-catch` block

▶ Throw the exception

▶ Handle the exception with a `try-catch` block and then throw it

Up to this point in the hour, you have seen how to handle exceptions. If you would like to throw an exception after handling it, you can use a `throw` statement followed by the exception object to throw.

The following statements handle a `NumberFormatException` error in a `catch` block, and then throw the exception:

```
float principal;
try {
    principal = Float.parseFloat(loanText) * 1.1F;
} catch (NumberFormatException e) {
    System.out.println(arguments[0] + " is not a number.");
    throw e;
}
```

This rewritten code handles all exceptions that could be generated in the `try` block and throws them:

```
float principal;
try {
    principal = Float.parseFloat(loanText) * 1.1F;
} catch (Exception e) {
    System.out.println("Error " + e.getMessage());
    throw e;
}
```

`Exception` is the parent of all exception subclasses. A `catch` statement will catch the class and any subclass below it in the class hierarchy.

When you throw an exception with `throw`, it generally means you have not done everything that needs to be done to take care of the exception.

An example of where this might be useful: Consider a hypothetical program called `CreditCardChecker`, an application that verifies credit card purchases. This application uses a class called `Database`, which has the following job:

1. Make a connection to the credit card lender's computer.

2. Ask that computer if the customer's credit card number is valid.

3. Ask the computer if the customer has enough credit to make the purchase.

As the `Database` class is doing its job, what happens if the credit card lender's computer doesn't respond to any attempts to connect? This kind of error is exactly the kind of thing that the `try-catch` block was designed for, and it is used within `Database` to handle connection errors.

If the `Database` class handles this error by itself, the `CreditCardChecker` application doesn't know that the exception took place at all. This isn't a good idea—the application should know when a connection cannot be made so it can report this to the person using the application.

One way to notify the `CreditCardChecker` application is for `Database` to catch the exception in a `catch` block, and then throw it again with a `throw` statement. The exception is thrown in `Database`, which must then deal with it like any other exception.

When you use `throw` in a `catch` block that catches a parent class, such as `Exception`, throwing the exception throws that class. This loses some detail of what kind of error occurred, because a subclass such as `NumberFormatException` tells you a lot more about the problem than simply the `Exception` class.

Java offers a way to keep this detail: the `final` keyword in a `catch` statement.

```
try {
    principal = Float.parseFloat(loanText) * 1.1F;
} catch (final Exception e) {
    System.out.println("Error " + e.getMessage());
    throw e;
}
```

That `final` keyword in `catch` causes `throw` to behave differently. The specific class that was caught is thrown.

Ignoring Exceptions

The next technique covered this hour is how to ignore an exception completely. A method in a class can ignore exceptions by using a `throws` clause as part of the method definition.

The following method throws a `MalformedURLException`, an error that can occur when you are working with web addresses in a Java program:

```
public void loadURL(String address) throws MalformedURLException {
    URL page = new URL(address);
    // code to load web page
}
```

The second statement in this example creates a `URL` object, which represents an address on the Web. The constructor of the `URL` class throws a `MalformedURLException` to indicate that an invalid address is used, so no object can be constructed. The following statement causes one of these exceptions to be thrown when you attempt to open a connection to that URL:

```
URL source = new URL("http:www.java24hours.com");
```

The string `http:www.java24hours.com` is not a valid URL because it's missing some punctuation: two slash characters (//) after the colon.

Since the `loadURL()` method has been declared to throw `MalformedURLException` errors, it does not have to deal with them inside the method. The responsibility for catching this exception falls to any method that calls the `loadURL()` method.

Exceptions That Don't Need `catch`

Although this hour has shown that exceptions need to be caught with `try-catch` or declared to be thrown with a `throws` clause, there's an exception.

Some exceptions that might occur in a Java program don't have to be handled in any way. The compiler won't come to a screeching halt when it detects that the exception is being ignored. These exceptions are called *unchecked* exceptions, while the others are *checked* exceptions.

Unchecked exceptions are all subclasses of `RuntimeException` in the `java.lang` package. A common example of an unchecked exception is `IndexOutOfBoundsException`, which indicates that the index used to access an array, string, or array list is not within its boundaries. If an array has five elements and you attempt to read element number 10, this exception occurs.

Another is `NullPointerException`, which occurs when an object that has no value is used. Object variables have the value `null` before they are assigned an object. Some methods also return `null` when an object can't be returned. If a statement incorrectly assumes an object has a value, a `NullPointerException` occurs.

Both errors are things a programmer could (and should) prevent in the code, not things that require exception handling. If you write a program that accesses an out-of-bounds array element, fix the code that does this and recompile it. If you expect an object and it equals `null`, check for that with an `if` conditional before using the object.

The rationale for unchecked exceptions in Java is that they either can be prevented by well-written code, or they could occur so often that catching them all the time would make programs unnecessarily complex. A `NullPointerException` could occur in every statement in a program where an object's methods are called.

Of course, just because an exception can be ignored doesn't mean it should be. You still have the option of using `try`, `catch`, and `throws` with unchecked exceptions.

Throwing and Catching Exceptions

For the hour's final project, you create a class that uses exceptions to tell another class about an error that has taken place.

The classes in this project are `HomePage`, a class that represents a personal home page on the Web, and `PageCatalog`, an application that catalogs these pages.

Enter the text of Listing 14.4 in a new Java file called `HomePage` in the `com.java24hours` package.

LISTING 14.4   The Full Text of `HomePage.java`

```
 1: package com.java24hours;
 2:
 3: import java.net.*;
 4:
 5: public class HomePage {
 6:     String owner;
 7:     URL address;
 8:     String category = "none";
 9:
10:     public HomePage(String inOwner, String inAddress)
11:         throws MalformedURLException {
12:
13:         owner = inOwner;
14:         address = new URL(inAddress);
15:     }
16:
17:     public HomePage(String inOwner, String inAddress, String inCategory)
18:         throws MalformedURLException {
19:
20:         this(inOwner, inAddress);
21:         category = inCategory;
22:     }
23: }
```

You can use the `HomePage` class in other programs. This class represents personal web pages. It has three instance variables: `address`, a `URL` object representing the address of the page; `owner`, the person who owns the page; and `category`, a short comment describing the page's primary subject matter.

Like any class that creates `URL` objects, `HomePage` must either deal with `MalformedURLException` errors in a `try-catch` block or declare that it is ignoring these errors.

The class takes the latter course, as shown in Listing 14.4 in Lines 10–11 and Lines 17–18. By using `throws` in the two constructor methods, `HomePage` removes the need to deal with `MalformedURLException` errors in any way.

To create an application that uses the `HomePage` class, return to NetBeans and create a Java file called `PageCatalog` in the `com.java24hours` package that contains the text of Listing 14.5.

LISTING 14.5   **The Full Text of** `PageCatalog.java`

```
 1: package com.java24hours;
 2:
 3: import java.net.*;
 4:
 5: public class PageCatalog {
 6:     public static void main(String[] arguments) {
 7:         HomePage[] catalog = new HomePage[5];
 8:         try {
 9:             catalog[0] = new HomePage("Mike Glyer",
10:                 "http://www.file770.com", "science fiction");
11:             catalog[1] = new HomePage("Shelley Powers",
12:                 "http://burningbird.net", "environment");
13:             catalog[2] = new HomePage("Rogers Cadenhead",
14:                 "http://workbench.cadenhead.org", "programming");
15:             catalog[3] = new HomePage("Taegan Goddard",
16:                 "https://politicalwire.com", "politics");
17:             catalog[4] = new HomePage("Manton Reese",
18:                 "www.manton.org");
19:             for (int i = 0; i < catalog.length; i++) {
20:                 System.out.println(catalog[i].owner + ": " +
21:                     catalog[i].address + " -- " +
22:                     catalog[i].category);
23:             }
24:         } catch (MalformedURLException e) {
25:             System.out.println("Error: " + e.getMessage());
26:         }
27:     }
28: }
```

When you run the compiled application, the output shown in Figure 14.4 is displayed.

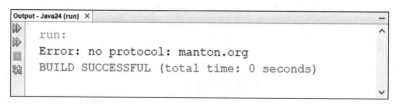

```
Output - Java24 (run)  ×
  run:
  Error: no protocol: manton.org
  BUILD SUCCESSFUL (total time: 0 seconds)
```

FIGURE 14.4
The erroneous output of the `PageCatalog` application.

The `PageCatalog` application creates an array of `HomePage` objects and then displays the contents of the array. Each `HomePage` object is created using up to three arguments:

▶ The name of the page's owner

▶ The address of the page (as a `String`, not a `URL`)

▶ The category of the page

The third argument is optional, and it is not used in Lines 17–18.

The constructors of the `HomePage` class throw `MalformedURLException` errors when they receive a string that cannot be converted into a valid `URL` object. These exceptions are handled in the `PageCatalog` application by using a `try-catch` block.

To correct the problem causing the "no protocol" error, edit Line 18 so the string begins with the text `http://` like the other web addresses in Lines 9–16. When you run the program again, you see the output shown in Figure 14.5.

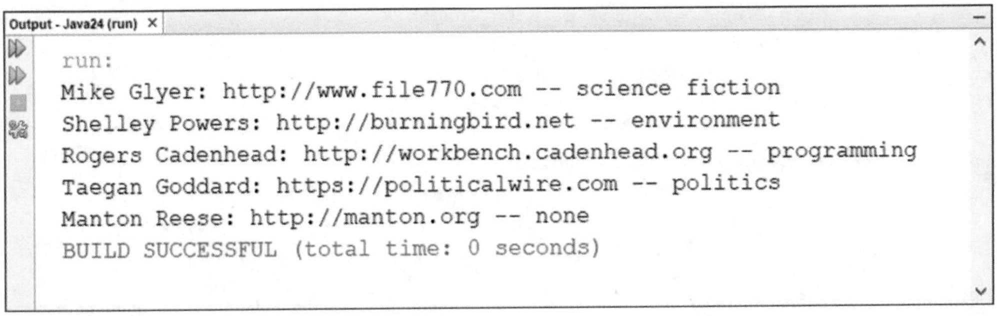

```
Output - Java24 (run)  ×

run:
Mike Glyer: http://www.file770.com -- science fiction
Shelley Powers: http://burningbird.net -- environment
Rogers Cadenhead: http://workbench.cadenhead.org -- programming
Taegan Goddard: https://politicalwire.com -- politics
Manton Reese: http://manton.org -- none
BUILD SUCCESSFUL (total time: 0 seconds)
```

FIGURE 14.5
The corrected output of the `PageCatalog` application.

Summary

Now that you have put Java's exception handling techniques to use, the subject of errors ought to be a bit more popular than it was at the beginning of the hour.

You can do a lot with these techniques:

▶ Catch an exception and deal with it.

▶ Ignore an exception, leaving it for another class or the Java Virtual Machine to take care of.

▶ Catch several different exceptions in the same `try-catch` block.

▶ Throw your own exception

Managing exceptions in your Java programs makes them more reliable, more versatile, and easier to use because you don't display any cryptic error messages to people who are running your software.

Workshop

Q&A

Q. Is it possible to create your own exceptions?

A. It's not just possible, it's a really good idea. Making your own exceptions for problems that may arise makes your classes more robust. You can create your own exceptions easily by making them a subclass of an existing exception, such as `Exception`, the superclass of all exceptions. In a subclass of `Exception`, there are only two constructors you might want to override: `Exception()` with no arguments and `Exception()` with a `String` as an argument. In the latter, the string should be a message describing the error that has occurred.

Q. Why doesn't this hour cover how to throw and catch errors in addition to exceptions?

A. Java divides problems into `Errors` and `Exceptions` because they differ in severity. Exceptions are less severe, so they are something that should be dealt with in your programs using `try-catch` or `throws` in the method declaration. Errors, on the other hand, are more serious and can't be dealt with adequately in a program.

Two examples of these errors are stack overflows and out-of-memory errors. These can cause the JVM to crash, and there's no way you can fix them in your own program as the JVM runs it.

Q. What is the oldest comic strip that's still running in newspapers?

A. *Katzenjammer Kids*, which was created by Rudolph Dirks in 1897 and is still offered today by King Features Syndicate. The strip was started only two years after the first comic strip, *The Yellow Kid*, and is the first to use speech balloons.

Dirks, a German immigrant to the United States, was inspired to create the rebellious kids Hans and Fritz by a children's story from his native country. He quit the strip in 1912 in a contractual dispute and was succeeded by Harold Knerr, who wrote and drew it until 1949. There have been five subsequent cartoonists working on it. Hy Eisman wrote and drew it from 1986 to 2006. Since then the strip has featured reprints.

The word *katzenjammer* literally means "the wailing of cats" in German, but it's more often used to describe a hangover.

Quiz

Although this hour is filled with errors, see if you can answer the following questions about them without making any errors of your own.

1. How many exceptions can a single `catch` statement handle?

    A. Only one.

    B. Several different exceptions.

    C. This answer intentionally left blank.

2. When are the statements inside a `finally` section run?

    A. After a `try-catch` block has ended with an exception

    B. After a `try-catch` block has ended without an exception

    C. Both A and B

3. With all this talk about throwing and catching, what do the Texas Rangers need to do in the off-season?

    A. Get more starting pitching

    B. Sign a left-handed power-hitting outfielder who can reach the.short porch in right

    C. Bring in new middle relievers

Answers

1. **B.** An `Exception` object in the `catch` statement can handle all exceptions of its own class and its superclasses or multiple classes separated by pipe "|" characters.

2. **C.** The statement or statements in a `finally` section always are executed after the rest of a `try-catch` block, whether or not an exception has occurred.

3. **A.** Every answer is correct, but A is more correct than the others and will probably be correct for the next 30 years.

Activities

To see whether you are an exceptional Java programmer, try to make as few errors as possible in completing the following activities:

▶ Modify the `NumberDivider` application so it throws any exceptions that it catches, and run the program to see what happens.

▶ Create a `Multiplier` application that takes three numbers as command-line arguments and throws exceptions for non-numeric arguments.

To see Java programs that implement these activities, visit the book's website at www.java24hours.com.

HOUR 15
Creating a Threaded Program

This Hour's To-Do List:

▶ Use an interface with a program.
▶ Create threads.
▶ Start, stop, and pause threads.
▶ Catch errors.

A computer term used often to describe the hectic pace of daily life is multitasking, which means to do more than one thing at once—such as browsing the Web at your desk while participating in a conference call and doing butt crunch exercises. A multitasking computer is one that can run more than one program at a time.

One sophisticated feature of the Java language is the ability to write programs that can multitask, which is made possible through a class of objects called *threads*.

Threads

In a Java program, each of the simultaneous tasks the computer handles is called a thread, and the overall process is called *multithreading*. Threading is useful in animation and many other tasks.

Threads are a way to organize a program so it does more than one thing at a time. Each task that must occur simultaneously is placed in its own thread, and this often is accomplished by implementing each task as a separate class.

Threads are represented by the `Thread` class and the `Runnable` interface, which are both part of the `java.lang` package of classes. Because they belong to this package, you don't have to use an `import` statement to refer to them in your programs.

One of the simplest uses of the `Thread` class is to slow down how fast a program does something.

Slowing Down a Program

The Thread class has a sleep() method that you can call in any program that should stop running for a short period of time. You often see this technique used in a program that features animation because it prevents images from being displayed faster than the Java Virtual Machine can handle them.

To use the sleep() method, call Thread.sleep() with the number of milliseconds to pause, as in the following statement:

```
Thread.sleep(5000);
```

The preceding statement causes the JVM to pause for five seconds (5,000 milliseconds) before doing anything else. If for some reason the JVM can't pause that long, an InterruptedException is thrown by the sleep() method.

Because this exception might be thrown, you must deal with it in some manner when using the sleep() method. One way to do this is to place the Thread.sleep() statement inside a try-catch block:

```
try {
    Thread.sleep(5000);
} catch (InterruptedException e) {
    // wake up early
}
```

When you want a Java program to handle more than one thing at a time, you must organize the program into threads. Your program can have as many threads as needed, and they all can run simultaneously without affecting each other.

Creating a Thread

A Java class that can be run as a thread is referred to as a runnable (or threaded) class. Although you can use threads to pause a program's execution for a few seconds, programmers often use them for the opposite reason—to speed up a program. If you put time-consuming tasks in their own threads, the rest of the program runs more quickly. This often is used to prevent a task from slowing down the responsiveness of a program's graphical user interface (GUI).

For example, if you have written an application that loads stock market price data from a file and compiles statistics, the most time-consuming task is to load the data. If threads are not used in the application, the program's interface might respond sluggishly as the data is being loaded. This can be extremely frustrating to a user.

Two ways to place a task in its own thread include

▶ Putting the task in a class that implements the Runnable interface

▶ Putting the task in a class that is a subclass of Thread

To support the `Runnable` interface, the `implements` keyword is used when the class is created, as in this example:

```
public class LoadStocks implements Runnable {
    // body of the class
}
```

When a class implements an interface, it indicates that the class contains some extra behavior in addition to its own methods.

Classes that implement the `Runnable` interface must include the `run()` method, which has the following structure:

```
public void run() {
    // body of the method
}
```

The `run()` method should take care of the task that the thread was created to accomplish. In the stock-market example, the `run()` method could contain statements to load data from disk and compile statistics based on that data.

When a threaded application is run, the statements in its `run()` method are not executed automatically. Threads can be started and stopped in Java, and a thread doesn't begin running until you do two things:

▶ Create an object of the threaded class by calling the `Thread` constructor

▶ Start the thread by calling its `start()` method

The `Thread` constructor takes a single argument: the object that contains the thread's `run()` method. Often, you use the `this` keyword as the argument, which indicates the current class includes the `run()` method.

Listing 15.1 contains a Java application that finds the first one million prime numbers, storing them in a `StringBuffer`. When it has found all of the primes, they are displayed. In NetBeans, create a new Java file named `PrimeFinder` in the `com.java24hours` package, enter the text from the listing in the file, and—wait for it—don't forget to save it.

LISTING 15.1   **The Full Text of** `PrimeFinder.java`

```
1: package com.java24hours;
2:
3: public class PrimeFinder implements Runnable {
4:     Thread go;
5:     StringBuffer primes = new StringBuffer();
6:     int time = 0;
7:
```

```
 8:      public PrimeFinder() {
 9:          start();
10:          while (primes != null) {
11:              System.out.println(time);
12:              try {
13:                  Thread.sleep(1000);
14:              } catch (InterruptedException exc) {
15:                  // do nothing
16:              }
17:              time++;
18:          }
19:      }
20:
21:      public void start() {
22:          if (go == null) {
23:              go = new Thread(this);
24:              go.start();
25:          }
26:      }
27:
28:      public void run() {
29:          int quantity = 1_000_000;
30:          int numPrimes = 0;
31:          // candidate: the number that might be prime
32:          int candidate = 2;
33:          primes.append("\nFirst ").append(quantity).append(" primes:\n\n");
34:          while (numPrimes < quantity) {
35:              if (isPrime(candidate)) {
36:                  primes.append(candidate).append(" ");
37:                  numPrimes++;
38:              }
39:              candidate++;
40:          }
41:          System.out.println(primes);
42:          primes = null;
43:          System.out.println("\nTime elapsed: " + time + " seconds");
44:      }
45:
46:      public static boolean isPrime(int checkNumber) {
47:          double root = Math.sqrt(checkNumber);
48:          for (int i = 2; i <= root; i++) {
49:              if (checkNumber % i == 0) {
50:                  return false;
51:              }
52:          }
53:          return true;
54:      }
55:
```

```
56:     public static void main(String[] arguments) {
57:         new PrimeFinder();
58:     }
59: }
```

Finding one million prime numbers is a time-consuming task, so that work is well-suited for its own thread in Java. While the thread is doing its work in the background, the `PrimeFinder` application displays how many seconds have elapsed. The thread ends by displaying the primes and the program ends. The start of the output is shown in Figure 15.1.

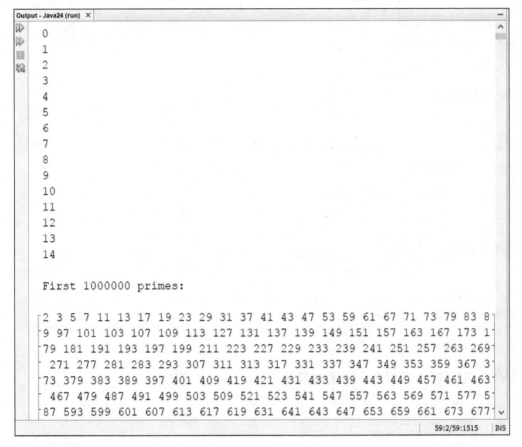

FIGURE 15.1
The output of the `PrimeFinder` application.

Most statements in the application are used to look for prime numbers. The following statements are used to implement threads in this program:

▶ Line 3—The `Runnable` interface is applied to the `PrimeFinder` class.

▶ Line 4—A `Thread` object variable is created with the name `go` but isn't assigned a value.

▶ Lines 22–25—If the `go` object variable has a value of `null`, which indicates the thread hasn't been created yet, a new `Thread` object is created and stored in the variable. The thread is started by calling the thread's `start()` method, which causes the `run()` method of the `PrimeFinder` class to be called.

▶ Lines 28–44—The `run()` method looks for a sequence of prime numbers beginning with 2, storing each one in the `primes` string buffer by calling its `append()` method.

There's something unusual in the `main()` method of this application when a `PrimeFinder` object is created to begin execution of the program. Here's the statement:

```
new PrimeFinder();
```

Normally you'd expect to see that object assigned to a variable, like so:

```
PrimeFinder frame = new PrimeFinder();
```

However, because there's no need to refer to that object again, storing it in a variable is not necessary. Calling `new` to create the object causes the program to run.

It's a good programming practice in Java to store objects in variables only when those objects are needed after their creation.

NOTE

The PrimeFinder application does something unusual with the `StringBuffer` object's `append()` method. A call to `append()` is followed by a period (.) character and another call to `append()`. This causes text to be appended in sequence. It's possible because a call to append() returns that buffer, which then can be called again.

Working with Threads

You can start a thread by calling its `start()` method, which might lead you to believe there's also a `stop()` method to bring it to a halt.

Although Java includes a `stop()` method in the `Thread` class, it has been deprecated. In Java, a *deprecated* element is a class, interface, method, or variable that has been replaced with something that works better.

CAUTION

It's a good idea to heed this deprecation warning. Oracle has deprecated the `stop()` method because it can cause problems for other threads running in the JVM. The `resume()` and `suspend()` methods of the class also are deprecated.

The next project you undertake shows how you can stop a thread. The program you are undertaking rotates through a list of website titles and the addresses used to visit them.

The title of each page and the web address are displayed in a continuous cycle. Users can visit the currently displayed site by clicking a button on the application's graphical user interface. This program operates over a period of time, displaying information about each website in sequence. Because of this time element, threads are the best way to control the program.

Instead of entering this program into the NetBeans source editor first and learning about it afterward, you get a chance to enter the full text of the `LinkRotator` application at the end of the hour. Before then, each section of the program is described.

The `class` Declaration

The first thing you need to do in this program is to use `import` for classes in the packages `java.awt`, `java.io`, `java.net`, `java.awt.event`, and `javax.swing`. This unusually large number of packages is required because the project uses Swing, a set of packages to support a graphical user interface in Java.

After you have used `import` to make some classes available, you're ready to begin the application with the following statement:

```
public class LinkRotator extends JFrame
    implements Runnable, ActionListener {
```

This statement creates the `LinkRotator` class as a subclass of the `JFrame` class, a simple graphical user interface that consists of an empty frame. The statement also indicates that two interfaces are supported by this class: `Runnable` and `ActionListener`. By implementing the `Runnable` class, you are able to use a `run()` method in this program to make a thread begin running. The `ActionListener` interface enables the program to respond to mouse clicks.

Setting Up Variables

The first thing to do in `LinkRotator` is create the variables and objects of the class. Create a six-element array of `String` objects called `pageTitle` and a six-element array of `URI` objects called `pageLink`:

```
String[] pageTitle = new String[6];
URI[] pageLink = new URI[6];
```

The `pageTitle` array holds the titles of the six websites that are displayed. The `URI` class of objects stores the value of a website address. `URI` has all the behavior and attributes needed to keep track of a web address.

The last three things to create are an integer variable, a `Thread` object, and a user interface label:

```
int current = 0;
Thread runner;
JLabel siteLabel = new JLabel();
```

The `current` variable keeps track of which site is being displayed so you can cycle through the sites. The `Thread` object `runner` represents the thread this program runs. You call methods of the `runner` object when you start, stop, and pause the operation of the program.

The Constructor

The program's constructor automatically is executed when the program is run. This method is used to assign values to the arrays `pageTitle` and `pageLink`. It also is used to create a clickable button that appears on the user interface. The method includes the following statements:

```
pageTitle = new String[] {
    "Oracle's Java site",
    "Server Side",
    "JavaWorld",
    "Java in 24 Hours",
    "Sams Publishing",
    "Workbench"
    };
pageLink[0] = getURI("http://www.oracle.com/technetwork/java");
pageLink[1] = getURI("http://www.theserverside.com");
pageLink[2] = getURI("http://www.javaworld.com");
pageLink[3] = getURI("http://www.java24hours.com");
pageLink[4] = getURI("http://www.samspublishing.com");
pageLink[5] = getURI("http://workbench.cadenhead.org");
Button visitButton = new Button("Visit Site");
goButton.addActionListener(this);
add(visitButton);
```

The title of each page is stored in the six elements of the `pageTitle` array, which is initialized using six strings. The elements of the `pageLink` array are assigned a value returned by the `getURI()` method, yet to be created.

The last three statements of the `init()` method create a button labeled "Visit Site" and add it to the application's frame.

Catching Errors as You Set Up URLs

When you set up a URI object, you must make sure the text used to set up the address is in a valid format: http://workbench.cadenhead.org and http://www.samspublishing.com are valid, but http:www.javaworld.com would not be because it is missing the two slash characters (//) after the colon.

The getURI(*String*) method takes a web address as an argument, returning a URI object representing that address. If the string is not a valid address, the method returns null instead:

```
URI getURI(String urlText) {
    URI pageURI = null;
    try {
        pageURI = new URI(urlText);
    } catch (URISyntaxException m) {
        // do nothing
    }
    return pageURI;
}
```

The try-catch block deals with any URISyntaxLException errors that occur when URI objects are created. Because nothing needs to happen if this exception is thrown, the catch block contains only a comment.

Starting the Thread

In this program, the runner thread starts when its start() method is called.

The start() method is called as the last statement of the constructor. Here's the method:

```
public void start() {
    if (runner == null) {
        runner = new Thread(this);
        runner.start();
    }
}
```

This method starts the runner thread if it is not already started.

The statement runner = new Thread(this) creates a new Thread object with one argument: the this keyword. The this keyword refers to the program itself, designating it as the class that runs within the thread.

The call to runner.start() causes the thread to begin running. When a thread begins, the run() method of that thread is called. Because the runner thread is the LinkRotator application itself, the run() method of the application is called.

Running the Thread

The run() method is where the main work of a thread takes place. In the LinkRotator program, the following represents the run() method:

```
public void run() {
    Thread thisThread = Thread.currentThread();
    while (runner == thisThread) {
        current++;
        if (current > 5) {
            current = 0;
        }
        siteLabel.setText(pageTitle[current]);
        repaint();
        try {
            Thread.sleep(1000);
        } catch (InterruptedException e) {
            // do nothing
        }
    }
}
```

The first thing that takes place in the run() method is the creation of a Thread object called thisThread. A class method of the Thread class, currentThread(), sets up the value for the thisThread object. The currentThread() method keeps track of the thread that's currently running.

All statements in this method are part of a while loop that compares the runner object to the thisThread object. Both objects are threads, and as long as they refer to the same object, the while loop continues looping. There's no statement inside this loop that causes the runner and thisThread objects to have different values, so it loops indefinitely unless something outside of the loop changes one of the Thread objects.

The run() method calls repaint(). Next, the value of the current variable increases by one, and if current exceeds 5, it is set to 0 again. The current variable is used to determine which website's information to display. It is used as the index to the pageTitle array of strings, and the title is set as the text of the siteLabel user interface component.

The run() method includes another try-catch block that handles errors. The Thread.sleep(1000) statement causes a thread to pause 1 second, long enough for users to read the name of the website and its address. The catch statement takes care of any InterruptedException errors that might occur while the Thread.sleep() statement is being handled. These errors would occur if something interrupted the thread as it slept.

Handling Mouse Clicks

The last thing to take care of in the LinkRotator program is event handling—the ability to detect user input. Whenever a user clicks the Visit Site button, the application should open the displayed website with a web browser. This is done with a method called actionPerformed(), required by the ActionListener interface. This method is called whenever the button is clicked.

The following is the actionPerformed() method of LinkRotator:

```
public void actionPerformed(ActionEvent event) {
    Desktop desktop = Desktop.getDesktop();
    if (pageLink[current] != null) {
        try {
            desktop.browse(pageLink[current]);
            runner = null;
            System.exit(0);
        } catch (IOException exc) {
            // do nothing
        }
    }
}
```

The first thing that happens in this method is that a Desktop object is created. The Desktop class in the java.awt package represents the desktop environment of the computer running the application. After you have this object, you can use it to launch an email client using a "mailto:" link, open a file for editing with another program, print a file, and make other programs outside of Java perform tasks.

Here, the Desktop object is used to open a web page with the computer's default web browser.

The browse(URI) method loads the specified web address in a browser. If pageLink[current] is a valid address, browse() requests that the browser load the page.

Displaying Revolving Links

You're now ready to create the program and test it. Create a new Java file named LinkRotator in the com.java24hours package and type in the text from Listing 15.2.

LISTING 15.2   The Full Text of LinkRotator.java

```
1: package com.java24hours;
2:
3: import java.awt.*;
4: import java.awt.event.*;
5: import java.io.*;
```

```
 6: import javax.swing.*;
 7: import java.net.*;
 8:
 9: public class LinkRotator extends JFrame
10:     implements Runnable, ActionListener {
11:
12:     String[] pageTitle = new String[6];
13:     URI[] pageLink = new URI[6];
14:     int current = 0;
15:     Thread runner;
16:     JLabel siteLabel = new JLabel();
17:
18:     public LinkRotator() {
19:         setDefaultCloseOperation(JFrame.EXIT_ON_CLOSE);
20:         setSize(300, 100);
21:         FlowLayout flo = new FlowLayout();
22:         setLayout(flo);
23:         add(siteLabel);
24:         pageTitle = new String[] {
25:             "Oracle's Java site",
26:             "Server Side",
27:             "JavaWorld",
28:             "Java in 24 Hours",
29:             "Sams Publishing",
30:             "Workbench"
31:         };
32:         pageLink[0] = getURI("http://www.oracle.com/technetwork/java");
33:         pageLink[1] = getURI("http://www.theserverside.com");
34:         pageLink[2] = getURI("http://www.javaworld.com");
35:         pageLink[3] = getURI("http://www.java24hours.com");
36:         pageLink[4] = getURI("http://www.samspublishing.com");
37:         pageLink[5] = getURI("http://workbench.cadenhead.org");
38:         Button visitButton = new Button("Visit Site");
39:         visitButton.addActionListener(this);
40:         add(visitButton);
41:         setVisible(true);
42:         start();
43:     }
44:
45:     private URI getURI(String urlText) {
46:         URI pageURI = null;
47:         try {
48:             pageURI = new URI(urlText);
49:         } catch (URISyntaxException ex) {
50:             // do nothing
51:         }
52:         return pageURI;
53:     }
```

```
54:
55:     public void start() {
56:         if (runner == null) {
57:             runner = new Thread(this);
58:             runner.start();
59:         }
60:     }
61:
62:     public void run() {
63:         Thread thisThread = Thread.currentThread();
64:         while (runner == thisThread) {
65:             current++;
66:             if (current > 5) {
67:                 current = 0;
68:             }
69:             siteLabel.setText(pageTitle[current]);
70:             repaint();
71:             try {
72:                 Thread.sleep(2000);
73:             } catch (InterruptedException exc) {
74:                 // do nothing
75:             }
76:         }
77:     }
78:
79:     public void actionPerformed(ActionEvent event) {
80:         Desktop desktop = Desktop.getDesktop();
81:         if (pageLink[current] != null) {
82:             try {
83:                 desktop.browse(pageLink[current]);
84:                 runner = null;
85:                 System.exit(0);
86:             } catch (IOException exc) {
87:                 // do nothing
88:             }
89:         }
90:     }
91:
92:     public static void main(String[] arguments) {
93:         new LinkRotator();
94:     }
95: }
```

Figure 15.2 shows two windows open on a computer desktop. The smaller window, which is shown in a rectangle, is the LinkRotator application running. The larger one behind is one of the links that can be opened with the program: the web page for Sams, the publisher of this book.

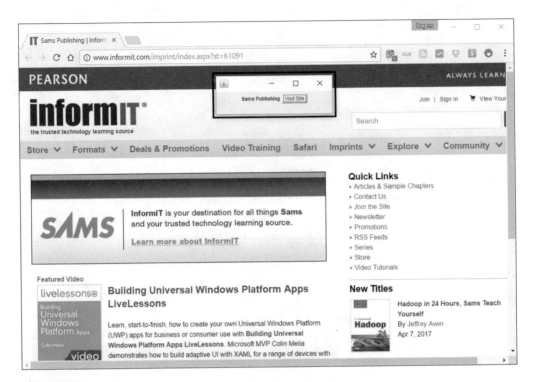

FIGURE 15.2
Displaying revolving links in an application.

Stopping a Thread

The `LinkRotator` application does not have a way to stop the thread, but it has been designed in a way that would make it simple to do so. Here's one method that could be called to end execution of the thread:

```
public void stop() {
    if (runner != null) {
        runner = null;
    }
}
```

The `if` statement tests whether the `runner` object is equal to `null`. If it is, there isn't an active thread that needs to be stopped. Otherwise, the statement sets `runner` equal to `null`.

Setting the `runner` object to a `null` value causes it to have a different value than the `thisThread` object. When this happens, the `while` loop inside the `run()` method stops running.

NOTE

This project might leave you feeling like new topics are rushing by too quickly. Swing and the graphical user interface techniques covered in this hour were used to demonstrate aspects of thread programming that required a user interface. You'll get a full introduction to creating graphical user interfaces in Java beginning in Hour 17, "Building a Simple User Interface in Swing."

Summary

Threads are a powerful concept implemented with a small number of classes and interfaces in Java. By supporting multithreading in your programs, you make them more responsive, and can speed up how quickly they perform tasks.

NOTE

Even if you learned nothing else from this hour, you now have a new term to describe your fast-paced, task-juggling, 21st century lifestyle. Use it in a few sentences to see if it grabs you:

▶ "Boy, I was really multithreading yesterday after we held up that string of liquor stores."

▶ "I multithreaded all through lunch, and it gave me gas."

▶ "Not tonight, dear, I'm multithreading."

Workshop

Q&A

Q. Are there any reasons to do nothing within a `catch` statement, as the `LinkRotator` application does?

A. It depends on the type of error or exception being caught. In the `LinkRotator` application, you know with both `catch` statements what the cause of an exception would be, so you can be assured that doing nothing always is appropriate. In the `getURI()` method, the `URISyntaxException` would be caused only if the URI sent to the method is invalid.

Another exception that likely requires no action in a `catch` block is `InterruptedException`. In over 20 years as a Java programmer I've never had a program throw that exception.

Most exceptions do necessitate at least logging the error.

Q. Whatever happened to the band that sang "My Future's So Bright, I Gotta Wear Shades"?

A. Their future was not bright. Timbuk3, a band formed by husband and wife Pat and Barbara K. MacDonald, never had another hit after the song that became a top 20 single in 1986. They produced six albums from 1986 to 1995, when they broke up the band and divorced.

Pat MacDonald continues to perform and release albums under his own name and with others as Purgatory Hill and the Legendary Sons of Crack Daniels. He's also written songs for Cher, Peter Frampton, Night Ranger, Aerosmith, and other musicians.

Barbara Kooyman performs as Barbara K and has several albums, one that reinterprets Timbuk3 songs. She also formed the artist's free speech charity Artists for Media Diversity.

Their best known song, widely taken to be a positive message about the future, was supposed to be ironic. The band said the bright future was actually an impending nuclear holocaust.

Quiz

Set aside your threads (in the Java sense, not the modesty sense) and answer the following questions about multithreading in Java.

1. What interface must be implemented for a program to use threads?

    A. `Runnable`

    B. `Thread`

    C. No interface is required

2. If an interface contains three different methods, how many of them must be included in a class that implements the interface?

    A. None of them.

    B. All of them.

    C. I know, but I'm not telling.

3. You're admiring the work of another programmer who has created a program that handles four simultaneous tasks. What should you tell him?

    A. "I'd buy that for a dollar."

    B. "You're the wind beneath my wings."

    C. "Nice threads!"

Answers

1. **A.** `Runnable` must be used with the `implements` statement. `Thread` is used inside a multithreaded program, but it is not needed in the class statement that begins a program.

2. **B.** An interface is a guarantee that the class includes all the interface's methods.

3. **C.** This compliment could be confusing if the programmer is well dressed, but let's be honest, what are the chances of that?

Activities

If this hour's material hasn't left you feeling threadbare, expand your skills with the following activities:

▶ Create a new version of the `LinkRotator` application and six of your own favorite websites.

▶ Add a second thread to the `PrimeFinder` application that finds the first million numbers not evenly divisible by 3. Only stop the time counter after both threads are finished doing their work.

To see Java programs that implement these activities, visit the book's website at www.java24hours.com.

HOUR 16
Using Inner Classes and Closures

This Hour's To-Do List:

- ▶ Add an inner class to an object.
- ▶ Explore why inner classes are useful.
- ▶ Create an anonymous inner class.
- ▶ Use an adapter class with interfaces.
- ▶ Write a lambda expression.
- ▶ Replace an anonymous inner class with a lambda expression.

When it was launched in 1995, the Java programming language was limited in scope and simple to master. There were only around 250 classes in the Java Class Library. The language was designed primarily so that interactive programs called applets could be run inside web browsers. Because no other technology had been introduced to do that, Java made an enormous splash and was quickly embraced by hundreds of thousands of programmers.

As a testament to how well the language was designed, it expanded beyond that one focus and became a general-purpose programming language to rival C++, which at the time was the most popular and widely implemented language on the planet.

Millions of programmers write in Java today as the language turns 23. With each new release, Java has supported its existing developers while expanding its capabilities to enable sophisticated new methodologies of software development.

One of the most exciting is a new way to write code called closures, or lambda expressions. These expressions make possible a methodology called functional programming.

During this hour, you learn about lambda expressions after covering two aspects of the language that are prerequisites to using them: inner classes and anonymous inner classes.

Inner Classes

When you create a class in Java, you define the attributes and behavior for that class. The attributes are the class and instance variables that hold data. The behavior is the methods that perform tasks with that data.

A class also can contain something that consists of both attributes and behavior: an inner class.

Inner classes are helper classes that are contained within an enclosing class. You may wonder why they're necessary, since it's easy to create a program out of as many new classes as you need. If you're writing a CheckBook program that needs objects for each check a person writes, you create a Check class. If the program supports recurring monthly payments, add an Autopayment class.

Inner classes aren't necessary. But when you learn all the things they can do, you'll find many situations where they're incredibly handy.

There are three reasons that Java includes inner classes:

1. When a helper class is only used by one other class, it makes sense to define it within that class.

2. They enable a helper class to access private methods and variables it could not access as a separate class.

3. They put a helper class as close as possible to where it is being used in another class.

An inner class is created with the class keyword, like any other class, but it is declared inside the containing class. Typically, this is placed with class and instance variables.

Here's an example of an inner class called InnerSimple being created inside a class called Simple:

```
public class Simple {

    class InnerSimple {
        InnerSimple() {
            System.out.println("I am an inner class!");
        }
    }

    public Simple() {
        // empty constructor
    }

    public static void main(String[] arguments) {
        Simple program = new Simple();
```

```
        Simple.InnerSimple inner = program.new InnerSimple();
    }
}
```

The inner class is structured like any other class, but placed inside the { and } brackets of the enclosing class.

Creating an inner class requires an object of the outer class. The new operator is called on the object:

```
Simple.InnerSimple inner = program.new InnerSimple();
```

The name of the class includes the name of the outer class, a period (.) character, and the inner class name. In the preceding statement, Simple.InnerSimple is the name.

The hour's first project is a rewrite of an application from Hour 14, "Handling Errors in a Program." The PageCatalog application from that hour required a helper class called HomePage. The Catalog application in Listing 16.1 revises that project to replace that separate class with an inner class.

Create a new Java file in the package com.java24hours with the name Catalog; then fill it with the source code in Listing 16.1.

LISTING 16.1 **The Full Text of** Catalog.java

```
 1: package com.java24hours;
 2:
 3: import java.net.*;
 4:
 5: public class Catalog {
 6:     class HomePage {
 7:         String owner;
 8:         URL address;
 9:         String category = "none";
10:
11:         public HomePage(String inOwner, String inAddress)
12:             throws MalformedURLException {
13:
14:             owner = inOwner;
15:             address = new URL(inAddress);
16:         }
17:
18:         public HomePage(String inOwner, String inAddress, String inCategory)
19:             throws MalformedURLException {
20:
21:             this(inOwner, inAddress);
```

```
22:                 category = inCategory;
23:             }
24:         }
25:
26:     public Catalog() {
27:         Catalog.HomePage[] catalog = new Catalog.HomePage[5];
28:         try {
29:             catalog[0] = new HomePage("Mike Glyer",
30:                 "http://www.file770.com", "science fiction");
31:             catalog[1] = new HomePage("Shelley Powers",
32:                 "http://burningbird.net", "environment");
33:             catalog[2] = new HomePage("Rogers Cadenhead",
34:                 "http://workbench.cadenhead.org", "programming");
35:             catalog[3] = new HomePage("Taegan Goddard",
36:                 "https://politicalwire.com", "politics");
37:             catalog[4] = new HomePage("Manton Reese",
38:                 "http://manton.org");
39:             for (int i = 0; i < catalog.length; i++) {
40:                 System.out.println(catalog[i].owner + ": " +
41:                     catalog[i].address + " -- " +
42:                     catalog[i].category);
43:             }
44:         } catch (MalformedURLException e) {
45:             System.out.println("Error: " + e.getMessage());
46:         }
47:     }
48:
49:     public static void main(String[] arguments) {
50:         new Catalog();
51:     }
52: }
```

The inner class is defined in Lines 6–24. It has two constructors, one that takes a website owner and site URI beginning in Line 11 and another that takes a site owner, URI, and category beginning in Line 18.

The Catalog class uses this inner class in Line 27, creating an array of HomePage objects. The inner class is referred to as Catalog.HomePage.

The application's output is shown in Figure 16.1.

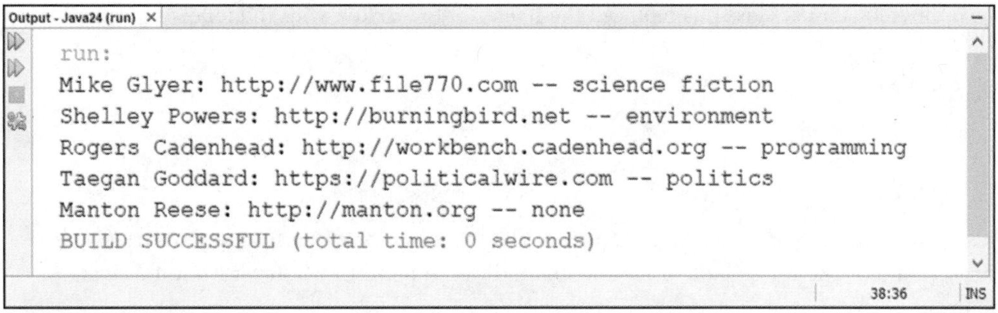

```
Output - Java24 (run)  ×                                                        —
run:                                                                           ^
Mike Glyer: http://www.file770.com -- science fiction
Shelley Powers: http://burningbird.net -- environment
Rogers Cadenhead: http://workbench.cadenhead.org -- programming
Taegan Goddard: https://politicalwire.com -- politics
Manton Reese: http://manton.org -- none
BUILD SUCCESSFUL (total time: 0 seconds)                                       v
                                                          38:36    INS
```

FIGURE 16.1
The output of the Catalog application.

Anonymous Inner Classes

A common task you undertake in Java programming is to create a class that will be used only once and has a simple purpose. A special kind of inner class is perfect for this purpose.

An anonymous inner class is one that has no name and is declared and created at the same time.

To use one, you replace a reference to an object with the new keyword, a call to a constructor, and the class definition inside { and } characters.

Here's some code that does not use an anonymous inner class:

```
WorkerClass worker = new WorkerClass();
Thread main = new Thread(worker);
main.start();
```

The worker object presumably implements the Runnable interface and can be run as a thread.

If the code in WorkerClass is short and simple, and the class only needs to be used once, it could be worthwhile to put it in an anonymous inner class. Here's a new version to do that:

```
Thread main = new Thread(new Runnable() {
    public void run() {
        // thread's work to perform goes here
    }
});
main.start();
```

The anonymous inner class has replaced the reference to `worker` with the following code:

```
new Runnable()   {
    public void run() {
        // thread's work to perform goes here
    }
}
```

This creates an anonymous class that implements the `Runnable` interface and overrides the `run()` method. The statements inside the method would perform whatever work the class requires.

This concept will be easier to comprehend with a full example of how an anonymous inner class is written and why it's useful.

A Java application can receive keyboard input with the Swing graphical user interface packages. The application monitors the keyboard with an object that implements the `KeyListener` interface.

A class that implements the interface must implement three methods: `keyTyped()`, `keyPressed()`, and `keyReleased()`, as in this code:

```
public void keyTyped(KeyEvent input) {
    char key = input.getKeyChar();
    keyLabel.setText("You pressed " + key);
}

public void keyPressed(KeyEvent txt) {
    // do nothing
}

public void keyReleased(KeyEvent txt) {
    // do nothing
}
```

In the same class as these statements, the key listener is set to use the class to monitor keyboard events:

```
keyText.addKeyListener(this);
```

With an anonymous inner class and the `KeyAdapter` class in the `java.awt.event` package, there's a better way to create the listener and add it to the graphical user interface.

The `KeyAdapter` class implements the `KeyListener` interface with do-nothing implementations of all three methods. It makes it easy to create a listener for keyboard events, because you can create a subclass that only overrides the method that actually does anything.

Here's the framework of a key listener for the `KeyViewer` application:

```
public class KeyViewerListener extends KeyAdapter {
    public void keyTyped(KeyEvent input) {
        // to do
    }
}
```

This listener could be created and set as a listener:

```
KeyViewerListener kvl = new KeyViewerListener();
keyText.addKeyListener(kvl);
```

This approach requires a separate helper class, `KeyViewerListener`, and an object of that class to be created and assigned to a variable.

Another way to do it is to create the listener as an anonymous inner class:

```
keyText.addKeyListener(new KeyAdapter() {
    public void keyTyped(KeyEvent input) {
        char key = input.getKeyChar();
        keyLabel.setText("You pressed " + key);
    }
});
```

The listener is created anonymously with the call to `new KeyAdapter()` followed by the definition of the class. The class overrides the `keyTyped()` method so that when a key is pressed, it is retrieved with a call to `getKeyChar()` and displayed by setting the value of `keyLabel`, which is a `JLabel` component.

The anonymous inner class does something that a normal helper class could not do: access the `keyLabel` instance variable. That variable belongs to the `KeyViewer` class. Inner classes can access the methods and variables of their enclosing class.

In NetBeans, create a new Java file named `KeyViewer` in the package `com.java24hours`. Enter the text of Listing 16.2 into the file and save it when you're done.

LISTING 16.2   The Full Text of `KeyViewer.java`

```
 1: package com.java24hours;
 2:
 3: import javax.swing.*;
 4: import java.awt.event.*;
 5: import java.awt.*;
 6:
 7: public class KeyViewer extends JFrame {
 8:     JTextField keyText = new JTextField(80);
 9:     JLabel keyLabel = new JLabel("Press any key in the text field.");
10:
```

```
11:    public KeyViewer() {
12:        super("KeyViewer");
13:        setSize(350, 100);
14:        setDefaultCloseOperation(JFrame.EXIT_ON_CLOSE);
15:        keyText.addKeyListener(new KeyAdapter() {
16:            public void keyTyped(KeyEvent input) {
17:                char key = input.getKeyChar();
18:                keyLabel.setText("You pressed " + key);
19:            }
20:        });
21:        BorderLayout bord = new BorderLayout();
22:        setLayout(bord);
23:        add(keyLabel, BorderLayout.NORTH);
24:        add(keyText, BorderLayout.CENTER);
25:        setVisible(true);
26:    }
27:
28:    public static void main(String[] arguments) {
29:        new KeyViewer();
30:    }
31: }
```

The anonymous inner class is created and used in Lines 15–20. It monitors keyboard input using the only method in the `KeyListener` interface the application requires and displays that input by updating the `keyLabel` instance variable.

The program's output is shown in Figure 16.2.

FIGURE 16.2
Monitoring keyboard input with the `KeyViewer` application.

Anonymous inner classes cannot define constructors, so they are more limited than a non-anonymous inner class.

They are a complex feature of the language that are harder to understand as you examine a program's source code, but they can make a program more concise. Experienced Java programmers often make use of them.

Closures

This next section introduces the most highly requested language feature for years: closures.

Closures, which also are called lambda expressions, allow an object with a single method to be created with only an -> operator, as long as other conditions are met.

Here's an example:

```
Runnable runner = () -> { System.out.println("Run!"); };
```

This single line creates an object that implements the Runnable interface and makes its run() method equivalent to the following code:

```
void run() {
    System.out.println("Run!");
}
```

In a lambda expression, the statement to the right of the arrow operator -> becomes the method that implements the interface.

This can be done only when the interface has a single method to implement, such as Runnable, which just contains run(). An interface in Java that has one method is now called a *functional interface.*

A lambda expression also has something to the left of the arrow operator. In the first example, it's an empty set of parentheses, and it refers to the arguments sent to the method of the functional interface. Since run() takes no arguments in the Runnable interface, no arguments are required in the expression.

Here's a second example of a lambda expression that does put something in those parentheses:

```
ActionListener al = (ActionEvent act) -> {
    System.out.println(act.getSource());
}
```

This is equivalent to the following code in an object that implements the ActionListener interface in the java.awt.event package:

```
public void actionPerformed(ActionEvent act) {
    System.out.println(act.getSource());
}
```

The ActionListener interface receives action events, such as when a user clicks a button. The only method in the functional interface is actionPerformed(*ActionEvent*). The argument is an ActionEvent object that describes the user action that triggered the event.

The right half of the lambda expression defines the `actionPerformed()` method as a single statement that displays information about the user interface component that triggered the event.

The left half of the expression declares that an `ActionEvent` object named `act` is the argument to the method.

This object, `act`, is used inside the body of the method. The left-half reference to `act` appears to be outside the scope of the right-half implementation of the method. This is because closures allow code to refer to the variables of another method outside the scope of those variables.

As you can see, one effect of lambda expressions is that they shorten code. A single expression creates an object and implements an interface.

This feature of Java can make the code even shorter through the language's support for target typing.

In a lambda expression, it's possible to infer the class of the argument or arguments sent to the method. Consider the last example. Because the `ActionListener` functional interface has a method that takes an `ActionEvent` object as its only argument, the name of that class can be omitted.

Here's a revised version of the lambda expression taking this into account:

```
ActionListener al = (act) -> {
    System.out.println(act.getSource());
}
```

The next two programs that you create should provide a more concrete demonstration of the difference wrought by the introduction of closures to Java.

The `ColorFrame` application in Listing 16.3 displays three buttons to change the color of a frame. This version of the application uses an anonymous inner class, not a lambda expression, to monitor user clicks on the three buttons.

Create a new program in NetBeans with the name ColorFrame in the package `com.java24hours`. Enter the text listing 16.3 into the file and save it when you're done.

LISTING 16.3   The Full Text of `ColorFrame.java`

```
1: package com.java24hours;
2:
3: import java.awt.*;
4: import java.awt.event.*;
5: import javax.swing.*;
6:
```

```
7: public class ColorFrame extends JFrame {
8:     JButton red, green, blue;
9:
10:     public ColorFrame() {
11:         super("ColorFrame");
12:         setSize(322, 122);
13:         setDefaultCloseOperation(JFrame.EXIT_ON_CLOSE);
14:         FlowLayout flo = new FlowLayout();
15:         setLayout(flo);
16:         red = new JButton("Red");
17:         add(red);
18:         green = new JButton("Green");
19:         add(green);
20:         blue = new JButton("Blue");
21:         add(blue);
22:         // begin anonymous inner class
23:         ActionListener act = new ActionListener() {
24:             public void actionPerformed(ActionEvent event) {
25:                 if (event.getSource() == red) {
26:                     getContentPane().setBackground(Color.RED);
27:                 }
28:                 if (event.getSource() == green) {
29:                     getContentPane().setBackground(Color.GREEN);
30:                 }
31:                 if (event.getSource() == blue) {
32:                     getContentPane().setBackground(Color.BLUE);
33:                 }
34:             }
35:         };
36:         // end anonymous inner class
37:         red.addActionListener(act);
38:         green.addActionListener(act);
39:         blue.addActionListener(act);
40:         setVisible(true);
41:     }
42:
43:     public static void main(String[] arguments) {
44:         new ColorFrame();
45:     }
46: }
```

This program is shown running in Figure 16.3.

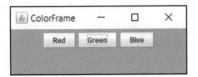

FIGURE 16.3
Monitoring action events with an anonymous inner class.

Lines 23–35 of the application create an event listener for the `ColorFrame` class using an anonymous inner class. It's an object of no name that implements the `ActionListener` interface's only method, `actionPerformed(ActionEvent)`.

Within that method, the frame's content pane is retrieved by calling its `getContentPane()` method. Anonymous inner classes have access to the methods and instance variables of their enclosing class. A separate helper class would not.

The content pane's `setBackground(Color)` method changes the frame's background to that color. The color of the three buttons does not change.

Now take a look at the `NewColorFrame` application in Listing 16.4. Create a new program in NetBeans with the name `NewColorFrame` in the package com.java24hours. Enter the text listing 16.4 into the file and save it when you're done.

LISTING 16.4   The Full Text of `NewColorFrame.java`

```
 1: package com.java24hours;
 2:
 3: import java.awt.*;
 4: import java.awt.event.*;
 5: import javax.swing.*;
 6:
 7: public class NewColorFrame extends JFrame {
 8:     JButton red, green, blue;
 9:
10:     public NewColorFrame() {
11:         super("NewColorFrame");
12:         setSize(322, 122);
13:         setDefaultCloseOperation(JFrame.EXIT_ON_CLOSE);
14:         FlowLayout flo = new FlowLayout();
15:         setLayout(flo);
16:         red = new JButton("Red");
17:         add(red);
```

```
18:            green = new JButton("Green");
19:            add(green);
20:            blue = new JButton("Blue");
21:            add(blue);
22:            // begin lambda expression
23:            ActionListener act = (event) -> {
24:                if (event.getSource() == red) {
25:                    getContentPane().setBackground(Color.RED);
26:                }
27:                if (event.getSource() == green) {
28:                    getContentPane().setBackground(Color.GREEN);
29:                }
30:                if (event.getSource() == blue) {
31:                    getContentPane().setBackground(Color.BLUE);
32:                }
33:            };
34:            // end lambda expression
35:            red.addActionListener(act);
36:            green.addActionListener(act);
37:            blue.addActionListener(act);
38:            setVisible(true);
39:        }
40:
41:        public static void main(String[] arguments) {
42:            new NewColorFrame();
43:        }
44: }
```

The `NewColorFrame` application implements the action listener in lines 23–33. You don't need to know the name of the method in the `ActionListener` interface to use it in the program and you don't need to specify the class of the `ActionEvent`.

Lambda expressions support functional programming, a methodology for software design that has until now been unavailable to Java programmers.

This section has introduced the basic syntax of lambda expressions and two of the more common ways they will be employed in programs.

But functional programming in Java is a topic so powerful and revolutionary that it's the subject of entire books.

At this point, you should be able to recognize lambda expressions and use them to implement any single-method interface, also called a functional interface.

Summary

Inner classes, anonymous inner classes, and lambda expressions are among the most complex parts of the Java language to learn. They appeal primarily to programmers who have been writing programs in the language for a while and can take advantage of powerful features to accomplish more in fewer lines of code.

But even before you reach a point where you're writing your own lambda expressions, you should be able to benefit from the use of inner classes and anonymous inner classes.

A non-anonymous inner class is structured like a separate helper class, but it's placed inside another class alongside the instance variables, class variables, instance methods, and class methods. Unlike a helper class, it can access the private variables and methods of the class that it is created inside.

An anonymous inner class removes the need to devote an object to a class that's only used once, such as an event listener attached to a user interface component in Swing.

Lambda expressions are deceptively similar in appearance, requiring only a new arrow operator -> to create. But the implications of what they enable a Java programmer to do are enormous. Programmers with experience in other languages have been clamoring for this functionality for years.

Workshop

Q&A

Q. Anonymous inner classes are confusing. Do I have to use them in my programs?

A. No. As with other complex features of the Java language, you don't have to use them if you can get the job done some other way.

But you should learn about them anyway, because you're likely to encounter them in Java code.

When you look at the Java programs written by experienced programmers, you often find both inner classes and anonymous inner classes. So even if you're not ready to create them yourself, it's worthwhile to learn what they are and how they work.

Q. Are the Hatfields and McCoys still feuding?

A. The West Virginia and Kentucky families are on good terms 126 years after the last casualty in their infamous 35-year conflict.

In 1979, Hatfields and McCoys got together to play the TV game show *Family Feud* for a week. A pig was kept on stage and awarded to the winning family.

In 2003, a formal peace treaty was reached between the families in Pikeville, KY.

The author of the best-selling 2016 memoir *Hillbilly Elegy*, J.D. Vance, is a descendant of the Hatfields.

The Hatfield-McCoy Trails, 500 miles of trails for recreational off-road driving, were established in West Virginia in 2000 and expanded over the next decade.

Quiz

To see whether you should go to the front of the class with the knowledge you've attained during this hour, answer the following questions about inner classes, anonymous inner classes, and lambda expressions.

1. What makes some inner classes anonymous?

    A. They implement an interface.

    B. They aren't given a name.

    C. Both.

2. What's another name for an interface that contains only one method?

    A. Abstract interface

    B. Class

    C. Functional interface

3. What is it called when a lambda expression guesses the class of an argument to a method?

    A. Target typing

    B. Type casting

    C. Class inference

Answers

1. **C.** An anonymous inner class implements an interface with the `new` keyword, skipping the creation and naming of a class that implements it.

2. **C.** Functional interface, as of Java 8. They were called single abstract method interfaces in earlier versions of the language.

3. **A.** Target typing can infer the class of any functional interface method argument.

Activities

To finish this hour with class, put its subjects to work with the following activities:

▶ Rewrite the `LinkRotator` class from Hour 15, "Creating a Threaded Program," to use a lambda expression for the event listener.

▶ Add a fourth background color, `Color.YELLOW`, to the `NewColorFrame` application.

To see Java programs that implement these activities, visit the book's website at www.java24hours.com.

Building a Simple User Interface

This Hour's To-Do List:

▶ Create user interface components such as buttons.

▶ Create labels, text fields, and other components.

▶ Group components together.

▶ Put components inside other components.

▶ Scroll components horizontally and vertically.

▶ Open and close windows.

Things are going to get pretty gooey during this hour. You will make an enormous mess creating your first graphical user interface (GUI) with Java.

Computer users have come to expect software to feature a GUI, take user input from a mouse, and work like other programs. Although some users still work in command-line environments such as a Linux or Unix shell, most would be confused by software that does not offer a point-and-click, drag-and-drop graphical interface like Microsoft Windows or Mac OS.

Java supports this kind of software with Swing, a collection of Java classes that represent all the different buttons, text fields, sliders, and other components that can be part of a GUI, as well as the classes needed to take user input from those components.

During this hour and the next, you create and organize GUIs in Java. Afterward, in Hour 19, "Responding to User Input," you enable those interfaces to receive mouse clicks and other user input.

Swing and the Abstract Windowing Toolkit

Because Java is a cross-platform language that enables you to write programs for many operating systems, its graphical user software must be flexible. Instead of catering only to the Windows style or the Mac version, it must handle both, along with other platforms.

With Java, the development of a program's user interface is based on Swing and an earlier set of classes called the Abstract Windowing Toolkit. These classes enable you to create a GUI and receive input from the user.

Swing includes everything you need to write programs that use a GUI. With Java's user interface classes, you can create a GUI that includes all the following and more:

- ▶ Buttons, check boxes, labels, and other simple components

- ▶ Text fields, sliders, and other more complex components

- ▶ Pull-down menus and pop-up menus

- ▶ Windows, frames, dialog boxes, panels, and applet windows

NOTE

Swing includes dozens of components that can be customized in far more ways than can be documented here. This book covers the most common components and their most useful methods. As you explore them in the next four hours, you can learn more about each component and find new methods in Oracle's official documentation for the Java Class Library. Read it on the web at http://download.java.net/jdk9/docs/api. It offers additional reference documentation on every class and interface in Java 9.

Using Components

In Java, every part of a GUI is represented by a class in the Swing package. There is a `JButton` class for buttons, a `JWindow` class for windows, a `JTextField` class for text fields, and so on.

To create and display an interface, you create objects, set their variables, and call their methods. The techniques are the same as those you used as you were introduced to object-oriented programming (OOP).

When you are putting a GUI together, you work with two kinds of objects: components and containers. A component is an individual element in a user interface, such as a button or slider. A container is a component that you can use to hold other components.

The first step in creating an interface is to create a container that can hold components. In an application, this container is often a window or a frame.

Windows and Frames

Windows and frames are containers that can be displayed in a user interface and hold other components. Windows are simple containers that do not have a title bar or any of the other buttons normally along the top edge of a GUI. Frames are windows that include all the common windowing features users expect to find when they run software—such as buttons to close, expand, and shrink the window.

You create these containers using Swing's `JWindow` and `JFrame` classes. To refer to Swing classes in a Java program without using their full package-and-class name, use the following statement:

```
import javax.swing.*;
```

This only imports the class names from the `javax.swing` package. There are other packages you'll be putting to work in Swing.

One way to make use of a frame in a Java application is to make the application a subclass of `JFrame`. Your program inherits the behavior it needs to function as a frame. The following statements create a subclass of `JFrame`:

```
import javax.swing.*;

public class MainFrame extends JFrame {
    public MainFrame() {
        // set up the frame
    }
}
```

This class creates a frame but doesn't set it up completely. In the frame's constructor, you must do several things when creating a frame:

- ▶ Call a constructor of the superclass, `JFrame`.

- ▶ Set up the title of the frame.

- ▶ Set up the size of the frame.

- ▶ Set the frame's look and feel.

- ▶ Define what happens when the frame is closed by a user.

You also must make the frame visible, unless for some reason it should not be displayed when the application begins running.

Most of these things can be handled in the frame's constructor. The first thing the method must contain is a call to one of the constructors of `JFrame`, using the `super` statement. Here's an example:

```
super();
```

The preceding statement calls the `JFrame` constructor with no arguments. You also can call it with the title of your frame as an argument:

```
super("Main Frame");
```

This sets the title of the frame, which appears in the title bar along the top edge, to the specified string. In this example, the text "Main Frame" appears.

If you don't set up a title in this way, you can call the frame's `setTitle(String)` method with the title as the argument:

```
setTitle("Main Frame");
```

The size of the frame can be established by calling its `setSize(int, int)` method with two arguments: the width and height. The following statement sets up a frame that is 350 pixels wide and 125 pixels tall:

```
setSize(350, 125);
```

Another way to set the size of a frame is to fill it with components and then call the frame's `pack()` method with no arguments:

```
pack();
```

The `pack()` method sets the frame big enough to hold the preferred size of each component inside the frame (but no bigger). Every interface component has a preferred size, though this is sometimes disregarded, depending on how components have been arranged within an interface. You don't need to explicitly set the size of a frame before calling `pack()`—the method sets it to an adequate size before the frame is displayed.

Every frame is displayed with a button along the title bar that can be used to close the frame. On a Windows system, this button appears as an X in the upper-right corner of the frame. To define what happens when this button is clicked, call the frame's `setDefaultCloseOperation(int)` method with one of four `JFrame` class variables as the argument:

- ▶ `EXIT_ON_CLOSE`—Exit the program when the button is clicked.

- ▶ `DISPOSE_ON_CLOSE`—Close the frame and keep running the application.

- ▶ `DO_NOTHING_ON_CLOSE`—Keep the frame open and continue running.

- ▶ `HIDE_ON_CLOSE`—Close the frame and continue running.

The first call to the method is the most common, because when an application's user interface closes, it means the application should complete its work and shut down:

```
setDefaultCloseOperation(JFrame.EXIT_ON_CLOSE);
```

A graphical user interface created with Swing can customize its appearance with a look and feel, a visual theme that controls how buttons and other components appear and how they behave.

Java includes an enhanced look and feel called Nimbus, but it must be turned on to be used in a class. Setting a look and feel is done by calling the `setLookAndFeel()` method of the `UIManager` class in the main Swing package.

The method takes one argument: the full name of the look and feel's class.

The following statement sets Nimbus as the look and feel:

UIManager.setLookAndFeel(

   "javax.swing.plaf.nimbus.NimbusLookAndFeel"

);

One last thing is required is to make the frame visible. Call its `setVisible()` method with `true` as an argument:

`setVisible(true);`

This opens the frame at the defined width and height. You also can call it with `false` to stop displaying a frame.

Listing 17.1 contains the source code described in this section. In a Java file named `SalutonFrame` in the `com.java24hours` package, enter these statements.

LISTING 17.1   The Full Text of `SalutonFrame.java`

```
 1: package com.java24hours;
 2:
 3: import javax.swing.*;
 4:
 5: public class SalutonFrame extends JFrame {
 6:     public SalutonFrame() {
 7:         super("Saluton mondo!");
 8:         setLookAndFeel();
 9:         setSize(450, 200);
10:         setDefaultCloseOperation(JFrame.EXIT_ON_CLOSE);
11:         setVisible(true);
12:     }
13:
14:     private void setLookAndFeel() {
15:         try {
16:             UIManager.setLookAndFeel(
17:                 "javax.swing.plaf.nimbus.NimbusLookAndFeel"
18:             );
19:         } catch (Exception exc) {
20:             // ignore error
21:         }
22:     }
23:
24:     public static void main(String[] arguments) {
25:         SalutonFrame frame = new SalutonFrame();
26:     }
27: }
```

Lines 24–26 of Listing 17.1 contain a `main()` method, which turns this frame class into an application. When you run the class, you see the frame shown in Figure 17.1.

FIGURE 17.1
Displaying a frame in an application.

The only thing that `SalutonFrame` displays is a title: the traditional programmer's greeting "Saluton mondo!" The frame is an empty window because it doesn't contain any other components yet.

To add components to a frame, you must create the component and add it to the container. Each container has an `add()` method that takes one argument: the component to display.

The `SalutonFrame` class includes a `setLookAndFeel()` method that designates Nimbus as the frame's look and feel. The `setLookAndFeel()` method of the `UIManager` class is called in lines 16–18 to accomplish this.

The call to this method is placed inside a `try-catch` block, which enables errors that might occur to be handled.

Calling `UIManager.setLookAndFeel()` sets a GUI's look and feel. Any error that might occur as a result would just cause a program to keep the default look and feel instead of Nimbus.

TIP

There's something you might not have seen before in Listing 13.1. Look at Lines 16–18 carefully. They are a single statement spread out over three lines. The statement could be on a single line, but it was spread out to make the code more readable—for humans. The Java compiler doesn't care about the extra whitespace. As long as the statement has the right things in it and ends with a semicolon, it can be on multiple lines.

Buttons

One simple component you can add to a container is a `JButton` object. `JButton`, like the other components you are working with during this hour, is part of the `java.awt.swing` package.

A `JButton` object is a clickable button with a label that describes what clicking the button does. This label can be text, graphics, or both. The following statement creates a `JButton` called okButton and gives it the text label OK:

```
JButton okButton = new JButton("OK");
```

After a component such as `JButton` is created, it should be added to a container by calling its `add()` method:

```
add(okButton);
```

When you add components to a container, you do not specify the place in the container where the component should be displayed. The arrangement of components is decided by an object called a *layout manager*. The simplest of these managers is the `FlowLayout` class, which is part of the `java.awt` package.

To make a container use a specific layout manager, you must first create an object of that layout manager's class. You can create a `FlowLayout` object by calling its constructor with no arguments:

```
FlowLayout flo = new FlowLayout();
```

After you create a layout manager, call the container's `setLayout` method to associate the specified manager with that container:

```
setLayout(flo);
```

This statement designates the `flo` object as the layout manager.

The next application you create, a class called `Playback` in the `com.java24hours` package, is a Java application that displays a frame with three buttons. Enter the text from Listing 17.2 into a new Java file and save the file.

LISTING 17.2   The Full Text of `Playback.java`

```
 1: package com.java24hours;
 2:
 3: import javax.swing.*;
 4: import java.awt.*;
 5:
 6: public class Playback extends JFrame {
 7:     public Playback() {
 8:         super("Playback");
 9:         setLookAndFeel();
10:         setSize(450, 200);
11:         setDefaultCloseOperation(JFrame.EXIT_ON_CLOSE);
12:         FlowLayout flo = new FlowLayout();
13:         setLayout(flo);
14:         JButton play = new JButton("Play");
```

```
15:         JButton stop = new JButton("Stop");
16:         JButton pause = new JButton("Pause");
17:         add(play);
18:         add(stop);
19:         add(pause);
20:         setVisible(true);
21:     }
22:
23:     private void setLookAndFeel() {
24:         try {
25:             UIManager.setLookAndFeel(
26:                 "javax.swing.plaf.nimbus.NimbusLookAndFeel"
27:             );
28:         } catch (Exception exc) {
29:             // ignore error
30:         }
31:     }
32:
33:     public static void main(String[] arguments) {
34:         Playback frame = new Playback();
35:     }
36: }
```

The `Playback` program creates a `FlowLayout` layout manager in line 12 and sets the frame to employ it in line 13. When three buttons are added to the frame in lines 17–19, they're arranged by this manager.

When you run the application, your output should resemble Figure 17.2. Though you can click the buttons, nothing happens in response because the program does not contain any methods to receive and respond to user input. That's covered during Hour 19.

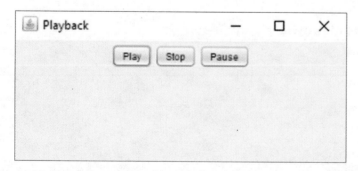

FIGURE 17.2
Displaying buttons on a GUI.

You can add many Swing user components to a container in this manner.

NOTE

Because so many different user interface components are introduced during this hour, the full source code used to create each figure is not listed here. You can find full versions of each program on the book's website at www.java24hours.com on the Hour 17 page.

Labels and Text Fields

A JLabel component displays information that the user cannot modify. This information can be text, a graphic, or both. These components are often used to label other components in an interface, hence the name. They often identify text fields.

A JTextField component is an area where a user can enter a single line of text. You can set up the width of the box when you create the text field.

The following statements create a JLabel component and JTextField component and add them to a container:

```
JLabel pageLabel = new JLabel("Web page address: ", JLabel.RIGHT);
JTextField pageAddress = new JTextField(20);
FlowLayout flo = new FlowLayout();
setLayout(flo);
add(pageLabel);
add(pageAddress);
```

Figure 17.3 shows this label and text field side-by-side. Both statements in this example use an argument to configure how the component should look.

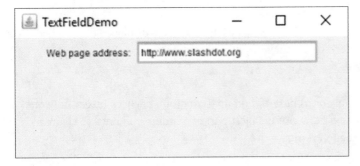

FIGURE 17.3
Displaying labels and text fields.

The pageLabel label is set up with the text "Web page address:" and a JLabel.RIGHT argument. This last value indicates that the label should appear flush right. JLabel.LEFT aligns the label text flush left, and JLabel.CENTER centers it. The argument used with

`JTextField` indicates the text field should be approximately 20 characters wide. You also can specify default text that appears in the text field with a statement such as the following:

```
JTextField country = new JTextField("Togolese Republic", 29);
```

This statement would create a `JTextField` object that is 20 characters wide and has the text "Togolese Republic" in the field.

You can retrieve the text contained within the object with the `getText()` method, which returns a string:

```
String countryChoice = country.getText();
```

As you might have guessed, you also can set the text with a corresponding method:

```
country.setText("Separate Customs Territory of Taiwan, Penghu, Kinmen, and Matsu");
```

This sets the text to the official name of Chinese Taipei, which is the longest country name in the world, edging out the second-place finisher: United Kingdom of Great Britain and Northern Ireland.

Check Boxes

A `JCheckBox` component is a box next to a line of text that can be checked or unchecked by the user. The following statements create a `JCheckBox` object and add it to a container:

```
JCheckBox jumboSize = new JCheckBox("Jumbo Size");
FlowLayout flo = new FlowLayout();
setLayout(flo);
add(jumboSize);
```

The argument to the `JCheckBox()` constructor indicates the text to be displayed alongside the box. If you want the box to be checked, use the following statement instead:

```
JCheckBox jumboSize = new JCheckBox("Jumbo Size", true);
```

You can present a `JCheckBox` singly or as part of a group. In a group of check boxes, only one can be checked at a time. To make a `JCheckBox` object part of a group, you have to create a `ButtonGroup` object. Consider the following:

```
JCheckBox frogLegs = new JCheckBox("Frog Leg Grande", true);
JCheckBox fishTacos = new JCheckBox("Fish Taco Platter", false);
JCheckBox emuNuggets = new JCheckBox("Emu Nuggets", false);
FlowLayout flo = new FlowLayout();
ButtonGroup meals = new ButtonGroup();
meals.add(frogLegs);
meals.add(fishTacos);
meals.add(emuNuggets);
```

```
setLayout(flo);
add(jumboSize);
add(frogLegs);
add(fishTacos);
add(emuNuggets);
```

This creates three check boxes that are all grouped under the `ButtonGroup` object called `meals`. The Frog Leg Grande box is checked initially, but if the user checked one of the other meal boxes, the check next to Frog Leg Grande would disappear automatically. Figure 17.4 shows the different check boxes from this section.

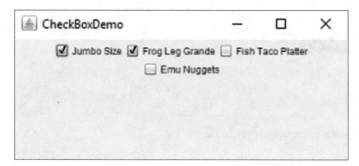

FIGURE 17.4
Displaying check box components.

Combo Boxes

A `JComboBox` component is a pop-up list of choices that also can be set up to receive text input. When both options are enabled, you can select an item with your mouse or use the keyboard to enter text instead. The combo box serves a similar purpose to a group of check boxes, except that only one of the choices is visible unless the pop-up list is being displayed.

To create a `JComboBox` object, you have to add each of the choices after creating the object, as in the following example:

```
JComboBox profession = new JComboBox();
FlowLayout flo = new FlowLayout();
profession.addItem("Butcher");
profession.addItem("Baker");
profession.addItem("Candlestick maker");
profession.addItem("Fletcher");
profession.addItem("Fighter");
profession.addItem("Technical writer");
setLayout(flo);
add(profession);
```

This example creates a single JComboBox component that provides six choices from which the user can make a selection. When one is selected, it appears in the display of the component. Figure 17.5 shows this example while the pop-up list of choices is being displayed.

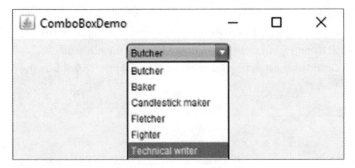

FIGURE 17.5
Displaying combo box components.

To enable a JComboBox component to receive text input, you must call its setEditable(*boolean*) method with an argument of true:

```
profession.setEditable(true);
```

You must call this method before the component is added to a container.

Text Areas

A JTextArea component is a text field that enables the user to enter more than one line of text. You can specify the width and height of the component. The following statements create a JTextArea component with a width of 40 characters and a height of 8 lines and add it to a container:

```
JTextArea comments = new JTextArea(8, 40);
FlowLayout flo = new FlowLayout();
setLayout(flo);
add(comments);
```

Figure 17.6 shows this example in a frame.

You can specify a string in the JTextArea() constructor to be displayed in the text area, using the newline character \n to send text to the next line, as in the following:

```
JTextArea comments = new JTextArea("I should have been a pair\n"
    + "of ragged claws.", 10, 25);
```

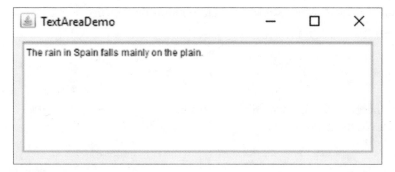

FIGURE 17.6
Displaying text area components.

Text areas have two methods that can be called to specify how the component behaves when a user types text past the right edge of a line. Call the `setLineWrap(boolean)` method with an argument of `true` to cause text to wrap to the next line:

```
comments.setLineWrap(true);
```

To determine how text wraps to the next line, use the `setWrapStyleWord(boolean)` method. Call it with the argument `true` to wrap based on where a word ends, or `false` to wrap based on characters.

If you don't call these methods, text will not wrap. A user can keep entering text on the same line until hitting the Enter key, going past the right edge of the area.

Text area components behave in ways you might not expect—they expand in size when the user reaches the bottom of the area and do not include scrollbars along the right edge or bottom edge. To implement them in a more well-behaved way, you must place the text area inside a container called a scroll pane.

Components in a GUI are often bigger than the area available to display them. To enable a component to move from one part of the component to another, you use vertical and horizontal scrollbars.

In Swing, you support scrolling by adding a component to a scroll pane, a container that is represented by the `JScrollPane` class.

You can create a scroll pane with the following constructors:

- ▶ `JScrollPane()`—Create a scroll pane with horizontal and vertical scrollbars that appear as needed.

- ▶ `JScrollPane(int, int)`—Create a scroll pane with the specified vertical scrollbar and horizontal scrollbars.

▶ JScrollPane(*Component*)—Create a scroll pane that contains the specified user interface component.

▶ JScrollPane(*Component, int, int*)—Create a scroll pane with the specified component, vertical scrollbar, and horizontal scrollbar.

The integer arguments to these constructors determine how scrollbars are used in the pane. Use the following class variables as these arguments:

▶ JScrollPane.VERTICAL_SCROLLBAR_AS_NEEDED or JScrollPane.HORIZONTAL_SCROLLBAR_AS_NEEDED

▶ JScrollPane.VERTICAL_SCROLLBAR_NEVER or JScrollPane.HORIZONTAL_SCROLLBAR_NEVER

▶ JScrollPane.VERTICAL_SCROLLBAR_ALWAYS or JScrollPane.HORIZONTAL_SCROLLBAR_ALWAYS

If you have created a scroll pane without a component in it, you can use the pane's add(*Component*) method to add components. After you have finished setting up a scroll pane, it should be added to a container in place of the component.

Here's the previous example rewritten to put the text area inside a scroll pane:

```
FlowLayout flo = new FlowLayout();
setLayout(flo);
JTextArea comments = new JTextArea(8, 40);
comments.setLineWrap(true);
comments.setWrapStyleWord(true);
JScrollPane scroll = new JScrollPane(comments,
    JScrollPane.VERTICAL_SCROLLBAR_ALWAYS,
    JScrollPane.HORIZONTAL_SCROLLBAR_NEVER);
add(scroll);
```

Figure 17.7 shows this example in a frame.

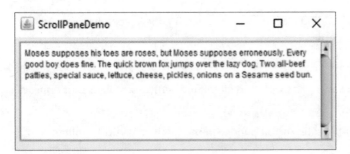

FIGURE 17.7
Displaying text area components in a scroll pane container.

Panels

The last component introduced this hour is a panel, which is created in Swing using the `JPanel` class. `JPanel` objects are the simplest kind of container available in a user interface. The purpose of `JPanel` objects is to subdivide a display area into different groups of components. When the display is divided into sections, you can use different layout managers in each section.

The following statements create a `JPanel` object and assign it a layout manager:

```
JPanel topRow = new JPanel();
FlowLayout flo = new FlowLayout();
topRow.setLayout(flo);
add(topRow);
```

Panels often are used when arranging the components in an interface, as you see in Hour 18, "Laying Out a User Interface."

You add components to a panel by calling its `add()` method. You can assign a layout manager directly to the panel by calling its `setLayout()` method.

You also can use panels when you need an area in an interface to draw something, such as an image from a graphics file.

Another convenient use of `JPanel` is to create your own components that can be added to other classes. This is demonstrated in the hour's final project.

Creating Your Own Component

An advantage of object-oriented programming is the capability to reuse classes in different projects. For the next project, you create a special panel component that you can reuse in other Java programs. The component, `FreeSpacePanel`, reports the disk space available on the computer running the application. The panel displays the amount of free space, the total space, and the percentage that is free.

The first step in creating your own user interface component is to decide the existing component from which to inherit. Your new component will have all of its existing attributes and behavior, aside from anything you modify and anything new you add.

The `FreeSpacePanel` component is a subclass of `JPanel` defined in Listing 17.3. Enter the text from Listing 17.3 into a new empty Java file and save the file.

LISTING 17.3   The Full Text of `FreeSpacePanel.java`

```
1: package com.java24hours;
2:
3: import java.io.IOException;
4: import java.nio.file.*;
5: import javax.swing.*;
```

```
 6:
 7: public class FreeSpacePanel extends JPanel {
 8:     JLabel spaceLabel = new JLabel("Disk space: ");
 9:     JLabel space = new JLabel();
10:
11:     public FreeSpacePanel() {
12:         super();
13:         add(spaceLabel);
14:         add(space);
15:         try {
16:             setValue();
17:         } catch (IOException ioe) {
18:             space.setText("Error");
19:         }
20:     }
21:
22:     private final void setValue() throws IOException {
23:         // get the current file storage pool
24:         Path current = Paths.get("");
25:         FileStore store = Files.getFileStore(current);
26:         // find the free storage space
27:         long totalSpace = store.getTotalSpace();
28:         long freeSpace = store.getUsableSpace();
29:         // get this as a percentage (with two digits)
30:         double percent = (double)freeSpace / (double)totalSpace * 100;
31:         percent = (int)(percent * 100) / (double)100;
32:         // set the label's text
33:         space.setText(freeSpace + " free out of " + totalSpace + " ("
34:             + percent + "%)");
35:
36:     }
37: }
```

This class is a component that can be added to any graphical user interface when you want to display information about available disk space. It cannot run on its own as an application.

The setValue() method in FreeSpacePanel sets the text of the label that presents disk space information. This method has the keyword final when it is declared in line 22:

```
private final void setValue() {
    // ...
}
```

Including the final keyword in a method declaration prevents the method from being overridden in a subclass. This is required for FreeSpacePanel to be a GUI component.

The panel is created in the constructor in Lines 11–20. The following things are taking place:

- Line 12—The super() method calls the constructor of the JPanel class, ensuring that it is set up properly.

- Line 13—The new label spaceLabel, which has the text "Disk space: " and was created as an instance variable in Line 8, is added to the panel by calling add(Component) with the label as an argument.

- Line 14—The space label, an instance variable with no text created in Line 9, also is added to the panel.

- Line 16—The setValue() method is called, which sets the text of the space label.

The call to setValue() in Line 16 is enclosed within another try-catch block like the one employed when setting a look and feel. You learn more about how to deal with errors during Hour 18, but here's the TLDR version: try-catch makes it possible to handle one or more errors that could occur in part of a Java program.

This is necessary because calling setValue() might cause an error to occur when the computer's file system is accessed to see how much free space it contains. The error has its own class in Java, IOException, which represents input/output errors.

The try block encloses the potential error-causing code. The catch block identifies the kind of error within parentheses and the code to execute if that error occurs.

If such an error is encountered as the application runs, Line 18 sets the space label's text to the text "Error" to let the user know something has gone wrong.

NOTE

The acronym "TLDR" stands for "too long; didn't read," and it appears on the Internet when people give an extremely brief summary of a long piece of writing for the people who don't want to read the whole thing.

I hope this book isn't TLDR for you. We tried to make it JRLRWTANIRJP (just-right length; read whole thing and now I'm rich Java programmer).

Giving the custom component something interesting to do requires a quick toe-dip into Java file handling, a subject that will be covered at length in Hour 20, "Reading and Writing Files."

To figure out how much disk space is free on a computer, you need four classes in the java.nio.file package, which is employed to access a computer's file system.

A `Path` object represents the location of a file or folder. The `Paths` class has a `get(String)` method that converts a string to a path matching that string. When called with `""` (an empty string), it returns the path of the current folder in which the Java application is running:

```
Path current = Paths.get("");
```

Storage information for a disk is represented in Java by a `FileStore` object, which is a file storage pool. After you have a path, you can get the file store where that path is located with a method in the `Files` class. Call the `getFileStore(Path)` method of `Files` to retrieve that file storage pool:

```
FileStore store = Files.getFileStore(current);
```

With this pool, you now can call its `getTotalSpace()` and `getUsableSpace()` methods to find out how much disk space is available on the current disk:

```
long totalSpace = store.getTotalSpace();
long freeSpace = store.getUsableSpace();
double percent = (double)freeSpace / (double)totalSpace * 100;
```

CAUTION

The expression that calculates the percentage includes a lot of references to `double`, which may seem weird. The second and third cast the `freeSpace` and `totalSpace` variables to double values before they are used in the expression. This is necessary to keep the expression from producing an integer value instead of a floating-point number. Java determines the data type of an expression's result by the types in the expression. A `long` divided by a `long` multiplied by the integer 100 would produce a `long`, not the desired percentage.

The percentage calculated in the final statement may be an extremely long number of digits past the decimal point, such as 64.8675309.

The following expression converts a `double` percentage to no more than two decimal places:

```
percent = (int)(percent * 100) / (double)100;
```

The first half of the expression multiplies the percentage by 100—moving the decimal two places to the right—and then converts it to an integer, so 64.8675309 becomes 6487.

The second half divides this by 100—moving the decimal back two places to the left—to restore an approximation of the percentage. This makes 6486 into 64.86.

With a percentage limited to two decimal places, the label's text can be set to report the available and occupied disk space:

```
space.setText(freeSpace + " free out of " + totalSpace + " ("
    + percent + "%)");
```

There's no way to see the panel you've just created until it is added to a graphical user interface. To try out FreeSpacePanel, create the FreeSpaceFrame application in the com.java24hours package as it's defined in Listing 17.4. Enter a new text file for a class called FreeSpaceFrame.

LISTING 17.4 **The Full Text of** FreeSpaceFrame.java

```
 1: package com.java24hours;
 2:
 3: import java.awt.*;
 4: import javax.swing.*;
 5:
 6: public class FreeSpaceFrame extends JFrame {
 7:     public FreeSpaceFrame() {
 8:         super("Disk Free Space");
 9:         setLookAndFeel();
10:         setSize(500, 120);
11:         setDefaultCloseOperation(JFrame.EXIT_ON_CLOSE);
12:         FlowLayout flo = new FlowLayout();
13:         setLayout(flo);
14:         FreeSpacePanel freePanel = new FreeSpacePanel();
15:         add(freePanel);
16:         setVisible(true);
17:     }
18:
19:     private void setLookAndFeel() {
20:         try {
21:             UIManager.setLookAndFeel(
22:                 "javax.swing.plaf.nimbus.NimbusLookAndFeel"
23:             );
24:         } catch (Exception exc) {
25:             // ignore error
26:         }
27:     }
28:
29:     public static void main(String[] arguments) {
30:         FreeSpaceFrame frame = new FreeSpaceFrame();
31:     }
32: }
```

This application creates a FreeSpacePanel component in Line 14 and adds the panel to its frame in Line 15.

When you run the application, it should resemble Figure 17.8 with values from your own computer.

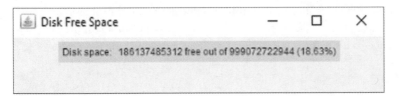

FIGURE 17.8
Displaying a custom disk space component.

Summary

Users have come to expect a point-and-click, visual environment for the programs they run. This expectation makes creating software more of a challenge, but Java puts these capabilities into your hands with Swing, which provides all the classes you need to provide a working, useful GUI—regardless of what kind of setup you're using to run Java programs.

Developing graphical Java applications with Swing is a good way to get some practice working with object-oriented programming. Every component, container, and layout manager is represented by its own class of object. Many of them inherit their common behavior from the same superclass. For instance, all user interface components introduced during this hour are subclasses of `javax.swing.JComponent`.

During the next hour, you learn more about the design of a GUI as you work with new layout managers that can specify the placement of components within a container in more sophisticated ways than `FlowLayout`.

Workshop

Q&A

Q. How are components arranged if I don't assign a layout manager to a container?

A. In a simple container such as a panel, components are arranged using `FlowLayout` by default. Each component is added in the same manner that words are displayed on a page in English, from left to right, then down to the next line when there's no more room. Frames, windows, and applets use the `BorderLayout` default layout style you learn about during the next hour.

Q. Why do so many of the graphical user interface classes have names preceded by a "J," such as `JFrame` and `JLabel`?

A. These classes are a part of the Swing framework, which was the second attempt at graphical user interface classes in the Java class library. The Abstract Windowing Toolkit (AWT) was first, and it had simpler class names, such as `Frame` and `Label`.

The AWT classes belong to the `java.awt` package and related packages, while Swing classes belong to `javax.swing` and the like, so they could have the same class names. The use of the "J" names keeps the classes from being mistaken for each other.

Swing classes also are called Java Foundation Classes (JFC).

Q. Where can I buy an uncut sheet of $1 bills?

A. The U.S. Bureau of Engraving and Printing sells sheets of real $1, $10, $20, and $50 bills at the website www.moneyfactorystore.gov.

A sheet of 25 $1 bills sells for $50.50, 16 $10 bills for $249, 16 $20 bills for $409, and 16 $50 bills for $920. Because the money is actual currency, these purchases are cheaper if you factor in the face value of those bills. You're paying an extra $25.50 for the ones, $89 for the tens, $89 for the twenties, and $100 for the fifties.

There's also a five-pound bag containing $10,000 of shredded bills that sells for $45.

The bureau is the only U.S. government agency that admits it is throwing money away.

Quiz

If your brain hasn't been turned into a GUI mush with this hour's toil, test your skills by answering the following questions.

1. Which user component is used as a container to hold other components?

    A. TupperWare

    B. `JPanel`

    C. Choice

2. Which of the following must be done first within a container?

    A. Establish a layout manager

    B. Add components

    C. Doesn't matter

3. What method determines how components are arranged within a container?

    A. `setLayout()`

    B. `setLayoutManager()`

    C. `setVisible()`

Answers

1. **B.** `JPanel`. You can add components to the panel and then add the panel to another container such as a frame.

2. **A.** You must specify the layout manager before the components so you can add them in the correct way.

3. **A.** The `setLayout()` method takes one argument: the layout manager object that has the job of deciding where components should be displayed.

Activities

To interface further with the subject of GUI design, undertake the following activities:

▶ Modify the `SalutonFrame` application so that it displays "Saluton Mondo!" in the frame's main area instead of the title bar.

▶ Enhance the `FreeSpacePanel` component by displaying commas every three places in the disk size figures. One way to do it uses a `StringBuilder` object, the `String` class method `charAt(int)`, and a `for` loop to iterate through the string.

To see Java programs that implement these activities, visit the book's website at www.java24hours.com.

HOUR 18
Laying Out a User Interface

This Hour's To-Do List:

▶ Create a layout manager.

▶ Assign a layout manager to a container.

▶ Use panels to organize components in an interface.

▶ Work with unusual layouts.

▶ Create a prototype for a Java application.

When you begin designing graphical user interfaces (GUIs) for your Java programs, one obstacle you face is that your components can move around. Whenever a container changes size—such as when a user resizes a frame—the components it holds may rearrange themselves to fit its new dimensions.

This fluidity works in your favor because it takes into account the differences in how interface components are displayed on different operating systems. A clickable button might look different in Windows than it does in Linux or Mac OS.

Components are organized in an interface by using a set of classes called *layout managers*. These classes define how components are displayed within a container. Each container in an interface can have its own layout manager.

Using Layout Managers

In Java, the placement of components within a container depends on the size of the component, the size of other components, and the height and width of the container. The layout of buttons, text fields, and other components can be affected by the following things:

▶ The size of the container

▶ The size of other components and containers

▶ The layout manager

There are several layout managers you can use to affect how components are shown. The default manager for panels is the FlowLayout class in the java.awt package, which was used during the previous hour.

Under FlowLayout, components are dropped onto an area in the same way words are organized on a page in English—from left to right and then down to the next line when there's no more space.

The following example could be used in a frame so that it employs flow layout when components are added:

```
FlowLayout topLayout = new FlowLayout();
setLayout(topLayout);
```

You also can set up a layout manager to work within a specific container, such as a JPanel object. You can do this by using the setLayout() method of that container object.

The hour's first project is Crisis, an application that has a GUI with five buttons. Create a new Java file for a class named Crisis in the package com.java24hours. Enter the text from Listing 18.1 into the file and save the file.

LISTING 18.1   The Full Text of Crisis.java

```
 1: package com.java24hours;
 2:
 3: import java.awt.*;
 4: import javax.swing.*;
 5:
 6: public class Crisis extends JFrame {
 7:     JButton panicButton;
 8:     JButton dontPanicButton;
 9:     JButton blameButton;
10:     JButton mediaButton;
11:     JButton saveButton;
12:
13:     public Crisis() {
14:         super("Crisis");
15:         setLookAndFeel();
16:         setSize(348, 128);
17:         setDefaultCloseOperation(JFrame.EXIT_ON_CLOSE);
18:         FlowLayout flo = new FlowLayout();
19:         setLayout(flo);
20:         panicButton = new JButton("Panic");
21:         dontPanicButton = new JButton("Don't Panic");
22:         blameButton = new JButton("Blame Others");
23:         mediaButton = new JButton("Notify the Media");
24:         saveButton = new JButton("Save Yourself");
25:         add(panicButton);
26:         add(dontPanicButton);
```

```
27:            add(blameButton);
28:            add(mediaButton);
29:            add(saveButton);
30:            setVisible(true);
31:        }
32:
33:        private void setLookAndFeel() {
34:            try {
35:                UIManager.setLookAndFeel(
36:                    "com.sun.java.swing.plaf.nimbus.NimbusLookAndFeel"
37:                );
38:            } catch (Exception exc) {
39:                // ignore error
40:            }
41:        }
42:
43:        public static void main(String[] arguments) {
44:            Crisis frame = new Crisis();
45:        }
46: }
```

Figure 18.1 shows the application running.

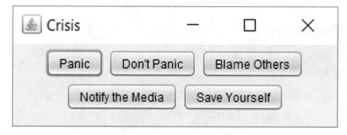

FIGURE 18.1
Arranging components using flow layout.

The `FlowLayout` class uses the dimensions of its container as the only guide for how to lay out components. Resize the window of the application to see how components are instantly rearranged in response. Make the window twice as wide, and all of the `JButton` components are shown on the same line. Make it narrow enough and they all stack vertically.

The `GridLayout` **Manager**

The `GridLayout` class in the `java.awt` package organizes all components in a container into a specific number of rows and columns. All components are allocated the same-sized space in the display area, so if you specify a grid that is three columns wide and three rows tall, the container is divided into nine areas of equal size.

GridLayout places all components as they are added into a place on a grid. Components are added from left to right until a row is full, and then the leftmost column of the next grid is filled.

The following statements create a container and set it to use a grid layout that is two rows wide and three columns tall:

```
GridLayout grid = new GridLayout(2, 3);
setLayout(grid);
```

Figure 18.2 shows what the Crisis application would look like if it used grid layout.

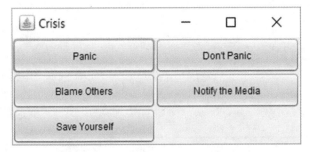

FIGURE 18.2
Arranging components using grid layout.

The BorderLayout **Manager**

The BorderLayout class, also in java.awt, arranges components at specific positions within the container that are identified by one of five directions: north, south, east, west, or center.

The BorderLayout manager arranges components into five areas: four denoted by compass directions and one for the center area. When you add a component under this layout, the add() method includes a second argument to specify where the component should be placed. This argument should be one of five class variables of the BorderLayout class: NORTH, SOUTH, EAST, WEST, and CENTER are used for this argument.

Like the GridLayout class, BorderLayout devotes all available space to the components. The component placed in the center is given all the space that isn't needed for the four border components, so it's usually the largest.

The following statements create a container that uses border layout:

```
BorderLayout crisisLayout = new BorderLayout();
setLayout(crisisLayout);
add(panicButton, BorderLayout.NORTH);
add(dontPanicButton, BorderLayout.SOUTH);
```

```
add(blameButton, BorderLayout.EAST);
add(mediaButton, BorderLayout.WEST);
add(saveButton, BorderLayout.CENTER);
```

Figure 18.3 shows how this looks in the Crisis application.

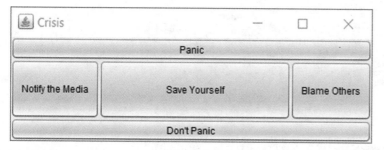

FIGURE 18.3
Arranging components using border layout.

The BoxLayout **Manager**

Another handy layout manager, BoxLayout in the javax.swing package, makes it possible to stack components in a single row horizontally or vertically.

To employ this layout, create a panel to hold components, and then create a layout manager with two arguments:

▶ The component to organize in box layout

▶ The value BoxLayout.Y_AXIS for vertical alignment and BoxLayout.X_AXIS for horizontal alignment

Here's code to stack the Crisis components:

```
JPanel pane = new JPanel();
BoxLayout box = new BoxLayout(pane, BoxLayout.Y_AXIS);
pane.setLayout(box);
pane.add(panicButton);
pane.add(dontPanicButton);
pane.add(blameButton);
pane.add(mediaButton);
pane.add(saveButton);
add(pane);
```

Figure 18.4 shows how this turns out.

FIGURE 18.4
Stacking components using box layout.

Separating Components with `Insets`

As you are arranging components within a container, you can move components away from the edges of the container using `Insets`, an object that represents the border area of a container.

The `Insets` class, which is part of the `java.awt` package, has a constructor that takes four arguments: the space to leave at the `top`, `left`, `bottom`, and `right` of the container. Each argument is specified using pixels, the same unit of measure employed when defining the size of a frame.

The following statement creates an `Insets` object:

```
Insets around = new Insets(10, 6, 10, 3);
```

The `around` object represents a container border that is 10 pixels inside the top edge, 6 pixels inside the left, 10 pixels inside the bottom, and 3 pixels inside the right.

To make use of an `Insets` object in a container, you must override the container's `getInsets()` method. This method has no arguments and returns an `Insets` object, as in the following example:

```
public Insets getInsets() {
    Insets squeeze = new Insets(50, 15, 10, 15);
    return squeeze;
}
```

Figure 18.5 shows how this would change the `FlowLayout`-managed interface shown in Figure 18.1.

FIGURE 18.5
Using insets to add space around components.

The container shown in Figure 18.5 has an empty border that's 15 pixels from the left edge, 10 pixels from the bottom edge, 15 pixels from the right edge, and 50 pixels from the top edge.

NOTE

A `JFrame` container has a built-in inset to make room for the frame's title bar. When you override `getInsets()` and set your own values, a low inset value causes the container to display components underneath the title bar.

Laying Out an Application

The layout managers you have seen thus far were applied to an entire frame. The `setLayout()` method of the frame was used, and all components followed the same rules. This setup can be suitable for some programs, but as you try to develop a GUI with Swing, you often find that none of the layout managers fit.

One way around this problem is to use a group of `JPanel` objects as containers to hold different sections of a GUI. You can set up different layout rules for each of these sections by using the `setLayout()` methods of each `JPanel`. After these panels contain all the components they need to contain, you can add the panels directly to the frame.

The next project develops a full interface for the program you write during the next hour. The program is a Lotto number cruncher that assesses a user's chance of winning one of the multimillion dollar Lotto contests in the span of a lifetime. This chance is determined by running random six-number Lotto drawings again and again until the user's numbers turn up as the big winner. Figure 18.6 shows the GUI you are developing for the application.

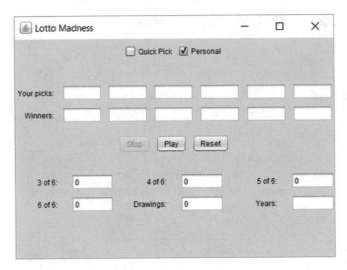

FIGURE 18.6
Displaying the GUI of the `LottoMadness` application.

Create a new Java file called `LottoMadness` in the package `com.java24hours`, enter text from Listing 18.2 into the source editor, and save the file.

LISTING 18.2 **The Full Text of** `LottoMadness.java`

```
 1: package com.java24hours;
 2:
 3: import java.awt.*;
 4: import javax.swing.*;
 5:
 6: public class LottoMadness extends JFrame {
 7:
 8:     // set up row 1
 9:     JPanel row1 = new JPanel();
10:     ButtonGroup option = new ButtonGroup();
11:     JCheckBox quickpick = new JCheckBox("Quick Pick", false);
12:     JCheckBox personal = new JCheckBox("Personal", true);
13:     // set up row 2
14:     JPanel row2 = new JPanel();
15:     JLabel numbersLabel = new JLabel("Your picks: ", JLabel.RIGHT);
16:     JTextField[] numbers = new JTextField[6];
17:     JLabel winnersLabel = new JLabel("Winners: ", JLabel.RIGHT);
18:     JTextField[] winners = new JTextField[6];
19:     // set up row 3
20:     JPanel row3 = new JPanel();
21:     JButton stop = new JButton("Stop");
22:     JButton play = new JButton("Play");
23:     JButton reset = new JButton("Reset");
```

```
24:     // set up row 4
25:     JPanel row4 = new JPanel();
26:     JLabel got3Label = new JLabel("3 of 6: ", JLabel.RIGHT);
27:     JTextField got3 = new JTextField("0");
28:     JLabel got4Label = new JLabel("4 of 6: ", JLabel.RIGHT);
29:     JTextField got4 = new JTextField("0");
30:     JLabel got5Label = new JLabel("5 of 6: ", JLabel.RIGHT);
31:     JTextField got5 = new JTextField("0");
32:     JLabel got6Label = new JLabel("6 of 6: ", JLabel.RIGHT);
33:     JTextField got6 = new JTextField("0", 10);
34:     JLabel drawingsLabel = new JLabel("Drawings: ", JLabel.RIGHT);
35:     JTextField drawings = new JTextField("0");
36:     JLabel yearsLabel = new JLabel("Years: ", JLabel.RIGHT);
37:     JTextField years = new JTextField();
38:
39:     public LottoMadness() {
40:         super("Lotto Madness");
41:
42:         setSize(550, 400);
43:         setDefaultCloseOperation(JFrame.EXIT_ON_CLOSE);
44:         GridLayout layout = new GridLayout(5, 1, 10, 10);
45:         setLayout(layout);
46:
47:         FlowLayout layout1 = new FlowLayout(FlowLayout.CENTER,
48:             10, 10);
49:         option.add(quickpick);
50:         option.add(personal);
51:         row1.setLayout(layout1);
52:         row1.add(quickpick);
53:         row1.add(personal);
54:         add(row1);
55:
56:         GridLayout layout2 = new GridLayout(2, 7, 10, 10);
57:         row2.setLayout(layout2);
58:         row2.add(numbersLabel);
59:         for (int i = 0; i < 6; i++) {
60:             numbers[i] = new JTextField();
61:             row2.add(numbers[i]);
62:         }
63:         row2.add(winnersLabel);
64:         for (int i = 0; i < 6; i++) {
65:             winners[i] = new JTextField();
66:             winners[i].setEditable(false);
67:             row2.add(winners[i]);
68:         }
69:         add(row2);
70:
71:         FlowLayout layout3 = new FlowLayout(FlowLayout.CENTER,
72:             10, 10);
```

```
73:            row3.setLayout(layout3);
74:            stop.setEnabled(false);
75:            row3.add(stop);
76:            row3.add(play);
77:            row3.add(reset);
78:            add(row3);
79:
80:            GridLayout layout4 = new GridLayout(2, 3, 20, 10);
81:            row4.setLayout(layout4);
82:            row4.add(got3Label);
83:            got3.setEditable(false);
84:            row4.add(got3);
85:            row4.add(got4Label);
86:            got4.setEditable(false);
87:            row4.add(got4);
88:            row4.add(got5Label);
89:            got5.setEditable(false);
90:            row4.add(got5);
91:            row4.add(got6Label);
92:            got6.setEditable(false);
93:            row4.add(got6);
94:            row4.add(drawingsLabel);
95:            drawings.setEditable(false);
96:            row4.add(drawings);
97:            row4.add(yearsLabel);
98:            years.setEditable(false);
99:            row4.add(years);
100:           add(row4);
101:
102:           setVisible(true);
103:       }
104:
105:       private static void setLookAndFeel() {
106:           try {
107:               UIManager.setLookAndFeel(
108:                   "com.sun.java.swing.plaf.nimbus.NimbusLookAndFeel"
109:               );
110:           } catch (Exception exc) {
111:               // ignore error
112:           }
113:       }
114:
115:       public static void main(String[] arguments) {
116:           LottoMadness.setLookAndFeel();
117:           LottoMadness frame = new LottoMadness();
118:       }
119: }
```

Even though you haven't added any statements that make the program do anything yet, you can run the application to make sure that the graphical interface is organized correctly and collects the information you need.

This application uses several layout managers. To get a clearer picture of how the application's user interface is laid out, take a look at Figure 18.7. The interface is divided into four horizontal rows that are separated by horizontal black lines in the figure. Each of these rows is a JPanel object, and the overall layout manager of the application organizes these rows into a GridLayout of four rows and one column.

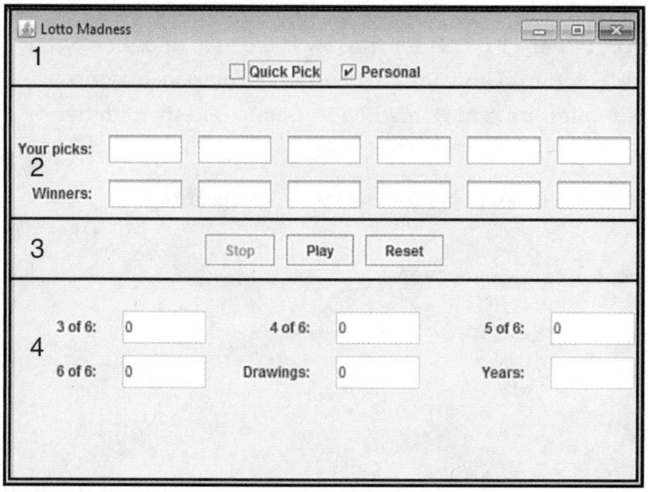

FIGURE 18.7
Dividing the LottoMadness application into panels.

Within the rows, different layout managers are used to determine how the components should appear. Rows 1 and 3 use FlowLayout objects. Lines 47–48 of the program show how these are created:

```
FlowLayout layout1 = new FlowLayout(FlowLayout.CENTER,
    10, 10);
```

Three arguments are used with the FlowLayout() constructor. The first argument, FlowLayout.CENTER, indicates that the components should be centered within their container—the horizontal JPanel on which they are placed. The last two components specify the width and height that each component should be moved away from other components. Using a width of 10 pixels and a height of 10 pixels puts a small amount of extra distance between the components.

Row 2 of the interface is laid out into a grid that is two rows tall and seven columns wide. The GridLayout() constructor also specifies that components should be set apart from other components by 10 pixels in each direction. Lines 56–57 set up this grid:

```
GridLayout layout2 = new GridLayout(2, 7, 10, 10);
row2.setLayout(layout2);
```

Row 4 uses GridLayout to arrange components into a grid that is two rows tall and three columns wide.

The LottoMadness application uses several components described during this hour. Lines 9–37 are used to set up objects for all the components that make up the interface. The statements are organized by row. First, a JPanel object for the row is created, and then each component that goes on the row is set up. This code creates all the components and containers, but they are not displayed unless an add() method is used to add them to the application's main frame.

In Lines 47–100, the components are added. Lines 47–54 are indicative of the entire LottoMadness() constructor:

```
FlowLayout layout1 = new FlowLayout(FlowLayout.CENTER,
    10, 10);
option.add(quickpick);
option.add(personal);
row1.setLayout(layout1);
row1.add(quickpick);
row1.add(personal);
add(row1);
```

After a layout manager object is created, it is used with the setLayout() method of the row's JPanel object—row1 in this case. When the layout has been specified, components are added to the JPanel by using its add() method. After all the components have been placed, the entire row1 object is added to the frame by calling its own add() method.

The LottoMadness application sets the look and feel of the graphical user interface differently from the way it did in previous Swing applications. The setLookAndFeel() method is created as a class method—note the static keyword in Line 105—and called in the main() method in Line 116.

Previous applications made setLookAndFeel() an object method and called it within the object's constructor. The reason this doesn't happen in LottoMadness is because the look and feel must be selected before any instance variables have been created and given values.

Summary

When you design a Java program's GUI for the first time, you might have trouble believing that it's an advantage for components to move around. They don't always go where you want them to go. Layout managers provide a way to develop an attractive GUI that is flexible enough to handle differences in presentation.

During the next hour, you learn more about the function of a GUI. You get a chance to see the `LottoMadness` interface in use as it churns through lottery drawings and tallies up winners.

Workshop

Q&A

Q. Why are some of the text fields in the LottoMadness application shaded in gray while others are white?

A. The `setEditable()` method has been used on the gray fields to make them impossible to edit. The default behavior of a text field is to enable users to change the value of the text field by clicking within its borders and typing any desired changes. However, some fields are intended to display information rather than take input from the user. The `setEditable()` method prevents users from changing a field they should not modify.

Q. Was there really a Willy Wonka golden ticket winner in *Willy Wonka and the Chocolate Factory* whose demise was too horrible for the movie?

A. The fate of Miranda Piker was so gruesome that she was dropped from the final draft of Roald Dahl's book *Charlie and the Chocolate* Factory, which inspired the 1971 movie and its 2005 remake. Piker was a smug child who believed children should never play so they could attend school all the time. Her father was a school headmaster.

Piker and the other golden ticket winners at Wonka's factory are introduced to Spotty Powder, a sugary concoction that causes the eater to break out in red spots so they can feign illness and miss school. Piker and her father become outraged and decide to destroy the machine that makes it.

As their screams are heard from the adjacent room, Wonka explains that they've gone into the place where the candy's ingredients are ground into powder. "That's part of the recipe," he tells Miranda's mother. "We've got to use one or two schoolmasters occasionally or it doesn't work."

The Oompa-Loompas celebrate her just deserts with song: "Oh, Miranda Mary Piker,/How could anybody like her,/Such a priggish and revolting little kid./So we said, 'Why don't we fix her/In the Spotty-Powder mixer/Then we're bound to like her better than we did.'/Soon this child who is so vicious/Will have gotten quite delicious,/And her classmates will have surely understood/That instead of saying, 'Miranda!/Oh, the beast! We cannot stand her!'/They'll be saying, 'Oh, how useful and how good!'"

Quiz

To see whether your brain cells are laid out properly, test your Java layout management skills by answering the following questions.

1. What container is often used when subdividing an interface into different layout managers?

     A. `JWindow`

     B. `JPanel`

     C. `Container`

2. What is the default layout manager for a panel?

     A. `FlowLayout`

     B. `GridLayout`

     C. No default

3. The `BorderLayout` class gets its name from where?

     A. The border of each component

     B. The way components are organized along the borders of a container

     C. Sheer capriciousness on the part of Java's developers

Answers

1. **B.** `JPanel`, which is the simplest of the containers.

2. **A.** Panels use flow layout, but the default manager for frames and windows is border layout.

3. **B.** You must specify the border position of components with the use of directional variables such as `BorderLayout.WEST` and `BorderLayout.EAST` as you add them to a container.

Activities

If you'd like to keep going with the flow (and the grid and the border), undertake the following activities:

▶ Create a modified version of the `Crisis` application with the `panic` and `dontPanic` objects organized under one layout manager and the remaining three buttons under another.

▶ Make a copy of the `LottoMadness.java` file that you can rename to `NewMadness.java`. Make changes to this program so the quick pick or personal choice is a combo box and the start, stop, and reset buttons are check boxes.

To see Java programs that implement these activities, visit the book's website at www.java24hours.com.

Responding to User Input

This Hour's To-Do List:

▶ Make your programs aware of events.

▶ Set up a component so it can cause events.

▶ Find out where events end up in a program.

▶ Store information in the interface.

▶ Convert values stored in text fields.

The graphical user interface (GUI) you developed during the past two hours can run on its own. Users can click buttons, fill text fields with text, and resize the window. Sooner or later, even the least discriminating user is going to be left wanting more. The GUI that a program offers has to cause things to happen when a mouse click or keyboard entry occurs.

These things become possible when your Java program can respond to user events. This is called event handling and is the main event for this hour.

Getting Your Programs to Listen

A user event in Java is something that happens when a user performs an action with the mouse, keyboard, or another input device.

Before you can receive events, you must learn how to make an object listen. Responding to user events requires the use of one or more `EventListener` interfaces. Interfaces are a feature of object-oriented programming in Java that enable a class to inherit behavior it would not be able to employ otherwise. They're like a contract agreement with other classes that guarantees the class will contain specific methods.

An `EventListener` interface contains methods that receive user input of a specific type.

Adding an `EventListener` interface requires two things. First, because the listening classes are part of the `java.awt.event` package, you must make them available with the following statement:

```
import java.awt.event.*;
```

Second, the class must use the `implements` keyword to declare that it supports one or more listening interfaces. The following statement creates a class that uses `ActionListener`, an interface for responding to button and menu clicks:

```
public class Graph implements ActionListener {
```

`EventListener` interfaces enable a component of a GUI to generate user events. Without one of the listeners in place, a component cannot do anything that can be heard by other parts of a program. A program must include a listener interface for each type of component to which it listens. To have the program respond to a mouse click on a button or the Enter key being pressed in a text field, you must include the `ActionListener` interface. To respond to the use of a choice list or check boxes, you need the `ItemListener` interface.

When you require more than one interface in the same class, separate their names with commas after the `implements` keyword, as in this code:

```
public class Graph3D implements ActionListener, MouseListener {
    // ...
}
```

Setting Up Components to Be Heard

After you have implemented the interface required for a particular component, you must cause that component to generate user events. The `ActionListener` interface listens for action events, such as a button click or the Enter key being pressed.

To make a `JButton` object generate an event, employ the `addActionListener()` method, as in the following statements:

```
JButton fireTorpedos = new JButton("Fire torpedos");
fireTorpedos.addActionListener(this);
```

This code creates the `fireTorpedos` button and calls the button's `addActionListener()` method. The `this` keyword used as an argument to the `addActionListener()` method indicates the current object receives the user event and handles it as needed.

NOTE

The `this` keyword confuses a lot of readers when it is first introduced. `this` refers to the object in which the keyword appears. So, if you create a `LottoMadness` class and use `this` in a statement inside that class, it refers to the `LottoMadness` object executing the code.

Handling User Events

When a user event is generated by a component that has a listener, a method is called automatically. The method must be found in the class specified when the listener was attached to the component.

Each listener has different methods that are called to receive their events. The `ActionListener` interface sends events to a method called `actionPerformed()`. The following is a short example of an `actionPerformed()` method:

```java
public void actionPerformed(ActionEvent event) {
    // method goes here
}
```

All action events sent in the program go to this method. If only one component in a program can possibly send action events, you can put statements in this method to handle the event. If more than one component can send these events, you need to check the object sent to the method.

An `ActionEvent` object is sent to the `actionPerformed()` method. Several classes of objects represent the user events that can be generated in a program. These classes have methods to determine which component caused the event to happen. In the `actionPerformed()` method, if the `ActionEvent` object is named `event`, you can identify the component with the following statement:

```java
String cmd = event.getActionCommand();
```

The `getActionCommand()` method sends back a string. If the component is a button, the string is the label on the button. If it's a text field, the string is the text entered in the field. The `getSource()` method sends back the object that caused the event.

You could use the following `actionPerformed()` method to receive events from three components: a `JButton` object called `start`, a `JTextField` called `speed`, and another `JTextField` called `viscosity`:

```java
public void actionPerformed(ActionEvent event) {
    Object source = event.getSource();
    if (source == speed) {
        // speed field caused event
    } else if (source == viscosity) {
        // viscosity field caused event
    } else {
        // start button caused event
    }
}
```

Call the `getSource()` method on all user events to identify the specific object that caused the event.

Check Box and Combo Box Events

Combo boxes and check boxes require the `ItemListener` interface. Call the component's `addItemListener()` method to make it generate these events. The following statements create a check box called `superSize` that sends out user events when selected or deselected:

```
JCheckBox superSize = new JCheckBox("Super Size", true);
superSize.addItemListener(this);
```

These events are received by the `itemStateChanged()` method, which takes an `ItemEvent` object as an argument. To see which object caused the event, you can call the event object's `getItem()` method.

To determine whether a check box is selected or deselected, compare the value returned by the `getStateChange()` method to the constants `ItemEvent.SELECTED` and `ItemEvent.DESELECTED`. The following code is an example for an `ItemEvent` object called `item`:

```
public void itemStateChanged(ItemEvent item) {
    int status = item.getStateChange();
    if (status == ItemEvent.SELECTED) {
        // item was selected
    }
}
```

To determine the value selected in a `JComboBox` object, use `getItem()` and convert that value to a string, as in the following:

```
Object which = item.getItem();
String answer = which.toString();
```

Keyboard Events

When a program must react immediately once a key is pressed, it uses keyboard events and the `KeyListener` interface.

The first step is to register the component that receives key presses by calling its `addKeyListener()` method. The argument of the method should be the object that implements the `KeyListener` interface. If it is the current class, use `this` as the argument.

An object that handles keyboard events must implement three methods:

▶ `keyPressed(KeyEvent)`—A method called the moment a key is pressed

▶ `keyReleased(KeyEvent)`—A method called the moment a key is released

▶ `keyTyped(KeyEvent)`—A method called after a key has been pressed and released

These methods all return `void` instead of a value. Each of these has a `KeyEvent` object as an argument, which has methods to call to find out more about the event. Call the `getKeyChar()`

method to find out which key was pressed. This key is returned as a char value, and it can be used only with letters, numbers, and punctuation.

To monitor any key on the keyboard, including Enter, Home, Page Up, and Page Down, you call getKeyCode() instead. This method returns an integer value representing the key. You then call getKeyText() with that integer as an argument to receive a String object containing the name of the key (such as Home, F1, and so on).

Listing 19.1 contains a Java application that draws the most recently pressed key in a label by using the getKeyChar() method. The application implements the KeyListener interface, so there are keyTyped(), keyPressed(), and keyReleased() methods in the class. The only one of these that does anything is keyTyped() in Lines 24–27. Create a new Java file called KeyViewer, in the com.java24hours package, enter the text from the listing in the file, and save it.

LISTING 19.1 The Full Text of KeyViewer.java

```
 1: package com.java24hours;
 2:
 3: import javax.swing.*;
 4: import java.awt.event.*;
 5: import java.awt.*;
 6:
 7: public class KeyViewer extends JFrame implements KeyListener {
 8:     JTextField keyText = new JTextField(80);
 9:     JLabel keyLabel = new JLabel("Press any key in the text field.");
10:
11:     public KeyViewer() {
12:         super("KeyViewer");
13:         setLookAndFeel();
14:         setSize(350, 100);
15:         setDefaultCloseOperation(JFrame.EXIT_ON_CLOSE);
16:         keyText.addKeyListener(this);
17:         BorderLayout bord = new BorderLayout();
18:         setLayout(bord);
19:         add(keyLabel, BorderLayout.NORTH);
20:         add(keyText, BorderLayout.CENTER);
21:         setVisible(true);
22:     }
23:
24:     @Override
25:     public void keyTyped(KeyEvent input) {
26:         char key = input.getKeyChar();
27:         keyLabel.setText("You pressed " + key);
28:     }
29:
30:     @Override
31:     public void keyPressed(KeyEvent txt) {
32:         // do nothing
```

```
33:     }
34:
35:     @Override
36:     public void keyReleased(KeyEvent txt) {
37:         // do nothing
38:     }
39:
40:     private void setLookAndFeel() {
41:         try {
42:             UIManager.setLookAndFeel(
43:                 "com.sun.java.swing.plaf.nimbus.NimbusLookAndFeel"
44:             );
45:         } catch (Exception exc) {
46:             // ignore error
47:         }
48:     }
49:
50:     public static void main(String[] arguments) {
51:         KeyViewer frame = new KeyViewer();
52:     }
53: }
```

When you run the application, it should resemble Figure 19.1. The application implements the three methods of the KeyListener interface in lines 24–38. Two of the methods are empty. They're not needed in the application but must be included to fulfill the contract between the class and interface established in line 7 with the `implements` keyword.

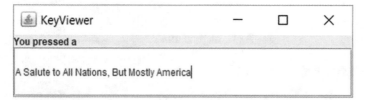

FIGURE 19.1
Handling keyboard events in a program.

Enabling and Disabling Components

You might have seen a component in a program that appears shaded instead of its normal appearance.

Shading indicates that users cannot do anything to the component because it is not enabled. Enabling and disabling components is accomplished with the `setEnabled()` method of the component. A Boolean value is sent as an argument to the method, so `setEnabled(true)` enables a component for use, and `setEnabled(false)` disables it.

The following statements create buttons with the labels Previous, Next, and Finish, and disable the first button:

```
JButton previousButton = new JButton("Previous");
JButton nextButton = new JButton("Next");
JButton finishButton = new JButton("Finish");
previousButton.setEnabled(false);
```

This method is an effective way to prevent a component from sending a user event when it shouldn't. For example, if you're writing a Java application that collects a user's address using text fields, you could disable a Save Address button until the user provided a street address, city, state, and ZIP code.

Completing a Graphical Application

To see how Swing's event-handling classes work in a Java program, you will finish LottoMadness, the lottery simulation begun during Hour 18, "Laying Out a User Interface."

At this point, LottoMadness is just a GUI. You can click buttons and enter text into text boxes, but nothing happens in response. In this workshop, you create LottoEvent, a new class that receives user input, conducts lotto drawings, and keeps track of the number of times you win. When the class is complete, you add a few lines to LottoMadness so that it makes use of LottoEvent. It often is convenient to divide Swing projects in this manner, with the GUI in one class and the event-handling methods in another.

The purpose of this application is to assess the user's chance of winning a six-number lotto drawing in a lifetime. Figure 19.2 shows a screen capture of the program as it runs.

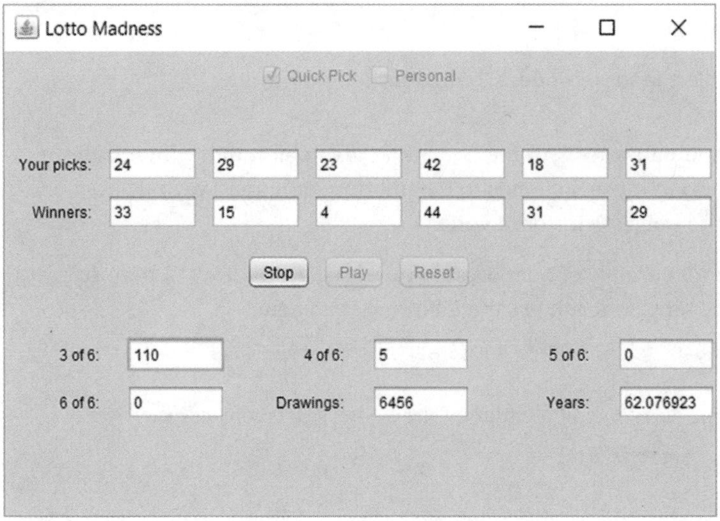

FIGURE 19.2
Running the LottoMadness application.

Instead of using probability to figure this problem out, the computer conducts drawings in rapid succession and doesn't stop until there's a winner. Because the 6-out-of-6 win is extremely unlikely, the program also reports on any combination of three, four, or five winning numbers.

The interface includes 12 text fields for lotto numbers and two check boxes labeled Quick Pick and Personal. Six text fields, disabled for input, are used to display the winning numbers of each drawing. The other six text fields are for the user's choice of numbers. Selecting the Quick Pick box chooses six random numbers for a user. Selecting the Personal box enables the user to select desired numbers.

Three buttons control the activity of the program: Stop, Play, and Reset. When the Play button is pressed, the program starts a thread called `playing` and generates Lotto drawings.

Pressing the Stop button stops the thread, and pressing Reset clears all fields so the user can start over. You learn about threads in Hour 15, "Creating a Threaded Program."

The `LottoEvent` class implements three interfaces: `ActionListener`, `ItemListener`, and `Runnable`. The `Runnable` interface relates to threads and was covered in Hour 15. The listeners are needed to listen to user events generated by the application's buttons and check boxes. The program does not need to listen to any events related to the text fields because they are used strictly to store the user's choice of numbers. The user interface handles this storage automatically.

The class requires the use of the main Swing package, `javax.swing`, and Java's event-handling package, `java.awt.event`.

The class has two instance variables:

▶ gui, a LottoMadness object

▶ playing, a Thread object used to conduct continuous lotto drawings

The gui variable is used to communicate with the `LottoMadness` object that contains the program's GUI. When you need to make a change to the interface or retrieve a value from one of its text fields, you use the gui object's instance variables.

For example, the play instance variable of `LottoMadness` represents the Play button. To disable this button in `LottoEvent`, you can use the following statement:

```
gui.play.setEnabled(false);
```

You can use the next statement to retrieve the value of the JTextField object got3:

```
String got3value = gui.got3.getText();
```

Listing 19.2 contains the full text of the LottoEvent class. Create a new Java file called LottoEvent in the com.java24hours package, enter the text from the listing in the file, and save it.

LISTING 19.2   The Full Text of LottoEvent.java

```
 1: package com.java24hours;
 2:
 3: import javax.swing.*;
 4: import java.awt.event.*;
 5:
 6: public class LottoEvent implements ItemListener, ActionListener,
 7:     Runnable {
 8:
 9:     LottoMadness gui;
10:     Thread playing;
11:
12:     public LottoEvent(LottoMadness in) {
13:         gui = in;
14:     }
15:
16:     @Override
17:     public void actionPerformed(ActionEvent event) {
18:         String command = event.getActionCommand();
19:         if (command.equals("Play")) {
20:             startPlaying();
21:         }
22:         if (command.equals("Stop")) {
23:             stopPlaying();
24:         }
25:         if (command.equals("Reset")) {
26:             clearAllFields();
26:         }
28:     }
29:
30:     void startPlaying() {
31:         playing = new Thread(this);
32:         playing.start();
33:         gui.play.setEnabled(false);
34:         gui.stop.setEnabled(true);
35:         gui.reset.setEnabled(false);
36:         gui.quickpick.setEnabled(false);
37:         gui.personal.setEnabled(false);
38:     }
39:
40:     void stopPlaying() {
41:         gui.stop.setEnabled(false);
```

```
42:            gui.play.setEnabled(true);
43:            gui.reset.setEnabled(true);
44:            gui.quickpick.setEnabled(true);
45:            gui.personal.setEnabled(true);
46:            playing = null;
47:        }
48:
49:    void clearAllFields() {
50:        for (int i = 0; i < 6; i++) {
51:            gui.numbers[i].setText(null);
52:            gui.winners[i].setText(null);
53:        }
54:        gui.got3.setText("0");
55:        gui.got4.setText("0");
56:        gui.got5.setText("0");
57:        gui.got6.setText("0");
58:        gui.drawings.setText("0");
59:        gui.years.setText("0");
60:    }
61:
62:    @Override
63:    public void itemStateChanged(ItemEvent event) {
64:        Object item = event.getItem();
65:        if (item == gui.quickpick) {
66:            for (int i = 0; i < 6; i++) {
67:                int pick;
68:                do {
69:                    pick = (int) Math.floor(Math.random() * 50 + 1);
70:                } while (numberGone(pick, gui.numbers, i));
71:                gui.numbers[i].setText("" + pick);
72:            }
73:        } else {
74:            for (int i = 0; i < 6; i++) {
75:                gui.numbers[i].setText(null);
76:            }
77:        }
78:    }
79:
80:    void addOneToField(JTextField field) {
81:        int num = Integer.parseInt("0" + field.getText());
82:        num++;
83:        field.setText("" + num);
84:    }
85:
86:    boolean numberGone(int num, JTextField[] pastNums, int count) {
87:        for (int i = 0; i < count; i++) {
88:            if (Integer.parseInt(pastNums[i].getText()) == num) {
89:                return true;
```

```
 90:                  }
 91:              }
 92:          return false;
 93:      }
 94:
 95:      boolean matchedOne(JTextField win, JTextField[] allPicks) {
 96:          for (int i = 0; i < 6; i++) {
 97:              String winText = win.getText();
 98:              if ( winText.equals( allPicks[i].getText() ) ) {
 99:                  return true;
100:              }
101:          }
102:          return false;
103:      }
104:
105:      @Override
106:      public void run() {
107:          Thread thisThread = Thread.currentThread();
108:          while (playing == thisThread) {
109:              addOneToField(gui.drawings);
110:              int draw = Integer.parseInt(gui.drawings.getText());
111:              float numYears = (float)draw / 104;
112:              gui.years.setText("" + numYears);
113:
114:              int matches = 0;
115:              for (int i = 0; i < 6; i++) {
116:                  int ball;
117:                  do {
118:                      ball = (int) Math.floor(Math.random() * 50 + 1);
119:                  } while (numberGone(ball, gui.winners, i));
120:                  gui.winners[i].setText("" + ball);
121:                  if (matchedOne(gui.winners[i], gui.numbers)) {
122:                      matches++;
123:                  }
124:              }
125:              switch (matches) {
126:                  case 3:
127:                      addOneToField(gui.got3);
128:                      break;
129:                  case 4:
130:                      addOneToField(gui.got4);
131:                      break;
132:                  case 5:
133:                      addOneToField(gui.got5);
134:                      break;
135:                  case 6:
136:                      addOneToField(gui.got6);
137:                      gui.stop.setEnabled(false);
```

```
138:                         gui.play.setEnabled(true);
139:                         playing = null;
140:                 }
141:             try {
142:                 Thread.sleep(100);
143:             } catch (InterruptedException e) {
144:                 // do nothing
145:             }
146:         }
147:     }
148: }
```

The LottoEvent class has one constructor: LottoEvent(*LottoMadness*). The LottoMadness object specified as an argument identifies the object that is relying on LottoEvent to handle user events and conduct drawings.

The following methods are used in the class:

▶ The clearAllFields() method causes all text fields in the application to be emptied out. This method is handled when the user clicks the Reset button.

▶ The addOneToField() method converts a text field to an integer, increments it by one, and converts it back into a text field. Because all text fields are stored as strings, you have to take special steps to use them in expressions.

▶ The numberGone() method takes three arguments: a single number from a lotto drawing, an array that holds several JTextField objects, and a count integer. This method makes sure that each number in a drawing hasn't been selected already in the same drawing.

▶ The matchedOne() method takes two arguments: a JTextField object and an array of six JTextField objects. This method checks to see whether one of the user's numbers matches the numbers from the current lotto drawing.

The application's actionPerformed() method receives the action events when the user clicks a button. The getActionCommand() method retrieves the label of the button to determine which component was clicked.

Clicking the "Play" button causes the startPlaying() method to be called. This method disables four components. Clicking Stop causes the stopPlaying() method to be called, which enables every component except for the Stop button.

The itemStateChanged() method receives user events triggered by the selection of the Quick Pick or Personal check boxes. The getItem() method sends back an Object that represents the check box that was clicked. If it's the "Quick Pick" check box, six random numbers from 1 to 50 are assigned to the user's lotto numbers. Otherwise, the text fields that hold the user's numbers are cleared out.

The `LottoEvent` class uses numbers from 1 to 50 for each ball in the lotto drawings. This is established in Line 118, which multiplies the `Math.random()` method by 50, adds 1 to the total, and uses this as an argument to the `Math.floor()` method. The end result is a random integer from 1 to 50. If you replace 50 with a different number here and on Line 69, you could use `LottoMadness` for lottery contests that generate a wider or smaller range of values.

The `LottoMadness` project lacks variables used to keep track of things such as the number of drawings, winning counts, and lotto number text fields. Instead, the interface stores values and displays them automatically.

To finish the project, reopen `LottoMadness.java` in NetBeans. You only need to add six lines to make it work with the `LottoEvent` class.

First, add a new instance variable to hold a `LottoEvent` object:

```
LottoEvent lotto = new LottoEvent(this);
```

Next, in the `LottoMadness()` constructor, call the `addItemListener()` and `addActionListener()` methods of each user interface component that can receive user input:

```
// Add listeners
quickpick.addItemListener(lotto);
personal.addItemListener(lotto);
stop.addActionListener(lotto);
play.addActionListener(lotto);
reset.addActionListener(lotto);
```

These statements should be added in the constructor right after the call to `setLayout()` that makes grid layout the manager for the application's frame.

Listing 19.3 contains the full text of `LottoMadness.java` after you have made the changes. The lines you added are shaded—the rest is unchanged from the previous hour.

LISTING 19.3   The Full Text of `LottoMadness.java`

```
 1: package com.java24hours;
 2:
 3: import java.awt.*;
 4: import javax.swing.*;
 5:
 6: public class LottoMadness extends JFrame {
 7:     LottoEvent lotto = new LottoEvent(this);
 8:
 9:     // set up row 1
10:     JPanel row1 = new JPanel();
```

```
11:      ButtonGroup option = new ButtonGroup();
12:      JCheckBox quickpick = new JCheckBox("Quick Pick", false);
13:      JCheckBox personal = new JCheckBox("Personal", true);
14:      // set up row 2
15:      JPanel row2 = new JPanel();
16:      JLabel numbersLabel = new JLabel("Your picks: ", JLabel.RIGHT);
17:      JTextField[] numbers = new JTextField[6];
18:      JLabel winnersLabel = new JLabel("Winners: ", JLabel.RIGHT);
19:      JTextField[] winners = new JTextField[6];
20:      // set up row 3
21:      JPanel row3 = new JPanel();
22:      JButton stop = new JButton("Stop");
23:      JButton play = new JButton("Play");
24:      JButton reset = new JButton("Reset");
25:      // set up row 4
26:      JPanel row4 = new JPanel();
27:      JLabel got3Label = new JLabel("3 of 6: ", JLabel.RIGHT);
28:      JTextField got3 = new JTextField("0");
29:      JLabel got4Label = new JLabel("4 of 6: ", JLabel.RIGHT);
30:      JTextField got4 = new JTextField("0");
31:      JLabel got5Label = new JLabel("5 of 6: ", JLabel.RIGHT);
32:      JTextField got5 = new JTextField("0");
33:      JLabel got6Label = new JLabel("6 of 6: ", JLabel.RIGHT);
34:      JTextField got6 = new JTextField("0", 10);
35:      JLabel drawingsLabel = new JLabel("Drawings: ", JLabel.RIGHT);
36:      JTextField drawings = new JTextField("0");
37:      JLabel yearsLabel = new JLabel("Years: ", JLabel.RIGHT);
38:      JTextField years = new JTextField("0");
39:
40:      public LottoMadness() {
41:          super("Lotto Madness");
42:
43:          setSize(550, 400);
44:          setDefaultCloseOperation(JFrame.EXIT_ON_CLOSE);
45:          GridLayout layout = new GridLayout(5, 1, 10, 10);
46:          setLayout(layout);
47:
48:          // Add listeners
49:          quickpick.addItemListener(lotto);
50:          personal.addItemListener(lotto);
51:          stop.addActionListener(lotto);
52:          play.addActionListener(lotto);
53:          reset.addActionListener(lotto);
54:
55:          FlowLayout layout1 = new FlowLayout(FlowLayout.CENTER,
56:              10, 10);
57:          option.add(quickpick);
58:          option.add(personal);
```

```
59:          row1.setLayout(layout1);
60:          row1.add(quickpick);
61:          row1.add(personal);
62:          add(row1);
63:
64:          GridLayout layout2 = new GridLayout(2, 7, 10, 10);
65:          row2.setLayout(layout2);
66:          row2.add(numbersLabel);
67:          for (int i = 0; i < 6; i++) {
68:              numbers[i] = new JTextField();
69:              row2.add(numbers[i]);
70:          }
71:          row2.add(winnersLabel);
72:          for (int i = 0; i < 6; i++) {
73:              winners[i] = new JTextField();
74:              winners[i].setEditable(false);
75:              row2.add(winners[i]);
76:          }
77:          add(row2);
78:
79:          FlowLayout layout3 = new FlowLayout(FlowLayout.CENTER,
80:              10, 10);
81:          row3.setLayout(layout3);
82:          stop.setEnabled(false);
83:          row3.add(stop);
84:          row3.add(play);
85:          row3.add(reset);
86:          add(row3);
87:
88:          GridLayout layout4 = new GridLayout(2, 3, 20, 10);
89:          row4.setLayout(layout4);
90:          row4.add(got3Label);
91:          got3.setEditable(false);
92:          row4.add(got3);
93:          row4.add(got4Label);
94:          got4.setEditable(false);
95:          row4.add(got4);
96:          row4.add(got5Label);
97:          got5.setEditable(false);
98:          row4.add(got5);
99:          row4.add(got6Label);
100:         got6.setEditable(false);
101:         row4.add(got6);
102:         row4.add(drawingsLabel);
103:         drawings.setEditable(false);
104:         row4.add(drawings);
105:         row4.add(yearsLabel);
106:         years.setEditable(false);
```

```
107:            row4.add(years);
108:            add(row4);
109:
110:            setVisible(true);
111:        }
112:
113:        private static void setLookAndFeel() {
114:            try {
115:                UIManager.setLookAndFeel(
116:                    "com.sun.java.swing.plaf.nimbus.NimbusLookAndFeel"
117:                );
118:            } catch (Exception exc) {
119:                // ignore error
120:            }
121:        }
122:
123:        public static void main(String[] arguments) {
124:            LottoMadness.setLookAndFeel();
125:            LottoMadness frame = new LottoMadness();
126:        }
127: }
```

After you add the shaded lines, you can run the application, which is capable of testing your lotto skills for thousands of years. As you might expect, these lotteries are an exercise in futility. The chance of winning a 6-out-of-6 lotto drawing in a lifetime is extremely slim, even if you live as long as a biblical figure.

NOTE

When the book's website at www.java24hours.com could be used to run the LottoMadness program, it completed 410,732,244 drawings equaling 3.9 million years of twice-weekly drawings. There were 6,364,880 3-out-of-6 winners, 337,285 4-out-of-6 winners, 6,476 5-out-of-6 winners, and 51 6-out-of-6 winners (roughly one out of every 8 million drawings). The first person to win the fictional lottery was Bill Teer. His numbers were 3, 7, 1, 15, 34, and 43, and it only took him 241,225 drawings (2,319.47 years) to win.

Summary

You can create a professional-looking program with a modest amount of programming by using Swing. Although the LottoMadness application is longer than many of the examples you have worked in during the last 19 hours, half of the program was composed of statements to build the interface.

If you spend some time running the application, you become even more bitter and envious about the good fortune of the people who win these six-number lottery drawings.

My most recent run of the program indicates that I could blow $17,000 and the best 165 years of my life buying tickets, only to win one 5-out-of-6, 10 4-out-of-6 and 264 3-out-of-6 prizes.

In comparison to those odds, the chance to make your Java programming skills pay off is practically a sure thing.

Workshop

Q&A

Q. Do you need to do anything with the `paint()` method or `repaint()` to indicate that a text field has been changed?

A. After the `setText()` method of a text component is used to change its value, you don't need to do anything else. Swing handles the updating necessary to show the new value.

Q. Why do you often import a class and also one of its subclasses, as in Listing 19.1 when you import `java.awt.*` and `java.awt.event.*`? Could the first of these statements include the second?

A. Though the names of the `java.awt` and `java.awt.event` packages look like they are related, there's no such thing as inheritance for packages in Java. One package cannot be a subpackage of another.

When you use an asterisk in an `import` statement, you are making all the classes in a package available in a program.

The asterisk works only on classes, not packages. The most a single `import` statement can load is the classes of a single package.

Q. Why is the actor Michael J. Fox identified by his middle initial?

A. There already was a Michael Fox in the Screen Actor's Guild, forcing the future *Family Ties* and *Back to the Future* star to choose another name for his professional work. Michael Andrew Fox is his real name, but he didn't like the sound of Andrew or Andy Fox—and calling himself Michael A. Fox sounded like he was admiring his own good looks.

He settled on Michael J. Fox as an homage to the character actor Michael J. Pollard.

The other Michael Fox was an actor who appeared on episodes of *Perry Mason, Burke's Law*, and numerous other TV shows and movies until his death in 1996.

Quiz

After the `LottoMadness` program has soured you on games of chance, play a game of skill by answering the following questions.

1. Why are action events called by that name?

    A. They occur in reaction to something else.

    B. They indicate that some kind of action should be taken in response.

    C. They honor cinematic adventurer Action Jackson.

2. What does `this` signify as the argument to an `addActionListener()` method?

    A. `this` listener should be used when an event occurs.

    B. `this` event takes precedence over others.

    C. `this` object handles the events.

3. Which text component stores user input as integers?

    A. `JTextField`

    B. `JTextArea`

    C. Neither A nor B

Answers

1. **B.** Action events include the click of a button and the selection of an item from a pull-down menu.

2. **C.** The `this` keyword refers to the current object. If the name of an object is used as an argument instead of the `this` statement, that object would receive the events and be expected to handle them.

3. **C.** `JTextField` and `JTextArea` components store their values as text, so you must convert their values before you can use them as integers, floating-point numbers, or other non-text values.

Activities

If the main event of this hour didn't provide enough action for your tastes, interface with the following activities:

▶ Add a text field to the `LottoMadness` application that works in conjunction with the `Thread.sleep()` statement in the `LottoEvent` class to slow down the rate that drawings are conducted.

▶ Modify the `LottoMadness` project so it draws five numbers from 1 to 90.

To see Java programs that implement these activities, visit the book's website at www.java24hours.com.

Reading and Writing Files

This Hour's To-Do List:

- ▶ Read bytes from a file into a program.
- ▶ Create a new file on your computer.
- ▶ Save an array of bytes to a file.
- ▶ Make changes to the data stored in a file.

There are numerous ways to represent data on a computer. You already have worked with one by creating objects. An object includes data in the form of variables and references to objects. It also includes methods that use the data to accomplish tasks.

To work with other kinds of data, such as files on your hard drive and documents on a web server, you can use the classes of the `java.io` package. The "io" part of its name stands for "input/output" and the classes are used to access a source of data, such as a hard drive, DVD, or the computer's memory.

You can bring data into a program and send data out by using a communications system called *streams*, which are objects that take information from one place to another.

Streams

To save data permanently within a Java program, or to retrieve that data later, you must use at least one stream.

A stream is an object that takes information from one source and sends it somewhere else, taking its name from water streams that take fish, boats, and industrial pollutants from one place to another.

Streams connect a diverse variety of sources, including computer programs, hard drives, Internet servers, computer memory, and thumb drives. After you learn how to work with one kind of data using streams, you can work with others in the same manner.

During this hour, you use streams to read and write data stored in files on your computer.

There are two kinds of streams:

▶ Input streams, which read data from a source

▶ Output streams, which write data to a source

All input and output streams are made up of bytes, individual integers with values ranging from 0 to 255. You can use this format to represent data, such as executable programs, word-processing documents, and MP3 music files, but those are only a small sampling of what bytes can represent. A byte stream is used to read and write these kinds of data.

NOTE

Java class files are stored as bytes in a form called bytecode. The Java Virtual Machine runs byte-code, which doesn't actually have to be produced by the Java language. It can run compiled bytecode produced by other languages, including Scala, Groovy, and Jython. You also hear the JVM referred to as the bytecode interpreter.

A more specialized way to work with data is in the form of characters—individual letters, numbers, punctuation, and the like. You can use a character stream when you are reading and writing a text source.

Whether you work with a stream of bytes, characters, or other kinds of information, the overall process is the same:

▶ Create a stream object associated with the data.

▶ Call methods of the stream to either put information in the stream or take information out of it.

▶ Close the stream by calling the object's `close()` method.

Files

In Java, files are represented by the `File` class, which also is part of the `java.io` package. Files can be read from hard drives, DVDs, and other storage devices.

A `File` object can represent files that already exist or files you want to create. To create a `File` object, use the name of the file as the constructor, as in this example:

```
File book = new File("address.dat");
```

This creates an object for a file named `address.dat` in the current folder. You also can include a path in the filename:

```
File book = new File("data\\address.dat");
```

This example works on a Windows system, which uses the backslash \ character as a separator in path and filenames. (There are two backslashes in these code examples because a backslash is a special character in Java.) Linux and other Unix-based systems use a forward slash / character instead. To write a Java program that refers to files in a way that works regardless of the operating system, use the class variable `File.pathSeparator` instead of a forward or backslash, as in this statement:

File book = new File("data" + File.pathSeparator

+ "address.dat");

Creating a `File` object doesn't create a file on your computer. It's just a reference to a file that may or may not yet exist.

When you have a `File` object, you can call several useful methods on that object:

- `exists()`—true if the file exists, `false` otherwise

- `getName()`—The name of the file, as a `String`

- `length()`—The size of the file, as a `long` value

- `createNewFile()`—Creates a file of the same name, if one does not exist already

- `delete()`—Deletes the file, if it exists

- `renameTo(File)`—Renames the file, using the name of the `File` object specified as an argument

You also can use a `File` object to represent a folder on your system rather than a file. Specify the folder name in the `File` constructor, which can be absolute (such as `C:\\Documents\\`) or relative (such as `java\\database`).

After you have an object representing a folder, call its `listFiles()` method to see what's inside the folder. This method returns an array of `File` objects representing every file and subfolder it contains.

Reading Data from a Stream

The first project of the hour is to read data from a file using an input stream. You can do this using the `FileInputStream` class, which represents input streams that are read as bytes from a file.

You can create a file input stream by specifying a filename or a `File` object as the argument to the `FileInputStream()` constructor.

Methods that read or write files can fail with an IOException if there's an error accessing the file. Many of the methods associated with reading and writing files generate this exception, so a try-catch block is often used. This exception belongs to the java.io package.

Streams are one of the resources in Java that must be closed when they're no longer being used. Leaving a stream open is a significant drain on resources in the JVM as a program runs.

A special try statement called try-with-resources makes it easy to ensure that a resource, such as a file input stream, will be closed when it's no longer needed. The try statement is followed by parentheses. Inside the parentheses are one or more Java statements that declare variables that read or write data through a resource.

Here's an example that reads a text file called cookie.web using a file input stream named stream:

```
File cookie = new File("cookie.web");
try (FileInputStream stream = new FileInputStream(cookie)) {
    System.out.println("Length of file: " + cookie.length());
} catch (IOException ioe) {
    System.out.println("Could not read file.");
}
```

Because stream is in the try statement, the stream is closed automatically when the try-catch block completes (if it hasn't been closed).

File input streams read data in bytes. You can read a single byte by calling the stream's read() method without an argument. If no more bytes are available in the stream because you have reached the end of the file, a byte value of –1 is returned.

When you read an input stream, it begins with the first byte in the stream, such as the first byte in a file. You can skip some bytes in a stream by calling its skip() method with one argument: an int representing the number of bytes to skip. The following statement skips the next 1,024 bytes in a stream named scanData:

```
scanData.skip(1024);
```

If you want to read more than one byte at a time, do the following:

▶ Create a byte array that is exactly the size of the number of bytes you want to read.

▶ Call the stream's read() method with that array as an argument. The array is filled with bytes read from the stream.

This first project reads ID3 data from an MP3 audio file. Because MP3 is such a popular format for music files, 128 bytes are often added to the end of an ID3 file to hold information about the song, such as the title, artist, and album.

The `ID3Reader` application reads an MP3 file using a file input stream, skipping everything but the last 128 bytes. The remaining bytes are examined to see if they contain ID3 data. If they do, the first three bytes are the numbers 84, 65, and 71.

NOTE

On the ASCII character set, which is included in the Unicode Standard character set supported by Java, those three numbers represent the capital letters "T," "A," and "G," respectively.

Create a new empty Java file called `ID3Reader` in the `com.java24hours` package and fill it with the text from Listing 20.1.

LISTING 20.1 **The Full Text of** `ID3Reader.java`

```
 1: package com.java24hours;
 2:
 3: import java.io.*;
 4:
 5: public class ID3Reader {
 6:     public static void main(String[] arguments) {
 7:         File song = new File(arguments[0]);
 8:         try (FileInputStream file = new FileInputStream(song)) {
 9:             int size = (int) song.length();
10:             file.skip(size - 128);
11:             byte[] last128 = new byte[128];
12:             file.read(last128);
13:             String id3 = new String(last128);
14:             String tag = id3.substring(0, 3);
15:             if (tag.equals("TAG")) {
16:                 System.out.println("Title: " + id3.substring(3, 32));
17:                 System.out.println("Artist: " + id3.substring(33, 62));
18:                 System.out.println("Album: " + id3.substring(63, 91));
19:                 System.out.println("Year: " + id3.substring(93, 97));
20:             } else {
21:                 System.out.println(arguments[0] + " does not contain"
22:                     + " ID3 info.");
23:             }
24:             file.close();
25:         } catch (IOException ioe) {
26:             System.out.println("Error -- " + ioe.toString());
27:         }
28:     }
29: }
```

Before running this class as an application, you must specify an MP3 file as a command-line argument (using Run, Set Project Configuration, Configure in NetBeans). The program can be run with any MP3, such as Come On and Gettit.mp3, the unjustly forgotten 1973 soul classic by Marion Black. If you have the song Come On and Gettit.mp3 on your system (and you really should), Figure 20.1 shows what the ID3Reader application displays.

```
Output - Java24 (run)  ×                                                    —
  run:
  Title: Come On and Gettit
  Artist: Marion Black
  Album: Eccentric Soul: The Prix Lab
  Year: 2007
  BUILD SUCCESSFUL (total time: 0 seconds)
```

FIGURE 20.1
Running the ID3Reader application.

TIP

If you don't have Come On and Gettit.mp3 on your computer (a big mistake, in my opinion), or any other MP3s, you can look for MP3 songs to examine using the Creative Commons license at http://search.creativecommons.org.

Creative Commons is a set of copyright licenses that stipulate how a work such as a song or book can be distributed, edited, or republished.

The application reads the last 128 bytes from the MP3 in Lines 11–12 of Listing 20.1, storing them in a byte array. This array is used in Line 13 to create a String object that contains the characters represented by those bytes.

If the first three characters in the string are "TAG," the MP3 file being examined contains ID3 information.

In Lines 16–19, the string's substring() method is called to display portions of the string. The ID3 format always puts the artist, song, title, and year information in the same positions in the last 128 bytes.

Some MP3 files either don't contain ID3 information at all or contain ID3 information in a different format that the application can't read.

The file Come On and Gettit.mp3 contains readable ID3 information if you created it from a copy of the *Eccentric Soul* CD that you purchased. Programs that create MP3 files from audio CDs read song information from a music industry database called CDDB.

After everything related to the ID3 information has been read from the MP3's file input stream, the stream is closed in Line 24. You should always close streams when you are finished with them to conserve JVM resources.

Buffered Input Streams

One of the ways to improve the performance of a program that reads input streams is to buffer the input. Buffering is the process of saving data in memory for use later when a program needs it. When a Java program needs data from a buffered input stream, it looks in the buffer first, which is faster than reading from a source such as a file.

To use a buffered input stream, you create an input stream such as a `FileInputStream` object, then use that object to create a buffered stream. Call the `BufferedInputStream` (`InputStream`) constructor with the input stream as the only argument. Data is buffered as it is read from the input stream.

To read from a buffered stream, call its `read()` method with no arguments. An integer from 0 to 255 is returned and represents the next byte of data in the stream. If no more bytes are available, –1 is returned instead.

As a demonstration of buffered streams, the next program you create adds a feature to Java that many programmers miss from other languages they have used: console input.

Console input is the ability to read characters from the console (also known as the command line) while running an application.

The `System` class, which contains the `out` variable used in the `System.out.print()` and `System.out.println()` statements, has a class variable called `in` that represents an `InputStream` object. This object receives input from the keyboard and makes it available as a stream.

You can work with this input stream like any other. The following statement creates a buffered input stream associated with the `System.in` input stream:

```
BufferedInputStream bin = new BufferedInputStream(System.in);
```

The next project, the `Console` class in the `com.java24hours` package, contains a class method you can use to receive console input in any of your Java applications. Enter the text from Listing 20.2 in a new Java file named `Console`.

LISTING 20.2 The Full Text of Console.java

```
1: package com.java24hours;
2:
3: import java.io.*;
4:
5: public class Console {
6:     public static String readLine() {
7:         StringBuilder response = new StringBuilder();
8:         try {
9:             BufferedInputStream bin = new
10:                 BufferedInputStream(System.in);
11:             int in = 0;
12:             char inChar;
13:             do {
14:                 in = bin.read();
15:                 inChar = (char) in;
16:                 if (in != -1) {
17:                     response.append(inChar);
18:                 }
19:             } while ((in != -1) & (inChar != '\n'));
20:             bin.close();
21:             return response.toString();
22:         } catch (IOException e) {
23:             System.out.println("Exception: " + e.getMessage());
24:             return null;
25:         }
26:     }
27:
28:     public static void main(String[] arguments) {
29:         System.out.print("You are standing at the end of the road ");
30:         System.out.print("before a small brick building. Around you ");
31:         System.out.print("is a forest. A small stream flows out of ");
32:         System.out.println("the building and down a gully.\n");
33:         System.out.print("> ");
34:         String input = Console.readLine();
35:         System.out.println("That's not a verb I recognize.");
36:     }
37: }
```

The Console class includes a main() method that demonstrates how it can be used. When you run the application, the output should resemble Figure 20.2.

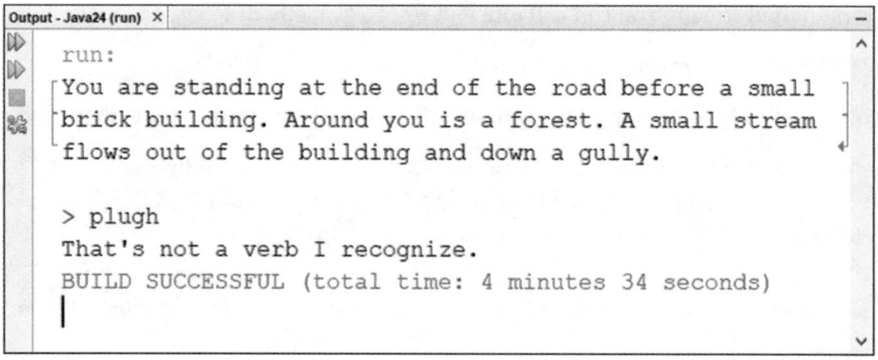

```
Output - Java24 (run)  ×                                                    —

   run:
  ⌈You are standing at the end of the road before a small ⌉
  ⌊brick building. Around you is a forest. A small stream ⌋
   flows out of the building and down a gully.


   > plugh
   That's not a verb I recognize.
   BUILD SUCCESSFUL (total time: 4 minutes 34 seconds)
   |
```

FIGURE 20.2
Running the Console application.

The Console class contains one class method, readLine(), that receives characters from the console. When the Enter key is hit, readLine() returns a string object containing the characters that are received.

NOTE
_____

The _Console_ application is also the world's least satisfying text adventure game. You can't enter the building, wade in the stream, or even wander off. For a more full-featured version of this game, which is called Adventure, visit Web-Adventures at www.web-adventures.org.
_____

Writing Data to a Stream

In the java.io package, the classes for working with streams come in matched sets. There are FileInputStream and FileOutputStream classes for working with byte streams, FileReader and FileWriter classes for working with character streams, and many other sets for working with other kinds of stream data.

To begin writing data, you first create a File object that is associated with an output stream. This file doesn't have to exist on your system.

You can create a FileOutputStream in two ways. If you want to append bytes onto an existing file, call the FileOutputStream() constructor with two arguments: a File object representing the file and the boolean of true. The bytes you write to the stream are tacked onto the end of the file.

If you want to write bytes into a new file, call the FileOutputStream() constructor with a File object as its only object.

After you have an output stream, you can call different write() methods to write bytes to it:

▶ Call write() with a byte as its only argument to write that byte to the stream.

▶ Call write() with a byte array as its only argument to write all the array's bytes to the stream.

▶ Specify three arguments to the write(*byte[]*, *int*, *int*) method: a byte array, an integer representing the first element of the array to write to the stream, and the number of bytes to write.

The following statement creates a byte array with 10 bytes and writes the last 4 to an output stream:

```
File dat = new File("data.dat");
FileOutputStream datStream = new FileOutputStream(dat);
byte[] data = new byte[] { 5, 12, 4, 13, 3, 15, 2, 17, 1, 18 };
datStream.write(data, 6, 4);
```

When writing bytes to a stream, you can convert text to an array of bytes by calling the String object's getBytes() method, as in this example:

```
String name = "Puddin N. Tane";
byte[] nameBytes = name.getBytes();
```

After you have finished writing bytes to a stream, you close it by calling the stream's close() method.

The next project you write is a simple application, ConfigWriter, that saves several lines of text to a file by writing bytes to a file output stream. Create a Java file of that name, assign it the package com.java24hours, and enter the text from Listing 20.3 into the source editor.

LISTING 20.3   The Full Text of ConfigWriter.java

```
 1: package com.java24hours;
 2:
 3: import java.io.*;
 4:
 5: public class ConfigWriter {
 6:     String newline = System.getProperty("line.separator");
 7:
 8:     public ConfigWriter() {
 9:         try {
10:             File file = new File("program.properties");
11:             FileOutputStream fileStream = new FileOutputStream(file);
12:             write(fileStream, "username=max");
13:             write(fileStream, "score=12550");
14:             write(fileStream, "level=5");
15:             fileStream.close();
16:         } catch (IOException ioe) {
17:             System.out.println("Could not write file");
```

```
18:          }
19:      }
20:
21:      void write(FileOutputStream stream, String output)
22:          throws IOException {
23:
24:          output = output + newline;
25:          byte[] data = output.getBytes();
26:          stream.write(data, 0, data.length);
27:      }
28:
29:      public static void main(String[] arguments) {
30:          new ConfigWriter();
31:      }
32: }
```

When this application is run, it creates a file called `program.properties` that contains the following three lines of text:

Output ▼

```
username=max
score=12550
level=5
```

The file is created in Line 10 and associated with a file output stream in Line 11. The three properties are written to the stream in Lines 12–14.

An application run in NetBeans will save the file (or files) it creates in the project's main folder if no other folder is specified. To see the `program.properties` file in NetBeans, in the Projects pane, click the Files tab to bring it to the front. The file is in the top `Java24` folder. In that tab, double-click `program.properties` to open the file, which is shown in Figure 20.3.

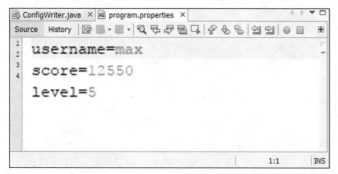

FIGURE 20.3
Finding the `program.properties` file.

Reading and Writing Configuration Properties

Java programs are more versatile when they can be configured using command-line arguments, as you have demonstrated in several applications created in earlier hours. The `java.util` package includes a class, `Properties`, that enables configuration settings to be loaded from another source: a text file.

The file can be read like other file sources in Java:

▶ Create a `File` object that represents the file.

▶ Create a `FileInputStream` object from that `File` object.

▶ Call `load()` to retrieve the properties from that input stream.

A properties file has a set of property names followed by an equal sign = and their values. Here's an example:

```
username=lepton
lastCommand=open database
windowSize=32
```

Each property has its own line, so this sets up properties named `username`, `lastCommand`, and `windowSize` with the values "lepton", "open database", and "32", respectively. (The same format was used by the `ConfigWriter` application.)

The following code loads a properties file called `config.dat`:

```
File configFile = new File("config.dat");
FileInputStream inStream = new FileInputStream(configFile);
Properties config = new Properties();
config.load(inStream);
```

Configuration settings, which are called *properties*, are stored as strings in the `Properties` object. Each property is identified by a key. The `getProperty()` method retrieves a property using its key, as in this statement:

```
String username = config.getProperty("username");
```

Because properties are stored as strings, you must convert them in some manner to use a numerical value, as in this code:

```
String windowProp = config.getProperty("windowSize");
int windowSize = 24;
try {
    windowSize = Integer.parseInt(windowProp);
} catch (NumberFormatException exception) {
    // do nothing
}
```

Properties can be stored by calling the setProperty() method with two arguments—the key and value:

```
config.setProperty("username", "max");
```

You can display all properties by calling the list(*PrintStream*) method of the Properties object. PrintStream is something you've been using throughout the book: It's the class of the out instance variable of the System class, which you've been using to display output in System.out.println() and System.out.print() statements. The following code calls list() to display all properties:

```
config.list(System.out);
```

After you have made changes to the properties, you can store them back to the file:

- ▶ Create a File object that represents the file.

- ▶ Create a FileOutputStream object from that File object.

- ▶ Call store(*OutputStream*, *String*) to save the properties to the designated output stream with a description of the properties file as the string.

For the hour's final project, you build on the ConfigWriter application, which wrote several program settings to a file. The Configurator application reads those settings into a Java properties file, adds a new property named runtime with the current date and time, and saves the altered file.

Create a new Java file to hold the Configurator class in the com.java24hours package and enter the text from Listing 20.4.

LISTING 20.4   The Full Text of Configurator.java

```
 1: package com.java24hours;
 2:
 3: import java.io.*;
 4: import java.util.*;
 5:
 6: public class Configurator {
 7:
 8:     public Configurator() {
 9:         try {
10:             // load the properties file
11:             File configFile = new File("program.properties");
12:             FileInputStream inStream = new FileInputStream(configFile);
13:             Properties config = new Properties();
14:             config.load(inStream);
15:             // create a new property
```

```
16:                Date current = new Date();
17:                config.setProperty("runtime", current.toString());
18:                // save the properties file
19:                FileOutputStream outStream = new FileOutputStream(configFile);
20:                config.store(outStream, "Properties settings");
21:                inStream.close();
22:                config.list(System.out);
23:            } catch (IOException ioe) {
24:                System.out.println("IO error " + ioe.getMessage());
25:            }
26:        }
27:
28:        public static void main(String[] arguments) {
29:            new Configurator();
30:        }
31: }
```

In this application, the `File` object for `program.properties` is created and associated with a file input stream in Lines 11–12. The contents of this file are loaded into a `Properties` object from the stream in Lines 13–14.

A new property for the current date and time is created in Lines 16–17. The file is then associated with an output stream in Line 19, and the entire properties file is written to that stream in Line 20.

The output of the `Configurator` application is shown in Figure 20.4.

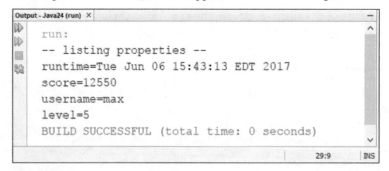

FIGURE 20.4
Running the `Configurator` application.

The `program.properties` file now contains the following text:

Output ▼

```
-- listing properties --
runtime=Tue Jun 06 15\:43\:13 EDT 2017
score=12550
username=max
level=5
```

The backslash character's \ formatting, which differs from the output of the application, ensures the properties file is stored properly.

Summary

During this hour, you worked with input streams and output streams that wrote bytes, the simplest way to represent data over a stream.

There are many more classes in the `java.io` package to work with streams in other ways. There's also a package of classes called `java.net` that enables you to read and write streams over an Internet connection.

Byte streams can be adapted to many uses because you can easily convert bytes into other data types, such as integers, characters, and strings.

The first project of this hour, the `ID3Reader` application, read bytes from a stream and converted them into a string to read the ID3 data in this format from a song such as "Come On and Gettit" by Marion Black off the album *Eccentric Soul*.

Have I mentioned yet that you should buy the song?

Workshop

Q&A

Q. Why do some of the byte stream methods in this hour use integers as arguments? Should they be using `byte` arguments?

A. There's a difference between the bytes in a stream and the bytes represented by the `byte` class. A `byte` in Java has a value ranging from −128 to 127, while a byte in a stream has a value from 0 to 255. You often have to use `int` when working with bytes for this reason—it can hold the values 128 to 255, whereas `byte` cannot.

Q. What is Mumblety-Peg?

A. It's a schoolyard game played by children with pocketknives.

In the simplest form, players stand and throw knives at their own feet. The one whose knife lands closest wins. Other versions involve throwing the knife at each other so the opponent has to stretch a foot to where it lands. The player who stretches too far and falls down loses.

The name comes from a rule that the winner could pound a peg into the ground with three blows of the knife. The loser had to "mumble the peg," removing it solely with his teeth.

The game faded from popularity in the early 20th century when the world reached the collective realization that children throwing knives at each other might not be the greatest idea in the world.

Quiz

To see whether you took a big enough byte from the tree of knowledge during this hour, answer the following questions about streams in Java.

1. Which of the following techniques can be used to convert an array of bytes into a string?

    A. Call the array's `toString()` method.

    B. Convert each byte to a character and then assign each one to an element in a `String` array.

    C. Call the `String()` constructor with the array as an argument.

2. What kind of stream is used to read from a file in a Java program?

    A. An input stream

    B. An output stream

    C. Either

3. What method of the `File` class can be used to determine the size of a file?

    A. `getSize()`

    B. `read()`

    C. `length()`

Answers

1. **C.** You can deal with each byte individually, as suggested in answer B, but you can easily create strings from other data types.

2. **A.** An input stream is created from a `File` object or by providing a filename to the input stream's constructor.

3. **C.** This method returns a `long`, representing the number of bytes in the stream.

Activities

To experience the refreshing feeling of wading through another stream, test the waters with the following activities:

▶ Write an application that reads the ID3 tags of all MP3 files in a folder and renames the files using the artist, song, and album information (when it is provided).

▶ Write a program that reads a Java source file and writes it back without any changes under a new name.

▶ Buy a copy of the song "Come On and Gettit" by Marion Black.

To see Java programs that implement these activities, visit the book's website at www.java24hours.com.

Using Java 9's New HTTP Client

This Hour's To-Do List:

▶ Add a module to a Java project.

▶ Create an HTTP web browser object.

▶ Make a GET request of a web server.

▶ Receive data from a web request.

▶ Download an image file from the web.

▶ Send data to a web server.

Though they were created to present websites, web servers have grown far beyond the browser since the early days of the World Wide Web. The ability to communicate over HTTP has been exploited by many types of software, including RSS readers, web services, software updaters, and operating systems.

Java 9 introduces an HTTP Client library to make sending and receiving data over the web easier, faster, and more reliable.

This library is not included automatically in the Java Class Library. Instead, it is added through an eagerly anticipated feature of the new language release called modules.

During this hour you'll learn about modules and making web connections over HTTP.

Java Modules

When Java programs are shipped, they are packaged into Java Archive (JAR) files with the class libraries used by the program. That JAR file and the other JAR files required by the project are all put on the Classpath accessed by the Java Virtual Machine (JVM) as it runs the program.

Over time, the inefficiencies in this process have become apparent. There could be hundreds or even thousands of Java classes in the JAR, organized only by package. The same class could be in two different places on the Classpath, leading to confusion about which one is used during the program's execution.

Java 9 brings more control in how programs are deployed through the use of modules.

The new HTTP Client Library included in Java 9 must be included in a module for it to be available in the programs that you write. The library is a package called `jdk.incubator.http`.

Follow these steps in NetBeans to add this module to the `Java24` project:

▶ Choose File, New File, then choose Java in the Categories pane. Something new appears in the File Types pane: Java Module Info.

▶ Choose Java Module Info, then click Next.

▶ The dialog displays the Class Name `module-info` and does not let a package name be chosen. Click Finish.

The file `module-info.java` opens for editing in the source code editor. It only needs these three lines:

```
module Java24 {
    requires jdk.incubator.httpclient;
}
```

When the file has been saved, the classes in the `jdk.incubator.httpclient` can be used in any Java program in this project.

Making an HTTP Request

A web server communicates with browsers and other types of web client software through a message called an HTTP request.

The request can be used to move information in both directions. Data can be received and sent between the server and client.

The hour's first project demonstrates the use of the HTTP Client Library to connect to a web server, request a document, and learn something about the server. This is a straightforward process, though it requires several classes.

Making a web request with this library requires these steps:

1. Create a browser object of the `HttpClient` class.

2. Create a request builder (the `HttpRequest.Builder` inner class).

3. Build the request as an `HttpRequest` object.

4. Use the browser to send the request to a web server.

5. Receive an `HttpResponse` object back.

The browser is created using a factory method of the `HttpClient` class:

```
HttpClient browser = HttpClient.newHttpClient();
```

As you might expect, the browser's job is to send the request to the server.

The request is created with a builder class. The builder requires the web address of the server. The URI class in the `java.net` package represents an address (also called a URI or URL) and can be created like this:

```
URI link = new URI("https://www.oracle.com/");
```

If the web address specified as the only argument isn't a properly formatted web address, a `URISyntaxException` (from `java.net`) is thrown.

With a URI object, you can call the factory method `HttpRequest.newBuilder(URI)` to create the builder:

```
HttpRequest.Builder bob = HttpRequest.newBuilder(uri);
```

The builder's `build()` method creates the request, which is an object of the `HttpRequest` class:

```
HttpRequest request = bob.build();
```

Now that you have a browser and a request, you can send it to the web server and get a response back. The response is an `HttpResponse` object that uses generics because it can receive information in multiple formats.

The browser's `send()` request takes two arguments:

▶ An `HttpRequest` object.

▶ A handler that sets the format of the response.

The handler is created by calling a class method of the `HttpResponse.BodyHandler` inner class, as in this statement:

```
HttpResponse<String> response = browser.send(request,
    HttpResponse.BodyHandler.asString());
```

The generic reference in `HttpResponse<String>` defines the response as a string. The handler's `asString()` method makes the call to the browser's `send()` method to return a string.

The handler also has an `asFile(Path)` method to return the response in a file and an `asByteArray()` method to return it as `byte[]`.

Every HTTP request has headers that provide more information about the response and the server that sent it. One of these headers, Server, contains the name and version number of the software that runs the server. Some servers omit the version number for security reasons.

The response's `headers()` method returns the headers as an `HttpHeaders` object. That object's `firstValue(String)` method is called with the header name to return the first header matching that name. Here's code to accomplish this:

```
HttpHeaders headers = response.headers();
Optional<String> server = headers.firstValue("Server");
```

The object returned by the call to `firstValue()` is a data structure from the `java.util` package that makes it easier to deal with something that has a `null` value when it isn't present. Using an object with no value causes a `NullPointerException`, one of the most common exceptions in Java.

The `Optional` class guards against this with an `isPresent()` method that returns `true` when there's a valid value and `false` otherwise.

The value of `server` is a string, as indicated by the generic in the `Optional<String>` portion of the statement. This string can be displayed while avoiding problems with `null` as follows:

```
if (server.isPresent()) {
    System.out.println("Server: " + server.get());
}
```

Putting these techniques into action, the `ServerCheck` application requests the home page of six companies in tech and reports what server software they use.

In NetBeans, create a new empty Java file called `ServerCheck` in the `com.java24hours` package. Enter Listing 21.1 into the source code editor.

LISTING 21.1   **The Full Text of** `ServerCheck.java`

```
 1: package com.java24hours;
 2:
 3: import java.io.*;
 4: import java.net.*;
 5: import java.util.*;
 6: import jdk.incubator.http.*;
 7:
 8: public class ServerCheck {
 9:     public ServerCheck() {
10:         String[] sites = {
11:             "https://www.apple.com",
```

```
12:                  "https://www.microsoft.com",
13:                  "http://www.compaq.com",
14:                  "http://www.hp.com",
15:                  "https://www.oracle.com/",
16:                  "http://www.informit.com/"
17:            };
18:            try {
19:                load(sites);
20:            } catch (URISyntaxException oops) {
21:                System.out.println("Bad URI: " + oops.getMessage());
22:            } catch (IOException | InterruptedException oops) {
23:                System.out.println("Error: " + oops.getMessage());
24:            }
25:        }
26:
27:        public void load(String[] sites) throws URISyntaxException, IOException,
28:                InterruptedException {
29:
30:            for (String site : sites) {
31:                System.out.println("\nSite: " + site);
32:                // create the web client
33:                HttpClient browser = HttpClient.newHttpClient();
34:                // build a request for a website
35:                URI uri = new URI(site);
36:                HttpRequest.Builder bob = HttpRequest.newBuilder(uri);
37:                HttpRequest request = bob.build();
38:                // execute the request
39:                HttpResponse<String> response = browser.send(request,
40:                    HttpResponse.BodyHandler.asString());
41:                // look for a server header
42:                HttpHeaders headers = response.headers();
43:                Optional<String> server = headers.firstValue("Server");
44:                if (server.isPresent()) {
45:                    System.out.println("Server: " + server.get());
46:                } else {
47:                    System.out.println("Server unidentified");
48:                }
49:            }
50:        }
51:
52:        public static void main(String[] arguments) {
53:            new ServerCheck();
54:        }
55: }
```

Save your work and run the application to produce the output shown in Figure 21.1.

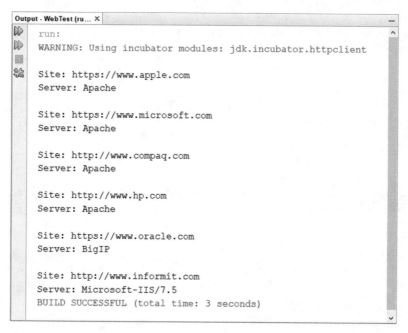

```
Output - WebTest (ru... ×                                              —
  run:
  WARNING: Using incubator modules: jdk.incubator.httpclient

  Site: https://www.apple.com
  Server: Apache

  Site: https://www.microsoft.com
  Server: Apache

  Site: http://www.compaq.com
  Server: Apache

  Site: http://www.hp.com
  Server: Apache

  Site: https://www.oracle.com
  Server: BigIP

  Site: http://www.informit.com
  Server: Microsoft-IIS/7.5
  BUILD SUCCESSFUL (total time: 3 seconds)
```

FIGURE 21.1
Using the HTTP client to request server headers.

Like the input and output classes you worked with in the previous hour, "Reading and Writing Files," the methods of these HTTP classes must deal with errors in the transmission of data. They throw the exceptions IOException and InterruptedException from the java.io package.

The ServerCheck application has a load() method that performs all of the HTTP tasks necessary to request the six home pages from their web servers and get a response back.

The three exceptions that may occur are put in the constructor in a try-catch block that uses a multi-class catch in line 22.

Saving a File from the Web

The data that can be retrieved over HTTP isn't limited to text files such as a web page. Any kind of data can be accessed as bytes, including images, videos, and executable files.

The next project of the hour uses the new HTTP Client library to download an image from the author's blog and save it to your computer.

The `ImageDownloader` application follows the same steps as the preceding example until to the point that the request is sent. A browser is created, a request builder is created using a URI, and the request is built.

Before the request is sent to the web server, some prep work must be done. A file must be created to hold the contents of the image when it is received:

```
Path temp = Files.createTempFile("lighthouse", ".jpg");
```

The `Files` class in the `java.nio` package can create a temporary file by calling its class method `createTempFile(String, String)`. The two arguments are a text identifier to use in the filename and the file extension. The filename is generated with the identifier followed by a number and the file extension, such as `lighthouse3994062538481620758.jpg`.

Once you have a file, the browser's `send()` method can use a response handler to specify this file as the second argument. The response from the server will be stored in that file. Here's a statement to do that:

```
HttpResponse<Path> response = browser.send(request,
    HttpResponse.BodyHandler.asFile(temp));
```

The `request` is the `HttpRequest` object created using a builder and the image file's web address (URI). The body handler's `asFile(Path)` method makes the specified file the destination for the image data.

This temporary file can be saved to a permanent file by renaming it:

```
File perm = new File("lighthouse.jpg");
temp.toFile().renameTo(perm);
```

In NetBeans, create an `ImageDownloader.java` empty Java file in the `com.java24hours` package, then fill it with the source code in Listing 21.2.

LISTING 21.2 **The Full Text of** `ImageDownloader.java`

```
 1: package com.java24hours;
 2:
 3: import java.io.*;
 4: import java.net.*;
 5: import java.nio.file.*;
 6: import jdk.incubator.http.*;
 7:
 8: public class ImageDownloader {
 9:     public ImageDownloader() {
10:         String uri = "http://workbench.cadenhead.org/media/lighthouse.jpg";
11:         try {
12:             load(uri);
13:         } catch (URISyntaxException oops) {
```

```
14:                    System.out.println("Bad URI: " + oops.getMessage());
15:            } catch (IOException | InterruptedException oops) {
16:                    System.out.println("Error: " + oops.getMessage());
17:            }
18:      }
19:
20:      public void load(String imageUri) throws URISyntaxException, IOException,
21:          InterruptedException {
22:
23:              // create the web client
24:              HttpClient browser = HttpClient.newHttpClient();
25:              // build a request for the image
26:              URI uri = new URI(imageUri);
27:              HttpRequest.Builder bob = HttpRequest.newBuilder(uri);
28:              HttpRequest request = bob.build();
29:              // create a file to hold the image data
30:              Path temp = Files.createTempFile("lighthouse", ".jpg");
31:              // execute the request and retrieve the data
32:              HttpResponse<Path> response = browser.send(request,
33:                  HttpResponse.BodyHandler.asFile(temp));
34:              System.out.println("Image saved to "
35:                  + temp.toFile().getAbsolutePath());
36:              // save the file permanently
37:              File perm = new File("lighthouse.jpg");
38:              temp.toFile().renameTo(perm);
39:              System.out.println("Image moved to " + perm.getAbsolutePath());
40:      }
41:
42:      public static void main(String[] arguments) {
43:          new ImageDownloader();
44:      }
45: }
```

When the `ImageDownloader` application is run, a file called `lighthouse.jpg` appears in the project's main folder. Click the Files tab to bring it to the front (this is in the same part of NetBeans as the Projects pane). Double-click the file to open it in the main pane, as shown in Figure 21.2.

The program displays the location of the temporary and permanent image files in lines 34–35 and 39, respectively.

FIGURE 21.2
Downloading an image file from the web.

Posting Data on the Web

So far, this hour has focused on using HTTP to get something from the web. Now it's time to give something back. The final project is SalutonVerkisto, a Java application to send a message to the author's web server using a POST request.

A POST request can encode large amounts of data to be received by the server, such as a weblog post or even an image or video file. A GET request also can carry information to the server, but it is limited by what can be included in a URI.

The application creates a URI for a script on my server that receives comments:

```
String site = "http://workbench.cadenhead.org/post-a-comment.php";
URI uri = new URI(site);
```

Two strings, yourName and yourMessage, contain the name and comment that will be sent:

```
String yourName = "Sam Snett of Indianapolis";
String yourMessage = "Your book is pretty good, if I do say so myself.";
```

The information will be sent to the web server using an HTTP request, just like the preceding projects. Before the comment can be sent, it must be encoded using a method of the HttpRequest.BodyProcessor inner class.

The class has a fromString() method called with a set of name-value pairs separated by "&" characters in a long string:

```
HttpRequest.BodyProcessor proc = HttpRequest.BodyProcessor.fromString(
    "name=" + URLEncoder.encode(yourName, "UTF-8") +
    "&comment=" + URLEncoder.encode(yourMessage, "UTF-8") +
    "&mode=" + URLEncoder.encode("demo", "UTF-8")
);
```

The encode(*String*, *String*) method of HttpRequest.BodyProcessor takes two arguments: the message and the character encoding to use. The proper encoding depends on what the web server can accept. The script on my server can accept UTF-8, so that's used here.

This method call specifies three name-value pairs: name, comment, and mode. The first two take their values from yourName and yourMessage. The third, mode, has the value "demo" and lets the server script know the purpose of the message. (It also helps weed out spammers who might send their junk messages to the script.)

The processed message proc can be used to create a request builder with a call to the newBuilder(*URI*) method followed by three more calls.

This will make more sense when the code is shown first:

```
HttpRequest.Builder newBuilder = HttpRequest.newBuilder(uri)
    .header("Content-Type", "application/x-www-form-urlencoded")
    .header("Accept", "text/plain")
    .POST(proc);
```

This method call stacks four calls together. This works because each one is a call to HttpRequest.Builder that returns the builder object. Here's what the calls accomplish, in order:

1. newBuilder(*URI*) creates a builder for that web address.

2. header(*String*, *String*) sets a request header called Content-Type to the value "application/x-www-form-urlencoded". This tells the server that a web form is being sent.

3. Another `header()` call sets `Accept` to "text/plain", the MIME type of the request.

4. `post(HttpRequest.BodyProcessor)` formats the encoded message as an HTTP POST request.

Now that the builder has been prepared, the request can be built:

```
HttpRequest request = newBuilder.build();
```

The request is sent with a browser `send(HttpRequest, HttpResponse.BodyHandler)` call with the request and a handler that gets the response back as a string:

```
HttpResponse<String> response = client.send(request,
    HttpResponse.BodyHandler.asString());
System.out.println(response.body());
```

The same technique was used in the `ServerCheck` application, but this time the response is displayed.

Create the `SalutonVerkisto` application as an empty Java file in the `com.java24hours` package, entering the source in Listing 21.3.

LISTING 21.3   **The Full Text of** `SalutonVerkisto.java`

```
 1: package com.java24hours;
 2:
 3: import java.io.*;
 4: import java.net.*;
 5: import jdk.incubator.http.*;
 6:
 7: public class SalutonVerkisto {
 8:
 9:     public SalutonVerkisto() {
10:         String site = "http://workbench.cadenhead.org/post-a-comment.php";
11:         try {
12:             postMessage(site);
13:         } catch (URISyntaxException oops) {
14:             System.out.println("Bad URI: " + oops.getMessage());
15:         } catch (IOException | InterruptedException oops) {
16:             System.out.println("Error: " + oops.getMessage());
17:         }
18:     }
19:
20:     public void postMessage(String server) throws IOException,
21:             URISyntaxException, InterruptedException {
22:
23:         HttpClient client = HttpClient.newHttpClient();
24:
25:         // address of the server
```

```
26:            URI uri = new URI(server);
27:
28:            // set up the message
29:            String yourName = "Sam Snett of Indianapolis";
30:            String yourMessage = "Your book is pretty good, if I do say so myself.";
31:
32:            // encode the message
33:            HttpRequest.BodyProcessor proc = HttpRequest.BodyProcessor.fromString(
34:                "name=" + URLEncoder.encode(yourName, "UTF-8") +
35:                "&comment=" + URLEncoder.encode(yourMessage, "UTF-8") +
36:                "&mode=" + URLEncoder.encode("demo", "UTF-8")
37:            );
38:
39:            // prepare the request
40:            HttpRequest.Builder newBuilder = HttpRequest.newBuilder(uri)
41:                .header("Content-Type", "application/x-www-form-urlencoded")
42:                .header("Accept", "text/plain")
43:                .POST(proc);
44:
45:            // finish the request
46:            HttpRequest request = newBuilder.build();
47:
48:            // get the response from the server
49:            System.out.println("Method: " + request.method() + "\n");
50:            HttpResponse<String> response = client.send(request,
51:                HttpResponse.BodyHandler.asString());
52:            System.out.println(response.body());
53:        }
54:
55:        public static void main(String[] arguments) {
56:            new SalutonVerkisto();
57:        }
58: }
```

Before you run the SalutonVerkisto application, edit lines 29–30. Put your name and location in yourName and something you'd like to tell me in yourMessage. These will be displayed publicly in a post on my weblog.

The application returns the text of the comments that have been received from readers (Figure 21.3).

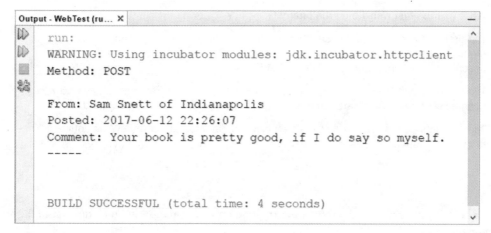

FIGURE 21.3
Sending data to a web server using a POST request.

Summary

The use of HTTP for software and web services was probably inevitable. The protocol is implemented everywhere and firewalls have to let the traffic through on port 80 or web browsers wouldn't work.

The new HTTP Client Library in Java 9 is an attempt to make it easier to exploit this useful two-way channel of information.

You might be confused about why the hour's final project was given the odd name `SalutonVerkisto`.

There's a clue in the program Saluton you created during Hour 2, "Writing Your First Program." That application displayed the message "Saluton, mondo!" which is the phrase "Hello, world!" in the Esperanto language. The word "saluton" translates to "hello."

"Saluton verkisto" means "Hello, author."

Q&A

Q. Why is there an incubation warning in the output of this hour's three programs?

A. The creators of Java have introduced the concept of an incubator in Java 9. The new HTTP Client library is in incubation, which means that it's still in an early stage of its development.

A project in incubation is likely to change in the next version of Java. This is something to keep in mind as you use the classes of the `jdk.incubator.http` package.

Q. What was the first website on the Internet?

A. The first site was http://info.cern.ch, which is still online today. Tim Berners-Lee, a British physicist at the European Organization for Nuclear Research (CERN), used the site to describe his new invention, the World Wide Web.

The first web page was at http://info.cern.ch/hypertext/WWW/TheProject.html and was updated daily as the Web attracted users, publishers, and software developers.

The site defined the Web as "a wide-area hypermedia information retrieval initiative aiming to give universal access to a large universe of documents."

Quiz

Check how well you've absorbed a web of information on HTTP programming by answering the following questions.

1. Which type of request can be used to send information to a web server?

    A. GET

    B. POST

    C. Both GET and POST

2. What class holds the information received from a server produced by a request?

    A. `HttpClient`

    B. `HttpResponse`

    C. `HttpRequest`

3. What's one reason to use the `Optional` data structure?

    A. To avoid `NullPointerException` errors.

    B. To hold a collection of `null` values.

    C. To run faster.

Answers

1. **C.** POST sends a large amount of data; GET sends data on a web address(URI).

2. **B.** The `HttpResponse` object is returned by a call to the browser's `send()` method.

3. **A.** Calling `isPresent()` checks whether this structure holds `null` instead of a valid object.

Activities

To further serve your knowledge of this hour's topic of web programming, do the following activities:

▶ Add five more tech company homepages to the `ServerCheck` program.

▶ Write a program that uses an HTTP response's "Content-Type" and "Content-Encoding" headers to report the MIME type and character encoding that the server employs.

To see Java programs that implement these activities, visit the book's website at www.java24hours.com.

HOUR 22
Creating Java2D Graphics

This Hour's To-Do List:

- ▶ Set the font and color of text.
- ▶ Set up a container's background color.
- ▶ Draw lines, rectangles, and other shapes.
- ▶ Draw GIF and JPEG graphics.
- ▶ Draw filled and unfilled shapes.

During this hour, you learn how to turn containers—the plain gray panels and frames that hold graphical user interface (GUI) components—into an artistic canvas on which you can draw fonts, colors, shapes, and graphics.

Using the Font Class

Colors and fonts are represented in Java by the Color and Font classes in the java.awt package. With these classes, you can present text in different fonts and sizes and change the color of text and graphics. Fonts are created with the Font(*String, int, int*) constructor, which takes three arguments:

- ▶ The typeface of the font as either a generic name ("Dialog," "DialogInput," "Monospaced," "SanSerif," or "Serif") or an actual font name ("Arial Black," "Helvetica," or "Courier New")

- ▶ The style as one of three class variables: Font.BOLD, Font.ITALIC, or Font.PLAIN

- ▶ The size of the font in points

The following statement creates a 12-point italic Serif font:

```
Font current = new Font("Serif", Font.ITALIC, 12);
```

If you use a specific font rather than one of the generic ones, it already must be installed on the computer of the user running your program.

You can combine the font styles by adding them together, as in the following example:

```
Font headline = new Font("Courier New", Font.BOLD + Font.ITALIC, 72);
```

When you have a font, you call the `Graphics2D` component's `setFont(Font)` method to designate it as the current font. All subsequent drawing operations use that font until another one is set. The following code creates a "Comic Sans" font object and designates it as the current font before drawing text:

```
public void paintComponent(Graphics comp) {
    Graphics2D comp2D = (Graphics2D) comp;
    Font font = new Font("Comic Sans", Font.BOLD, 15);
    comp2D.setFont(font);
    comp2D.drawString("Potrzebie!", 5, 50);
}
```

Java supports antialiasing to draw fonts and graphics more smoothly and less blocky in appearance. To enable this functionality, you must set a rendering hint. A `Graphics2D` object has a `setRenderingHint(int, int)` method that takes two arguments:

- ▶ The key of the rendering hint
- ▶ The value to associate with that key

These values are class variables in the `RenderingHints` class of `java.awt`. To activate antialiasing, call `setRenderingHint()` with two arguments:

```
comp2D.setRenderingHint(RenderingHints.KEY_ANTIALIASING,
    RenderingHints.VALUE_ANTIALIAS_ON);
```

The `comp2D` object in this example is the `Graphics2D` object that represents a container's drawing environment.

Using the `Color` **Class**

Colors in Java are represented by the `Color` class, which includes the following constants as class variables: `black`, `blue`, `cyan`, `darkGray`, `gray`, `green`, `lightGray`, `magenta`, `orange`, `pink`, `red`, `white`, and `yellow`.

In a container, you can set the background color of the component using these constants by calling the `setBackground(Color)` method like this:

```
setBackground(Color.orange);
```

The current color, like the current font, must be set before drawing takes place using the `setColor(Color)` method. The following code includes a statement to set the current color to blue and draw text in that color:

```
public void paintComponent(Graphics comp) {
    Graphics2D comp2D = (Graphics2D) comp;
    comp2D.setColor(Color.blue);
    comp2D.drawString("Go, Owls!", 5, 50);
}
```

Unlike the setBackground() method, which you can call directly on a container, you must call the setColor() method on a Graphics2D object.

Creating Custom Colors

You can create custom colors in Java by specifying their Red Green Blue (RGB) value. RGB defines a color by the amount of red, green, and blue present in the color. Each value ranges from 0 (none of that color) to 255 (the maximum amount).

The constructor Color(int, int, int) takes arguments representing the red, green, and blue values. The following code draws a panel that displays gold text (159 red, 121 green, 44 blue) on a teal (0 red, 101 green, 118 blue) background:

```
import java.awt.*;
import javax.swing.*;

public class Jacksonville extends JPanel {
    Color gold = new Color(159, 121, 44);
    Color teal = new Color(0, 101, 118);

    public void paintComponent(Graphics comp) {
        Graphics2D comp2D = (Graphics2D) comp;
        comp2D.setColor(teal);
        comp2D.fillRect(0, 0, 200, 100);
        comp2D.setColor(gold);
        comp2D.drawString("Go, Jaguars!", 5, 50);
    }
}
```

This example calls the fillRect() method of Graphics2D to draw a filled-in rectangle using the current color.

NOTE

RGB values enable the creation of 16.5 million possible combinations, although most computer monitors offer only a close approximation for most of them. For guidance on whether burnt-midnight blue goes well with medium-faded-baby green, read *Sams Teach Yourself Color Sense While Waiting in Line at This Bookstore.*

Drawing Lines and Shapes

Drawing shapes such as lines and rectangles is as easy in a Java program as displaying text. All you need is a `Graphics2D` object to define the drawing surface and objects that represent things to draw.

The `Graphics2D` object has methods used to draw text with a command such as the following:

```
comp2D.drawString("Draw, pardner!", 15, 40);
```

This draws the text "Draw, pardner!" at the coordinates (15, 40). Drawing methods use the same (x, y) coordinate system as text. The (0, 0) coordinate is at the upper-left corner of the container, x values increase to the right, and y values increase as you go down. You can determine the maximum (x, y) value you can use in a frame or another container with the following statements:

```
int maxXValue = getSize().width;
int maxYValue = getSize().height;
```

With the exception of lines, shapes you draw can be filled or unfilled. A filled shape is drawn with the current color completely filling the space taken up by the shape. Unfilled shapes draw a border with the current color.

Drawing Lines

A 2D drawing of an object is created and represents the shape that is being drawn.

The objects that define shapes belong to the `java.awt.geom` package of classes.

The `Line2D.Float` class creates a line connecting a beginning (x, y) point and an ending (x, y) point. The following statement creates a line from the point (40, 200) to the point (70, 130):

```
Line2D.Float line = new Line2D.Float(40F, 200F, 70F, 130F);
```

The arguments are followed by the letter F to indicate they are floating-point values. If this was omitted, Java would treat them as integers.

NOTE

`Line2D.Float` has a period in the middle of its class name, which differs from most classes you've worked with before. That's because `Float` is a static inner class of the `Line2D` class, a subject covered in Hour 16, "Using Inner Classes and Closures."

All shapes except for lines are drawn by calling a method of the `Graphics2D` class: `draw()` for outlines and `fill()` for filled shapes.

The following statement draws the `line` object created in the previous example:

```
comp2D.draw(line);
```

Drawing Rectangles

Rectangles can be filled or unfilled and have rounded or square corners. They are created using the `Rectangle2D.Float(int, int, int, int)` constructor with these arguments:

- ▶ The x coordinate at the upper left of the rectangle
- ▶ The y coordinate at upper left
- ▶ The width of the rectangle
- ▶ The height

The following statement draws an unfilled rectangle with square corners:

```
Rectangle2D.Float box = new Rectangle2D.Float(245F, 65F, 20F, 10F);
```

This statement creates a rectangle with its upper-left corner at the (x, y) coordinates (245, 65) with a width of 20 pixels and a height of 10. To draw this rectangle as an outline, you could use the following statement:

```
comp2D.draw(box);
```

If you want to make the rectangle filled in, use the `fill()` method instead:

```
comp.fill(box);
```

You can create rectangles with rounded corners instead of square ones by using the `RoundRectangle2D.Float` class.

The constructor to this class starts with the same four arguments as the `Rectangle2D.Float` class and adds the following two arguments:

- ▶ The number of pixels in the x direction away from the corner of the rectangle
- ▶ The number of pixels in the y direction away from the corner

These distances are used to determine where the rounding of the rectangle's corner should begin.

The following statement creates a rounded rectangle:

```
RoundRectangle2D.Float ro = new RoundRectangle2D.Float(
     10F, 10F,
     100F, 80F,
     15F, 15F);
```

This rectangle has its upper-left corner at the (10, 10) coordinate. The third and fourth arguments specify how wide and tall the rectangle should be. In this case, it should be 100 pixels wide and 80 pixels tall.

The last two arguments to `drawRoundRect()` specify that all four corners should begin rounding 15 pixels away from the corner at (10, 10).

Drawing Ellipses and Circles

You can create ellipses and circles with the same class, `Ellipse2D.Float`, which takes four arguments:

- ▶ The x coordinate of the ellipse
- ▶ The y coordinate of the ellipse
- ▶ Its width
- ▶ Its height

The (x, y) coordinates do not indicate a point at the center of the ellipse or circle, as you might expect. Instead, the (x, y) coordinates, width, and height describe an invisible rectangle inside which the ellipse fits. The (x, y) coordinate is the upper-left corner of this rectangle. If it has the same width and height, the ellipse is a circle.

The following statement creates a circle inside the rectangle at the (245, 45) coordinate with a height and width of 5 pixels each:

```
Ellipse2D.Float cir = new Ellipse2D.Float(
    245F, 45F, 5F, 5F);
```

Drawing Arcs

Another circular shape you can draw in Java is an arc, a partial ellipse or circle. Arcs are created using the `Arc2D.Float` class, which has a constructor with many of the same arguments. You draw the arc by specifying an ellipse, the portion of the ellipse that should be visible (in degrees), and the place the arc should begin on the ellipse.

To create an arc, specify the following integer arguments to the constructor:

- ▶ The x coordinate of the invisible rectangle that the ellipse fits into
- ▶ The y coordinate of the rectangle
- ▶ The width of the rectangle
- ▶ The height of the rectangle

▶ The point on the ellipse where the arc should begin (in degrees from 0 to 359)

▶ The size of the arc (also in degrees)

▶ The type of arc it is

The arc's starting point and size range from 0 to 359 degrees in a counterclockwise direction, beginning with 0 degrees at the 3 o'clock position, as shown in Figure 22.1.

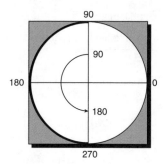

FIGURE 22.1
How arcs are defined in degrees.

The type of arc is specified using class variables: PIE for pie graph slices, CLOSED if the endpoints are connected with a straight line, and OPEN if the endpoints should not be connected.

The following statement draws an open arc at (100, 50) that is 120 degrees long, begins at the 30-degree mark, and has a width of 65 and a height of 75:

```
Arc2D.Float smile = new Arc2D.Float(100F, 50F, 65F, 75F,
    30F, 120F, Arc2D.Float.OPEN);
```

Baking a Pie Graph

To draw this hour to a close, you create PiePanel, a GUI component that displays a pie graph. This component is a subclass of JPanel, a simple container that's useful as a place to draw something.

One way to begin creating a class is to define the way objects of the class are created. Programs that use the PiePanel class must undertake the following steps:

▶ Create a PiePanel object by using the constructor method PiePanel(*int*). The integer specified as an argument is the number of slices the pie graph contains.

▶ Call the object's addSlice(*Color*, *float*) method to give a slice the designated color and value.

The value of each slice in `PiePanel` is the quantity represented by that slice.

For example, Table 22.1 displays data about the status of student loan repayments in the United States for the first 38 years of the program, according to the Office of Postsecondary Education.

TABLE 22.1 U.S. Student Loan Repayments

Amount repaid by students	$101 billion
Amount loaned to students still in school	$68 billion
Amount loaned to students making payments	$91 billion
Amount loaned to students who defaulted	$25 billion

You could use `PiePanel` to represent this data in a pie graph with the following statements:

```
PiePanel loans = new PiePanel(4);
loans.addSlice(Color.green, 101F);
loans.addSlice(Color.yellow, 68F);
loans.addSlice(Color.blue, 91F);
loans.addSlice(Color.red, 25F);
```

Figure 22.2 shows the result in an application frame that contains one component:, a `PiePanel` created with the student loan data.

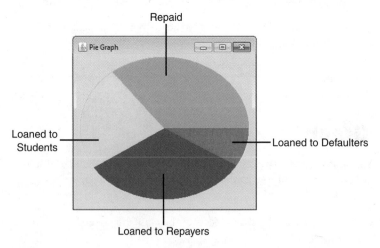

FIGURE 22.2
Displaying student loan data on a pie graph.

When a `PiePanel` object is created, the number of slices is specified in the constructor. You need to know three more things to draw each slice:

▶ The color of the slice, represented by a `Color` object

▶ The value represented by each slice

▶ The total value represented by all slices

A new helper class, `PieSlice`, is used to represent each slice in the pie graph:

```java
import java.awt.*;

class PieSlice {
    Color color = Color.lightGray;
    float size = 0;

    PieSlice(Color pColor, float pSize) {
        color = pColor;
        size = pSize;
    }
}
```

Each slice is constructed by calling `PieSlice(Color, float)`. The combined value of all slices is stored as a private instance variable of the `PiePanel` class, `totalSize`. There also are instance variables for the panel's background color (`background`) and a counter used to keep track of slices (`current`):

```java
private int current = 0;
private float totalSize = 0;
private Color background;
```

Now that you have a `PieSlice` class to work with, you can create an array of `PieSlice` objects with another instance variable:

```java
private PieSlice[] slice;
```

When you create a `PiePanel` object, none of the slices have an assigned a color or size. The only things that you must do in the constructor are define the size of the `slice` array and save the background color of the panel:

```java
public PiePanel(int sliceCount) {
    slice = new PieSlice[sliceCount];
    background = getBackground();
}
```

Use the addSlice(`Color`, `float`) method to add a slice of the pie to the panel:

```
public void addSlice(Color sColor, float sSize) {
    if (current <= slice.length) {
        slice[current] = new PieSlice(sColor, sSize);
        totalSize += sSize;
        current++;
    }
}
```

The current instance variable is used to put each slice into its own element of the slice array. The length variable of an array contains the number of elements the array has been defined to hold; as long as current is not larger than slice.length, you can continue adding slices to the panel.

The PiePanel class handles all drawing operations in its paintComponent() method, as you might expect. The trickiest thing about this task is drawing the arcs that represent each slice of the pie.

This is handled in the following statements:

```
float start = 0;
for (int i = 0; i < slice.length; i++) {
    float extent = slice[i].size * 360F / totalSize;
    comp2D.setColor(slice[i].color);
    Arc2D.Float drawSlice = new Arc2D.Float(
        xInset, yInset, width, height, start, extent,
        Arc2D.Float.PIE);
    start += extent;
    comp2D.fill(drawSlice);
}
```

The start variable keeps track of where to start drawing an arc, and extent keeps track of the size of an arc. If you know the total size of all pie slices and the size of a specific slice, you can figure out extent by multiplying the arc's size by 360 and dividing that by the total of all slices.

All the arcs are drawn in a for loop: After each arc's extent is calculated, the arc is created and then extent is added to start. This causes each slice to begin right next to the last one. A call to the Graphics2D method fill() draws the arc.

To bring all this together, create a new empty Java file named PiePanel in the com. java24hours package and enter into it the full text from Listing 22.1.

LISTING 22.1   The Full Text of PiePanel.java

```
1: package com.java24hours;
2:
3: import java.awt.*;
4: import javax.swing.*;
```

```
 5: import java.awt.geom.*;
 6:
 7: public class PiePanel extends JPanel {
 8:     private PieSlice[] slice;
 9:     private int current = 0;
10:     private float totalSize = 0;
11:     private Color background;
12:
13:     public PiePanel(int sliceCount) {
14:         slice = new PieSlice[sliceCount];
15:         background = getBackground();
16:     }
17:
18:     public void addSlice(Color sColor, float sSize) {
19:         if (current <= slice.length) {
20:             slice[current] = new PieSlice(sColor, sSize);
21:             totalSize += sSize;
22:             current++;
23:         }
24:     }
25:
26:     public void paintComponent(Graphics comp) {
27:         super.paintComponent(comp);
28:         Graphics2D comp2D = (Graphics2D) comp;
29:         int width = getSize().width - 10;
30:         int height = getSize().height - 15;
31:         int xInset = 5;
32:         int yInset = 5;
33:         if (width < 5) {
34:             xInset = width;
35:         }
36:         if (height < 5) {
37:             yInset = height;
38:         }
39:         comp2D.setColor(background);
40:         comp2D.fillRect(0, 0, getSize().width, getSize().height);
41:         comp2D.setColor(Color.lightGray);
42:         Ellipse2D.Float pie = new Ellipse2D.Float(
43:             xInset, yInset, width, height);
44:         comp2D.fill(pie);
45:         float start = 0;
46:         for (int i = 0; i < slice.length; i++) {
47:             float extent = slice[i].size * 360F / totalSize;
48:             comp2D.setColor(slice[i].color);
49:             Arc2D.Float drawSlice = new Arc2D.Float(
50:                 xInset, yInset, width, height, start, extent,
51:                 Arc2D.Float.PIE);
52:             start += extent;
```

```
53:                 comp2D.fill(drawSlice);
54:             }
55:         }
56: }
57:
58: class PieSlice {
59:     Color color = Color.lightGray;
60:     float size = 0;
61:
62:     PieSlice(Color pColor, float pSize) {
63:         color = pColor;
64:         size = pSize;
65:     }
66: }
```

Listing 22.1 defines a `PiePanel` class in lines 1–56 and a `PieSlice` helper class in lines 58–66. The `PiePanel` class can be used as a component in any Java program's GUI. To test `PiePanel`, you need to create a class that uses it.

Listing 22.2 contains an application that uses these panels, `PieFrame`. Create a new empty Java file in the `com.java24hours` package and enter the source code for this class from the listing.

LISTING 22.2   The Full Text of `PieFrame.java`

```
1: package com.java24hours;
2:
3: import javax.swing.*;
4: import java.awt.*;
5:
6: public class PieFrame extends JFrame {
7:     Color uneasyBeingGreen = new Color(0xCC, 0xCC, 0x99);
8:     Color zuzusPetals = new Color(0xCC, 0x66, 0xFF);
9:     Color zootSuit = new Color(0x66, 0x66, 0x99);
10:    Color sweetHomeAvocado = new Color(0x66, 0x99, 0x66);
11:    Color shrinkingViolet = new Color(0x66, 0x66, 0x99);
12:    Color miamiNice = new Color(0x33, 0xFF, 0xFF);
13:    Color inBetweenGreen = new Color(0x00, 0x99, 0x66);
14:    Color norwegianBlue = new Color(0x33, 0xCC, 0xCC);
15:    Color purpleRain = new Color(0x66, 0x33, 0x99);
16:    Color freckle = new Color(0x99, 0x66, 0x33);
17:
18:    public PieFrame() {
19:        super("Pie Graph");
20:        setLookAndFeel();
21:        setSize(320, 290);
22:        setDefaultCloseOperation(JFrame.EXIT_ON_CLOSE);
23:        setVisible(true);
24:
```

```
25:          PiePanel pie = new PiePanel(10);
26:          pie.addSlice(uneasyBeingGreen, 1350);
27:          pie.addSlice(zuzusPetals, 1221);
28:          pie.addSlice(zootSuit, 316);
29:          pie.addSlice(sweetHomeAvocado, 251);
30:          pie.addSlice(shrinkingViolet, 201);
31:          pie.addSlice(miamiNice, 193);
32:          pie.addSlice(inBetweenGreen, 173);
33:          pie.addSlice(norwegianBlue, 164);
34:          pie.addSlice(purpleRain, 143);
35:          pie.addSlice(freckle, 127);
36:          add(pie);
37:      }
38:
39:      private void setLookAndFeel() {
40:          try {
41:              UIManager.setLookAndFeel(
42:                  "com.sun.java.swing.plaf.nimbus.NimbusLookAndFeel"
43:              );
44:          } catch (Exception exc) {
45:              // ignore error
46:          }
47:      }
48:
49:      public static void main(String[] arguments) {
50:          PieFrame pf = new PieFrame();
51:      }
52: }
```

The PieFrame class is a simple graphical user interface that contains one component: a PiePanel object created in line 25. The object's addSlice() method is called 10 times in lines 26–35 to add slices to the pie graph.

When you run the application, PieFrame displays a pie graph showing the population of the 10 most populated countries (in millions), using figures from a June 2017 U.S. Census International Data Base report. In order, they are China (1.379 billion), India (1.282 billion), United States (327 million), Indonesia (261 million), Brazil (207 million), Pakistan (205 million), Nigeria (191 million), Bangladesh (158 million), Russia (142 million), and Japan (126 million).

Because Java only has a few colors defined in the Color class, 10 new ones are created for use here and given descriptive names. The colors are expressed as hexadecimal values—in Java, hexadecimal literals are preceded by 0x—but they also could have been specified as decimal values in each Color() constructor.

Figure 22.3 shows this application running.

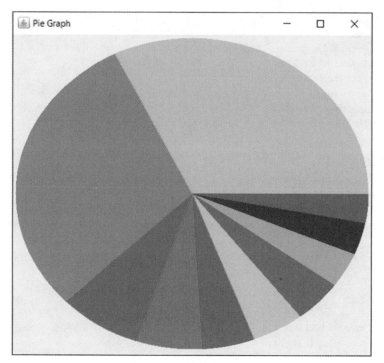

FIGURE 22.3
Displaying population figures in a pie graph.

NOTE

You can find the current U.S. Census world population figures by visiting www.cadenhead.org/ census, which redirects to a page on www.census.gov where you can request population reports for countries.

Summary

By using fonts, colors, and graphics, you can draw more attention to elements of your programs and make them more compelling for users.

Drawing something using the shapes available with Java might seem like more trouble than it's worth. However, graphics depicted with polygons have two advantages over graphics that are loaded from image files:

▶ Speed—Even a small graphic, such as an icon, would take longer to load and display than a series of polygons.

▶ Scaling—You can change the size of an entire image that uses polygons simply by changing the values to create it. For example, you could add a function to the `Sign` class that multiplies all (x, y) points in each shape by two before they are created, and it would result in an image twice as large. Polygon images scale much more quickly than image files and produce better results.

Workshop

Q&A

Q. How can I draw arcs that go clockwise rather than counterclockwise?

A. You can accomplish this by specifying the size of the arc as a negative number. The arc begins at the same point but goes in the opposite direction in an elliptical path. For example, the following statement draws an open arc at (35, 20) that is 90 degrees long, begins at the 0 degree mark, goes clockwise, and has a height of 20 and a width of 15:

```
Arc2D.Float smile = new Arc2D.Float(35F, 20F, 15F, 20F,
    0F, -90F, Arc2D.Float.OPEN);
```

Q. Ellipses and circles don't have corners. What are the (x, y) coordinates specified with the `Ellipses.Float` constructor?

A. The (x, y) coordinates represent the smallest x value and smallest y value of the oval or circle. If you drew an invisible rectangle around it, the upper-left corner of the rectangle would be the x and y coordinates used as arguments to the method.

Q. Why do photographers ask you to say "cheese"?

A. The word "cheese" forces your mouth into a smile, as do the words whiskey, breeze, and money. Words that end with a long "e" generally cause the sides of your lips to curl upwards and your teeth to show.

Another word that photographers sometimes use is "grin." Though it doesn't end in an "e", it contorts the mouth and the meaning makes people smile.

Spanish photographers tell people to say "patata" (potato), French "ouistiti" (marmoset) and Germans "Käsekuchen" (cheesecake).

Quiz

Test whether your font and color skills are MAH-ve-lous by answering the following questions.

1. Which one of the following is *not* a constant used to select a color?

    A. `Color.cyan`

    B. `Color.purple`

    C. `Color.magenta`

2. When you change the color of something and redraw it on a container, what must you do to make it visible?

    A. Use the `drawColor()` method.

    B. Use the `repaint()` statement.

    C. Do nothing.

3. What do the initials RGB stand for?

    A. Roy G. Biv

    B. Red Green Blue

    C. Lucy in the Sky with Diamonds

Answers

1. B. The primary color of Orlando City SC, prideful purple, has gone unrepresented in `Color`.

2. B. The call to `repaint()` causes the `paintComponent()` method to be called manually.

3. B. If **C.** were the right answer, you could use colors that would only be visible years later during flashbacks.

Activities

To further explore the spectrum of possibilities when using fonts and color in your programs, do the following activities:

▶ Create a version of the `PieFrame` class that takes color values and pie slice values as command-line arguments instead of including them in the source code of the application.

▶ Create an application that draws a stop sign on a panel using colors, shapes, and fonts.

To see Java programs that implement these activities, visit the book's website at www.java24hours.com.

HOUR 23
Creating Minecraft Mods with Java

This Hour's To-Do List:

- ▶ Install a Minecraft server on your computer.
- ▶ Write a script to start the server.
- ▶ Set up NetBeans for Minecraft mod programming.
- ▶ Create a framework for mods.
- ▶ Design a mod that spawns a mob.
- ▶ Make one mob the rider of another.
- ▶ Find every mob in the game and attack it.
- ▶ Write a mod that digs enormous scoops out of the world.

This hour of the book covers something that has become a phenomenon in recent years.

I have teenaged sons who are avid gamers, and they all play the multiplayer building game Minecraft. Most of the cousins around their age play the game, too. When I tell any young person that I write books on Java programming, they all ask me the same question: Will it teach me how to create Minecraft mods?

Mods are extensions to the game that are designed and shared by players. The game Minecraft is written in Java, and mods must be programmed in the same language.

Learning Java is the first step in creating Minecraft mods.

This hour is the second.

By the end of this hour, you will have your own Minecraft server downloaded, installed, and running on your computer. You will also be able to create mods in the Java language, deploy them on the server, and use them as you play the game.

But be careful. There are creepers about.

Setting Up a Minecraft Server

Developing mods requires access to a Minecraft server. The best way to do this when you're starting out as a mod developer is to install and run a server on your own computer. Because there's not yet a standard way to add mods to the game, different servers have different ways to make this possible.

The easiest to use when creating mods comes from the Spigot Project, a Minecraft server and Java class library designed specifically for this purpose. Spigot is free and can be downloaded from the website www.javaminecraft.com/spigot. Look for—the file `spigotserver.jar`.

This file contains the Minecraft server and class library packaged as a JAR file.

The Spigot API is a set of Java packages that will be used when creating mods.

When the download is complete, create a new folder on your computer and store the files in it. On my Windows PC I created `c:\minecraft\server` and copied the JAR file into it.

Next, copy `spigotserver.jar` to the same folder. This is the file you run to start the Minecraft server.

The following command starts the server:

```
java -Xms1024M -Xmx1024M -jar spigotserver.jar
```

This command tells the Java Virtual Machine to run the application packaged as the JAR file `spigotserver.jar`, allocating 1,024MB of memory to the program.

To avoid typing this command every time you run the server, you can create a batch or shell file that contains it and then run that file instead.

On Windows, open a text editor such as Notepad and enter the text of Listing 23.1 into the file, saving it as `start-server.bat` in the same folder where you put `spigotserver.jar`.

LISTING 23.1   The Full Text of `start-server.bat`

```
1: java -Xms1024M -Xmx1024M -jar spigotserver.jar
2: pause
```

Double-click this file to run the server. If it runs successfully, a window opens that displays what the server is doing as it starts.

You will see an error message, "Failed to load eula.txt," as shown in Figure 23.1. This is supposed to happen.

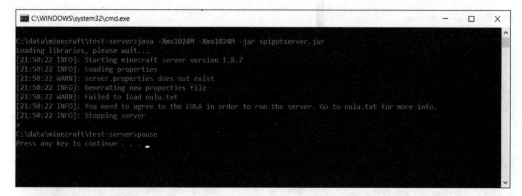

FIGURE 23.1
The server fails a EULA check.

Minecraft has an end-user license agreement (EULA) that is required to accept before you can run the server. Visit this web page to review this agreement: https://account.mojang.com/documents/minecraft_eula.

There's now a file called eula.txt in the same folder as the server. This file has a line that contains the following text:

`eula=false`

If you agree to the EULA, open the file in an editor, change this line to `eula=true`, save the file, and run the server again.

The first time the server runs, it creates more than a dozen files and subfolders and builds the world map. If it is successful, you see the final message "[Info] Done" and a blinking cursor next to a > prompt.

The `help` command lists commands you can use that control the server and the game world. The `stop` command shuts down the server (don't do this yet!).

Figure 23.2 shows a running Spigot server.

This window must be kept open while the server is running. If your server window looks like this, you can skip the next section and proceed to "Connecting to the Server."

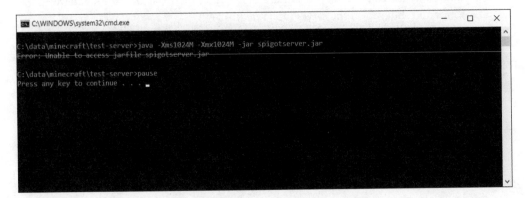

```
C:\WINDOWS\system32\cmd.exe                                              —  □  ×
[22:15:21 INFO]: Custom Map Seeds:  Village: 10387312 Feature: 14357617
[22:15:21 INFO]: Tile Max Tick Time: 50ms Entity max Tick Time: 50ms
[22:15:21 INFO]: Max TNT Explosions: 100
[22:15:21 INFO]: Entity Tracking Range: Pl 48 / An 48 / Mo 48 / Mi 32 / Other 64
[22:15:21 INFO]: Random Lighting Updates: false
[22:15:21 INFO]: Structure Info Saving: true
[22:15:21 INFO]: Hopper Transfer: 8 Hopper Check: 8 Hopper Amount: 1
[22:15:21 INFO]: Sending up to 10 chunks per packet
[22:15:21 INFO]: Max Entity Collisions: 8
[22:15:21 INFO]: Preparing start region for level 0 (Seed: -2171463313270444984)
[22:15:22 INFO]: Preparing spawn area: 7%
[22:15:23 INFO]: Preparing spawn area: 12%
[22:15:24 INFO]: Preparing spawn area: 20%
[22:15:25 INFO]: Preparing spawn area: 26%
[22:15:26 INFO]: Preparing spawn area: 34%
[22:15:27 INFO]: Preparing spawn area: 43%
[22:15:28 INFO]: Preparing spawn area: 53%
[22:15:29 INFO]: Preparing spawn area: 65%
[22:15:30 INFO]: Preparing spawn area: 77%
[22:15:31 INFO]: Preparing spawn area: 90%
[22:15:32 INFO]: Preparing start region for level 1 (Seed: -2171463313270444984)
[22:15:33 INFO]: Preparing spawn area: 14%
[22:15:34 INFO]: Preparing spawn area: 38%
[22:15:35 INFO]: Preparing spawn area: 59%
[22:15:37 INFO]: Preparing spawn area: 80%
[22:15:37 INFO]: Preparing start region for level 2 (Seed: -2171463313270444984)
[22:15:38 INFO]: Preparing spawn area: 48%
[22:15:39 INFO]: Preparing spawn area: 98%
[22:15:39 INFO]: Done (18.775s)! For help, type "help" or "?"
```

FIGURE 23.2
Running a Minecraft server for the first time.

Fixing Problems Running the Server

There are two common errors that prevent a server from running successfully after you download and install it.

The first error displays the message "Unable to access jar file spigotserver.jar," as shown in Figure 23.3.

```
C:\WINDOWS\system32\cmd.exe                                              —  □  ×
C:\data\minecraft\test-server>java -Xms1024M -Xmx1024M -jar spigotserver.jar
Error: Unable to access jarfile spigotserver.jar

C:\data\minecraft\test-server>pause
Press any key to continue . . .
```

FIGURE 23.3
The Spigot JAR file can't be found.

To fix this problem, make sure the file `spigotserver.jar` is in the same folder as the file you ran to start the server (`start-server.bat`). Then try to start the server again.

The second error displays the message "'java' is not recognized as an internal or external command" as in Figure 23.4.

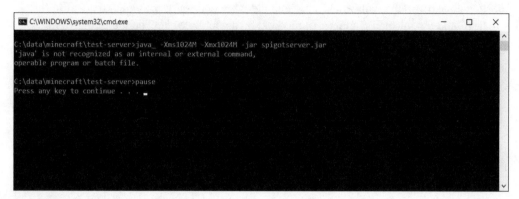

FIGURE 23.4
The Java Virtual Machine (JVM) can't be found.

The JVM is in a file called `java.exe`, which is in the `bin` subfolder of the folder where Java is installed on your computer. When the `java` command is not recognized, this means the computer doesn't know where to find `java.exe`.

On a Windows system, this problem can be fixed by adding the name of the folder that contains `java.exe` to a Control Panel setting called the Path environmental variable.

First, find your Java folder. Go to the top-level folder of your main hard drive, then open the `Program Files` or `Program Files (x86)` folder to see if either one contains a `Java` subfolder. If you find it, open that folder.

The `Java` folder may contain several versions of the Java Development Kit (JDK), each with a version number. On my computer, there are `jdk1.8.0` and `jdk-9` folders. The higher number contains the most current JDK.

Open that folder, and then open its `bin` subfolder. There should be a couple dozen applications, including one called `java`.

Your computer's Path variable needs to be updated to include the full name of this folder, which is something like `C:\Program Files\jdk-9\bin` (with your own JDK version number).

To add the JVM to the Path, perform these steps:

1. Open the Control Panel on the Start Menu or by typing it in the search box.

2. Choose System, and then choose Advanced System Settings. The Advanced dialog opens.

3. Click Environment Variables. A dialog opens that lists a group of user variables and a group of system variables.

4. In the System Variables panel, scroll down until you find Path, click it, and then click the Edit button below the panel. The Edit System Variable dialog opens.

5. If you see a Variable Value field, carefully place your cursor at the end of the text in this field. Add a semicolon character (;) followed by the folder where you found the `java` program. (Don't forget that semicolon!)

6. If you don't see a Variable Value field, click New. The cursor moves to a field below a list of folders. Enter the folder where you found the `java` program.

7. Click OK to close each of the three dialogs, then close the Control Panel.

Try running the server again. If it still isn't working, you might be able to fix the problem by reinstalling the JDK. Visit Oracle's website at http://jdk9.java.net and look for the Downloads section, which contains links to get the JDK for several operating systems.

After reinstalling the JDK, reboot your computer and try to run the Minecraft server again.

Connecting to the Server

Because you want to make Minecraft mods, you presumably already have a Minecraft client on your computer that you use to play the game. If not, you can buy and download the game from the website www.minecraft.net. The current price is $26.95. There are versions of the game for Windows, Mac OS, videogame consoles, and mobile devices, but mod programming requires the version for Windows or Mac.

Start Minecraft and choose Multiplayer. You should see your new server as one of the options (Figure 23.5).

The server is called "Minecraft Server" (you can change this to something cooler later). The client will send a ping message to the server and report back the speed, which is displayed as a set of green connection bars (as shown in Figure 23.5).

These green bars mean you are ready to connect. If you see them, choose the server (by clicking it) and click the Join Server button. You now have a new Minecraft world running on your own server. Proceed to the section "Creating Your First Mod."

When the client can't connect to the server, a red X is displayed instead of green connection bars. The next section describes how to troubleshoot this issue.

FIGURE 23.5
Your new Minecraft server is ready for connections.

Fixing a Server Connection Problem

Sometimes a Minecraft client has a problem sending a ping to the server and getting a response back. This is indicated by the red X shown in Figure 23.6.

FIGURE 23.6
Your new Minecraft server has a connection problem.

The most common cause of this problem is that the server is running a different version of Minecraft than the client. In the server window, the first message indicates the version the server is running. It says "Starting Minecraft version 1.8.7."

The Minecraft client normally runs the most up-to-date version. You can edit your profile to use an older version instead. Exit the Minecraft client completely. You need to reload it to change this.

Run the client again and follow these steps to choose a different version in your profile:

1. In the Minecraft Launcher dialog, click the Launch Options button, then click Add New.

2. In the Version drop-down, choose Release 1.8.7.

3. Click Save.

4. Click Settings.

5. Click the arrow on the green Play button, then choose Unnamed Configuration 1.8.7.

Click Play, and then choose Multiplayer. You should see your server with green connection bars.

CAUTION
_____

Changing your player profile affects all Minecraft servers you use, including the ones you play when you're not creating and testing mods. Make sure to change the configuration on the Play button back to the current version when you aren't connecting to your own Spigot server (or create a second player profile so one is for mod work and one is for playing).
_____

Creating Your First Mod

Now that you've got a Spigot server for Minecraft set up and running, you're ready to begin developing mods for that server.

Mods have to be packaged as Java archive files, also called JAR files. NetBeans, the free integrated development environment from Oracle used throughout this book, automatically creates JAR files every time you build a project.

When you have finished writing a mod, you will be adding to the server's folder in a subfolder named `plugins`.

This hour's first mod is a simple one that demonstrates the framework you'll use in every mod you create for Spigot. The mod adds a "/siamesecat" command to the game that creates a Siamese cat mob, adds it to the world, and makes you (the player) its owner.

Each mod will be its own project in NetBeans. To begin this project, follow these steps:

1. In NetBeans, choose the menu command File, New Project. The New Project wizard opens.

2. In the Categories pane, choose Java, and in the Projects pane, choose Java Application. Then click Next.

3. In the Project Name field, enter SiameseCat (with no spaces and capitalized as shown).

4. Click the Browse button next to the Project Folder field. The Select Project Location dialog appears.

5. Find the folder where you installed the Minecraft server. Select it and click Open. The folder appears in the Project Location field.

6. Deselect the Create Main Class check box.

7. Click Finish.

The SiameseCat project is created and two folders appear in the Projects pane, Source Packages and Libraries, as shown in Figure 23.7.

FIGURE 23.7
Adding libraries to a Java project.

1. On each mod project, you must add a Java class library before you begin writing Java code: the Spigot JAR file you downloaded when you installed the In the Projects pane, right-click the Libraries folder and choose the menu command Add Library. The Add Library dialog opens.

2. Click the Create button. The Create New Library dialog appears.

3. In the Library Name field, enter Spigot and click OK. The Customize Library dialog opens.

4. Click the Add JAR/Folder button. The Browse JAR/Folder dialog opens.

5. Use the dialog to find and open the folder where you installed the server.

6. Click spigotserver.jar to select that file.

   7. Click Add JAR/Folder.

   8. Click OK.

   9. The Available Libraries pane now has a Spigot item. Select it and click Add Library.

The Projects pane now contains the JAR file for Spigot in the Libraries folder (click the + next to Libraries to see it). You're ready to begin writing the mod program.

Follow these steps to create the program:

   1. Click File, New File. The New File dialog appears.

   2. In the Categories pane, choose Java.

   3. In the File Types pane, choose Empty Java File; then click Next.

   4. In the Class Name field, enter SiameseCat.

   5. In the Package field, enter org.cadenhead.minecraft.

   6. Click Finish.

The file SiameseCat.java opens in the NetBeans source code editor.

Every mod you create for Spigot begins with a simple framework of standard code. After the package statement and several import statements, you will start every mod with these statements:

```java
public class SiameseCat extends JavaPlugin {
    public static final Logger log = Logger.getLogger("Minecraft");

    public boolean onCommand(CommandSender sender, Command command,
        String label, String[] arguments) {

        if (label.equalsIgnoreCase("siamesecat")) {
            if (sender instanceof Player) {
                // do something cool here
                log.info("[SiameseCat] Meow!");
                return true;
            }
        }
        return false;
    }
}
```

Mod programs all are subclasses of JavaPlugin from the org.bukkit.plugin.java package. Looking at this framework, the only things that will change when you use it for a different mod are the three things that refer to a Siamese cat, because those are specific to this project.

The name of the program is `SiameseCat`.

The argument inside the method call, `label.equalsIgnoreCase("siamesecat")`, is the command the user will type in the game to run the mod. So this program implements the command `/siamesecat` (commands are preceded by a slash `/` character). The `label` object, which is sent as an argument to `onCommand()`, is a string that holds the text of a command entered by the user.

The statement that calls `log.info()` with the message "[SiameseCat] Meow!" sends a log message that is displayed in the Minecraft server window.

The `Logger` object created as an instance variable sends messages to the server.

The `sender` object is another argument sent to the `onCommand()` method. It represents the entity in Minecraft that entered the command. Checking to make sure that `sender` is an instance of the `Player` class verifies that the player issued that command.

Everything a mod does when its command is entered goes at the spot marked by the comment `// do something cool here`.

The first thing the SiameseCat mod needs to do is learn more about the game world, using these three statements:

```
Player me = (Player) sender;
Location spot = me.getLocation();
World world = me.getWorld();
```

An object called `me` is created by casting the `sender` object to the `Player` class. This object is the character controlled by the person playing the game.

With this `Player` object, you can call its `getLocation()` method with no objects to learn the exact spot where the player is standing. This spot is represented by the `Location` class. Three things you can learn about a location are its (x,y,z) coordinates on the three-dimensional game map.

The `Player` object also has a `getWorld()` object that returns a `World` object representing the entire game world.

Most of the mods you create will need these `Player`, `Location`, and `World` objects.

This mod creates a new mob that's a Siamese cat, using the `spawn()` method of the `World` class:

```
Ocelot cat = world.spawn(spot, Ocelot.class);
```

There's a class for every type of mob in the game. The two arguments to `spawn()` are the location where the cat should be placed and the class of the mob to create.

This statement creates an `Ocelot` object named `cat` at the same spot as the player.

At this point, the cat is an ocelot, but it can be changed to a Siamese cat with this statement:

```
cat.setCatType(Ocelot.Type.SIAMESE_CAT);
```

The cat's setCatType() method determines whether the cat is a wild ocelot or a Siamese, black, or red cat.

Cats in Minecraft are one of the mobs that can be tamed by an owner. This relationship is established by calling the cat's setOwner() method with the player as the argument:

```
cat.setOwner(me);
```

Put all this together by entering Listing 23.2 into the source code editor and clicking the Save All button in the NetBeans toolbar (or choosing File, Save).

LISTING 23.2   The Full Text of SiameseCat.java

```
 1: package org.cadenhead.minecraft;
 2:
 3: import java.util.logging.*;
 4: import org.bukkit.*;
 5: import org.bukkit.command.*;
 6: import org.bukkit.entity.*;
 7: import org.bukkit.plugin.java.*;
 8:
 9: public class SiameseCat extends JavaPlugin {
10:     public static final Logger log = Logger.getLogger("Minecraft");
11:
12:     public boolean onCommand(CommandSender sender, Command command,
13:         String label, String[] arguments) {
14:
15:         if (label.equalsIgnoreCase("siamesecat")) {
16:             if (sender instanceof Player) {
17:                 // get the player
18:                 Player me = (Player) sender;
19:                 // get the player's current location
20:                 Location spot = me.getLocation();
21:                 // get the game world
22:                 World world = me.getWorld();
23:
24:                 // spawn one ocelot
25:                 Ocelot cat = world.spawn(spot, Ocelot.class);
26:                 // make it a Siamese cat
27:                 cat.setCatType(Ocelot.Type.SIAMESE_CAT);
28:                 // make the player its owner
29:                 cat.setOwner(me);
30:                 log.info("[SiameseCat] Meow!");
31:                 return true;
```

```
32:                    }
33:             }
34:             return false;
35:       }
36: }
```

The `import` statements in Lines 3–7 of Listing 23.2 make five packages available in the program: one from the Java Class Library and four from Spigot.

The `return` statements in Lines 31 and 34 are part of the standard mod framework. Your mods should return the value `true` inside the `onCommand()` method when the mod handles a user command and `false` when it doesn't.

You have created your first mod, but it can't be run yet by Spigot. It needs a file called `plugin.yml` that tells the Minecraft server about the mod.

This file is a text file, which you also can create with NetBeans using these steps:

1. Choose File, New File. The New File dialog opens.

2. In the Categories pane, choose Other.

3. In the File Types pane, choose Empty File and click Next.

4. In the File Name field, enter `plugin.yml`.

5. In the Folder field, enter `src`.

6. Click Finish.

A blank file named `plugin.yml` opens in the source code editor. Enter the text of Listing 23.3 into the file, and make sure to use the same number of spaces in each line. Don't use Tab characters instead of spaces.

LISTING 23.3   **The Full Text of this Project's** `plugin.yml`

```
1: name: SiameseCat
2:
3: author: Your Name Here
```

```
 4:
 5: main: org.cadenhead.minecraft.SiameseCat
 6:
 7: commands:
 8:     siamesecat:
 9:         description: Spawn a Siamese cat.
10:
11: version: 1.0
```

Replace "Your Name Here" with your own name (unless your name is Your Name Here already).

To double-check that you have entered the spaces correctly, there are four spaces in Line 8 before the text `siamesecat` and eight spaces in Line 9 before `description`.

The `plugin.yml` file describes the mod's name, author, Java class file, version, command, and a short description of what the command does.

This file must be in the right place in the project. Look in the Projects pane, where it should be inside the `Source Libraries` folder under a subheading called `<default package>`. This is shown in Figure 23.8.

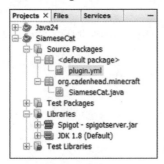

FIGURE 23.8
Checking the location of plugin.yml.

If the file is in the wrong place, such as under the `org.cadenhead.minecraft` heading, you can use drag and drop to move it. Click and hold the file, drag it to the Source Libraries folder icon, and drop it there.

You're now ready to build your mod. Choose the menu command Run, Clean, and Build Project. If this is successful, the message "Finished Building SiameseCat (clean jar)" will appear in the lower-left corner of the NetBeans user interface.

The mod is packaged as a file called `SiameseCat.jar` in a subfolder of the project. To find it, click the Files tab in the Projects pane, and then expand the `dist` subfolder. The Files tab lists all the files that make up the project, as shown in Figure 23.9.

FIGURE 23.9
Finding the SiameseCat mod's JAR file.

This `SiameseCat.jar` file needs to be copied from the project folder to the Minecraft server. Follow these steps:

1. If the Minecraft server is running, stop it by going to the server window Outside of NetBeans, open the folder where you installed the Minecraft server.

2. Open the `SiameseCat` subfolder.

3. Go back to the Minecraft server folder.

4. Open the `plugins` subfolder.

5. Press Ctrl+v to copy `SiameseCat` into it.

You have deployed your new mod on the Minecraft server. Start the server the same way you did before—by clicking the `start-server` file you created—and you will see two new messages in the log file that displays as it runs:

```
[SiameseCat] Loading SiameseCat v1.0
[SiameseCat] Enabling SiameseCat v1.0
```

If you don't see these messages, but instead see some long, really complicated error messages, double-check everything from `SiameseCat.java` and `plugin.yml` to make sure they were entered correctly; then redeploy the mod.

When you run the Minecraft client and connect to your server, enter the command `/siamesecat`. You now have a new pet cat who will follow you around. Enter the command as many times as you like to keep adding cats.

Figure 23.10 shows me and 23 cats. Creepers want nothing to do with us.

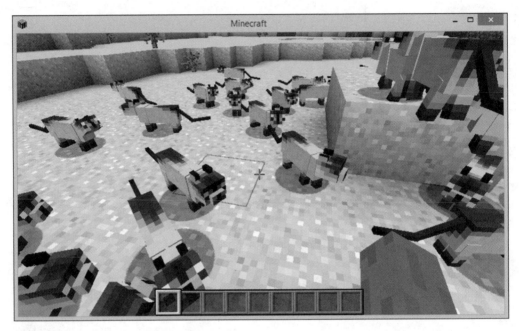

FIGURE 23.10
Come to me, Siamese cat friends!

Teaching Zombies to Ride Horses

The first mod you created required a lot of work because you were going through the process for the first time. The rest should be easier because you will repeat a lot of the same steps.

Each mod you develop during the hour will be more complex than the preceding one. For this project, you'll create a cavalry of horses ridden by zombies.

Get things rolling with these tasks:

1. Choose File, New Project to create a new Java Application project called CrazyHorse in the same folder as the Minecraft server, just like the last project. Make sure that Create Main Class is deselected.

2. Right-click Libraries in the Projects pane, click Add Library, and add the Spigot library to the project.

3. Choose File, New File, and create an empty Java file with the class name CrazyHorse and the package name org.cadenhead.minecraft.

Enter the text of Listing 23.4 into the source code editor for the file CrazyHorse.java. The new concepts used in the program will be explained after it has been entered.

LISTING 23.4 The Full Text of CrazyHorse.java

```
 1: package org.cadenhead.minecraft;
 2:
 3: import java.util.logging.*;
 4: import org.bukkit.*;
 5: import org.bukkit.command.*;
 6: import org.bukkit.entity.*;
 7: import org.bukkit.plugin.java.*;
 8: import org.bukkit.potion.*;
 9:
10: public class CrazyHorse extends JavaPlugin {
11:     public static final Logger log = Logger.getLogger("Minecraft");
12:
13:     public boolean onCommand(CommandSender sender, Command command,
14:         String label, String[] arguments) {
15:
16:         if (label.equalsIgnoreCase("crazyhorse")) {
17:             if (sender instanceof Player) {
18:                 Player me = (Player) sender;
19:                 Location spot = me.getLocation();
20:                 World world = me.getWorld();
21:
22:                 // spawn some horse-riding zombies
23:                 int quantity = (int) (Math.random() * 10) + 1;
24:                 log.info("[CrazyHorse] Creating " + quantity
25:                     + " zombies and horses");
26:                 for (int i = 0; i < quantity; i++) {
27:                     // set horse and zombie location
28:                     Location horseSpot = new Location(world,
29:                         spot.getX() + (Math.random() * 15),
30:                         spot.getY() + 20,
31:                         spot.getZ() + (Math.random() * 15));
32:                     Horse horse = world.spawn(horseSpot, Horse.class);
33:                     Zombie zombie = world.spawn(horseSpot, Zombie.class);
34:                     horse.setPassenger(zombie);
35:                     horse.setOwner(me);
36:                     // set the horse's color
37:                     int coat = (int) (Math.random() * 7);
38:                     switch (coat) {
39:                         case 0:
40:                             horse.setColor(Horse.Color.WHITE);
41:                             break;
42:                         case 1:
43:                             horse.setColor(Horse.Color.GRAY);
44:                             break;
```

```
45:                          case 2:
46:                              horse.setColor(Horse.Color.CREAMY);
47:                              break;
48:                          case 3:
49:                              horse.setColor(Horse.Color.CHESTNUT);
50:                              break;
51:                          case 4:
52:                              horse.setColor(Horse.Color.BROWN);
53:                              break;
54:                          case 5:
55:                              horse.setColor(Horse.Color.DARK_BROWN);
56:                              break;
57:                          case 6:
58:                              horse.setColor(Horse.Color.BLACK);
59:                          }
60:                          // increase the horse's speed
61:                          PotionEffect potion = new PotionEffect(
62:                              PotionEffectType.SPEED,
63:                              Integer.MAX_VALUE,
64:                              10 + (coat * 10));
65:                          horse.addPotionEffect(potion);
66:                      }
67:                  return true;
68:              }
69:          }
70:      return false;
71:      }
72: }
```

Save this file after entering the listing by choosing File, Save or clicking Save All.

This mod adds a /crazyhorse command to Minecraft that drops a random number of horse-riding zombies from the sky. Lines 18–65 do something cool when the command is entered. The rest of the program surrounding those lines is the standard mod framework.

After retrieving the player, location, and world, the mod stores a random number from 1 to 11 in a variable:

```
int quantity = (int) (Math.random() * 10) + 1;
```

The random() method in Java's Math class generates a random floating-point number between 0.0 and 1.0. It can be multiplied by an integer to produce a random integer ranging from 0 to that integer.

This number is the number of zombies and horses that are created.

A `for` loop that begins in Line 26 loops once for each zombie-horse pair.

Their location is set by calling the `Location()` constructor with four arguments: the game world, x coordinate, y coordinate, and z coordinate.

```
Location horseSpot = new Location(world,
    spot.getX() + (Math.random() * 15),
    spot.getY() + 20,
    spot.getZ() + (Math.random() * 15));
```

The player's location in the `spot` variable is used to help pick a location for each zombie and horse. For the x coordinate, the player's `getX()` coordinate is retrieved and a random number from 0 to 14 is added. For the z coordinate, `getY()` and a number from 0 to 14 are added. For the y coordinate, 20 is added.

This means that the mobs will appear 20 blocks above the player in the sky and within 14 blocks in the other two directions.

Horses and zombies are created the same way as ocelots. Call the world's `spawn()` method with the mob's location and its class, which is `Horse` for horses and `Zombie` for zombies.

Every mob that can be ridden in Minecraft has a `setPassenger()` method, which takes the rider as the only argument:

```
horse.setPassenger(zombie);
```

If you stopped here, the zombie would appear on the horse, but the horse would quickly buck it off. This can be prevented by making the player that horse's owner:

```
horse.setOwner(me);
```

A tamed horse does not buck its rider, even if the rider is a zombie that hungers for human brains. When you create a mob, it inherits the default behavior of that mob from the game.

Like ocelots, horses can be customized in several ways. One is to give the horse a different color coat by calling its `setColor()` method. There are seven possibilities.

After a random number from 0 to 6 is generated, that number is used in a `switch-case` statement in Lines 38–59 to set that horse's color.

To make the horses a little crazier, you can customize their speed as well. The effects of a game potion can be applied to a mob. There are 23 different effects, which are indicated by the `PotionEffectType` class.

A potion effect is created by calling the `PotionEffect` constructor with three arguments: the effect type, the duration the potion should be in effect, and the value of that effect.

This statement creates a speed potion of the maximum possible duration—the highest value an integer can hold in Java:

```
PotionEffect potion = new PotionEffect(
    PotionEffectType.SPEED,
    Integer.MAX_VALUE,
    10 + (coat * 10));
```

The third argument to `PotionEffect()` sets the speed of the horse. It has a base value of 10 plus 10 times the random number used to determine the horse's color. Because the colors in the `switch`-`case` statement are ordered from lightest to darkest, the formula `10 + (coat * 10)` causes horses to run faster the darker their coloration.

Now that the mod's Java class is done, it needs a plug-in description file. Choose New File, select Other in the Categories pane, and create an empty file called `plugin.yml` in the `src` folder.

Enter Listing 23.5 into this file, being careful to format it exactly as shown with spaces instead of tabs.

LISTING 23.5   The Full Text of this Project's `plugin.yml`

```
 1: name: CrazyHorse
 2:
 3: author: Your Name Here
 4:
 5: main: org.cadenhead.minecraft.CrazyHorse
 6:
 7: commands:
 8:     crazyhorse:
 9:         description: Spawn 1-11 horse-riding zombies.
10:
11: version: 1.0
```

When you're done, choose Run, Clean and Build Project to create the mod's JAR file.

In the Projects pane there should be two files under the `Source Packages` heading: `CrazyHorse.java` under `org.cadenhead.minecraft` and `plugin.yml` under `<default package>`.

Outside of NetBeans, go to your file folders and copy the `CrazyHorse.jar` file from this project's `dist` folder to the server's `plugins` folder. Restart your server (by stopping it and running it again), and you should be able to enter a `/crazyhorse` command.

From 1–11 zombies on horseback will drop around you, landing with a thud. If you issue the command during the game's daytime, the living dead are in for an unpleasant surprise. A screen capture is shown in Figure 23.11.

FIGURE 23.11
Two zombies riding horseback.

The designers of Spigot did a good job of making Java classes match the things in the game. As you developed these first two mods, you probably started thinking of things that could be changed with a little tinkering.

Here's a one-line change to Line 33 of Listing 23.4 of the CrazyHorse mod that puts an entirely different mob on horseback:

```
Creeper creeper = world.spawn(horseSpot, Creeper.class);
```

This change creates a cavalry of creepers instead of zombies.

Although you can guess at class names and see what happens, Spigot has extensive online documentation for all its Java classes. You can view the documentation for Spigot 1.8.7 at www.javaminecraft.com/bukkitapi.

Use this guide to learn about every class and interface in Spigot, their instance variables, and their instance and class methods.

By poking around the documentation and tinkering with the CrazyHorse mod, you can try different mobs and potion effects.

Here's a mod-ification that makes the horse invisible, causing zombies to appear as if they're floating in air:

```
PotionEffect potion2 = new PotionEffect(
    PotionEffectType.INVISIBILITY,
    Integer.MAX_VALUE,
    1);
horse.addPotionEffect(potion2);
```

Finding All Mobs (and Killing Them)

The first two mods added mobs to the game world. The next project examines the mobs that already exist, finds each of their locations, and hits that spot with a lightning bolt.

To get started:

1. Choose File, New Project to create the new project LightningStorm in the Minecraft server folder. Make sure that Create Main Class is deselected.

2. In the Projects pane, right-click Libraries, click Add Library, and add the Spigot library.

3. Choose File, New File and create an Empty Java File with the class name LightningStorm and the package name org.cadenhead.minecraft.

Enter the text of Listing 23.6 into NetBeans' source code editor, remembering to save the file when you're done.

LISTING 23.6   The Full Text of LightningStorm.java

```
 1: package org.cadenhead.minecraft;
 2:
 3: import java.util.*;
 4: import java.util.logging.*;
 5: import org.bukkit.*;
 6: import org.bukkit.command.*;
 7: import org.bukkit.entity.*;
 8: import org.bukkit.plugin.java.*;
 9:
10: public class LightningStorm extends JavaPlugin {
11:     public static final Logger log = Logger.getLogger("Minecraft");
12:
13:     public boolean onCommand(CommandSender sender, Command command,
14:         String label, String[] arguments) {
15:
16:         Player me = (Player) sender;
17:         World world = me.getWorld();
```

```
18:         // get every living mob in the game
19:         List<LivingEntity> mobs = world.getLivingEntities();
20:
21:         // process lightningstorm command
22:         if (label.equalsIgnoreCase("lightningstorm")) {
23:             if (sender instanceof Player) {
24:                 int myId = me.getEntityId();
25:                 // loop through each mob one at a time
26:                 for (LivingEntity mob : mobs) {
27:                     log.info("[LightningStorm]" + mob.getType());
28:                     // is this mob the player?
29:                     if (mob.getEntityId() == myId) {
30:                         // yes, so don't strike him
31:                         continue;
32:                     }
33:                     // get the mob's location
34:                     Location spot = mob.getLocation();
35:                     // lightning strike!
36:                     world.strikeLightning(spot);
37:                     // set the mob's health to 0 (dead)
38:                     mob.setHealth(0);
39:                 }
40:             }
41:             return true;
42:         }
43:
44:         // process mobcount command
45:         if (label.equalsIgnoreCase("mobcount")) {
46:             if (sender instanceof Player) {
47:                 me.sendMessage("There are " + mobs.size() + " living mobs.");
48:                 return true;
49:             }
50:         }
51:         return false;
52:     }
53: }
```

The LightningStorm mod does something new with the mod framework: It monitors two commands instead of one. The /lightningstorm command rains down a massive number of lightning bolts on mobs. The /mobcount command counts how many living mobs are in the game world.

A Minecraft mod for Spigot can implement as many commands as desired. The /lightningstorm command is implemented in Lines 22–42 of Listing 23.6. The /mobcount command is implemented in Lines 45–50.

These commands need both a player object and world object. They also need a list of every living mob, which is accomplished in Line 19:

```
List<LivingEntity> mobs = world.getLivingEntities();
```

This statement calls the world's `getLivingEntitities()` method, which returns a `List` object containing each mob. The mobs are represented as objects that implement the `LivingEntity` interface.

`List` also is an interface. It is implemented by array lists, stacks, and other data structures. The methods and techniques used on array lists can be used with this list as well.

After you have this list, you can implement the `/mobcount` command with a single statement (Line 47):

```
me.sendMessage("There are " + mobs.size() + " living mobs.");
```

A list's `size()` command returns the number of elements in that list.

This information is sent to the player as a message that appears in the game. This is accomplished by calling the player's `sendMessage()` method with the information to display as the only argument.

The `/lightningstorm` command is more complicated.

Data structures in Java have special `for` loops that make it easy to loop through every item in the structure. Line 26 starts such a loop for each mob in the `mobs` list:

```
for (LivingEntity mob : mobs) {
```

This stores the current mob in a `LivingEntity` object named `mob`.

When sending lightning bolts at every mob on the map, it's important to recall that the player is a mob. Raining lightning down on yourself is never a good idea.

Every mob in the game has a unique ID. Before the `for` loop began, Line 24 stored the player's ID:

```
int myId = me.getEntityId();
```

This integer is compared inside the loop to the current mob's ID, by calling its `getEntityID()` method in Lines 29–32:

```
if (mob.getEntityId() == myId) {
    continue;
}
```

The `continue` statement causes the loop to go back to Line 26 and continue with the next mob.

Now that the player is safe, you find out where a mob is by calling its `getLocation()` method:

```
Location spot = mob.getLocation();
```

Then call the world's `strikeLightning()` method with that location:

```
world.strikeLightning(spot);
```

Hitting a mob with lightning isn't always fatal—some mobs are tough little critters—but that makes this effect less impressive. Calling a mob's `setHealth()` method with an argument of 0 sets its health to that amount, killing it:

```
mob.setHealth(0);
```

The `plugin.yml` file that should be entered for this mod can be found in Listing 23.7. Create an empty file called `plugin.yml` in the project's `src` folder, and then fill it with this listing.

LISTING 23.7 **The Full Text of This Project's** `plugin.yml`

```
 1: name: LightningStorm
 2:
 3: author: Your Name Here
 4:
 5: main: org.cadenhead.minecraft.LightningStorm
 6:
 7: commands:
 8:     lightningstorm:
 9:         description: Hit every living mob with lightning.
10:     mobcount:
11:         description: Count of living mobs.
12:
13: version: 1.0
```

Build the project (choose Run, Build, and Clean Project), then deploy the mod on your Minecraft server by copying the `LightningStorm.jar` file from the project's `dist` folder to the server's `plugins` folder. The next time you start the server and play the game, you'll see a lightning storm like the one in Figure 23.12.

Actually, it would spoil the surprise to show it in this book. Figure 23.12 is a cow that is about to become flame-broiled.

FIGURE 23.12
This is not a lightning storm.

Writing a Mod that Can Build Things

The first three mods you created were about mobs, the mobile entities that roam Minecraft. This hour's final mod explores how to use Java to perform the most fundamental activities of the game: building and destroying blocks.

You will create a new command, /icecreamscoop, that digs a circular hole around the player. The size of the hole will be determined by the player as an argument to the command.

Here's how to start building the mod:

1. Create the new project IceCreamScoop in the Minecraft server folder, keeping Create Main Class deselected.

2. In the Projects pane, right-click Libraries and add the Spigot library.

3. Create an empty Java file for a class named IceCreamScoop in the package org.cadenhead.minecraft.

Enter the text of Listing 23.8 as the IceCreamScoop class. It will be explained after you've typed it in.

LISTING 23.8   **The Full Text of** `IceCreamScoop.java`

```
 1: package org.cadenhead.minecraft;
 2:
 3: import java.util.logging.*;
 4: import org.bukkit.*;
 5: import org.bukkit.block.*;
 6: import org.bukkit.command.*;
 7: import org.bukkit.entity.*;
 8: import org.bukkit.plugin.java.*;
 9:
10: public class IceCreamScoop extends JavaPlugin {
11:     public static final Logger log = Logger.getLogger("Minecraft");
12:
13:     public boolean onCommand(CommandSender sender, Command command,
14:         String label, String[] arguments) {
15:
16:         // set the default scoop radius
17:         double radius = 15;
18:         if (arguments.length > 0) {
19:             try {
20:                 // read the user-provided radius (if any)
21:                 radius = Double.parseDouble(arguments[0]);
22:                 // make sure it's an acceptable size (5-25)
23:                 if ((radius < 5) | (radius > 25)) {
24:                     radius = 15;
25:                 }
26:             } catch (NumberFormatException exception) {
27:                 // do nothing (use the default);
28:             }
29:         }
30:
31:         if (label.equalsIgnoreCase("icecreamscoop")) {
32:             if (sender instanceof Player) {
33:                 scoopTerrain(sender, radius);
34:             }
35:             return true;
36:         }
37:         return false;
38:     }
39:
40:     // dig a circular scoop out of the world
41:     private void scoopTerrain(CommandSender sender, double rad) {
42:         Player me = (Player) sender;
43:         Location spot = me.getLocation();
44:         World world = me.getWorld();
45:
46:         // loop through a 3-D square with sides twice the radius width
```

```
47:          for (double x = spot.getX() - rad; x < spot.getX() + rad; x++) {
48:            for (double y = spot.getY() - rad; y < spot.getY() + rad; y++) {
49:              for (double z = spot.getZ() - rad; z < spot.getZ() + rad; z++) {
50:                // get a location in that square
51:                Location loc = new Location(world, x, y, z);
52:                // see how far it is from the player
53:                double xd = x - spot.getX();
54:                double yd = y - spot.getY();
55:                double zd = z - spot.getZ();
56:                double distance = Math.sqrt(xd * xd + yd * yd + zd * zd);
57:                // is it within the radius?
58:                if (distance < rad) {
59:                  // yes, so turn that block into air
60:                  Block current = world.getBlockAt(loc);
61:                  current.setType(Material.AIR);
62:                }
63:              }
64:            }
65:          }
66:
67:          // play a sound after the scoop is scooped
68:          world.playSound(spot, Sound.BURP, 30, 5);
69:          log.info("[IceCreamScoop] Scooped at ("
70:            + spot.getX() + ","
71:            + spot.getY() + ","
72:            + spot.getZ() + ")");
73:        }
74: }
```

This mod digs out a circle with a radius from 5 to 25 blocks in size. The player determines the size by following the /icecreamscoop command with a space and a number, as in this example:

/icecreamscoop 10

Mods can take arguments just like Java applications. The arguments are stored in the fourth argument to the onCommand() method, a String array.

After a double called radius is created in Line 17 and given the value 15, the following statement sets the radius to the value of the first argument:

radius = Double.parseDouble(arguments[0]);

The parseDouble() method of Java's standard Double class converts a string to a double value, if such a conversion is possible.

To guard against bad input from a user, you put `parseDouble()` inside a `try-catch` block. A `NumberFormatException` occurs when the user's value isn't numeric.

If the user's value is a number, that becomes the radius. But there's one more check: an `if` conditional in Lines 23–25 that makes sure the radius falls into the acceptable range of values from 5 to 25.

The `IceCreamScoop` class has a `scoopTerrain()` method that digs out the circle.

Like other mods, this one requires player, player location, and world objects.

There are different techniques that could be used to dig out a circle around a player in a three-dimensional grid like the Minecraft World.

This mod accomplishes it by looking at every block in a square around the player that has sides a little bigger than twice the radius. The center of the square is the spot where the player is standing.

Three nested `for` loops that begin in Lines 47–49 loop through all the squares. There's a loop for the X axis, one for the Y axis, and one for the Z axis.

A `Location` object is created to represent the spot that's being examined in one trip through the loop:

```
loc = new Location(world, x, y, z);
```

The player's location was previously stored in the `spot` object in Line 43:

```
Location spot = me.getLocation();
```

Three statements measure the distance between the current spot and the player, on all three axes:

```
double xd = x - spot.getX();
double yd = y - spot.getY();
double zd = z - spot.getZ();
```

Using the Pythagorean Theorem, you can calculate the distance by squaring xd, yd, and zd, adding them together, and using the `Math` method `sqrt()` to get the square root of that sum:

```
double distance = Math.sqrt(xd * xd + yd * yd + zd * zd);
```

If the distance from the current block to the player is within the player's chosen radius, that block is turned into air with these two statements:

```
Block current = world.getBlockAt(loc);
current.setType(Material.AIR);
```

First, a `Block` object is created that represents the block.

Next, the block's `setType()` method is called with `Material.AIR`, which is one of several dozen values that represent the things a block can be made of in Minecraft.

The same technique that's used to destroy a block by turning it into air can be used to build things. The only thing that changes is the type of material. If you had wanted to dig out a scoop of the game and turn it into diamond instead of air, this statement would be used:

```
current.setType(Material.DIAMOND);
```

When a scoop has been dug from the world, the mod does two things to note the accomplishment: A sound is played and a message is sent to the server log.

Sounds are played by calling a `world` object's `playSound()` method with four arguments—the sound's location, type, volume, and pitch:

```
world.playSound(spot, Sound.BURP, 30, 5);
```

As you might have guessed, the sound is a burp. There are dozens of possible sounds that could be used.

A message is logged on the server by calling the `Logger` object's `info()` command with the text of the message:

```
log.info("[IceCreamScoop] Scooped at " + spot);
```

The project's `plugin.yml` file is shown in Listing 23.9. Create an empty file called `plugin.yml` in the project's `src` folder to match this listing.

LISTING 23.9   The Full Text of This Project's `plugin.yml`

```
 1: name: IceCreamScoop
 2:
 3: author: Your Name Here
 4:
 5: main: org.cadenhead.minecraft.IceCreamScoop
 6:
 7: commands:
 8:     icecreamscoop:
 9:         description: Scoop away land around the player.
10:
11: version: 1.0
```

After you build the mod and deploy its JAR file on the Minecraft server, using the same steps as in the previous projects, you can move through the game world digging huge scoops out of the landscape. Figure 23.13 show what happens when you are standing on a flat stretch of land and type this command:

```
/icecreamscoop 10
```

FIGURE 23.13
Scooping circles out of the Minecraft world.

While testing this mod, I discovered that it doesn't take long to dig yourself down past the bottom of the world. You also can fall far enough to be killed, so it's not the best idea to do any scooping at the spawn point.

By changing the material from AIR to another material, you can make spheres in the world. The full list of substances can be found in Spigot's Java documentation at www.javaminecraft.com/bukkitapi, but here are four to get you started:

▶ Material.DIRT

▶ Material.COBBLESTONE

▶ Material.WOOD

▶ Material.GRAVEL

If you turn blocks into anything other than air, the mod will take away the air in the location where you are standing. That's gotta hurt. You can teleport to a new location with these two statements:

```
Location newSpot = new Location(world,
    spot.getX(),
    spot.getY() + rad + 1,
    spot.getZ());
me.teleport(newSpot);
```

Because the Y axis in Minecraft is the vertical position, this moves the player to a spot right above the sphere.

Summary

In all the years I've been writing Java programs and teaching people how to use this language, I never expected that I would put those skills to work making a zombie ride a horse.

Or that the horse would buck that zombie if not trained.

Or the zombie would immediately catch fire because the sun was out.

Or you could dig a hole so large you fell out of the world.

This is the *funnest* kind of Java programming. I know that isn't a word, but it should be one, and it should be used to describe putting your own Java objects into a three-dimensional world where you fight monsters, dig tunnels, build houses, and dodge the legions of the living dead.

Minecraft also is an excellent way to learn about object-oriented programming, one of the toughest aspects of the language to master. Everything you do in Java is accomplished with objects. You create them with constructors, give them knowledge in instance variables, and tell them to do things by calling methods. Objects indicate the tasks they can perform by implementing interfaces.

All these concepts directly relate to mod programming. Need a zombie? Create a `Zombie` object. Want the player to move to a new spot? Call his `teleport()` method. Did you lose your horse? Call its `getLocation()` method.

So dig as deep into Minecraft mod programming as you like. You're going to be able to use these skills far beyond the realm of creepers and wither skeletons and pig zombies.

Workshop

Q&A

Q. I made an enormous mess of my server's world with the IceCreamScoop mod. How can I start over?

A. The Minecraft server makes it easy to create a new world from scratch or switch from one world to another.

To start over and delete the old world, stop the server, open the Minecraft server's folder, and delete the `world` subfolder. When you start the server, Minecraft figures out the world is gone and creates a new one. This process is a little slower than usual. The server log explains what it is doing.

To switch to a new world while keeping the old one around, stop the server and rename the `world` subfolder to something else. The server will build a new world, and you can switch back to the old one by editing the `server.properties` file in the server's main folder.

If you named the original world `world2`, you can switch back this way: Open the file `server.properties` with any text editor and change the line `level-name=world` to `level-name=world2`. Save the file and restart the server.

Quiz

Test whether you're made of the right material by answering the following questions about Minecraft mod programming.

1. What is the superclass of all mods created for a Minecraft server that uses Spigot?

    A. `Player`

    B. `JavaPlugin`

    C. `Mod`

2. What class is used to create a special effect and apply it to a mob?

    A. `Type`

    B. `Effect`

    C. `Potion`

3. What class represents each square in the game, whether it is filled with air or something else?

    A. `Location`

    B. `Block`

    C. `Spot`

Answers

1. **B.** All mods you create use `extends JavaPlugin` in their class declaration.

2. **C.** A `Potion` object is created with a `PotionEffect` value such as `SPEED` or `INVISIBILITY`.

3. **B.** Each square is called a block and can be accessed in a mod with the `Block` class. Answer A is almost correct—it represents the location of any square.

Activities

To dig deeper into mod programming, do the following activities:

▶ Create a mod that summons all the chickens in the world to the player's side.

▶ Using Spigot's Java documentation, create a mod that spawns a mob that wasn't mentioned during this hour.

To see Java programs that implement these activities, visit the book's website at www.java24hours.com.

HOUR 24
Writing Android Apps

This Hour's To-Do List:

▶ Learn why Android was created.
▶ Create an Android app.
▶ Learn how an Android app is structured.
▶ Run an app on an emulator.
▶ Run an app on an Android phone.

Java's a general-purpose programming language that can run on a wide variety of platforms. One of those platforms has arisen in recent years to become an enormously successful spark for new Java development.

The Android operating system, which started out on cell phones and has spread to a variety of other devices, exclusively runs programs written in Java.

These programs, called apps, are built on an open source mobile platform that's completely free for developers to build on. Anyone can write, deploy, and sell Android apps.

During this hour, you learn about how Android came about, what makes it special, and why so many programmers are developing on the platform. You also create an app and run it on an Android phone (if you own one) and an emulator (if you don't).

Introduction to Android

Android was begun in 2003, acquired by Google, and launched in 2007 as part of an industry-wide effort to establish a new mobile phone platform that was non-proprietary and open, unlike the technology that drives RIM BlackBerry and Apple iPhone. Some of the biggest names in mobile phones and technology—Google, Intel, Motorola, Nvidia, Samsung, and other companies—formed the Open Handset Alliance to promote the new platform for mutual benefit.

Google released the Android Software Development Kit (SDK), a free set of tools for developing Android apps. The first phone running Android, the T-Mobile G1, came out in June 2008.

This effort started slowly, but since early 2010 has exploded and become a genuine rival to iPhone and other mobile platforms. All major phone carriers now offer Android phones. There's also a growing market for tablet and ebook readers.

Before Android, mobile application development required expensive programming tools and developer programs. The makers of the phone had control over who'd be allowed to create apps for them and whether the apps could be sold to users.

Android tears down that wall.

The open source and non-proprietary nature of Android means that anyone can develop, release, and sell apps. The only cost involved is a nominal fee to submit apps to Google's marketplace. Everything else is free.

The place to download the Android SDK and find out more about creating programs for the platform is the Android Developer site at https://developer.android.com. You will consult it often as you write your own apps, because it documents every class in Android's Java class library and serves as an extensive online reference.

Writing Android apps is easier if you're using an integrated development environment (IDE) that's equipped to support the Android SDK. The recommended IDE for Android programming is Android Studio, which also is free and open source.

You can use Android Studio to write Android apps, test them in an emulator that acts like an Android phone, and even deploy them on an actual device.

For most of its existence, the Java language has been used to write programs that run in one of three places: a desktop computer, a web server, or a web browser.

Android puts Java everywhere. Your programs can be deployed on millions of phones and other mobile devices.

This fulfills the original design goal of Java back when James Gosling invented the language in the mid-1990s. He was tasked with creating a language that could run everywhere on devices such as phones, smart cards, and appliances.

Java's developers set aside those dreams when the language became popular first as a means of running interactive web browser programs, and then as a general-purpose language.

Two decades later, the Android platform is hosting as many as 3 billion Java programs around the world, according to one industry estimate.

Android has the potential to be the most pervasive—and lucrative—area of Java programming for years to come.

Creating an Android App

Android apps are ordinary Java programs that use an application framework, a core set of classes and files that all apps have in common. The framework embodies a set of rules for how apps must be structured in order to run properly on Android devices.

To get started writing apps, you must install Android Studio. To download the software, visit https://developer.android.com. Run the installation wizard and follow the instructions to set up the software on your computer.

To begin using the IDE on a project:

1. Run Android Studio.

2. In the dialog that appears at startup, choose Start a New Android Project. The Create New Project wizard opens, as shown in Figure 24.1.

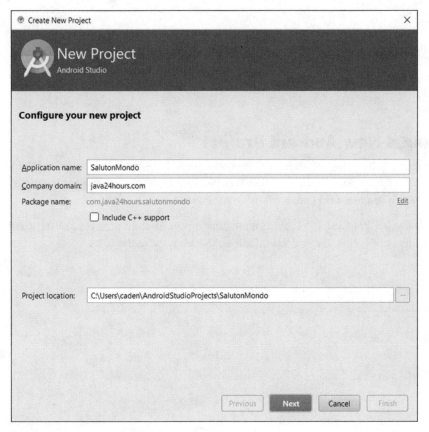

FIGURE 24.1
Creating a new Android project in Android Studio.

1. In the Application Name field, enter `SalutonMondo`.

2. In the Company Domain field, enter `java24hours.com`. The Package Name field will be updated to use this and the application name, becoming `com.java24hours.saluton-mondo`.

3. You can accept the default Project Location (a subfolder of `AndroidStudioProjects` in your user folder) or choose a different one with the "…" button to the right of the field.

4. Click Next.

5. Every Android project requires a target platform. The target represents the oldest version of Android that can run your app. Because each new Android release has enhanced features, your target choice determines which features you can use. Choose Phone and Tablet as the target and API 15 as the Minimum SDK (or the lowest if API 15 isn't available).

6. Click Next. The wizard asks about the application's activity to create. Choose Fullscreen Activity and click Next.

7. In the Activity Name field, enter `SalutonActivity`. This changes the Layout Name and Title fields. Keep those changes.

8. Click Finish. The new app is created and a SalutonMondo item appears in the Package Explorer pane.

Exploring a New Android Project

A new Android project consists of about 20 files and folders that always are organized the same way in an Android app. There might be more files you add depending on the capabilities of the app, but these starting files and folders always must be present.

Figure 24.2 shows Android Studio's Projects pane after a new Android project has been created. If you don't see this pane, click the Projects tab along the left edge of the IDE.

Project pane

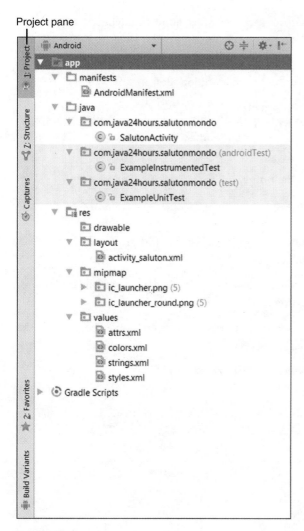

FIGURE 24.2
Viewing the parts of an Android project.

You can use the folder to explore the file and folder structure of the project. The new SalutonMondo app starts out with the following components:

▶ /javar—The root folder for the app's Java source code.

▶ /src/com.java24hours.salutonmondo/SalutonActivity.java—The class for the activity that launches by default when the app is run.

▶ /res—The folder for application resources such as strings, numbers, layout files, graphics, and animation. There are subfolders for specific resource types: layout, values, drawable, and mipmap.

▶ AndroidManifest.xml—The app's primary configuration file.

These files and folders form the application framework. The first thing you undertake as an Android programmer is to learn how to modify the framework so you can discover what each component can accomplish.

There are additional files that are added to the framework to suit specific purposes.

Creating an App

Although you haven't done anything to it yet, you could successfully run the new Android project. The framework functions as a working app.

Because there's no fun in that, you will customize the SalutonMondo app to offer the traditional computer programming greeting "Saluton Mondo!"

In Hour 2, "Writing Your First Program," you displayed the text "Saluton Mondo!" as a string by calling the method System.out.println().

Android apps display strings that have been stored first in a resource file called strings.xml. You can find this file in the /res/values folder.

Use the Package Explorer to navigate to this folder. Double-click strings.xml. The XML file opens in a text editor, as shown in Figure 24.3.

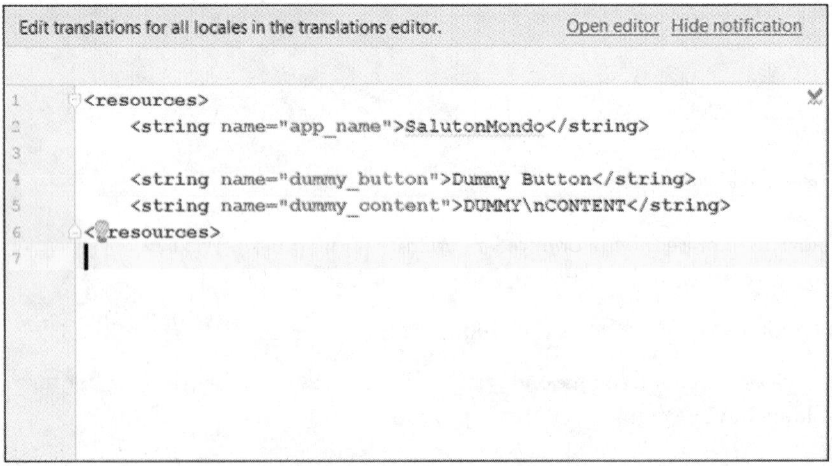

```
   Edit translations for all locales in the translations editor.        Open editor   Hide notification

1   <resources>
2        <string name="app_name">SalutonMondo</string>
3
4        <string name="dummy_button">Dummy Button</string>
5        <string name="dummy_content">DUMMY\nCONTENT</string>
6   <resources>
7
```

FIGURE 24.3
Editing an Android app's string resources.

Strings and other resources are given a name and a value, just like a variable in Java. There are three string resources represented as XML data in the editing pane: `app_name`, `dummy_button`, and `dummy_content`.

The names of resources follow three rules:

▶ They must be all lowercase.

▶ They must have no spaces.

▶ They must only use the underscore character ("_") as punctuation.

Resources are stored in XML files. The Resources editor is a simple XML editor. You also can directly edit the XML itself.

Here's what `strings.xml` looks like at the moment:

Output ▼

```
<resources>
    <string name="app_name">SalutonMondo</string>
    <string name="dummy_button">Dummy Button</string>
    <string name="dummy_content">DUMMY\nCONTENT</string>
</resources>
```

This is a `resources` element with three `string` child elements. Each `string` element has a name attribute that holds its name. There's also text between an opening `<string>` tag and a closing `</string>` tag that holds its value.

These serve the same purpose as variables: one named dummy_content has the value "DUMMY\nCONTENT."

This editor allows everything in the XML file to be edited, even the markup tags. Change "DUMMY\nCONTENT" to "Saluton Mondo!"—but take care not to change any of the surrounding characters. When you've made the change, here's what the XML file should contain:

Output ▼

```
<resources>
    <string name="app_name">SalutonMondo</string>
    <string name="dummy_button">Dummy Button</string>
    <string name="dummy_content">Saluton Mondo!</string>
</resources>
```

Click the Save button in the Android Studio toolbar (or choose File, Save All) to save your change to the file `strings.xml`.

With that modification, you're almost ready to run the app.

Setting Up an Android Emulator

Before you can build an Android app, you must set up its debugging environment. This can be handled within Android Studio. You must set up an Android Virtual Device (AVD) that can run the app on your desktop as an emulator. You also must create the project's debug configuration. When you're done, you can build the app and run it in the emulator.

To configure an Android Virtual Device, first click the green Android phone icon in the Android Studio toolbar, which is shown in Figure 24.4.

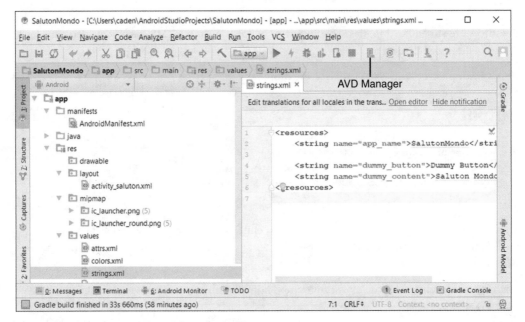

FIGURE 24.4
Configuring an Android Virtual Device.

This launches the Android Virtual Device Manager, one of the tools in the Android SDK. The emulators that you've created are listed to the left. The manager is shown in Figure 24.5.

FIGURE 24.5
Creating a new Android emulator.

To add a new emulator, click Create Virtual Device and follow these steps:

1. Choose a device from the list, such as the Galaxy Nexus, and click Next.

2. Choose a release from the list, such as Nougat, and click Next.

3. In the AVD Name field, give it the name SimpleAVD.

4. Click Finish.

5. The new emulator is created, which might take a little while (no longer than a minute, generally).

You can create as many emulators as you need. They can be customized for different versions of Android and different kinds of displays.

Close the Android Virtual Device Manager to return to the main Android Studio interface.

Running the App

Now that you have an Android emulator, you can run your first app. Choose the menu command Run, Run App. The Select Deployment Target dialog opens. Under Available Virtual Devices, choose SimpleAVD and click OK.

You may be asked to install the platform. Click Install and Continue.

The Android emulator loads in its own window. This can take a minute or more, so wait patiently as the fake phone boots up. (The emulator loads so slowly it gives you time to ponder a Chinese proverb: "The oxen are slow, but the earth is patient.")

The app you have installed will appear with an Android icon and the label SalutonMondo. Click the icon to run the app.

The emulator displays "Saluton Mondo!" as the text of the app, as shown in Figure 24.6. Controls enable the emulator to be used like a phone, but with a mouse instead of your finger. Click the back button to close the app and see how the Android device is emulated.

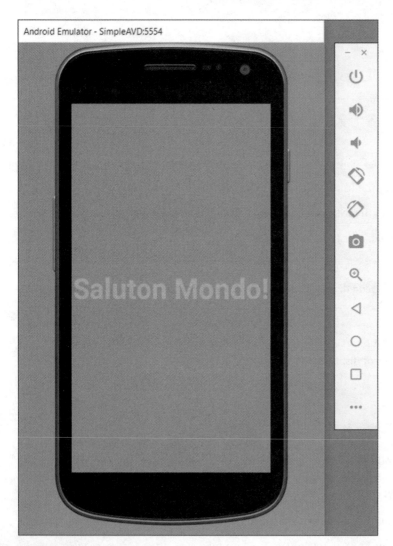

FIGURE 24.6
Running an app in the Android emulator.

An emulator can do many of the things a real device can do, including connect to the Internet if the computer has an active connection. It also can receive fake phone calls and SMS messages, but making real calls and sending messages requires the real thing.

Because it's not a fully functional device, the apps that you develop must be tested on actual Android phones and tablets.

If you can connect an Android phone (or other device) to your computer using a USB cord, you should be able to run the app if the phone is set to debugging mode. Apps developed with the Android SDK can only be deployed on a phone in this mode.

On the phone, enter this mode by choosing Home, Settings, Applications, Development (or Home, Settings, Developer Options). The Development settings are displayed. Choose the USB debugging option.

Connect your Android phone to your computer with the USB cord. An Android bug icon should appear on the bar at the top of the phone's screen. If you drag this bar down, you should see the message "USB Debugging Connected." Next, in Android, follow these steps:

1. Choose RunRun App.

2. Under Connected Devices, choose your phone.

3. Click OK.

The app runs on the phone as it did on the emulator.

Like the first program you wrote in Java back in Hour 2, the first app you created on Android is exceptionally non-exceptional. The next project is more ambitious.

Close this project by choosing the menu command File, Close Project.

Designing a Real App

Android apps can exploit all of the device's functionality, such as SMS messaging, location-based services, and touch input. In this book's final programming project, you create a real app called Take Me to Your Leader.

This app takes advantage of an Android's phone capabilities to make a phone call, visit a website, and load a location in Google Maps. The app puts you in touch with the White House via phone, Web, and maps. (If the president of the United States is not your leader, the app can be customized.)

To get started, you create a new project in Android Studio by performing these steps:

1. Choose Start a New Android Studio Project. (If you don't see this, close the last project with the menu command File, Close Project.)

2. In the Application Name field, enter `Leader`. This also will enter automatically in the Project Location field.

3. The Company Domain field already should be `java24hours.com`. Make sure it is, then click Next.

4. Choose Phone and Tablet, choose the Minimum SDK value API 15 (or the lowest possible if that's not available), then click Next.

5. Choose Fullscreen Activity; then click Next.

6. In the Activity Name field, enter `LeaderActivity`.

7. Click Finish.

The project appears in the Android Studio Project pane.

TIP
_____

This project covers a lot of ground. As you work through it, you'll find it handy to keep a browser open to the Android Developer site's reference section at https://developer.android.com/reference. You can search for the Java classes in the Android class library and the filenames of the files in the project to learn more.
_____

Organizing Resources

Creating an Android app requires Java programming, but a lot of the work is done in the Android Studio interface. When you are fully versed in the capabilities of the Android SDK, you can accomplish a great deal without writing a single line of Java code.

One thing you do without programming is create resources that will be used by the app. Every new Android project starts out with several folders where resources are placed. To see these folders, expand the Leader folder in the Package Explorer, and then expand the /res folder and all its subfolders.

Resources consist of graphics in the PNG, JPG, or GIF format; strings stored in a file called `strings.xml`; user interface layout files in XML format; and other files you can create. Two others are `colors.xml` for colors used in the app and `styles.xml` to define the appearance of user interface components.

The /res folder of a new project contains folders called `ic_launcher.png` and ic_launcher_round.png that have different versions of the app's icon. The icon's the small graphic used to launch the app.

The multiple versions of `ic_launcher.png` are the same graphic, sized for different-resolution displays. You won't be using these icons. A new graphics file, `appicon.png`, will be added to the project and designated as its icon in the file `AndroidManifest.xml`, the app's main configuration file.

This book's website contains `appicon.png` and four other graphics files needed by this app: `browser.png`, `maps.png`, `phone.png`, and `whitehouse.png`. Visit www.java24hours.com and go to the Hour 24 page for this edition of the book. Download all five files and save them in a temporary folder on your computer.

Android's support for multiple resolutions is handy, but it's not necessary here.

Files can be added to resources using cut and paste. Open the temporary folder containing the five files, select `appicon.png` and hit Ctrl-C to copy it. In Android Studio, select the folder `mipmap` in the Project pane, right-click and choose Paste. Next, go back to the temporary folder, select the other four files and copy them. Then in Android Studio, select the folder `drawable` and paste the files in it.

CAUTION

Resources are identified in an app using an ID formed from their filename with the extension removed. `appicon.png` has the ID `appicon`, `browser.png` has the ID `browser`, and so on. No two resources can have the same ID (with the exception of the same graphic being stored at different resolutions in the `mipmap` folders, because they count as a single resource).

If two resources have the same name without the extension, such as `appicon.png` and `appicon.gif`, Android Studio will flag the error and the app won't compile.

Resources also must have names that contain only lowercase letters, numbers, underscores (_), and periods (.). The files in this project follow these rules.

Now that the project has a new icon, you can set it as the app's icon. This will be handled by editing `AndroidManifest.xml`.

Configuring the App's Manifest File

The primary configuration tool in an Android app is a file called `AndroidManifest.xml` in the app's `manifests` folder. Double-click `AndroidManifest.xml` to open the XML file for editing.

The Icon field identifies the app's icon, which currently has the incorrect value `@mipmap/ic_launcher`.

Find the line in the file that reads as follows:

```
android:icon="@mipmap/ic_launcher"
```

This sets the app's icon and contains a folder and resource name. Change it to this:

```
android:icon="@mipmap/appicon"
```

Designing a User Interface

An app's graphical user interface consists of layouts, which are containers that hold widgets such as text fields, buttons, graphics, and custom widgets of your own design. Each screen displayed to a user can have one layout or multiple layouts contained within each other. There are layouts to stack components vertically or horizontally, organize them in a table, and other arrangements.

An app can be as simple as a single screen or contain multiple screens. A game could be organized into these screens:

- ▶ A splash screen that displays as the game is loading

- ▶ A main menu screen with buttons to view the other screens

- ▶ A help screen explaining how to play

- ▶ A scores screen that lists the highest player scores

- ▶ A credits screen naming the game's developers

- ▶ A game screen for actual play

The Leader app consists of a single screen, which holds buttons for contacting the president of the United States or a leader to be named later.

All of an app's screens are kept in the `/res/layout` folder. This project has an `activity_leader.xml` file in this folder that's designated as the screen to display when the app loads.

To begin editing this screen's layout, double-click `activity_leader.xml` in Package Explorer. The screen opens in the main Android Studio editing pane, as shown in Figure 24.7.

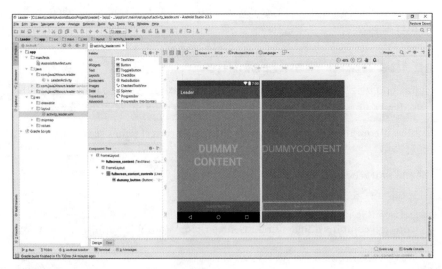

FIGURE 24.7
Editing an activity's graphical user interface.

The editing window includes a Palette pane with several categories of user interface components that can be expanded. These can be dragged and dropped onto the screen at right.

Follow these steps to add three graphical buttons to the screen:

1. Delete the widget that displays the "Dummy Button" text by clicking this widget at the bottom of the screen in the editing pane and pressing the Delete key.

2. Click the Layouts folder in the Palette pane. The subpane expands.

3. Drag the LinearLayout (vertical) widget from the Palette to the screen. A Properties pane appears to the right of the editing pane with a Linear Layout label above an Orientation drop-down. Choose the value vertical if it isn't already selected. The layout widget determines how user interface elements placed on it will be arranged.

4. In the Palette pane, click the Images folder. The subpane expands.

5. Drag an ImageButton widget from the Palette to the app screen in the editing pane. A Resource dialog opens, asking you to choose an image to display on the button. Choose phone and click OK. The button now has a graphic of a phone.

6. In the Properties pane, set Layout_Width to wrap_content.

7. Drag another ImageButton widget and drop it to the right of the phone button. Choose the browser resource for this one. A browser button is added.

8. Drag one more ImageButton widget and drop it to the right of browser, assigning it the maps resource.

The Component pane lists the widgets on the screen. Select the imageButton1 item. The properties of the button open in the Properties pane.

1. Scroll down the Properties pane until you see an ID property. Its value currently is set to imageButton1. Change this to phoneButton.

2. In the On Click property, enter the value processClicks. (This will be explained in the next section.)

3. Repeat steps 8–11 for imageButton2, giving it the ID webButton and the On Click property processClicks.

4. Repeat steps 8–11 for imageButton3, giving it the ID mapButton and the On Click property processClicks.

5. Click the LinearLayout item in the Component Tree. The properties for the screen appear in the Properties pane.

6. In the Properties pane, click the View All Properties link.

7. Click the value for Background; then click the ... button. The Resources dialog opens.

8. Choose `whitehouse`, and click OK. A graphic of the White House becomes the screen's background.

9. Click the Save button.

The finished screen is shown in Figure 24.8.

FIGURE 24.8
Previewing an app's graphical user interface.

Writing Java Code

At this point, you've done the bulk of the work on the new app, but you haven't written a single line of Java code. App development is easier when you utilize as many capabilities of the Android SDK as possible without resorting to programming.

Apps are organized into Activities, which represent things an app can do. Each Activity is defined by its own Java class. When you created this app, you specified that an Activity named `LeaderActivity` should be created. A class matching this name runs automatically when the app is loaded.

The source code for `LeaderActivity.java` can be found in Package Explorer in the `/java/com.java24hours.leader` folder. Double-click this file to edit it.

When you start, the class has a lot of existing source code.

Like all Activities, the `LeaderActivity` class is a subclass of an activity `class that` contains the behavior necessary to display a screen, collect user input, save user preferences, and so on.

The `onCreate()` method defined in the class is called when the class is loaded.

The first thing the method does is use `super()` to call the same method in its superclass:

```
super.onCreate(savedInstanceState);
```

Next, it calls `setContentView()`, a method that selects the screen that will be displayed. The argument to this method is an instance variable, `R.layout.activity_leader`, that refers to the file `activity_leader.xml` in `/res/layout`. As you may recall, the ID of a resource is its filename without the extension.

When you designed the app's user interface earlier, you set the On Click property of each button to `processClicks`. This indicated that a method called `processClicks()` would be called when a user clicked a widget on the screen.

Now it's time to implement that method. Add these statements to `LeaderActivity` above the `onCreate()` method:

```
public void processClicks(View display) {
    Intent action = null;
    int id = display.getId();
}
```

Add this `import` statement at the top of the file:

```
import android.content.Intent;
```

Return to the `processClicks()` method. It is called with one argument: a `View` object from the `android.view` package. A `View` is a visual display of some kind in an app. In this case, it's the screen containing the Dialer, Browser, and Map buttons.

The `View` object's `getId()` method returns the ID of the button that was clicked: `phoneButton`, `webButton`, or `mapButton`.

This ID is stored in the `id` variable so it can be used in a `switch` statement to take action based on the click. After the line where you called `display.getId()`, add these statements:

```
switch (id) {
    case (R.id.phoneButton):
        // ...
        break;
```

```
case (R.id.webButton):
    // ...
    break;
case (R.id.mapButton):
    // ...
    break;
default:
    break;
}
```

This code will take one of three actions, using the integer of each ID as the conditional in the `switch`.

The first statement in the `processClicks()` method creates a variable to hold an `Intent` object, a class in Android's `android.content` package:

```
Intent action;
```

Intents in Android are how Activities tell another Activity what to do. They're also the way an app communicates with the Android device.

Here are the three Intents employed in this method:

```
action = new Intent(Intent.ACTION_DIAL, Uri.parse("tel:202-456-1111"));

action = new Intent(Intent.ACTION_VIEW, Uri.parse("http://whitehouse.gov"));

action = new Intent(Intent.ACTION_VIEW, Uri.parse("geo:0,0?q=White House,
Washington, DC"));
```

The `Intent()` constructor takes two arguments:

▶ The action to take, represented by one of its class variables

▶ The data associated with the action

These three Intents tell the Android device to set up an outgoing phone call to the White House public phone line at (202) 456-1111, visit the website `http://whitehouse.gov`, and load Google Maps with the partial address "White House, Washington, DC," respectively.

Take these three Intent constructors and put them in place of the comments in the `switch` conditional. One statement goes in each case—the phone call in the `phoneButton` block, web visit in the `webButton` block, and address in the `mapButton` block.

After you have created an Intent, the following statement makes it do something:

```
startActivity(action);
```

Put this statement after the end of the `switch` block.

Because you deleted the Dummy Button on the activity, you must remove this line of code, which is the last one in the onCreate() method:

```
findViewById(R.id.dummy_button).setOnTouchListener(mDelayHideTouchListener);
```

An easy way to remove it is to put // in front of it, turning it into a comment that's ignored by the compiler.

The following import statement must be added to the class for the code you've added to function properly:

```
import android.net.Uri;
```

The full text of the processClicks() method in LeaderActivity class is shown in Listing 24.1. Make sure the method in your code matches the listing. (Note that this is not the entire source code of LeaderActivity.java, just the processClicks() method.)

LISTING 24.1 Partial Text of LeaderActivity.java

```
 1:      public void processClicks(View display) {
 2:          Intent action = null;
 3:          int id = display.getId();
 4:          switch (id) {
 5:              case (R.id.phoneButton):
 6:                  action = new Intent(Intent.ACTION_DIAL,
 7:                      Uri.parse("tel:202-456-1111"));
 8:                  break;
 9:              case (R.id.webButton):
10:                  action = new Intent(Intent.ACTION_VIEW,
11:                      Uri.parse("http://whitehouse.gov"));
12:                  break;
13:              case (R.id.mapButton):
14:                  action = new Intent(Intent.ACTION_VIEW,
15:                      Uri.parse("geo:0,0?q=White House, Washington, DC"));
16:                  break;
17:              default:
18:                  break;
19:          }
20:          startActivity(action);
21:      }
```

Save the file when you're done. Choose the menu comment Build, Make Project to compile it. If not, error messages are displayed and red lines appear in files in the Project pane where the errors were found.

To run the app, choose Run, Run App, and SimpleAVD as the virtual device. The emulator loads (which takes time) and then automatically runs the app.

An emulator does not emulate everything an Android device can do. The Leader app's Dialer and Browser buttons should work properly, but you might encounter problems with Maps.

The app also can be run on an Android phone, if you have one working with the Android SDK and the phone has been set to debugging mode.

Choose Run, Run App, then choose your phone as the device instead of a virtual one. Click OK.

Figure 24.9 shows the app running on my phone. When the phone is shifted from portrait mode to landscape mode, the app shifts accordingly.

FIGURE 24.9
Take me to your leader!

The Leader app also has been added to the phone's applications with its own "Take Me to Your Leader" icon. It will stay on the phone even after you disconnect the USB cable.

Congratulations! The world now has one billion and one Android apps.

NOTE

As you might have surmised, there's a lot more to Android programming than can be covered in a single hour. Sams offers another book that takes the Java programming you've learned here and extends it with another 24 hours of Android-specific coverage: *Sams Teach Yourself Android Application Development*, Fourth Edition, by Carmen Delessio, Lauren Darcey, and Shane Conder (ISBN 978-0-672-33739-0).

Summary

The goal of *Sams Teach Yourself Java in 24 Hours* has been to help you become comfortable with the concepts of programming and confident in your ability to write your own programs whether they run on a desktop computer, web server, or even a phone. Java has an approach that is somewhat difficult to master. (Feel free to scratch out the word *somewhat* in the previous sentence.)

As you build experience in Java, you're building experience that grows increasingly relevant, because concepts such as object-oriented programming, virtual machines, and secure environments are on the leading edge of software development.

If you haven't already, you should check out the appendices for additional useful information.

At the conclusion of this hour, you can explore Java in several places. Programmers are discussing the language on the weblogs at www.planetnetbeans.org. Numerous Java job openings are displayed in the database of employment websites such as www.careerbuilder.com. There's also a website for this book at www.java24hours.com where you can send email to the author and read answers to reader questions, clarifications to the book, and (gulp) corrections.

One way to continue building your skills as a Java programmer is to read *Sams Teach Yourself Java in 21 Days*. I wrote that book also, and it expands on the subjects covered here and introduces new ones, such as JDBC, Java servlets, and network programming.

If you didn't skip ahead and have just completed all 24 hours, kudos. Please use your newfound programming skills to get a great job and rebuild the world economy.

Workshop

Q&A

Q. Why is Android Studio used to create Android apps instead of NetBeans?

A. You can use NetBeans to develop apps, but it's a more cumbersome and less well-supported IDE for Android programming. Android Studio has been designated by Google as the preferred Android IDE. The official documentation and tutorials on the Android Developer site at http://developer.android.com all use Android Studio.

Most programming books for Android also employ Android Studio. Although there's a learning curve required to switch from NetBeans to Android Studio when you dive into Android, after you master the basics of writing, debugging, and deploying an app, you should find Android Studio easier to use because it's so much better supported by Android programmers and technical writers.

Q. Why do so many movies have the same exact sound of a man screaming in anguish?

A. That sound is the Wilhelm scream, a sound effect that was heard first in the 1951 movie *Distant Drums*. It turns up most often when somebody falls from a great height, is shot by a gun, or is knocked back by an explosion. Two famous uses are in the original *Star Wars*, when a stormtrooper is shot by Luke Skywalker and falls off a ledge, and in the animated movie *Toy Story* when Sheriff Woody knocks Buzz Lightyear out the window.

The sound was popularized by movie sound designer Ben Burtt, who found it in a Warner Brothers stock library when developing sound for *Star Wars* and included it in every Steven Spielberg and George Lucas movie he worked on. It has since become a tradition among sound designers and can be heard in more than 140 movies.

The voice actor who screamed is believed to be Sheb Wooley, an actor and singer who recorded the 1958 novelty song "Purple People Eater."

The scream being named Wilhelm comes from the third movie to use the sound effect. In the 1953 film *The Charge at Feather River*, Private Wilhelm yells in anguish as he's shot by an arrow.

Quiz

If you would like to dial up the knowledge you've just acquired in Android development, answer the following questions.

1. Which of the following companies was not part of the Open Handset Initiative, the group that championed Android?

    A. Google

    B. Apple

    C. Motorola

2. What object is used for one Activity to tell another Activity what to do?

   A. An `Intent`

   B. An `Action`

   C. A `View`

3. Which of the following tasks can an Android emulator not perform?

   A. Receiving an SMS message

   B. Connecting to the Internet

   C. Making a phone call

Answers

1. **B.** Apple, because Android was created in part as an open source, non-proprietary alternative to the Apple iPhone.

2. **A.** An `Intent` also is the way an Activity communicates with the Android device.

3. **C.** Emulators can't do everything an actual device can do, so they're only part of the testing process for apps.

Activities

To make your Android knowledge go for longer distance, undertake the following activities:

▶ Change the text of the SalutonMondo app to "Hello, Android" and run the app in the emulator and on an Android device (if one is available to you).

▶ Create a new version of Take Me to Your Leader for a different world leader, customizing the phone, Web, and map destinations.

To see Java programs that implement these activities, visit the book's website at www.java24hours.com.

APPENDIX A
Using the NetBeans Integrated Development Environment

Although it's possible to create Java programs with nothing more than the Java Development Kit and a text editor, the experience is considerably more pleasant when you use an integrated development environment (IDE).

Most of this book employs NetBeans, a free IDE offered by Oracle for Java programmers. NetBeans is a program that makes it easier to organize, write, compile, and debug Java software. It includes a project and file manager, graphical user interface designer, and many other tools. One killer feature is a code editor that automatically detects Java syntax errors as you type.

Now in version 8.2, NetBeans has become a favorite of professional Java developers, offering functionality and performance that would be worth the money at 10 times the price. (See what I did there?) NetBeans also is one of the easiest IDEs for Java novices to use.

In this appendix, you learn enough about NetBeans to install the software and put it to use throughout this book.

Installing NetBeans

From inauspicious beginnings, the NetBeans IDE has grown to become one of the leading programming tools for Java developers. James Gosling, the creator of the Java language, gave it the ultimate vote of confidence in his book *NetBeans Field Guide*: "I use NetBeans for all my Java development." After trying most of the IDEs available for the language over the years, I've become a convert as well.

NetBeans supports all facets of Java programming for the three editions of the language—Java Standard Edition (JSE), Java Enterprise Edition (JEE), and Java Mobile Edition (JME). It also supports web application development, web services, and JavaBeans. This book focuses on the JSE.

You can download NetBeans, available for Windows, Mac OS, and Linux, from https://netbeans. org. The software is available for download bundled with the Java Development Kit and can be downloaded separately. You must have NetBeans and the JDK installed on your computer. NetBeans is available in several bundles. Choose the one that supports Java SE.

CAUTION

Having trouble loading the NetBeans website? You are probably trying to load www.netbeans.org (which does not work) instead of https://netbeans.org.

If you'd like to ensure that you're downloading the same versions of NetBeans and the JDK used in the preparation of this book, visit the book's website at www.java24hours.com. Click the cover of this book to open the site for this edition and then look for the Download JDK and Download NetBeans links. You'll be steered to the proper sites.

Creating a New Project

The JDK and NetBeans are downloaded as installation wizards that set up the software on your system. You can install the software in any folder and menu group you like, but it's best to stick with the default setup options unless you have a good reason to do otherwise.

When you run NetBeans for the first time after installation, you see a start page that displays links to demos and programming tutorials (see Figure A.1). You can read these within the IDE using NetBeans' built-in web browser.

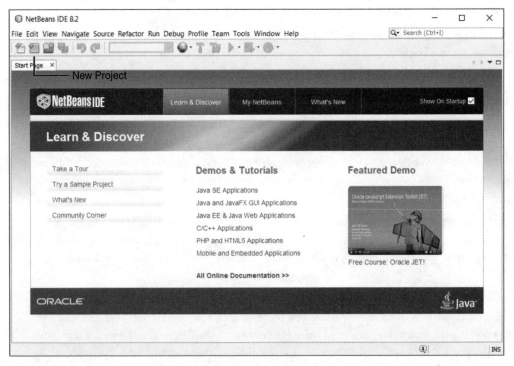

FIGURE A.1
The NetBeans user interface.

A NetBeans project consists of a set of related Java classes, files used by those classes, and Java class libraries. Each project has its own folder, which you can explore and modify outside NetBeans using text editors and other programming tools.

To begin a new project, click the New Project button shown in Figure A.1 or choose the File, New Project menu command. The New Project Wizard opens, as shown in Figure A.2.

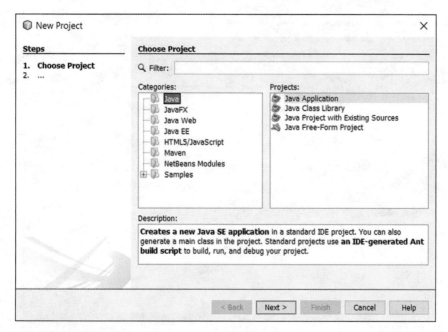

FIGURE A.2
The New Project Wizard.

NetBeans can create several types of Java projects, but during this book you can focus on one type: Java Application.

For your first project (and most of the projects in this book), choose the project type Java Application and click Next. The wizard asks you to choose a name and location for the project.

The Project Location text field identifies the root folder of the programming projects you create with NetBeans. On Windows, this may be a subfolder of your My Documents (or Documents) folder named NetBeansProjects. All projects you create are stored inside this folder, each in its own subfolder.

In the Project Name text field, enter Java24. The Create Main Class text box changes in response to the input, recommending java24.Java24 as the name of the main Java class in the project. Change this to Spartacus and click Finish, accepting all other defaults. NetBeans creates the project and its first class.

Creating a New Java Class

When NetBeans creates a new project, it sets up all the necessary files and folders and creates the main class. Figure A.3 shows the first class in your project, Spartacus.java, open in the source editor.

FIGURE A.3
The NetBeans source editor.

Spartacus.java is a bare-bones Java class that consists only of a main() method. All the light gray lines in the class are comments that explain the purpose and function of the class. Comments are ignored when the class is run.

To make the new class do something, add the following line of code on a new line right below the comment // TODO code application logic here:

```
System.out.println("I am Spartacus!");
```

The method System.out.println() displays a string of text, in this case the sentence "I am Spartacus!"

Make sure to enter this exactly as it appears. After you make sure you typed the line correctly and ended it with a semicolon, click the Save All toolbar button (or the menu command File, Save All) to save the class.

NOTE

As you type, the source editor figures out what you're doing and pops up helpful information related to the System class, the `out` instance variable, and the `println()` method. You'll love this helpfulness later, but for now try your best to ignore it.

Java classes must be compiled into an executable form called bytecode before you can run them. NetBeans tries to compile classes automatically. You also can manually compile this class in two ways:

▶ Choose the menu command Run, Compile File.

▶ Right-click `Spartacus.java` in the Projects pane to open a pop-up menu and choose Compile File.

If NetBeans doesn't allow you to choose either of these options, it already has compiled the class automatically.

If the class does not compile successfully, a red exclamation point appears next to the filename `Spartacus.java` in the Projects pane. To fix the error, compare what you've typed in the text editor to the full source code of `Spartacus.java` in Listing A.1 and save the file again. The line numbers in Listing A.1 should not appear in your program—they're used in this book when describing how the code works. (Also, Line 9 will have your own username in place of the word "User.")

LISTING A.1   **The Java Class** `Spartacus.java`

```
 1: /*
 2:  * To change this license header, choose License Headers in Project Properties.
 3:  * To change this template file, choose Tools | Templates
 4:  * and open the template in the editor.
 5:  */
 6:
 7: /**
 8:  *
 9:  * @author User
10:  */
11: public class Spartacus {
12:
13:     /**
14:      * @param args the command line arguments
15:      */
16:     public static void main(String[] args) {
17:         // TODO code application logic here
18:         System.out.println("I am Spartacus!");
19:
20:     }
21:
22: }
```

The Java class is defined in lines 11–22. Everything above Line 11 is a comment included by NetBeans in every new class when you choose Java Application as the project type. These comments help explain things about the program to humans reading the source code. The compiler ignores them.

Running the Application

After you've created the Java class `Spartacus.java` and compiled it successfully, you can run it within NetBeans in two ways:

▶ Choose Run, Run File from the menu.

▶ Right-click `Spartacus.java` in the Projects pane and choose Run File.

When you run a Java class, its `main()` method is called by the Java Virtual Machine. The string "I am Spartacus!" appears in the Output pane, as shown in Figure A.4.

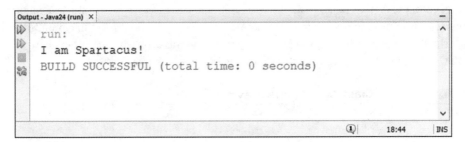

```
Output - Java24 (run)  X                                    —
  run:
  I am Spartacus!
  BUILD SUCCESSFUL (total time: 0 seconds)

                                          ①  18:44  INS
```

FIGURE A.4
Output of the Spartacus application.

A Java class must have a `main()` method to be run. If you attempt to run a class that lacks one, NetBeans responds with an error.

When you're finished reviewing the program's output, close the Output pane by clicking the X on the pane's tab (the place with the title Output – Java24 (run). This makes the source editor larger so that more lines are displayed, which comes in handy when you are creating a program.

Fixing Errors

Now that the Spartacus application has been written, compiled, and run, it's time to break something to get some experience with how NetBeans responds when things go terribly wrong.

Like any programmer, you'll have plenty of practice screwing things up on your own, but pay attention here anyway.

Return to `Spartacus.java` in the source editor and take the semicolon off the end of the line that calls `System.out.println()` (line 18 in Listing A.1). Even before you save the file, NetBeans spots the error and displays a red alert icon to the left of the line (see Figure A.5).

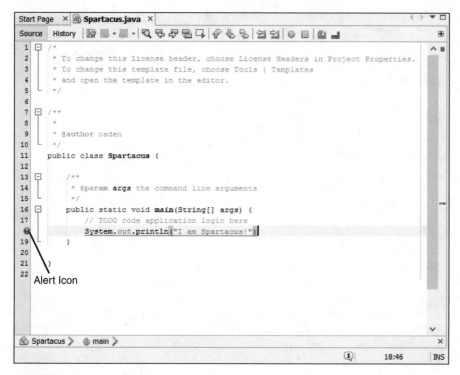

FIGURE A.5
Flagging errors in the source editor.

Hover over the alert icon to see a dialog appear that describes the error NetBeans thinks it has spotted.

The NetBeans source editor can identify most of the common programming errors and typos that it encounters as you write a Java program. The detection of an error stops the file from being compiled until the error has been fixed.

Put the semicolon back at the end of the line. The alert icon disappears and you can save and run the class again.

These basic features are all you need to create and compile the Java programs in this book.

NetBeans is capable of a lot more than these features, but you should focus on learning Java before diving too deeply into the IDE. Use NetBeans as if it was just a simple programming project manager and text editor. Write classes, flag errors, and make sure you can compile and run each project successfully.

When you're ready to learn more about NetBeans, the Start page offers resources to learn how to use it. Oracle also offers training and documentation resources at https://netbeans.org/kb.

APPENDIX B

Where to Go from Here: Java Resources

After you have finished this book, you might be wondering where you can turn to improve your Java programming skills. This appendix lists some books, websites, Internet discussion sites, and other resources you can use to expand your Java knowledge.

Other Books to Consider

Sams Publishing and other publishers offer several useful books on Java programming, including some that follow up on the material covered in this book. Use these ISBN numbers at bookstores if they don't currently carry the book that you're looking for:

▶ *Sams Teach Yourself Java in 21 Days*, by Rogers Cadenhead (me! me! me!), ISBN: 978-0-672-33795-6. Although some of the material in the first seven chapters of this book is redundant, it covers Java in more depth and adds a lot of advanced topics. If you're ready to make another 504-hour commitment to learning Java, this should be a suitable book.

▶ *Java Phrasebook,* by Timothy R. Fisher. ISBN 0-67232-907-7. A collection of more than 100 snippets of code for use in your own Java projects, created by a professional programmer and *Java Developer's Journal* contributor.

▶ *Agile Java Development with Spring, Hibernate and Eclipse* by Anil Hemrajani. ISBN 0-672-32896-8. A book for Java Enterprise Edition that shows how to use the Spring framework, Hibernate library, and Eclipse IDE to reduce the complexity of enterprise application programming.

▶ *Android How to Program, 3rd Edition* by Paul and Harvey Deitel. ISBN 0-13-444430-2. An extensive introduction to Android programming for phones and tablets updated for Android version 6 and the Android Studio IDE. Readers of the book learn to create eight apps.

▶ *Java 9 for Programmers, 4th Edition* by Paul and Harvey Deitel. ISBN 978-0-134-77756-6. An advanced exploration of Java 9 that includes coverage of lambda expressions, the Java module system, animation, video, and database programming with JDBC and JPA.

Chapters and other material from many Sams Publishing Java books have been made freely available on www.informit.com, a website for information technology professionals that is produced in collaboration with Sams.

The Sams Publishing website, www.informit.com/sams, is a good place to see what's coming from Sams Publishing and other imprints of the Pearson Technology Group.

Oracle's Official Java Site

The Java software division of Oracle maintains three websites of interest to programmers and users of its language.

The Oracle Technology Network for Java Developers, which is published at www.oracle.com/technetwork/java, is the first place to visit when looking for Java-related information. New versions of the Java Development Kit and other programming resources are available for download, along with documentation for the entire Java class library. There's also a bug database, a directory of local face-to-face user groups, and support forums.

Java.com at www.java.com promotes the benefits of the language to consumers and non-programmers. You can download the Java runtime environment from the site, which enables users to run programs created with Java on their computers. There's also a help section for running Java and addressing security concerns.

Planet NetBeans at www.planetnetbeans.org is a collection of several dozen blogs that cover Java programming with the NetBeans IDE. The latest posts from the blogs appear on the site and you can subscribe to their RSS feeds in a reader such as Feedly.

Java Class Documentation

Perhaps the most useful part of Oracle's Java site is the documentation for every class, variable, and method in the Java class library. Thousands of pages are available online at no cost to you to show you how to use the classes in your programs.

To visit the class documentation for Java 9, go to http://download.java.net/jdk9/docs/api.

Other Java Websites

Because so much of the Java phenomenon was originally inspired by its use on web pages, a large number of websites focus on Java and Java programming.

This Book's Official Site

This book's official website is www.java24hours.com and is described fully in Appendix C, "This Book's Website."

Workbench

I also publish a weblog, Workbench, which covers Java, Internet technology, computer books, and similar topics along with other subjects. You can find it at http://workbench.cadenhead.org.

Slashdot

The technology news site Slashdot has been a go-to place for programmers and other computer industry professionals since 1997. The site selects the best user-submitted stories for its front page and allows users to rank comments so you can filter out the noise. To see its latest Java-related stories, visit www.slashdot.org/tag/java.

Other Java Weblogs

Hundreds of other weblogs cover Java programming, either as their primary focus or part of more diverse subject matter.

WordPress.Com, a host for thousands of blogs, categorizes the latest Java-related posts on these sites at https://en.wordpress.com/tag/java.

On Twitter, you can locate Java blogs and news with a search for the hashtag "#java" at https://twitter.com/search?q=%23java. Some of the results will be about coffee or the island of Java instead of the programming language.

InformIT

The tech reference site InformIT, available at www.informit.com, is a comprehensive resource supported by the publisher of this book. The site devotes sections to several dozen subjects related to software development and the Internet. InformIT's Java section includes how-to articles and a beginner's reference. Visit www.informit.com/topics/topic.aspx?st=66497 to access it directly.

Stack Overflow

The online community Stack Overflow is a place where programmers can ask questions and rate the answers provided by other users. The site is tagged so you can narrow your search to the language or topic that's of interest. To see Java-related questions, visit https://stackoverflow.com/questions/tagged/java.

JavaWorld Magazine

A magazine that has been around since the inception of the language in the 1990s, *JavaWorld*, publishes frequent tutorial articles along with Java development news and other features. There also are video and audio podcasts. Visit www.javaworld.com.

Developer.com's Java Directory

Because Java is an object-oriented language, it's easy to use resources created by other developers in your own programs. Before you start a Java project of any significance, you should scan the Web for resources you might be able to use in your program.

A good place to start is Developer.com's Java directory. This site catalogs Java programs, programming resources, and other information at www.developer.com/java.

Java Meetings

The website Meetup.com contains thousands of meetings of formal and informal groups shared on the site by users seeking people to attend.

Many Java users groups and other Java events are announced on the site. To find a meetup within 100 miles of your location, visit www.meetup.com/find/?keywords=Java&radius=100.

In my region of Florida, there are regularly held meetings of Java user's groups, developer's groups, and social gatherings over coffee.

Job Opportunities

If you're one of those folks learning Java as a part of your plan to become a captain of industry, several of the resources listed in this appendix have a section devoted to job opportunities. Check out some of the Java-related job openings that might be available.

The job posting search engine Indeed has a section devoted to Java jobs. Visit www.indeed.com/q-Java-jobs.html to see the latest help-wanted ads for programmers proficient in the language. Another good job site for Java programmers is Dice, which lists Java employment postings at www.dice.com/jobs?q=java.

Although it isn't specifically a Java employment resource, the CareerBuilder website enables you to search the job classifieds of more than two dozen job databases, including newspaper classifieds and many other sources. You can search more than 100,000 job postings using keywords such as Java, Internet, or snake charmer. Go to www.careerbuilder.com.

If you get a job in Java programming after reading this book, I'd love to hear about it. Come to the book's website and use the Feedback link to contact me, or send a message on Twitter to @rcade.

APPENDIX C
This Book's Website

As much as I'd like to think otherwise, there are undoubtedly some things you're not clear about after completing the 24 hours of this book.

Programming is a specialized technical field that throws strange concepts and jargon at you, such as "instantiation," "ternary operators," and "big- and little-endian byte order."

If you're unclear about any of the topics covered in the book, or if I was unclear about a topic (sigh), visit the book's website at www.java24hours.com for assistance.

The website offers the following:

▶ Error corrections and clarifications—When errors are brought to my attention, they are described on the site with the corrected text and any other material that could help.

▶ Answers to reader questions—If readers have questions that aren't covered in this book's Q&A sections, many are presented on the site.

▶ The source code, class files, and resources required for all programs you create during the 24 hours of this book.

▶ Solutions, including source code, for activities suggested at the end of each hour.

▶ Updated links to the sites mentioned in this book: If sites mentioned in the book have changed addresses and I know about the new link, I'll share it on the website.

You also can send me email by visiting the book's site. Click the Feedback link to go to a page where you can send email directly from the Web. I also can be reached on Twitter as @rcade.

Feel free to voice all opinions positive, negative, indifferent, undecided, enraged, enthused, peeved, amused, irked, intrigued, bored, captivated, enchanted, disenchanted, flummoxed, and flabbergasted.

—Rogers Cadenhead

Fixing a Problem with the Android Studio Emulator

The free Android Studio integrated development environment (IDE) has become the official tool for creating Android apps since its release in 2015. You learn how to create mobile apps in Java with this IDE during Hour 24, "Writing Android Apps."

If you already have read that chapter and successfully run an app in an Android emulator, you don't need to read this appendix.

But if you couldn't make the emulator work at all, you're in the right place.

Problems Running an App

When you are working on an Android project in Android Studio and you want to run the app, you can choose the menu command Run, Run App.

This command opens a Choose Device dialog that asks for the device where the app should be executed. The device can be a real Android phone or tablet, if it's connected to your computer over a USB cord and configured to test apps. The device also can be an Android emulator.

An Android emulator in Android Studio can act like actual phones and tablets that run the mobile OS. A virtual device can be set up for multiple Android virtual devices.

Some users experience problems running an Android app for the first time with an emulator in Android Studio. The emulator crashes with this ominous message:

output ▼

```
ERROR: x86 emulation currently requires hardware acceleration!
Please ensure Intel HAXM is properly installed and usable. CPU
acceleration status: HAX kernel module is not installed!
```

This error occurs on Windows computers and indicates that they need a hardware acceleration program from Intel called the Hardware Accelerated Execution Manager (HAXM) before the emulator will work. This program can be downloaded in Android Studio, but you must install it outside of the IDE.

HAXM is a hardware virtualization engine for computers with Intel processors that speeds up Android development by making emulators run faster. One of the biggest bottlenecks in app programming for Android is how slowly emulators load.

Before you set up HAXM, you must add it to the Android SDK in Android Studio.

CAUTION

HAXM only should be installed on computers with an Intel processor. This appendix resolves a problem where Android Studio indicates that it needs HAXM to run the Android emulator. If the emulator is failing with an error message that does not mention HAXM, don't use this appendix to fix it.

Install HAXM in Android Studio

HAXM can be downloaded and added to the Android SDK as you're running Android Studio. Click the SDK Manager button in the Android Studio toolbar, which is identified in Figure D.1.

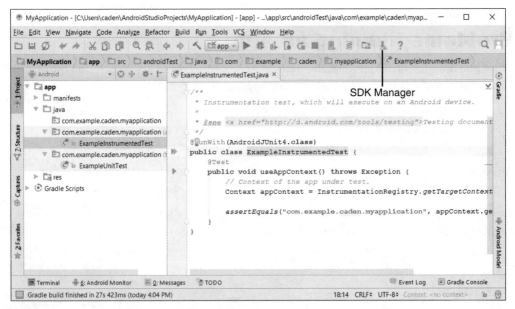

FIGURE D.1
Running the Android SDK Manager.

The SDK Manager is used to enhance the SDK with additional versions of Android and useful SDK tools. Click the SDK Tools tab to bring it to the front.

The tools available for the SDK will be listed along with a check mark next to the ones you already have installed. Look for the item Intel x86 Emulator Accelerator (HAXM Installer).

If there's no check mark next to this item, it hasn't been added to the Android SDK in your copy of Android Studio. (If there is a check mark, it already has been installed, so you should proceed to the next section, "Install HAXM on Your Computer.")

The Android SDK Manager is shown in Figure D.2.

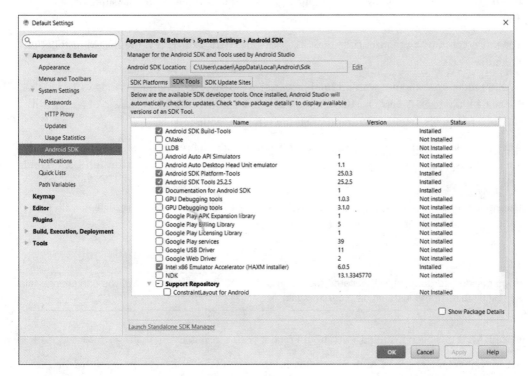

FIGURE D.2
Adding an SDK tool.

Select Intel x86 Emulator Accelerator (HAXM Installer) and click OK. You will be asked to confirm this change. Click OK.

Android Studio will download HAXM and report its progress. If it installs correctly, you're ready to proceed to the next step and install it on your computer.

Install HAXM on Your Computer

To begin setting up HAXM on your computer, first close Android Studio.

In your file system, find the folder where you told the Android Studio installation wizard to store the Android SDK.

If you don't remember where you put it, the default on Windows is to put the SDK in your personal user folder in a subfolder called `AppData\Local\Android\sdk`. So if your Windows username is Catniss, the suggested SDK location is `\Users\Catniss\AppData\Local\Android\sdk`.

If you find the SDK's folder on your computer, open that folder, then open the subfolder `extras\intel\Hardware_Accelerated_Execution_Manager`.

The folder contains a program called `intelhaxm-android.exe`. This is the HAXM installation program.

HAXM requires a computer with an Intel processor, 1G of disk space, and a Windows 7 or higher, or the 64-bit Mac OS X versions 10.8 through 10.11. A text file called `Release Notes.txt` in this folder contains detailed information on the software requirements.

After you've reviewed the release notes file, if you are ready to install HAXM, run the program `intelhaxm-android.exe`. The installer will check whether your computer can run HAXM and exit if it can't.

During installation you'll be asked how much memory to allow HAXM to use. The default value of 2G should be sufficient. Complete the installation.

TIP
___
If you decide later that you've allocated too much or too little memory for HAXM, you can change this setting by running the installation program again.
___

Once HAXM has been installed, you should reboot your computer.

When that's complete, load Android Studio and try to run your Android app again by choosing Run, Run App.

The app should run in an emulator. The Android emulator looks like a phone, displays an "Android" boot screen while it's loading and then runs the app. Figure D.3 shows what the SalutonMondo app looks like when it has been run successfully.

FIGURE D.3
Success! The emulator loads and runs an app.

If it worked, you're ready to go back to Hour 24.

If it failed with the same error message asking you to "ensure Intel HAXM is properly installed and usable," there's one more thing you can check. However, it requires checking your computer's BIOS settings and making changes to them.

Checking BIOS Settings

For HAXM to work, your computer's BIOS must have Intel Virtualization Technology enabled in its settings. If you are comfortable making changes to BIOS, this is a straightforward thing to check and change.

Because changes to BIOS can affect how your computer boots up—or even stop it from booting up Windows at all—you should only poke around in BIOS if you have made BIOS changes to a computer before. Otherwise, you should recruit the help of someone else who is an expert and can guide you through the process.

BIOS is the software that controls a Windows computer when you turn it on, taking care of booting the computer and other necessary hardware functions.

While your computer is booting up, you briefly will see a message about hitting a function key to check your BIOS settings.

If you don't hit this key, BIOS completes its work and Windows loads.

If you do hit the key, you see a screen like the one in Figure D.4.

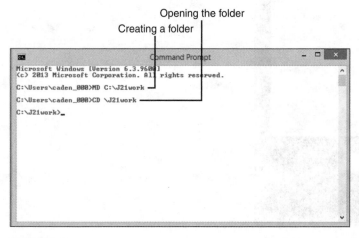

FIGURE D.4
Looking at a computer's BIOS settings.

Your computer's main menu for BIOS probably looks different than the one in Figure D.4. It varies depending on your computer manufacturer and the version of BIOS it uses.

On my Dell desktop PC, I found out whether Intel Virtualization Technology was enabled by choosing BIOS Setup, Advanced, Processor Configuration. A list of processor settings was presented with "[Enabled]" or "[Disabled]" next to each one. These could be toggled from one setting to the other.

If you enable Intel Virtualization Technology in BIOS and save the change, your computer should be able to run HAXM and the emulator problem should be resolved.

APPENDIX E
Fixing Package Not Visible Errors in NetBeans

One of the most interesting features introduced in Java 9 is modules, which enable Java programs to indicate which parts of the Java Class Library they require and what class packages they export.

Modules also can be used to access Java packages in the class library that aren't normally available. In Hour 21, "Using Java 9's New HTTP Client," the experimental support for the new HTTP Client was not usable in a programming project until the module `jdk.incubator.httpclient` was added to that project.

The modules that are standard in Java 9—]and thus don't require special effort to use—are still being decided by Oracle and the other companies finalizing the new release of the Java language.

This appendix covers what to do when a Java project in NetBeans experiences an error because a module is not available.

Adding Module Info

The Java Class Library includes hundreds of packages. A small number of them are only usable when their module has been added to a project.

If you try to `import` a class or group of classes that are in a module not yet available, the `import` statement will cause an error flagged in the NetBeans source code editor.

Here's an example of such a statement:

```
import jdk.incubator.http.*;
```

If this causes an error flagged by a red stop sign icon along the left edge of the source editor, hover over the icon to see the error message:

```
Package jdk.incubator.http is not visible
(package jdk.incubator.http is declared in module
jdk.incubator.httpclient, which is not in the module
graph)
```

This error message reveals the name of the module that must be added to the project to resolve the problem. In this example, it's `jdk.incubator.http`.

Modules are set in a Java class called `module-info` in the default package (in other words, a class with no `package` statement at all).

Follow these steps to add a module to the `Java24` project in NetBeans:

- ▶ Choose File, New File, then choose Java in the Categories pane.

- ▶ In the File Types pane, choose Java Module Info.

- ▶ Choose Java Module Info, then click Next.

- ▶ The dialog displays the Class Name `module-info` and does not let a package name be chosen. Click Finish.

The file `module-info.java` opens for editing in the source code editor. It only needs three statements of this form:

```
module Java24 {
    requires jdk.incubator.httpclient;
}
```

The `module` keyword is followed by `Java24` because that's the project's name. If you were adding a module to a different project, the statement should be revised accordingly.

Inside the `module` block within the { and } squiggly brackets, the `requires` keyword is followed by the module name `jdk.incubator.httpclient`. If your project requires a different module, edit this statement to reflect that.

A project can have more than one `requires` statement.

When the `module-info.java` file has been saved, the classes in the module (or modules) can be used by any Java program in the project. The `import` statements that add packages in that module will have no error and the program can be compiled and run.

Index

Symbols

Accessing the Free Web Edition

Your purchase of this book in any format, print or electronic, includes access to the corresponding Web Edition, which provides several special features to help you learn:

▶ The complete text of the book online

▶ Updates and corrections as they become available

The Web Edition can be viewed on all types of computers and mobile devices with any modern web browser that supports HTML5.

To get access to the Web Edition of *Sams Teach Yourself Java in 24 Hours, Eighth Edition,* all you need to do is register this book:

1. Go to www.informit.com/register

2. Sign in or create a new account

3. Enter ISBN: 9780672337949

4. Answer the questions as proof of purchase

The Web Edition will appear under the Digital Purchases tab on your Account page.

Click the Launch link to access the product.